Thackray's 2023 Investor's Guide

THACKRAY'S
2023
INVESTOR'S
GUIDE

Brooke Thackray MBA, CIM

Copyright ©2022 by Brooke Thackray

Published in 2022 by: MountAlpha Media:
alphamountain.com

Brooke Thackray is a research analyst for Horizons ETFs Management (Canada) Inc. All of the views expressed herein are the personal views of the author and are not necessarily the views of Horizons ETFs Management (Canada) Inc., although any of the strategies/recommendations found herein may be reflected in positions or transactions in the various client portfolios managed by Horizons ETFs Management (Canada) Inc. Securities (if any) discussed in this publication are meant to highlight investment strategies for educational purposes only not investment advice.

Horizons ETFs is a Member of Mirae Asset Global Investments. Commissions, management fees and expenses all may be associated with an investment in exchange traded products managed by Horizons ETFs Management (Canada) Inc. (the "Horizons Exchange Traded Products"). The Horizons Exchange Traded Products are not guaranteed, their values change frequently and past performance may not be repeated. The prospectus contains important detailed information about the Horizons Exchange Traded Products. **Please read the relevant prospectus before investing**.

ISBN13: 978-1-989125-08-3
Printed and Bound in Canada by Marquis.

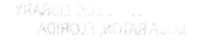

To my wife Jane

Acknowledgments

This book is the product of many years of research and could not have been written without the help of many people. I would like to thank my wife, Jane Steer-Thackray, and my children Justin, Megan, Carly and Madeleine, for the help they have given me and their patience during the many hours that I have devoted to writing this book.

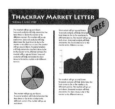

INTRODUCTION

2023 THACKRAY'S INVESTOR'S GUIDE
Technical Commentary

The seasonal strategies that I have included in my previous books have proven to be very successful. The buy and sell dates are based upon iterative comparisons of different time periods measured by gain and frequency of success. Although the buy and sell dates are the optimal dates on which seasonal investors should focus on making their investment decisions, the markets have different dynamics from year to year, shifting the optimal buy and sell dates. Combining technical analysis with seasonal trends helps to adjust the decision process, allowing seasonal investors to enter and exit trades early or late, depending on market conditions.

The universe of technical indicators and techniques is huge. It is impossible to use all of the indicators. Only a small number of indicators and techniques that suit an investment style should be used. In the case of seasonal investing, a lot of long-term indicators provide little benefit. For example, the standard Moving Average Convergence Divergence (MACD), is too slow to be of use in shorter term seasonal strategies. In this book I have chosen to illustrate three technical indicators that can provide value in fine-tuning the dates for seasonal investing: Full Stochastic Oscillator (FSO), Relative Strength Index (RSI) and Relative Strength. The indicators are used in conjunction with the price pattern and moving averages of the security being considered. Investors must remember that technical analysis is not absolute and there will be exceptions when utilizing indicators and price patterns.

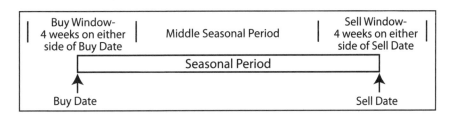

To combine technical indicators with seasonal trends, it is best that the indicators be used within the windows of the buy and sell dates. The indicators should be ignored outside the seasonal buy/sell windows. An exception to this occurs when an indicator gives a signal during its middle seasonal period, which is in the seasonal period, but after the buy window and before the sell window. In this case a technical signal can support selling a full position based upon a fundamental breakdown in the price action of a security. By itself, a FSO or RSI indicator showing weakness in a security during its middle seasonal period, does not necessarily warrant action, it can be used to support a decision being made in conjunction with underperformance relative to the broad market, or a major price action break.

Below are short descriptions of three technical indicators that can be used with seasonal analysis. Full evaluation of the indicators and their uses with seasonal analysis is beyond the scope of this book.

Full Stochastic Oscillator (FSO)

A stochastic oscillator is a range bound momentum indicator that tracks the location of the close price relative to the high-low range, over a set number of periods. It tracks the momentum of price change and helps to indicate the strength and direction of price movement.

I have found that generally the best method to combine the FSO with seasonal trends is to buy an early partial position when the FSO turns up above 20 within four weeks of the seasonal buy date. Additionally, the best time to sell an early partial position occurs when the FSO turns below 80, within four weeks of the seasonal exit date.

Relative Strength Index (RSI)

The RSI is a momentum oscillator that measures the speed and change of price movements. I have found that the best method to combine the RSI with seasonal trends is to buy an early partial position when the RSI turns up above 30 within four weeks of the seasonal buy date. The best time to sell an early partial position occurs when the RSI turns below 70, within four weeks of the seasonal exit date. Compared with the FSO, the RSI is less useful as it is slower and gives too few signals in the buy/sell windows.

Relative Strength

Relative strength calculates the performance of one security versus another security. When the relative strength is increasing, it indicates the seasonal security is outperforming. When the relative strength is declining, the seasonal security is underperforming. When a downward trend line is broken to the upside by the performance of the seasonal security, relative to the benchmark, this is a positive signal. This action carries a lot of weight and can justify a full early entry into a position if other technical evidence is positive. Likewise, if an upward trend line is broken to the downside, a negative technical signal is given and can justify a full early exit from a position if other technical evidence is negative.

THACKRAY'S 2023 INVESTOR'S GUIDE

You can choose great companies to invest in and still underperform the market. Unless you are in the market at the right time and in the best sectors, your investment expertise can be all for naught.

Successful investors know when they should be in the market. Very successful investors know when they should be in the market, and the best sectors in which to invest. *Thackray's 2023 Investor's Guide* is designed to provide investors with the knowledge of when and what to buy, and when to sell.

The goal of this book is to help investors capture extra profits by taking advantage of the seasonal trends in the markets. This book is straightforward. There are no complicated rules and there are no complex algorithms. The strategies put forward are intuitive and easy to understand.

It does not matter if you are a short-term or long-term investor, this book can be used to help establish entry and exit points. For the short-term investor, specific periods are identified that can provide profitable opportunities. For the long-term investor best buy dates are identified to launch new investments on a sound footing.

The stock market has its seasonal rhythms. Historically, the broad markets, such as the S&P 500, have a seasonal trend of outperforming during certain times of the year. Likewise, different sectors of the market have their own seasonal trends of outperformance. When oil stocks tend to do well in the springtime before "driving season," health care stocks tend to underperform the market. When utilities do well in the summertime, industrials do not. With different markets and different sectors having a tendency to outperform at different times of the year, there is always a place to invest.

Until recently, investors did not have access to the information necessary to analyse and create sector strategies. In recent years there have been a great number of sector Exchange Traded Funds (ETFs) and sector indexes introduced into the market. For the first time, investors are now able to easily implement a sector rotation strategy. This book provides a seasonal road map of what sectors tend to do well at different times of the year. It is a first of its kind, revealing new sector-based strategies that have never before been published.

In terms of market timing there are ample strategies in this book to help determine the times when equities should be over or underweight. During a favorable time for the market, investments can be purchased to overweight equities relative to their target weight in a portfolio (staying within risk tolerances). During an unfavorable time, investments can be sold to underweight equities relative to their target.

A large part of the book is devoted to sector seasonality – the underpinnings for a sector rotation strategy. The most practical rotation strategy is to create a core part of a portfolio that represents the broad market and then set aside an allocation to be rotated between favored sectors from one time period to the next.

It does not makes sense to apply any investment strategy only once with a large investment. Seasonal strategies are no exception. The best way to apply an investment strategy is to use a disciplined methodology that allows for diversification and a large enough number of investments to help remove the anomalies of the market. This reduces risk and increases the probability of a long term gain.

Following the specific buy and sell dates put forth in this book would have netted an investor large, above market returns. To "turbo-charge" gains, an investor can combine seasonality with technical analysis. As the seasonal periods are never exactly the same, technical analysis can help investors capture the extra gains when a sector turns up early, or momentum extends the trend.

IMPORTANT: Strategy Buy and Sell Dates
The beginning date of every strategy period in this book represents a full day in the market; therefore, investors should buy at the end of the preceding market day. For example the *Biotech Summer Solstice* seasonal period of strength is from June 23rd to September 13th. To be in the sector for the full seasonal period, an investor would enter the market before the closing bell on June 22nd. If the buy date landed on a weekend or holiday, then the buy would occur at the end of the preceding trading day.

The last day of a trading strategy is the sell date. For example, the Biotech sector investment would be sold at the end of the day on September 13th. If the sell date is a holiday or weekend, then the investment would be sold at the close on the preceding trading day.

What is Seasonal Investing?

In order to properly understand seasonal investing in the stock market, it is important to look briefly at its evolution. It may surprise investors to know that seasonal investing at the broad market level, i.e. Dow Jones or S&P 500, has been around for a long time. The initial seasonal strategies were written by Fields (1931, 1934) and Watchel (1942), who focused on the *January Effect*. Coincidentally, this strategy is still bantered about in the press every year.

Yale Yirsch Senior has been largely responsible for the next stage in the evolution, producing the *Stock Trader's Almanac* for more than forty years. This publication focuses on broad market trends such as the best six months of the year and tendencies of the market to do well depending on the political party in power and holiday trades.

In 2000, Brooke Thackray and Bruce Lindsay wrote, *Time In Time Out: Outsmart the Market Using Calendar Investment Strategies*. This work focused on a comprehensive analysis of the six month seasonal cycle and other shorter seasonal cycles in the broad markets such as the S&P 500.

Seasonal investing has changed over time. The focus has shifted from broad market strategies to taking advantage of sector rotation opportunities – investing in different sectors at different times of the year, depending on their seasonal strength. This has created a whole new set of investment opportunities. Rather than just being "in or out" of the market, investors can now always be invested by shifting between different sectors and asset classes, taking advantage of both up and down markets.

Definition – Seasonal investing is a method of investing in the market at the time of the year when it typically does well, or investing in a sector of the market when it typically outperforms the broad market such as the S&P 500.

The term seasonal investing is somewhat of a misnomer, and it is easy to see why some investors might believe that the discipline relates to investing based upon the seasons of the year – winter, spring, summer and autumn. Other than some agricultural commodities where the price is often correlated to growing seasons, generally seasonal investment strategies use the calendar as a reference for buy and sell dates. It is usually a specific event, i.e. Christmas sales, that occurs on a recurring annual basis that creates the seasonal opportunity.

The discipline of seasonal investing is not restricted to the stock market. It has been used successfully for a number of years in the commodities market. The opportunities in this market tend to be based upon changes in supply and/or demand that occur on a yearly basis. Most commodities, especially the agricultural commodities, tend to have cyclical supply cycles, i.e., crops are harvested only at certain times of the year. The supply bulge that occurs at the same time every year provides seasonal investors with profit opportunities. Recurring increased seasonal demand for commodities also plays a major part in providing opportunities for seasonal investors. This applies to most metals and many other commodities, whether the end-product is industrial or consumer based.

Seasonal investment strategies can be used with a lot of different types of investments. The premise is the same, outperformance during a certain period of the year based upon a repeating event in the markets or economy. In my past writings I have developed seasonal strategies that have been used successfully in the stock, commodity, bond and foreign exchange markets. Seasonal investing is still relatively new for most markets with a lot of new opportunities waiting to be discovered.

How Does Seasonal Investing Work?

Most stock market sector seasonal trends are the result of a recurring annual catalyst: an event that affects the sector positively. These events can range from a seasonal spike in demand, seasonal inventory lows, weather effects, conferences and other events. Mainstream investors very often anticipate a move in a sector and incorrectly try to take a position just before an event takes place that is supposed to drive a sector higher. A good example of this would be investors buying oil just before the cold weather sets in. Unfortunately, their efforts are usually unsuccessful as they are too late to the party and the opportunity has already passed.

By the time the anticipated event occurs, a substantial amount of investors have bought into the sector – fully pricing in the expected benefit. At this time there is little potential left in the short-term. Unless there is a strong positive surprise, the sector's outperformance tends to slowly roll over. If the event produces less than its desired result, the sector can be severely punished.

So how does the seasonal investor take advantage of this opportunity? "Be there" before the mainstream investors, and get out before they do. Seasonal investors usually enter a sector two or three months before an event is anticipated to have a positive effect on a sector and get out before the actual event takes place. In essence, seasonal investors are benefiting from the mainstream investor's tendency to "buy in" too late.

Seasonality in the markets occurs because of three major reasons: money flow, changing market analyst expectations and the *Anticipation-Realization Cycle*. First, money flows vary throughout the year and at different times of the month. Generally, money flows increase at the end of the year and into the start of the next year. This is a result of year end bonuses and tax related investments. In addition, money flows increase at month end from money managers "window dressing" their portfolios. As a result of these money flows, the months around the end of the year and the days around the end of the month, tend to have a stronger performance than the other times of the year.

Second, the analyst expectations cycle tends to push markets up at the end of the year and the beginning of the next year. Stock market analysts tend to be a positive bunch – the large investment houses pay them to be positive. They start the year with aggressive earnings for all of their favorite companies. As the year progresses, they generally back off their earnings forecast, which decreases their support for the market. After a lull in the summer and early autumn months, they start to focus on the next year with another rosy forecast. As a result, the stock market tends to rise once again at the end of the year.

Third, at the sector level, sectors of the market tend to be greatly influenced by the *Anticipation-Realization Cycle*. Although some investors may not be familiar with the term "anticipation-realization," they probably are familiar with the concept of "buy the rumor – sell the fact," or in the famous words of Lord Rothschild "Buy on the sound of the war-cannons; sell on the sound of the victory trumpets."

The *Anticipation-Realization Cycle* as it applies to human behavior has been much studied in psychology journals. In the investment world, the premise of this cycle rests on investors anticipating a positive event in the market to drive prices higher and buying in ahead of the event. When the event takes place, or is realized, upward pressure on prices decreases as there is very little impetus for further outperformance.

A good example of the *Anticipation-Realization Cycle* takes place with the "conference effect." Very often large industries have major conferences that occur at approximately the same time every year. Major companies in the industry often hold back positive announcements and product introductions to be released during the conference.

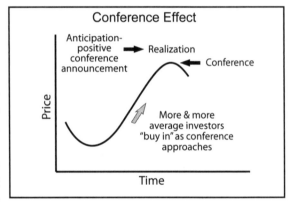

Two to three months prior to the conference, seasonal investors tend to buy into the sector. Shortly afterwards, the mainstream investors anticipate "good news" from the conference and start to buy in. As a result, prices are pushed up. Just before the conference starts, seasonal investors capture their profits by exiting their positions. As the conference unfolds, company announcements are made (realized), but as the potential good news has already been priced into the sector, there is little to push prices higher and the sector typically starts to rolls over.

The same *Anticipation-Realization Cycle* takes place with increased demand for oil to meet the "summer driving season", increased sales of goods at Christmas time, increased demand for gold jewellery to meet the autumn and winter demand, and many other events that tend to drive the outperformance of different sectors.

Does Seasonal Investing ALWAYS Work?

The simple answer to the above question is "No." There is not any investment system in the world that works all of the time. When following any investment system, it is probability of success that counts. It has often been said that "being correct in the markets 60% of the time will make you rich." Investors tend to forget this and become too emotionally attached to their losses. Just about every investment trading book states that investors typically fail to let their profits run and cut their losses quickly. I concur. In my many years in the investment industry, the biggest mistake that I have found with investors is not being able to cut their losses. Everyone wants to be right, that is how we have been raised. Investors feel that if they sell at a loss they have failed, and as a result, often suffer bigger losses by waiting for their position to trade at profit. With any investment system, investors should let probability work for them. This means that investors should be able to enter and exit positions capturing both gains and losses without becoming emotionally attached to any positions. Emotional attachment clouds judgement, which leads to errors.

XOI vs S&P 500 1984 to 2022			
Feb 25 to May 9	S&P 500	positive XOI	Diff
1984	1.7 %	5.6 %	3.9 %
1985	1.4	4.9	3.5
1986	6.0	7.7	1.7
1987	3.7	25.5	21.8
1988	-3.0	5.6	8.6
1989	6.3	8.1	1.8
1990	5.8	-0.6	-6.3
1991	4.8	6.8	2.0
1992	0.9	5.8	4.9
1993	0.3	6.3	6.0
1994	-4.7	3.2	7.9
1995	7.3	10.3	3.1
1996	-2.1	2.2	4.3
1997	1.8	4.7	2.9
1998	7.5	9.8	2.3
1999	7.3	35.4	28.1
2000	4.3	22.2	17.9
2001	0.8	10.2	9.4
2002	-1.5	5.3	6.9
2003	12.1	5.7	-6.4
2004	-3.5	4.0	7.5
2005	-1.8	-1.0	0.8
2006	2.8	9.4	6.6
2007	4.2	10.1	5.8
2008	2.6	7.6	5.0
2009	20.2	15.8	-4.4
2010	0.5	-2.3	-2.8
2011	3.1	-0.6	-3.7
2012	-0.8	-13.4	-12.5
2013	7.3	3.8	-3.5
2014	1.7	9.1	7.4
2015	0.3	1.2	1.1
2016	6.7	11.1	4.4
2017	1.3	-4.0	-5.2
2018	-1.8	15.4	17.2
2019	2.8	-2.6	-5.4
2020	-9.2	-25.2	-16.0
2021	7.8	7.0	-0.7
2022	-6.9	12.0	18.9
Avg	2.5 %	6.2 %	3.7 %
Fq > 0	74 %	80 %	72 %

When all of the trades are put together, the goal is for profits to be larger than losses in a way that minimizes risks and beats the market.

If we examine the winter oil stock trade, we can see how probability has worked in an investor's favor. This trade is based upon the premise that at the tail end of winter, the refineries drive up demand for oil in order to produce enough gas for the approaching "driving season" that starts in the spring. As a result, oil stocks tend to increase and outperform the market (from February 25 to May 9). The oil stock sector, represented by the NYSE

Arca Oil Index (XOI), has been very successful at this time of year, producing an average return of 6.2% and beating the S&P 500 by 3.7%, from 1984 to 2022. In addition it has been positive 30 out of 39 times. Investors should always evaluate the strength of seasonal trades before applying them to their own portfolios.

If an investor started using the seasonal investment discipline in 1984 and chose to invest in the winter-oil trade, they would have been very happy with the results. If an investor started using the strategy in 2010 a loss would have occurred following the strategy. The fact that the strategy did not produce gains in 2010, 2011 and 2012, does not mean that the seasonal trade no longer works. All seasonal trades go through periods, sometimes multiple years where they do not work. An investor can start any methodology of trading at the "wrong time," and be unsuccessful in a particular trade. In fact, if an investor started the oil-winter trade in 1990 and had given up in the same year, they would have missed the following successful twelve years. Investors have to remember that it is the final score that counts, after all of the gains have been weighed against the losses.

In practical terms, investors should not put all of their investment strategies in one basket. If one or two large investments were made based upon seasonal strategies, it is possible that the seasonal methodology might be inappropriately evaluated and its use discontinued. A much more prudent strategy is to use a larger number of strategic seasonal investments with smaller investments. The end result will be to put the seasonal probability to work with a much greater chance of success.

Measuring Seasonal Performance

How do you determine if a seasonal strategy has been successful? Many people feel that ten years of data is a good sample size, others feel that fifteen years is better, and yet others feel that the more data the better. I tend to fall into the camp that, if possible, it is best to use fifteen or twenty years of data for sectors and more data for the broad markets, such as the S&P 500. Although the most recent data in almost any analytical framework is the most relevant, it is important to get enough data to reflect a sector's performance across different economic conditions. Given that historically the economy has performed on an eight year cycle, four years of expansion and then four years of contraction, using a short data set does not provide for enough exposure to different economic conditions.

A data set that is too long can run into the problem of older data having too much of an influence on the numbers when fundamental factors affecting a sector have changed. It is important to look at trends over time and assess if there has been a change that should be considered in determining the dates for a seasonal cycle. Each sector should be judged on its own merit. The analysis tables in this book illustrate the performance level for each year in order to provide the opportunity for readers to determine any relevant changes.

In order to determine if a seasonal strategy is effective there are two possible benchmarks, absolute and relative performance. Absolute performance measures if a profit is made and relative performance measures the performance of a sector in relationship to a major market. Both measurements have their merits and depending on your investment style, one measurement may be more valuable than another. This book provides both sets of measurement in tables and graphs.

It is not just the average percent gain of a sector over a certain time period that determines success. It is possible that one or two spectacular years of performance skew the results substantially (particularly with a small data set). The frequency of success is also very important: the higher the percentage of success the better. Also, the fewer large drawdowns the better. There is no magic number (percent success rate) per se of what constitutes a successful strategy. The success rate should be above fifty percent, otherwise it would be better to just invest in the broad market. Ideally speaking a strategy should have a high percentage success rate on both an absolute and relative basis. Some strategies are stronger than others, but that does not mean that the weaker strategies should not be used. Prudence should be used in determining the ideal portfolio allocation.

Illustrating the strength of a sector's seasonal performance can be accomplished through either an absolute yearly average performance graph, or a relative yearly average performance graph. The absolute graph shows the average yearly cumulative gain for a set number of years. It lets a reader visually identify the strong periods during the year. The relative graph shows the average yearly cumulative gain for the sector relative to the benchmark index.

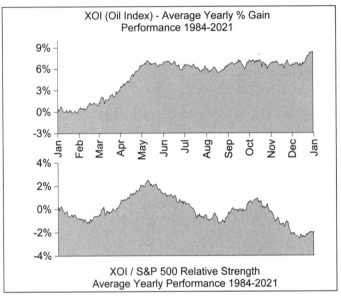

Both graphs are useful in determining the strength of a particular seasonal strategy. In the above diagram, the top graph illustrates the average year for the NYSE Arca Oil Index (XOI) from 1984 to 2021. Essentially it illustrates the cumulative average gain if an investment were made in the index. The steep rising line starting in January/February shows the overall price rise that typically occurs in this sector at this time of year. In May the line flattens out and then rises very modestly starting in July.

The bottom graph is a ratio graph, illustrating the strength of the XOI Index relative to the S&P 500. It is derived by dividing the average year of the XOI by the average year of the S&P 500. When the line in the graph is rising, the XOI is outperforming the S&P 500, and vise versa when it is declining. This is an important graph and should be used in considering seasonal investments because the S&P 500 is a viable alternative to the energy sector. If both markets are increasing, but the S&P 500 is increasing at a faster rate, the S&P 500 represents a more attractive opportunity. This is particularly true when measuring the risk of a volatile sector relative to the broad market. If both investments were expected to produce the same rate of return, generally the broad market is a better investment because of its diversification.

Who Can Use Seasonal Investing?

Any investor from novice to expert, from short-term trader to long-term investor can benefit from using seasonal analysis. Seasonal investing is unique because it is an easy to understand system that can be used by itself or as a complement to another investment discipline. For the novice it provides an easy to follow strategy that makes intuitive sense. For the expert it can be used as a stand-alone system or as a complement to an existing system.

Seasonal investing is easily understood by all levels of investors, which allows investors to make rational decisions. This may seem obvious, but it is very common for investors to listen to a "guru of the market", be impressed and blindly follow his advice. When the advice works there is no problem. When the advice does not work investors wonder why they made the investment in the first place. When investors do not understand their investments it causes stress, bad decisions and a lack of "stick-to-it ness" with any investment discipline. Even expert investors realize the importance of understanding your investments. Peter Lynch of Fidelity Investments used to say "Never invest in any idea that you can't illustrate with a crayon." Investors do not need to go that far, but they should understand their investments.

Novice investors find seasonal strategies very easy to understand because they are intuitive. They do not have to be investing for years to understand why seasonal strategies work. They understand that an increase in demand for gold every year at the same time causes a ripple effect in the stock market pushing up gold stocks at the same time every year.

Most expert investors use information from a variety of sources in making their decisions. Even experts that primarily use fundamental analysis can benefit from using seasonal trends to get an edge in the market. Fundamental analysis is a very crude tool and provides very little in the way of timing an investment. Using seasonal trends can help with the timing of the buy and sell decisions and produce extra profit.

Seasonal investing can be used by both short-term and long-term investors, but in different ways. For short-term investors it provides a complete trade – buy and sell dates. For long-term investors it can provide a buy date for a sector of interest.

Combining Seasonal Analysis with other Investment Disciplines

Seasonal investing used by itself has historically produced above average market returns. Depending on an investor's particular style, it can be combined with one of the other three investment disciplines: fundamental, quantitative and technical analysis. There are two basic ways to combine seasonal analysis with other investment methodologies – as the primary or secondary method. If it is used as a primary method, seasonally strong time periods are established for a number of sectors and then appropriate sectors are chosen based upon fundamental, quantitative or technical screens. If it is used as a secondary method, sector selections are first made based upon one of three methods and then final sectors are chosen based upon which ones are in their seasonally strong period.

Technical analysis is an ideal mate for seasonal analysis. Unlike fundamental and quantitative analysis, which are very blunt timing tools at best, seasonal and technical analysis can provide specific trigger points to buy and sell. The combination can turbo-charge investment strategies, adding extra profits by fine-tuning entry and exit dates.

Seasonal analysis provides both buy and sell dates. Although a sector in the market can sometimes bottom on the exact seasonal buy date, it more often bottoms a bit early or a bit late. After all, the seasonal buy date is based upon an average of historical performance. Depending on the sector, buying opportunities start to develop approximately one month before and after the seasonal buy date. Using technical analysis gives an investor the advantage of buying into a sector when it turns up early or waiting when it turns up late. Likewise, technical analysis can be used to trigger a sell signal when the market turns down before or after the sell date.

The sell decision can be extended with the help of a trailing stop-loss order. If a sector has strong momentum and the technical tools do not provide a sell signal, it is possible to let the sector "run." When a trailing stop-loss is used, a profitable sell point is established. If the price continues to run, then the selling point is raised. If, on the other hand, the price falls through the stop-loss point, the position is sold.

Sectors of the Market

Standard & Poor's has done an excellent job in categorizing the U.S. stock market into its different parts. Although the demand for this service initially came from institutional investors, many individual investors now seek the same information. Knowing the sector breakdown in the market allows investors to see how different their portfolio is relative to the market. As a result, they are able to make conscious decisions on what parts of the stock market to overweight based upon their beliefs of which sectors will outperform. It also helps control the amount of desired risk.

Standard & Poor's uses four levels of detail in its Global Industry Classification Standard (GICS©) to categorize stock markets around the world. From the most specific, it classifies companies into sub-industries, industries, industry groups and finally economic sectors. All companies in the Standard & Poor's global family of indices are classified according to the GICS structure.

This book focuses on the U.S. market, analysing the trends of the venerable S&P 500 index and its economic sectors and industry groups. The following diagram illustrates the index classified according to its economic sectors.

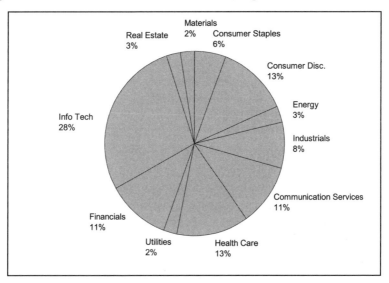

Standard and Poor's, Understanding Sectors, June 30, 2021

For more information on Standard and Poor's Global Industry Classification Standard (GICS©), refer to www.standardandpoors.com

Investment Products – Which One Is The Right One?

There are many ways to take advantage of the seasonal trends at the broad stock market and sector levels. Regardless of the investment products that you currently use, whether exchange traded funds, mutual funds, stocks or options, all can be used with the strategies in this book. Different investments offer different risk-reward relationships and return potential.

Exchange Traded Funds (ETFs)

Exchange Traded Funds (ETFs) offer the purest method of seasonal investment. The broad market ETFs are designed to track the major indices and the sector ETFs are designed to track specific sectors without using active management. Relatively new, ETFs are a great way to capture both market and sector trends. They were originally introduced into the Canadian market in 1993 to represent the Toronto stock market index. Shortly afterward they were introduced to the U.S. market and there are now hundreds of ETFs to represent almost every market, sector, style of investing and company capitalization. Originally ETFs were mainly of interest to institutional investors, but individual investors have fast realized the merits of ETF investing and have made some of the broad market ETFs the most heavily traded securities in the world.

An ETF is a single security that represents a market, such as the S&P 500; a sector of the market, such as the financial sector; or a commodity, such as gold. In the case of the S&P 500, an investor buying one security is buying all 500 stocks in the index. By investing into a financial ETF, an investor is buying the companies that make up the financial sector of the market. By investing into a gold commodity ETF, an investor is buying a security that represents the price of gold.

ETFs trade on the open market just like stocks. They have a bid and an ask, can be shorted and many are option eligible. They are a very low cost, tax efficient method of targeting specific parts of the market.

Mutual Funds

Mutual funds are a good way to combine market or sector investing with active management. In recent years, many mutual fund companies have added sector funds to accommodate an increasing appetite in this area.

As the seasonal strategies put forward in this book have a short-term nature, it is important to make sure that there are no fees (or a nominal charge) for getting into and out of a position in the market.

Stocks

Stocks provide an opportunity to make better returns than the market or sector. If the market increases during its seasonal period, some stocks will increase dramatically more than the index. Choosing one of the outperforming stocks will greatly enhance returns; choosing one of the underperforming stocks can create substantial loses. Using stocks requires increased attention to diversification and security selection.

Options

Disclaimer: Options involve risk and are not suitable for every investor. Because they are cash-settled, investors should be aware of the special risks associated with index options and should consult a tax advisor. Prior to buying or selling options, a person must receive a copy of Characteristics and Risks of Standardized Options and should thoroughly understand the risks involved in any use of options. Copies may be obtained from The Options Clearing Corporation, 440 S. LaSalle Street, Chicago, IL 60605.

Options, for more sophisticated investors, are a good tool to take advantage of both market and sector opportunities. An option position can be established with either stocks or ETFs. There are many different ways to use options for seasonal trends: establish a long position on the market during its seasonally strong period, establish a short position during its seasonally weak period, or create a spread trade to capture the superior gains of a sector over the market.

THACKRAY'S 2023 INVESTOR'S GUIDE

CONTENTS

JANUARY

	MONDAY	TUESDAY	WEDNESDAY
WEEK 01	**2** 29 CAN Market Closed - New Year's Day USA Market Closed - New Year's Day	**3** 28	**4** 27
WEEK 02	**9** 22	**10** 21	**11** 20
WEEK 03	**16** 15 USA Market Closed- Martin Luther King Jr. Day	**17** 14	**18** 13
WEEK 04	**23** 8	**24** 7	**25** 6
WEEK 05	**30** 1	**31**	1

THURSDAY	FRIDAY
5 26	**6** 25
12 19	**13** 18
19 12	**20** 11
26 5	**27** 4
2	3

FEBRUARY

M	T	W	T	F	S	S
		1	2	3	4	5
6	7	8	9	10	11	12
13	14	15	16	17	18	19
20	21	22	23	24	25	26
27	28					

MARCH

M	T	W	T	F	S	S
		1	2	3	4	5
6	7	8	9	10	11	12
13	14	15	16	17	18	19
20	21	22	23	24	25	26
27	28	29	30	31		

APRIL

M	T	W	T	F	S	S
					1	2
3	4	5	6	7	8	9
10	11	13	13	14	15	16
17	18	19	20	21	22	23
22	23	26	27	28	29	30

MAY

M	T	W	T	F	S	S
1	2	3	4	5	6	7
8	9	10	11	12	13	14
15	16	17	18	19	20	21
22	23	24	25	26	27	28
29	30	31				

JANUARY SUMMARY

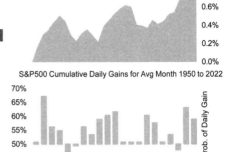

S&P500 Cumulative Daily Gains for Avg Month 1950 to 2022

	Dow Jones	S&P 500	Nasdaq	TSX Comp
Month Rank	5	5	1	4
# Up	45	43	33	23
# Down	27	29	17	14
% Pos	63	60	66	62
% Avg. Gain	1.0	1.1	2.6	1.2

Dow & S&P 1950-2021, Nasdaq 1972-2021, TSX 1985-2021

Prob. of Daily Gain

♦ Over the last ten years, the stock market in January has had large moves up or down on a number of occasions. ♦ In January there is typically a lot of sector rotation. ♦ January is often a pivotal month, for the stock market. The year 2022 was no exception. ♦ Small caps tend to perform well. ♦ The technology sector finishes its seasonal period. ♦ The industrials, materials, metals and mining sectors start the second part of their seasonal periods. ♦ The retail sector starts its strongest seasonal period.

BEST / WORST JANUARY BROAD MKTS. 2013-2022

BEST JANUARY MARKETS
- ♦ Russell 2000 (2019) 11.2%
- ♦ Nasdaq (2019) 9.7%
- ♦ TSX Comp. (2019) 8.5%

WORST JANUARY MARKETS
- ♦ Russell 2000 (2022) -9.7%
- ♦ Nasdaq (2022) -9.0%
- ♦ Russell 2000 (2016) - 8.8%

Index Values End of Month

	2013	2014	2015	2016	2017	2018	2019	2020	2021	2022
Dow	13,861	15,699	17,165	16,466	19,864	26,149	25,000	28,256	29,983	35,132
S&P 500	1,498	1,783	1,995	1,940	2,279	2,824	2,704	3,226	3,714	4,516
Nasdaq	3,142	4,104	4,635	4,614	5,615	7,411	7,282	9,151	13,071	14,240
TSX Comp.	12,685	13,695	14,674	12,822	15,386	15,952	15,541	17,318	17,337	21,098
Russell 1000	832	996	1,112	1,070	1,265	1,562	1,498	1,784	2,101	2,495
Russell 2000	902	1,131	1,165	1,035	1,362	1,575	1,499	1,614	2,074	2,028
FTSE 100	6,277	6,510	6,749	6,084	7,099	7,534	6,969	7,286	6,407	7,464
Nikkei 225	11,139	14,915	17,674	17,518	19,041	23,098	20,773	23,205	27,663	27,002

Percent Gain for January

	2013	2014	2015	2016	2017	2018	2019	2020	2021	2022
Dow	5.8	-5.3	-3.7	-5.5	0.5	5.8	7.2	-1.0	-2.0	-3.3
S&P 500	5.0	-3.6	-3.1	-5.1	1.8	5.6	7.9	-0.2	-1.1	-5.3
Nasdaq	4.1	-1.7	-2.1	-7.9	4.3	7.4	9.7	2.0	1.4	-9.0
TSX Comp.	2.0	0.5	0.3	-1.4	0.6	-1.6	8.5	1.5	-0.6	-0.6
Russell 1000	5.3	-3.3	-2.8	-5.5	1.9	5.4	8.2	0.0	-0.9	-5.7
Russell 2000	6.2	-2.8	-3.3	-8.8	0.3	2.6	11.2	-3.3	5.0	-9.7
FTSE 100	6.4	-3.5	2.8	-2.5	-0.6	-2.0	3.6	-3.4	-0.8	1.1
Nikkei 225	7.2	-8.5	1.3	-8.0	-0.4	1.5	3.8	-1.9	0.8	-6.2

January Market Avg. Performance 2013 to 2022[1]

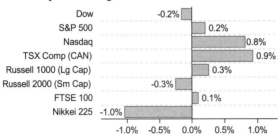

Dow	-0.2%
S&P 500	0.2%
Nasdaq	0.8%
TSX Comp (CAN)	0.9%
Russell 1000 (Lg Cap)	0.3%
Russell 2000 (Sm Cap)	-0.3%
FTSE 100	0.1%
Nikkei 225	-1.0%

Interest Corner Jan[2]

	Fed Funds %[3]	3 Mo. T-Bill %[4]	10 Yr %[5]	20 Yr %[6]
2022	0.25	0.22	1.79	2.17
2021	0.25	0.06	1.11	1.68
2020	1.75	1.55	1.51	1.83
2019	2.50	2.41	2.63	2.83
2018	1.50	1.46	2.72	2.83

(1) Russell Data provided by Russell (2) Federal Reserve Bank of St. Louis- end of month values (3) Target rate set by FOMC (4)(5)(6) Constant yield maturities.

January 2022 % Sector Performance

S&P GIC Sectors	2022 % Gain	1990-2022[1] GIC[2] % Avg Gain	1990-2022[1] Fq% Gain >S&P 500
Information Technology	-6.9 %	2.4 %	73 %
Consumer Discretionary	-9.7	0.6	55
Health Care	-6.9	0.5	58
Energy	19.0	0.1	42
Financials	-0.1	-0.2	58
Industrials	-4.8	-0.2	33
Utilities	-3.3	-0.4	39
Materials	-6.9	-0.9	36
Telecom	-6.4	-1.0	42
Consumer Staples	-1.5 %	-1.1 %	33 %
S&P 500	-5.3 %	0.1 %	N/A %

Sector Commentary

♦ In January 2022, the S&P 500 moved sharply lower with a loss of 5.3% ♦ The energy sector was the only sector with a gain. The gain was large at 19%. ♦ The financial sector was the next best performing sector, producing a loss of 0.1%. ♦ The consumer discretionary was the worst performing sector, with a loss of 9.7%. ♦ The information technology sector and the materials sector were tied for the second worst performing sectors, with both sectors losing 6.9%. ♦ Generally, the growth sectors of the stock market performed poorly as investors shifted to a risk-off mode.

Sub-Sector Commentary

♦ In January 2022, the agriculture sub-sector produced a strong gain of 11%. ♦ Rising interest rates hurt the homebuilders sub-sector, which produced a loss of 14.6%. ♦ Both gold and silver were slightly negative in January, despite rising interest rates. The banks benefited from rising interest rates and produced a gain of 1.4%.

SELECTED SUB-SECTORS[3]

Silver	-2.6 %	3.8 %	73 %
SOX (1995-2022)	-11.7	3.0	57
Homebuilders	-14.6	2.8	61
Gold	-0.6	1.8	58
Biotech (1993-2022)	-4.1	1.4	55
Railroads	-5.8	1.1	55
Auto	-10.7	0.8	48
Retail	-10.0	0.3	55
Agriculture (1994-2022)	11.0	0.1	45
Banks	1.4	-0.1	52
Steel	-11.2	-0.1	45
Pharma	-4.2	-0.2	55
Transportation	-5.6	-0.2	45
Metals & Mining	-7.6	-1.0	42
Chemicals	-7.9	-1.0	36

FASTENAL

FAST (NEW)

① Jan 17 to May 5 ② Oct 28 to Dec 31

Fastenal engages in the wholesale distribution of industrial and construction supplies. The company's stock price tends to follow a similar seasonal pattern as the industrial sector. Its strong seasonal periods exists within the favorable six-month period for stocks which lasts from late October to early May.

25% gain & 84% of the time positive

In its strong seasonal period from January 17 to May 5, from 1990 to 2021, Fastenal has outperformed the S&P 500 in most years. The outperformance has been fairly consistent over the years. In this strong seasonal period, Fastenal has produced gains over 10%, eighteen times. In comparison, it has only produced one loss greater than 10%.

In its strong seasonal period from October 28 to December 31, in the years from 1990 to 2021, Fastenal has produced gains greater than 10%, seventeen times and losses greater than 10%, twice.

Overall, combining the two strong seasonal periods for Fastenal has produced an average gain of 25.1% and an 84% frequency of positive performance.

2021/22 Performance Update.

In 2021, Fastenal strongly outperformed the S&P 500 in its strong seasonal period from January 17 to May 5.

In 2022, Fastenal started its January 17 to May 5 seasonal period underperforming the S&P 500, but strong performance in March, helped Fastenal to outperform the S&P 500.

Fastenal vs S&P 500 - 1990 to 2021 Positive

Year	Jan 17-May 5 S&P 500	Jan 17-May 5 FAST	Oct 28-Dec 31 S&P 500	Oct 28-Dec 31 FAST	Compound Growth S&P 500	Compound Growth FAST
1990	-0.7 %	59.6 %	8.4 %	7.4 %	7.6 %	71.4 %
1991	20.4	21.7	8.6	31.5	30.8	60.1
1992	-0.3	0.8	4.1	18.6	3.8	19.5
1993	1.7	15.4	0.4	0.8	2.1	16.3
1994	-5.0	0.0	-1.4	-5.8	-6.3	-5.8
1995	10.8	22.3	6.3	22.0	17.7	49.3
1996	5.5	26.1	5.7	-1.3	11.4	24.4
1997	7.9	-7.1	10.7	-21.1	19.4	-26.7
1998	16.0	39.5	15.4	32.1	33.9	84.2
1999	8.4	18.3	13.3	24.0	22.8	46.7
2000	-2.2	46.6	-4.3	4.0	-6.4	52.5
2001	-4.5	31.3	3.9	10.3	-0.8	44.9
2002	-4.8	31.6	-2.0	8.3	-6.7	42.5
2003	1.3	0.5	7.8	11.0	9.2	11.6
2004	-1.6	6.2	7.7	13.1	6.0	20.1
2005	-1.0	-10.4	5.9	15.7	4.8	3.7
2006	3.0	17.6	3.0	-11.9	6.0	3.6
2007	5.1	10.5	-4.4	-6.4	0.6	3.4
2008	2.5	45.4	6.4	9.4	9.1	59.0
2009	6.3	11.7	4.9	14.1	11.5	27.4
2010	2.6	16.2	6.4	16.8	9.2	35.7
2011	3.2	10.1	-2.1	13.7	1.1	25.2
2012	6.2	-4.9	1.0	7.9	7.3	2.6
2013	9.6	1.8	5.0	-6.2	15.1	-4.4
2014	2.1	4.4	5.0	11.8	7.2	16.7
2015	3.5	-8.0	-1.1	6.5	2.4	-2.0
2016	9.1	23.6	5.0	22.2	14.5	51.0
2017	5.5	-4.9	3.6	15.9	9.3	10.2
2018	-4.1	-8.6	-5.7	6.0	-9.5	-3.2
2019	12.6	31.0	6.9	-0.6	20.4	30.1
2020	-13.5	-1.8	10.8	12.0	-4.2	10.0
2021	10.6	7.3	4.7	15.3	15.8	23.7
Avg.	3.6 %	14.2 %	4.4 %	9.3 %	8.3 %	25.1 %
Fq>0	69 %	75 %	78 %	78 %	81 %	84 %

Fastenal Avg. Year 1990 to 2021

Fastenal / S&P 500 Rel Str.- Avg Yr. 1990-2021

Fastenal Performance

FAST Monthly % Gain (1990-2021)

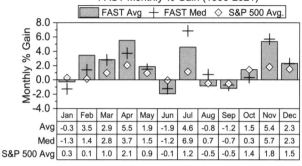

Legend: FAST Avg + FAST Med ◇ S&P 500 Avg.

	Jan	Feb	Mar	Apr	May	Jun	Jul	Aug	Sep	Oct	Nov	Dec
Avg	-0.3	3.5	2.9	5.5	1.9	-1.9	4.6	-0.8	-1.2	1.5	5.4	2.3
Med	-1.3	1.4	2.8	3.7	1.5	-1.2	6.9	0.7	-0.7	0.3	5.7	2.3
S&P 500 Avg	0.3	0.1	1.0	2.1	0.9	-0.1	1.2	-0.5	-0.5	1.4	1.8	1.5

Fq % FAST Gain > 0% (1990-2021)

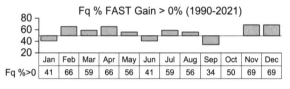

	Jan	Feb	Mar	Apr	May	Jun	Jul	Aug	Sep	Oct	Nov	Dec
Fq %>0	41	66	59	66	56	41	59	56	34	50	69	69

Fq % FAST Gain > S&P 500 % (1990-2021)

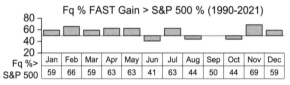

	Jan	Feb	Mar	Apr	May	Jun	Jul	Aug	Sep	Oct	Nov	Dec
Fq %> S&P 500	59	66	59	63	63	41	63	44	50	44	69	59

FAST % Gain 5 Year (2017-2021)

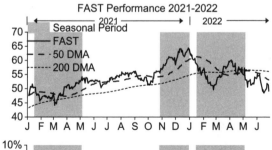

Legend: Hi/Lo — Avg. ■ Med. ◇ S&P 500 Avg.

FAST Performance 2021-2022

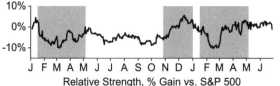

Relative Strength, % Gain vs. S&P 500

Market Indices & Rates
Weekly Values**

Stock Markets	2021	2022
Dow	31,098	36,232
S&P500	3,825	4,677
Nasdaq	13,202	14,936
TSX	18,042	21,084
FTSE	6,873	7,485
DAX	14,050	15,948
Nikkei	28,139	28,479
Hang Seng	27,878	23,493

Commodities	2021	2022
Oil	52.24	78.90
Gold	1862.9	1792.6

Bond Yields	2021	2022
USA 5 Yr Treasury	0.49	1.50
USA 10 Yr T	1.13	1.76
USA 20 Yr T	1.67	2.15
Moody's Aaa	2.48	2.88
Moody's Baa	3.32	3.54
CAN 5 Yr T	0.45	1.51
CAN 10 Yr T	0.81	1.72

Money Market	2021	2022
USA Fed Funds	0.25	0.25
USA 3 Mo T-B	0.08	0.10
CAN tgt overnight rate	0.25	0.25
CAN 3 Mo T-B	0.06	0.20

Foreign Exchange	2021	2022
EUR/USD	1.22	1.14
GBP/USD	1.36	1.36
USD/CAD	1.27	1.26
USD/JPY	103.94	115.56

JANUARY

M	T	W	T	F	S	S
						1
2	3	4	5	6	7	8
9	10	11	12	13	14	15
16	17	18	19	20	21	22
23	24	25	26	27	28	29
30	31					

FEBRUARY

M	T	W	T	F	S	S
	1	2	3	4	5	
6	7	8	9	10	11	12
13	14	15	16	17	18	19
20	21	22	23	24	25	26
27	28					

MARCH

M	T	W	T	F	S	S
	1	2	3	4	5	
6	7	8	9	10	11	12
13	14	15	16	17	18	19
20	21	22	23	24	25	26
27	28	29	30	31		

TOROMONT
① Jan 31 to Mar 7 ② Oct 14 to Dec 14

Toromont's revenue generation on average ramps up from Q1 to Q4 of the year. The first quarter of the year tends to be the weakest for Toromont. Revenue tends to take a large jump from Q1 to Q2 and then from Q3 to Q4. Investors tend to try and front run these trends.

14% gain & 96% of the time positive

The result of investor behavior has created two seasonal periods for Toromont. The first seasonal period is from January 31 to March 7. In this time period, from 1997 to 2021, Toromont has produced an average gain of 8.7% and has been positive 88% of the time.

Investors should note the juxtaposition with weakest month of the year being December and the strongest month being January. The strong seasonal period starts at the end of January, but in any one year, could start earlier or later.

The second seasonal period is from October 14 to December 14. In this time period, from 1997 to 2021, Toromont has produced an average gain of 4.9% and has been positive 76% of the time.

It should also be noted that the end of this seasonal period, occurs just before the weakest month of the year.

2021/22 Performance Update.
Toromont outperformed the S&P/ TSX Composite Index in 2021, but slightly underperformed during its strong seasonal periods. In 2022, Toromont strongly outperformed in its Jan 31 to Mar 7 strong seasonal period.

ⓘ *Source: TIH- stock symbol for The Microsoft which trades on the Toronto Stock Exchange, adjusted for stock splits.*

Toromont vs TSX Comp.- 1997 to 2021   Positive ☐

Year	Jan 31-Mar 7 S&P 500	Jan 31-Mar 7 TIH	Oct 14-Dec 14 S&P 500	Oct 14-Dec 14 TIH	Compound Growth S&P 500	Compound Growth TIH
1997	3.0 %	0.4 %	-6.6 %	6.2 %	-3.8 %	6.5 %
1998	7.2	23.8	12.1	4.8	20.3	29.7
1999	-4.7	6.5	12.7	-1.2	7.4	5.2
2000	12.3	8.5	-12.1	14.5	-1.3	24.2
2001	-11.2	15.8	5.6	4.7	-6.2	21.2
2002	5.4	21.1	11.5	-2.0	17.5	18.7
2003	-2.8	1.1	4.5	9.0	1.6	10.2
2004	3.8	15.8	4.1	2.3	8.0	18.5
2005	8.1	0.7	6.4	6.9	15.0	7.7
2006	-1.1	3.2	9.3	4.6	8.1	8.0
2007	-0.2	18.2	-4.3	11.5	-4.5	31.8
2008	2.2	19.8	-6.1	-2.1	-4.0	17.3
2009	-12.7	-0.9	1.2	12.5	-11.7	11.5
2010	7.9	7.9	4.8	8.0	13.1	16.6
2011	4.9	-0.9	-3.1	11.5	1.6	10.5
2012	-0.7	7.4	0.8	8.8	0.1	16.8
2013	0.3	8.1	1.8	17.4	2.1	26.9
2014	4.1	1.9	-3.5	5.9	0.5	8.0
2015	1.9	13.5	-8.3	-7.8	-6.6	4.6
2016	4.4	16.0	3.8	9.6	8.3	27.2
2017	1.3	9.2	1.3	-5.2	2.7	3.5
2018	-3.0	1.9	-5.3	-15.6	-8.2	-14.0
2019	3.7	16.5	3.6	5.6	7.4	23.0
2020	-7.5	-4.2	5.3	13.0	-2.6	8.2
2021	6.0	5.7	0.1	0.0	6.2	5.7
Avg.	1.3 %	8.7 %	1.6 %	4.9 %	2.8 %	13.8 %
Fq>0	64 %	88 %	68 %	76 %	64 %	96 %

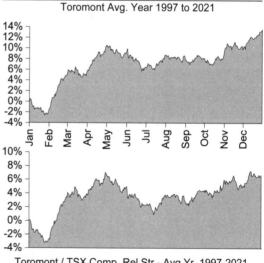

Toromont Avg. Year 1997 to 2021

Toromont / TSX Comp. Rel Str.- Avg Yr. 1997-2021

Toromont Performance

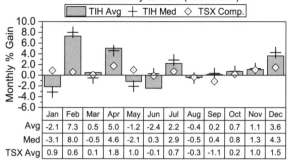

TIH Monthly % Gain (1997-2021)

Legend: TIH Avg □ + TIH Med ◇ TSX Comp.

	Jan	Feb	Mar	Apr	May	Jun	Jul	Aug	Sep	Oct	Nov	Dec
Avg	-2.1	7.3	0.5	5.0	-1.2	-2.4	2.2	-0.4	0.2	0.7	1.1	3.6
Med	-3.1	8.0	-0.5	4.6	-2.1	0.3	2.9	-0.5	0.4	0.8	1.3	4.3
TSX Avg	0.9	0.6	0.1	1.8	1.0	-0.1	0.7	-0.3	-1.1	0.2	1.0	1.5

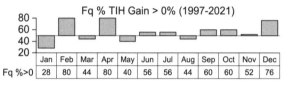

Fq % TIH Gain > 0% (1997-2021)

	Jan	Feb	Mar	Apr	May	Jun	Jul	Aug	Sep	Oct	Nov	Dec
Fq %>0	28	80	44	80	40	56	56	44	60	60	52	76

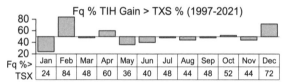

Fq % TIH Gain > TXS % (1997-2021)

	Jan	Feb	Mar	Apr	May	Jun	Jul	Aug	Sep	Oct	Nov	Dec
Fq %> TSX	24	84	48	60	36	40	48	44	48	52	44	72

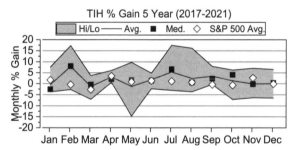

TIH % Gain 5 Year (2017-2021)

Legend: Hi/Lo — Avg. ■ Med. ◇ S&P 500 Avg.

Jan Feb Mar Apr May Jun Jul Aug Sep Oct Nov Dec

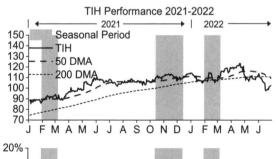

TIH Performance 2021-2022

Legend: Seasonal Period, TIH, 50 DMA, 200 DMA

Relative Strength, % Gain vs. S&P 500

Market Indices & Rates
Weekly Values**

Stock Markets	2021	2022
Dow	30,814	35,912
S&P500	3,768	4,663
Nasdaq	12,999	14,894
TSX	17,909	21,358
FTSE	6,736	7,543
DAX	13,788	15,883
Nikkei	28,519	28,124
Hang Seng	28,574	24,383

Commodities	2021	2022
Oil	52.36	83.82
Gold	1839.0	1823.0

Bond Yields	2021	2022
USA 5 Yr Treasury	0.46	1.55
USA 10 Yr T	1.11	1.78
USA 20 Yr T	1.66	2.18
Moody's Aaa	2.46	2.92
Moody's Baa	3.24	3.57
CAN 5 Yr T	0.43	1.57
CAN 10 Yr T	0.81	1.77

Money Market	2021	2022
USA Fed Funds	0.25	0.25
USA 3 Mo T-B	0.09	0.13
CAN tgt overnight rate	0.25	0.25
CAN 3 Mo T-B	0.05	0.27

Foreign Exchange	2021	2022
EUR/USD	1.21	1.14
GBP/USD	1.36	1.37
USD/CAD	1.27	1.26
USD/JPY	103.85	114.19

JANUARY

M	T	W	T	F	S	S
						1
2	3	4	5	6	7	8
9	10	11	12	13	14	15
16	17	18	19	20	21	22
23	24	25	26	27	28	29
30	31					

FEBRUARY

M	T	W	T	F	S	S
	1	2	3	4	5	
6	7	8	9	10	11	12
13	14	15	16	17	18	19
20	21	22	23	24	25	26
27	28					

MARCH

M	T	W	T	F	S	S
	1	2	3	4	5	
6	7	8	9	10	11	12
13	14	15	16	17	18	19
20	21	22	23	24	25	26
27	28	29	30	31		

SILVER – SHINES
① LONG (Dec27 to Feb22)
② SELL SHORT (April12-Jun29)

Gold and silver have a high degree of price correlation, with silver typically mirroring the direction of gold's price changes. When gold increases in price, silver typically increases in price and vice versa. Despite this relationship, the seasonal profiles for gold and silver are different because of silver's use in industrial products

9% growth

Although the period of seasonal strength for silver finishes in late February, under favorable conditions of rising base metal prices, silver can perform well into late March.

Historically, when silver has corrected sharply in December, it has often rallied strongly at the beginning of its seasonal period. This phenomenon has taken place a few times over the last few years. Over the last twenty years, silver has been positive eighteen times in its strong seasonal period from late December to late February.

2021/22 Performance Update.
In 2021, silver declined throughout most of the year and underperformed the S&P 500.

In the first half of 2022, silver started the year on positive note, performing well in its strong seasonal period. Rising interest rates and a stronger US dollar had a negative impact on silver and it performed poorly in its weak seasonal period from April 12 until June 29.

Silver* vs. S&P 500 1983/84 to 2021/22

Positive Long   Negative Short

Year	Dec 27 to Feb 22 S&P 500	Dec 27 to Feb 22 Silver	April 12 to Jun 29 S&P 500	April 12 to Jun 29 Silver	Compound Growth S&P 500	Compound Growth Silver
1983/84	-5.5	6.6%	-1.2 %	-9.7%	-6.6 %	17.0%
1984/85	7.7	-6.4	6.5	-8.5	14.7	1.6
1985/86	8.4	1.7	5.8	-6.8	14.7	8.7
1986/87	15.6	2.6	5.3	0.8	21.7	1.8
1987/88	5.4	-5.1	0.3	4.7	5.7	-9.6
1988/89	4.7	-2.9	7.1	-9.4	12.1	6.2
1989/90	-6.1	-5.5	4.7	-4.8	-1.7	-1.0
1990/91	10.5	-10.4	-1.7	11.7	8.6	-20.9
1991/92	1.6	5.2	1.2	-3.4	2.8	8.7
1992/93	-1.0	-2.8	2.0	14.9	1.0	-17.3
1993/94	0.9	2.7	-0.5	-3.4	0.4	6.2
1994/95	5.5	0.1	7.6	1.0	13.5	-0.9
1995/96	7.3	9.2	6.3	-9.1	14.0	19.2
1996/97	6.1	8.2	20.3	-0.9	27.6	9.1
1997/98	10.4	7.9	2.5	-17.2	13.2	26.5
1998/99	3.7	13.7	0.2	4.8	4.0	8.2
1999/00	-7.3	1.0	-3.9	-2.7	-10.9	3.7
2000/01	-4.7	-3.8	5.0	0.1	0.0	-3.9
2001/02	-5.2	-2.1	-10.3	5.5	-15.0	-7.5
2002/03	-4.7	0.5	12.4	1.3	7.2	-0.9
2003/04	4.4	15.5	-0.3	-27.1	4.1	46.9
2004/05	-2.1	9.7	1.6	-1.6	-0.6	11.4
2005/06	1.9	12.1	-1.1	-18.1	0.8	32.4
2006/07	2.8	14.0	4.5	-9.9	7.4	25.3
2007/08	-9.7	25.0	-4.1	-3.1	-13.3	28.8
2008/09	-11.8	38.8	8.3	14.4	-4.5	18.8
2009/10	-1.6	-5.1	-12.8	1.3	-14.3	-6.3
2010/11	4.7	13.1	-1.3	-16.9	3.3	32.2
2011/12	7.3	16.6	-0.5	-14.6	6.8	33.6
2012/13	6.7	-4.6	0.8	-31.6	7.6	25.5
2013/14	-0.3	12.1	8.0	4.7	7.7	6.8
2014/15	1.0	3.6	-2.1	-4.4	-1.1	8.1
2015/16	-5.6	5.6	1.4	17.0	-4.3	-12.4
2016/17	4.4	14.4	2.8	-6.2	7.3	21.4
2017/18	0.9	1.8	2.9	-3.2	3.8	5.1
2018/19	13.2	8.1	1.9	0.4	15.3	7.7
2019/20	3.0	5.5	9.4	18.0	12.7	-13.4
2020/21	4.7	6.5	3.9	2.9	8.8	3.4
2021/22	-8.9	5.9	-13.5	-16.3	-21.2	23.2
Avg.	1.8 %	5.6%	2.0 %	-3.2%	3.9 %	9.1%
Fq>0	64 %	74 %	67 %	41 %	72 %	72 %

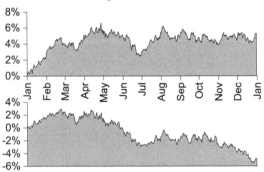

Silver - Avg. Year 1984 to 2021

Silver / S&P 500 Rel. Strength- Avg Yr. 1984-2021

Silver Performance

Silver Monthly % Gain (1984-2021)

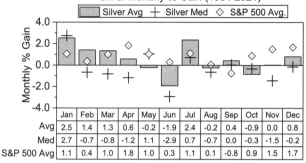

Legend: Silver Avg | Silver Med | S&P 500 Avg.

	Jan	Feb	Mar	Apr	May	Jun	Jul	Aug	Sep	Oct	Nov	Dec
Avg	2.5	1.4	1.3	0.6	-0.2	-1.9	2.4	-0.2	0.4	-0.9	0.0	0.8
Med	2.7	-0.7	-0.8	-1.2	1.1	-2.9	0.7	-0.7	0.0	-0.3	-1.5	-0.2
S&P 500 Avg	1.1	0.4	1.0	1.8	1.0	0.3	1.1	0.1	-0.8	0.9	1.5	1.7

Fq % Silver Gain > 0% (1984-2021)

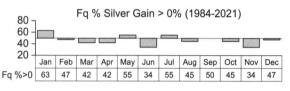

	Jan	Feb	Mar	Apr	May	Jun	Jul	Aug	Sep	Oct	Nov	Dec
Fq %>0	63	47	42	42	55	34	55	45	50	45	34	47

Fq % Silver Gain > S&P 500 % (1984-2021)

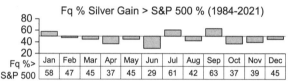

	Jan	Feb	Mar	Apr	May	Jun	Jul	Aug	Sep	Oct	Nov	Dec
Fq %> S&P 500	58	47	45	37	45	29	61	42	63	37	39	45

Silver % Gain 5 Year (2017-2021)

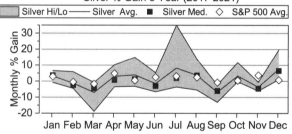

Legend: Silver Hi/Lo | Silver Avg. | Silver Med. | S&P 500 Avg.

Silver Performance 2021-2022

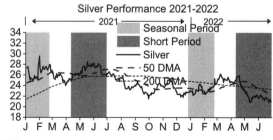

Seasonal Period | Short Period | Silver | 50 DMA | 200 DMA

Relative Strength, % Gain vs. S&P 500

Market Indices & Rates
Weekly Values**

Stock Markets	2021	2022
Dow	30,997	34,265
S&P500	3,841	4,398
Nasdaq	13,543	13,769
TSX	17,846	20,621
FTSE	6,695	7,494
DAX	13,874	15,604
Nikkei	28,631	27,522
Hang Seng	29,448	24,966

Commodities	2021	2022
Oil	52.25	86.24
Gold	1852.7	1837.6

Bond Yields	2021	2022
USA 5 Yr Treasury	0.44	1.54
USA 10 Yr T	1.10	1.75
USA 20 Yr T	1.66	2.13
Moody's Aaa	2.51	2.95
Moody's Baa	3.24	3.59
CAN 5 Yr T	0.44	1.63
CAN 10 Yr T	0.85	1.79

Money Market	2021	2022
USA Fed Funds	0.25	0.25
USA 3 Mo T-B	0.08	0.17
CAN tgt overnight rate	0.25	0.25
CAN 3 Mo T-B	0.06	0.42

Foreign Exchange	2021	2022
EUR/USD	1.22	1.13
GBP/USD	1.37	1.36
USD/CAD	1.27	1.26
USD/JPY	103.78	113.68

JANUARY

M	T	W	T	F	S	S
						1
2	3	4	5	6	7	8
9	10	11	12	13	14	15
16	17	18	19	20	21	22
23	24	25	26	27	28	29
30	31					

FEBRUARY

M	T	W	T	F	S	S
	1	2	3	4	5	
6	7	8	9	10	11	12
13	14	15	16	17	18	19
20	21	22	23	24	25	26
27	28					

MARCH

M	T	W	T	F	S	S
	1	2	3	4	5	
6	7	8	9	10	11	12
13	14	15	16	17	18	19
20	21	22	23	24	25	26
27	28	29	30	31		

TJX COMPANIES INC.
January 22 to March 30

TJX is an off-price apparel and home fashion retailer that typically reports its fourth quarter earnings in approximately the third week of February. The company, like the retail sector, benefits from investors expecting positive results from the Christmas season.

Over the long-term, TJX has typically outperformed the retail sector when the sector has been positive, making it an excellent complement to a retail sector investment during retail's strong seasonal period that also starts in January.

TJX's period of seasonal strength is similar to the seasonal period for the retail sector. The best time to invest in TJX has been from January 22 to March 30. In this time period, positive economic forecasts by investment analysts tend to increase expected consumption forecasts in the economy helping to drive the retail sector and TJX higher.

10% gain & positive 70% of the time

Since 1990, TJX has produced large gains in its seasonal period, and very few large losses. In the last thirty-two years, TJX has only had two losses of 10% or greater. In the same time period, TJX has had thirteen gains of 10% or greater.

TJX* vs. Retail vs. S&P 500 1990 to 2021			
Jan 22 to Mar 30	S&P 500	Retail	TJX (Positive)
1990	0.2%	6.3%	6.7%
1991	13.3	21.7	61.9
1992	-2.3	1.7	16.2
1993	3.8	3.0	21.7
1994	-6.1	-0.1	-2.8
1995	8.1	9.7	-6.9
1996	5.5	19.7	43.6
1997	-1.1	10.4	-0.3
1998	12.6	19.7	25.4
1999	5.3	16.5	18.9
2000	3.2	5.1	35.4
2001	-13.6	1.7	16.4
2002	1.8	4.7	2.9
2003	-2.7	6.6	-6.7
2004	-1.8	5.4	3.5
2005	1.2	-0.6	-1.6
2006	3.1	4.5	3.8
2007	-0.7	-2.7	-10.2
2008	-0.8	1.4	13.1
2009	-6.3	8.1	29.0
2010	5.1	12.5	17.2
2011	3.5	3.5	6.1
2012	7.1	12.9	19.3
2013	5.6	6.2	4.5
2014	0.8	-2.7	-0.2
2015	2.7	12.5	6.8
2016	10.4	10.2	16.0
2017	4.3	5.4	5.7
2018	-6.0	1.6	3.4
2019	6.1	6.7	8.2
2020	-20.9	-10.8	-23.7
2021	2.7	-0.1	-2.3
2022	4.7	7.0	-8.1
Avg	1.5%	6.3%	9.7%
Fq > 0	67%	82%	70%

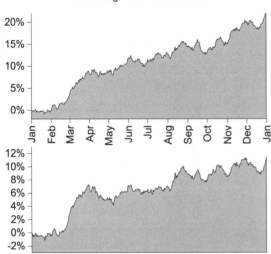

TJX - Avg. Year 1990 to 2021

TJX / S&P 500 Relative Strength - Avg Yr. 1990-2021

2021/22 Performance Update.

In 2021, TJX underperformed the S&P 500 for the full year and slightly underperformed in its strong seasonal period.

In the first part of 2022, retail stocks performed poorly as poor earnings and forecasts weighed on the sector. TJX underperformed the S&P 500 in the first half of the year and in its strong seasonal period.

This was the third year in a row that TJX underperformed in its strong seasonal period.

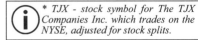
TJX - stock symbol for The TJX Companies Inc. which trades on the NYSE, adjusted for stock splits.

TJX Performance

TJX Monthly % Gain (1990-2021)

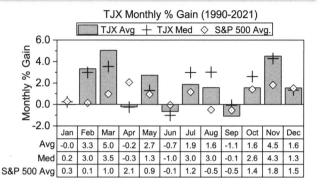

	Jan	Feb	Mar	Apr	May	Jun	Jul	Aug	Sep	Oct	Nov	Dec
Avg	-0.0	3.3	5.0	-0.2	2.7	-0.7	1.9	1.6	-1.1	1.6	4.5	1.6
Med	0.2	3.0	3.5	-0.3	1.3	-1.0	3.0	3.0	-0.1	2.6	4.3	1.3
S&P 500 Avg	0.3	0.1	1.0	2.1	0.9	-0.1	1.2	-0.5	-0.5	1.4	1.8	1.5

Fq % TJX Gain > 0% (1990-2021)

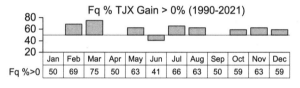

	Jan	Feb	Mar	Apr	May	Jun	Jul	Aug	Sep	Oct	Nov	Dec
Fq %>0	50	69	75	50	63	41	66	63	50	59	63	59

Fq % TJX Gain > S&P 500 % (1990-2021)

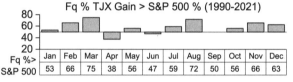

	Jan	Feb	Mar	Apr	May	Jun	Jul	Aug	Sep	Oct	Nov	Dec
Fq %> S&P 500	53	66	75	38	56	47	59	72	50	56	66	63

TJX % Gain 5 Year (2017-2021)

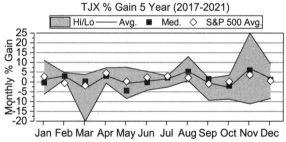

TJX Performance 2021-2022

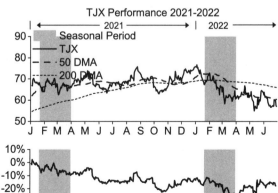

Relative Strength, % Gain vs. S&P 500

Market Indices & Rates
Weekly Values**

Stock Markets	2021	2022
Dow	29,983	34,725
S&P500	3,714	4,432
Nasdaq	13,071	13,771
TSX	17,337	20,742
FTSE	6,407	7,466
DAX	13,433	15,319
Nikkei	27,663	26,717
Hang Seng	28,284	23,550

Commodities	2021	2022
Oil	52.20	86.82
Gold	1863.8	1788.2

Bond Yields	2021	2022
USA 5 Yr Treasury	0.45	1.61
USA 10 Yr T	1.11	1.78
USA 20 Yr T	1.68	2.14
Moody's Aaa	2.51	3.05
Moody's Baa	3.28	3.69
CAN 5 Yr T	0.42	1.63
CAN 10 Yr T	0.89	1.76

Money Market	2021	2022
USA Fed Funds	0.25	0.25
USA 3 Mo T-B	0.06	0.19
CAN tgt overnight rate	0.25	0.25
CAN 3 Mo T-B	0.07	0.29

Foreign Exchange	2021	2022
EUR/USD	1.21	1.12
GBP/USD	1.37	1.34
USD/CAD	1.28	1.28
USD/JPY	104.68	115.26

JANUARY

M	T	W	T	F	S	S
						1
2	3	4	5	6	7	8
9	10	11	12	13	14	15
16	17	18	19	20	21	22
23	24	25	26	27	28	29
30	31					

FEBRUARY

M	T	W	T	F	S	S
	1	2	3	4	5	
6	7	8	9	10	11	12
13	14	15	16	17	18	19
20	21	22	23	24	25	26
27	28					

MARCH

M	T	W	T	F	S	S
	1	2	3	4	5	
6	7	8	9	10	11	12
13	14	15	16	17	18	19
20	21	22	23	24	25	26
27	28	29	30	31		

SNAP-ON

SNA ①LONG (Jan24-May5) ②SELL SHORT (Aug1-Oct8)
③LONG (Oct9-Dec31)

Snap-On has a seasonal trend that generally follows the seasonal six month trend of the stock market, performing well from October into early May. There are some differences, with Snap-On performing much worse than the S&P 500 from August into early October. This is generally a slower time for automobile maintenance and the purchase of automobile maintenance tools.

22% gain & positive 84% of the time

After its weak summer seasonal period, Snap-On tends to perform well from October 9 to the end of the year as automobile maintenance tends to increase at this time. This strong seasonal period occurs right after its weak seasonal period and as such it has typically been best to use technical indicators to help navigate the seasonal transition.

2021/22 Performance Update.

In the first part of 2021, Snap-On performed extremely well and strongly outperformed the S&P 500 in its strong seasonal period from Jan 24 to May 5. The strong performance more than made up for its weaker performance from Oct 9 to Dec 31. In 2022, Once again Snap-On performed well from Jan 24 to May 5.

(i) *SNA - stock symbol for Snap-On, which trades on the NYSE, adjusted for stock splits.*

Snap-On vs. S&P 500 1990 to 2021

Negative Short ☐   Positive Long ▨

Year	Jan 24 to May 5 S&P 500	SNA	Aug 1 to Oct 8 S&P 500	SNA	Oct 9 to Dec 31 S&P 500	SNA	Compound Growth S&P 500	SNA
1990	2.0 %	8.1 %	-12.0 %	-20.3 %	5.3 %	13.4 %	-5.4 %	47.5 %
1991	15.3	7.4	-1.8	-1.9	9.6	0.8	24.0	10.3
1992	0.5	-2.2	-3.9	-4.0	6.9	3.7	3.2	5.5
1993	1.9	12.2	2.7	-11.8	1.3	-1.3	6.1	23.8
1994	-4.9	-8.8	-0.7	-5.5	0.9	-4.0	-4.7	-7.6
1995	11.7	16.3	3.6	-7.8	5.7	17.5	22.4	47.3
1996	4.7	3.3	9.5	10.7	5.7	8.8	21.2	0.3
1997	6.8	7.4	2.0	6.4	-0.4	-0.6	8.6	0.0
1998	16.5	9.4	-14.4	-17.3	28.1	18.5	27.8	52.0
1999	10.0	0.2	0.5	-7.1	10.0	-18.3	21.6	-12.3
2000	-0.6	-5.6	-1.5	-27.1	-6.3	26.7	-8.3	52.0
2001	-6.9	3.9	-12.3	-9.5	8.1	37.8	-11.7	56.8
2002	-4.9	4.1	-12.4	-17.9	10.2	26.1	-8.2	54.7
2003	4.4	14.7	4.4	2.5	7.6	11.0	17.2	24.1
2004	-1.8	7.4	1.9	-11.0	8.0	20.2	8.1	43.3
2005	0.4	-0.1	-3.1	-2.3	4.4	4.8	1.6	7.0
2006	4.9	7.4	5.7	7.0	5.1	6.0	16.5	5.8
2007	5.4	14.7	6.7	-5.4	-5.4	-2.5	6.4	17.8
2008	5.1	44.7	-22.3	-22.9	-8.3	-9.3	-25.1	61.2
2009	8.6	2.7	7.9	0.8	4.7	17.7	22.7	19.9
2010	6.8	7.2	5.8	6.0	7.9	19.5	21.9	20.4
2011	4.0	7.6	-10.6	-19.9	8.8	11.2	1.2	43.4
2012	4.0	14.5	5.6	7.4	-2.0	8.5	7.6	15.0
2013	8.0	7.4	-1.8	0.8	11.7	14.5	18.4	22.0
2014	3.1	11.8	2.0	-0.1	4.6	13.8	9.9	27.3
2015	1.8	12.7	-4.3	-1.9	1.5	6.0	-1.1	21.7
2016	7.5	3.5	-0.9	-4.4	4.0	14.0	10.8	23.1
2017	5.9	-1.8	3.2	-3.2	4.9	16.8	14.6	18.3
2018	-6.2	-20.5	2.4	5.7	-13.1	-19.0	-16.5	-39.2
2019	11.6	5.1	-2.9	-0.5	11.7	11.5	21.0	17.7
2020	-13.7	-27.8	5.4	8.6	9.0	8.1	-0.9	-28.6
2021	8.4	38.0	-0.1	-1.1	8.5	-0.1	17.6	39.4
Avg.	3.8 %	6.4 %	-1.1 %	-4.6 %	5.0 %	8.8 %	7.8 %	21.6 %
Fq>0	78 %	78 %	50	31 %	81 %	75 %	72 %	84 %

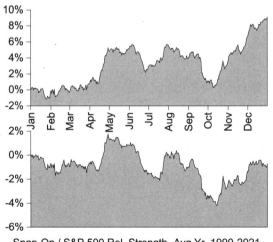

Snap-On - Avg. Year 1990 to 2021

Snap-On / S&P 500 Rel. Strength- Avg Yr. 1990-2021

Snap-On Performance

SNA Monthly % Gain (1990-2021)

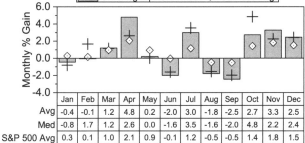

SNA Avg   + SNA Med   ◇ S&P 500 Avg.

	Jan	Feb	Mar	Apr	May	Jun	Jul	Aug	Sep	Oct	Nov	Dec
Avg	-0.4	-0.1	1.2	4.8	0.2	-2.0	3.0	-1.8	-2.5	2.7	3.3	2.5
Med	-0.8	1.7	1.2	2.6	0.0	-1.6	3.5	-1.6	-2.0	4.8	2.2	2.4
S&P 500 Avg	0.3	0.1	1.0	2.1	0.9	-0.1	1.2	-0.5	-0.5	1.4	1.8	1.5

Fq % SNA Gain > 0% (1990-2021)

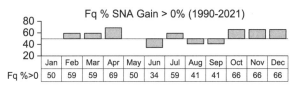

	Jan	Feb	Mar	Apr	May	Jun	Jul	Aug	Sep	Oct	Nov	Dec
Fq %>0	50	59	59	69	50	34	59	41	41	66	66	66

Fq % SNA Gain > S&P 500 % (1990-2021)

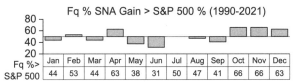

	Jan	Feb	Mar	Apr	May	Jun	Jul	Aug	Sep	Oct	Nov	Dec
Fq %> S&P 500	44	53	44	63	38	31	50	47	41	66	66	63

SNA % Gain 5 Year (2017-2021)

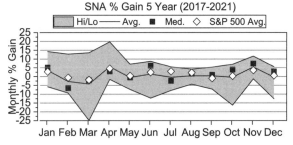

Hi/Lo —— Avg. ■ Med. ◇ S&P 500 Avg.

SNA Performance 2021-2022

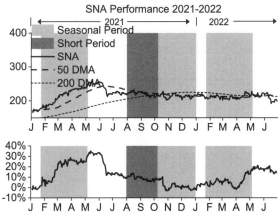

Relative Strength, % Gain vs. S&P 500

Market Indices & Rates
Weekly Values**

Stock Markets	2021	2022
Dow	31,148	35,090
S&P500	3,887	4,501
Nasdaq	13,856	14,098
TSX	18,136	21,272
FTSE	6,489	7,516
DAX	14,057	15,100
Nikkei	28,779	27,440
Hang Seng	29,289	24,573

Commodities	2021	2022
Oil	56.85	92.31
Gold	1803.0	1804.7

Bond Yields	2021	2022
USA 5 Yr Treasury	0.47	1.78
USA 10 Yr T	1.19	1.93
USA 20 Yr T	1.79	2.29
Moody's Aaa	2.63	3.22
Moody's Baa	3.37	3.85
CAN 5 Yr T	0.48	1.71
CAN 10 Yr T	1.00	1.86

Money Market	2021	2022
USA Fed Funds	0.25	0.25
USA 3 Mo T-B	0.03	0.23
CAN tgt overnight rate	0.25	0.25
CAN 3 Mo T-B	0.06	0.28

Foreign Exchange	2021	2022
EUR/USD	1.20	1.14
GBP/USD	1.37	1.35
USD/CAD	1.28	1.28
USD/JPY	105.39	115.26

JANUARY

M	T	W	T	F	S	S
						1
2	3	4	5	6	7	8
9	10	11	12	13	14	15
16	17	18	19	20	21	22
23	24	25	26	27	28	29
30	31					

FEBRUARY

M	T	W	T	F	S	S
	1	2	3	4	5	
6	7	8	9	10	11	12
13	14	15	16	17	18	19
20	21	22	23	24	25	26
27	28					

MARCH

M	T	W	T	F	S	S
	1	2	3	4	5	
6	7	8	9	10	11	12
13	14	15	16	17	18	19
20	21	22	23	24	25	26
27	28	29	30	31		

FEBRUARY

	MONDAY	TUESDAY	WEDNESDAY
WEEK 05	30	31	**1** 27
WEEK 06	**6** 22	**7** 21	**8** 20
WEEK 07	**13** 15	**14** 14	**15** 13

WEEK 08	**20** 8
	
	CAN Market Closed -
	      Family Day
	
	USA Market Closed -
	      Presidents' Day
		21 7	**22** 6

WEEK 09	**27** 1	**28**	1

THURSDAY	FRIDAY
2 26	**3** 25
9 19	**10** 18
16 12	**17** 11
23 5	**24** 4
2	3

MARCH

M	T	W	T	F	S	S
		1	2	3	4	5
6	7	8	9	10	11	12
13	14	15	16	17	18	19
20	21	22	23	24	25	26
27	28	29	30	31		

APRIL

M	T	W	T	F	S	S
					1	2
3	4	5	6	7	8	9
10	11	13	13	14	15	16
17	18	19	20	21	22	23
22	23	26	27	28	29	30

MAY

M	T	W	T	F	S	S
1	2	3	4	5	6	7
8	9	10	11	12	13	14
15	16	17	18	19	20	21
22	23	24	25	26	27	28
29	30	31				

JUNE

M	T	W	T	F	S	S
			1	2	3	4
5	6	7	8	9	10	11
12	13	14	15	16	17	18
19	20	21	22	23	24	25
26	27	28	29	30		

FEBRUARY SUMMARY

S&P500 Cumulative Daily Gains for Avg Month 1950 to 2022

	Dow Jones	S&P 500	Nasdaq	TSX Comp
Month Rank	8	11	10	7
# Up	42	40	27	23
# Down	30	32	23	14
% Pos	58	56	54	59
% Avg. Gain	0.3	0.0	0.6	0.9

Dow & S&P 1950-2021, Nasdaq 1972-2021, TSX 1985-2021

♦ Historically, over the long-term, February has been one of the weaker months of the year for the S&P 500. Over the last ten years, the S&P 500 has bucked this trend and has been positive six out of ten times. ♦ The energy sector typically starts to outperform in late February, helping to boost the S&P/TSX Composite. ♦ The consumer discretionary sector tends to be one of the better performing sectors. ♦ In February 2022, the S&P 500 produced a loss of 3.1%, which followed on January's loss of 5.3%.

BEST / WORST FEBRUARY BROAD MKTS. 2013-2022

BEST FEBRUARY MARKETS
- ♦ Nasdaq (2015) 7.1%
- ♦ Nikkei 225 (2015) 6.4%
- ♦ Russell 2000 (2021) 6.1%

WORST FEBRUARY MARKETS
- ♦ Dow (2020) -10.1%
- ♦ FTSE 100 (2020) -9.7%
- ♦ Nikkei 225 (2020) -8.9%

Index Values End of Month

	2013	2014	2015	2016	2017	2018	2019	2020	2021	2022
Dow	14,054	16,322	18,133	16,517	20,812	25,029	25,916	25,409	30,932	33,893
S&P 500	1,515	1,859	2,105	1,932	2,364	2,714	2,784	2,954	3,811	4,374
Nasdaq	3,160	4,308	4,964	4,558	5,825	7,273	7,533	8,567	13,192	13,751
TSX Comp.	12,822	14,210	15,234	12,860	15,399	15,443	15,999	16,263	18,060	21,126
Russell 1000	841	1,041	1,173	1,067	1,311	1,501	1,546	1,635	2,159	2,423
Russell 2000	911	1,183	1,233	1,034	1,387	1,512	1,576	1,476	2,201	2,048
FTSE 100	6,361	6,810	6,947	6,097	7,263	7,232	7,075	6,581	6,483	7,458
Nikkei 225	11,559	14,841	18,798	16,027	19,119	22,068	21,385	21,143	28,966	26,527

Percent Gain for February

	2013	2014	2015	2016	2017	2018	2019	2020	2021	2022
Dow	1.4	4.0	5.6	0.3	4.8	-4.3	3.7	-10.1	3.2	-3.5
S&P 500	1.1	4.3	5.5	-0.4	3.7	-3.9	3.0	-8.4	2.6	-3.1
Nasdaq	0.6	5.0	7.1	-1.2	3.8	-1.9	3.4	-6.4	0.9	-3.4
TSX Comp.	1.1	3.8	3.8	0.3	0.1	-3.2	2.9	-6.1	4.2	0.1
Russell 1000	1.1	4.5	5.5	-0.3	3.6	-3.9	3.2	-8.3	2.8	-2.9
Russell 2000	1.0	4.6	5.8	-0.1	1.8	-4.0	5.1	-8.5	6.1	1.0
FTSE 100	1.3	4.6	2.9	0.2	2.3	-4.0	1.5	-9.7	1.2	-0.1
Nikkei 225	3.8	-0.5	6.4	-8.5	0.4	-4.5	2.9	-8.9	4.7	-1.8

February Market Avg. Performance 2013 to 2022[1]

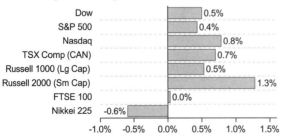

Dow	0.5%
S&P 500	0.4%
Nasdaq	0.8%
TSX Comp (CAN)	0.7%
Russell 1000 (Lg Cap)	0.5%
Russell 2000 (Sm Cap)	1.3%
FTSE 100	0.0%
Nikkei 225	-0.6%

Interest Corner Feb[2]

	Fed Funds %[3]	3 Mo. T-Bill %[4]	10 Yr %[5]	20 Yr %[6]
2022	0.25	0.35	1.83	2.25
2021	0.25	0.04	1.44	2.08
2020	1.75	1.27	1.13	1.46
2019	2.50	2.45	2.73	2.94
2018	1.50	1.65	2.87	3.02

(1) Russell Data provided by Russell (2) Federal Reserve Bank of St. Louis- end of month values (3) Target rate set by FOMC (4)(5)(6) Constant yield maturities.

FEBRUARY SECTOR PERFORMANCE

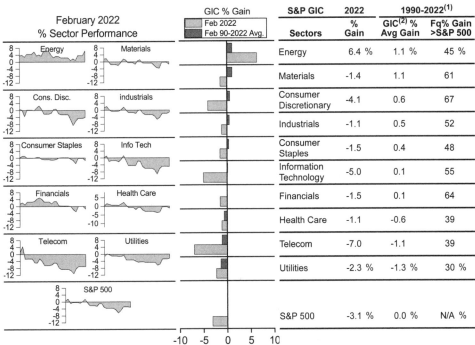

S&P GIC Sectors	2022 % Gain	1990-2022[1] GIC[2] % Avg Gain	1990-2022[1] Fq% Gain >S&P 500
Energy	6.4 %	1.1 %	45 %
Materials	-1.4	1.1	61
Consumer Discretionary	-4.1	0.6	67
Industrials	-1.1	0.5	52
Consumer Staples	-1.5	0.4	48
Information Technology	-5.0	0.1	55
Financials	-1.5	0.1	64
Health Care	-1.1	-0.6	39
Telecom	-7.0	-1.1	39
Utilities	-2.3 %	-1.3 %	30 %
S&P 500	-3.1 %	0.0 %	N/A %

Sector Commentary

♦ In February 2022, most of the sectors were positive. ♦ Generally, the sectors followed their seasonal trends with their relative performance compared to the S&P 500. ♦ The energy sector performed particularly well with a gain of 6.4%. ♦ The telecom sector was hit particularly hard from rising interest rates, losing 7% in February. ♦ The information technology sector was also hit hard by rising rates, losing 5% in February.

Sub-Sector Commentary

♦ In February 2022, the stock market was in a risk-off mode; nevertheless, the cyclical sub-sectors, metals & mining and steel, both produced gains over 20%. A lot of the gains were generated as the Russia-Ukraine war started to unfold. ♦ The auto sub-sector, produced a loss of 7.9% as supply chain issues continued to affect the sub-sector. ♦ After a poor performance in January, the homebuilders continued to lose ground in February, with a loss of 5.7%.

SELECTED SUB-SECTORS[3]

Silver	8.2 %	3.1 %	64 %
SOX (1995-2022)	-1.5	2.6	68
Metals & Mining	20.3	2.3	58
Steel	29.8	1.9	55
Retail	-2.6	1.4	70
Chemicals	-4.7	1.2	64
Gold	6.4	1.1	48
Agriculture (1994-2022)	4.6	0.5	52
Transportation	-0.5	0.5	55
Railroads	-1.2	0.3	48
Banks	-2.6	0.3	58
Homebuilders	-5.7	-0.4	52
Auto	-7.9	-0.4	39
Pharma	-4.2	-0.8	36
Biotech (1993-2022)	-0.4	-1.0	48

COPPER
Cu

① Jan 29 to Mar 5   ② Jun 24 to Jul 31

Copper has a strong seasonal period early in the year as economic activity tends to increase at this time. In addition, copper demand tends to increase in China before the Chinese New Year' holidays. Investors front run the increase in Chinese copper demand. As a result, once the Chinese economy starts to increase after the holidays, copper tends to lose momentum. From 1990 to 2021, in the period from January 29 to March 5, copper has produced an average gain of 4.2% and has been positive 72% of the time.

**8% gain &
75% of the time positive**

Copper also tends to perform well from late June until the end of July. The positive trend in copper somewhat aligns with strong stock market performance that tends to occur from late June into mid-July as investors move to a risk-on mode, in the period leading up to the Q2 earnings season.

From 1990 to 2021, in the period from June 24 to Jul 31, copper has produced an average gain of 3.9% and has been positive 72% of the time. It should be noted that after its strong seasonal period finishes, copper on average has declined in price in August, which tends to be one of the weaker months of the year for copper.

2021/22 Performance Update.
In 2021, copper was positive in both of its strong seasonal periods.

In 2022, copper performed well in its seasonal period from Jan 29 to Mar 5. As the strong seasonal period finished, copper turned abruptly lower.

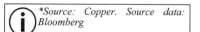

Source: Copper. Source data: Bloomberg

Copper vs S&P 500 - 1990 to 2021   Positive ▢

Year	Jan 29-Mar 5 S&P 500	Jan 29-Mar 5 Copper	Jun 24-Jul 31 S&P 500	Jun 24-Jul 31 Copper	Compound Growth S&P 500	Compound Growth Copper
1990	2.4 %	18.8 %	0.2 %	12.1 %	2.6 %	33.1 %
1991	12.1	4.0	2.7	0.4	15.1	4.4
1992	-2.0	2.8	5.0	6.7	2.9	9.6
1993	1.7	-4.8	1.1	4.7	2.8	-0.4
1994	-2.9	4.5	1.9	-1.9	-1.1	2.6
1995	3.2	-3.9	2.2	-2.5	5.5	-6.4
1996	5.5	3.1	-4.0	2.2	1.2	5.4
1997	4.8	4.0	8.6	-7.9	13.9	-4.2
1998	5.9	-0.2	0.1	2.5	6.0	2.3
1999	0.8	-1.5	-0.3	15.5	0.5	13.8
2000	3.6	-3.8	-0.7	7.9	2.8	3.8
2001	-8.4	-0.2	-1.2	-4.5	-9.4	-4.7
2002	1.2	5.7	-7.8	-8.3	-6.8	-3.1
2003	-3.3	1.0	0.9	7.0	-2.5	8.0
2004	2.5	18.6	-3.7	9.3	-1.3	29.6
2005	4.3	3.9	2.8	7.7	7.2	11.8
2006	0.3	1.4	2.6	13.3	2.9	14.9
2007	-3.4	1.3	-3.1	7.8	-6.4	9.2
2008	-1.5	24.8	-3.8	-3.8	-5.3	20.0
2009	-21.9	10.5	10.3	19.3	-13.9	31.9
2010	5.0	10.3	0.9	12.8	5.9	24.4
2011	3.5	2.6	0.7	11.0	4.2	13.9
2012	3.6	-0.6	3.3	3.5	7.1	2.9
2013	2.6	-3.9	5.9	0.6	8.7	-3.3
2014	4.5	-1.5	-1.6	2.4	2.8	0.8
2015	4.9	7.9	-1.0	-9.9	3.9	-2.8
2016	5.6	10.0	2.9	2.5	8.6	12.8
2017	3.9	0.3	1.3	10.2	5.2	10.5
2018	-5.3	-2.2	2.2	-6.5	-3.2	-8.5
2019	5.5	9.5	1.0	-1.4	6.6	7.9
2020	-7.7	-0.3	4.5	7.9	-3.6	7.6
2021	1.4	13.9	3.6	3.5	5.1	17.9
Avg.	1.0 %	4.2 %	1.2 %	3.9 %	2.1 %	8.3 %
Fq>0	72 %	66 %	69 %	72 %	69 %	75 %

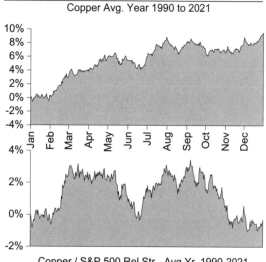

Copper Avg. Year 1990 to 2021

Copper / S&P 500 Rel Str.- Avg Yr. 1990-2021

Copper Performance

Copper Monthly % Gain (1990-2021)

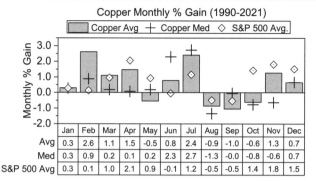

	Jan	Feb	Mar	Apr	May	Jun	Jul	Aug	Sep	Oct	Nov	Dec
Avg	0.3	2.6	1.1	1.5	-0.5	0.8	2.4	-0.9	-1.0	-0.6	1.3	0.7
Med	0.3	0.9	0.2	0.1	0.2	2.3	2.7	-1.3	-0.0	-0.8	-0.6	0.7
S&P 500 Avg	0.3	0.1	1.0	2.1	0.9	-0.1	1.2	-0.5	-0.5	1.4	1.8	1.5

Fq % Copper Gain > 0% (1990-2021)

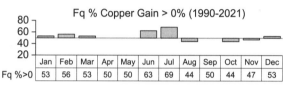

	Jan	Feb	Mar	Apr	May	Jun	Jul	Aug	Sep	Oct	Nov	Dec
Fq %>0	53	56	53	50	50	63	69	44	50	44	47	53

Fq % Copper Gain > S&P 500 % (1990-2021)

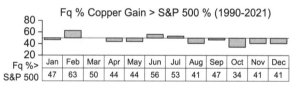

	Jan	Feb	Mar	Apr	May	Jun	Jul	Aug	Sep	Oct	Nov	Dec
Fq %> S&P 500	47	63	50	44	44	56	53	41	47	34	41	41

Copper % Gain 5 Year (2017-2021)

Copper Performance 2021-2022

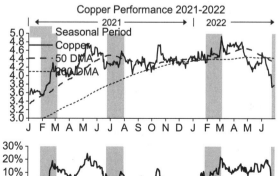

Relative Strength, % Gain vs. S&P 500

Market Indices & Rates
Weekly Values**

Stock Markets	2021	2022
Dow	31,458	34,738
S&P500	3,935	4,419
Nasdaq	14,095	13,791
TSX	18,460	21,549
FTSE	6,590	7,661
DAX	14,050	15,425
Nikkei	29,520	27,696
Hang Seng	30,174	24,907

Commodities	2021	2022
Oil	59.47	93.10
Gold	1816.4	1831.2

Bond Yields	2021	2022
USA 5 Yr Treasury	0.50	1.84
USA 10 Yr T	1.20	1.92
USA 20 Yr T	1.83	2.30
Moody's Aaa	2.65	3.22
Moody's Baa	3.39	3.92
CAN 5 Yr T	0.50	1.72
CAN 10 Yr T	1.03	1.85

Money Market	2021	2022
USA Fed Funds	0.25	0.25
USA 3 Mo T-B	0.04	0.36
CAN tgt overnight rate	0.25	0.25
CAN 3 Mo T-B	0.07	0.31

Foreign Exchange	2021	2022
EUR/USD	1.21	1.14
GBP/USD	1.38	1.36
USD/CAD	1.27	1.27
USD/JPY	104.94	115.42

FEBRUARY

M	T	W	T	F	S	S
		1	2	3	4	5
6	7	8	9	10	11	12
13	14	15	16	17	18	19
20	21	22	23	24	25	26
27	28					

MARCH

M	T	W	T	F	S	S
		1	2	3	4	5
6	7	8	9	10	11	12
13	14	15	16	17	18	19
20	21	22	23	24	25	26
27	28	29	30	31		

APRIL

M	T	W	T	F	S	S
				1	2	3
4	5	6	7	8	9	10
11	13	13	14	15	16	17
18	20	20	21	22	23	24
25	27	27	28	29	30	

EASTMAN CHEMICAL COMPANY

EMN
① LONG (Jan28 to May5)
② SELL SHORT (May30-Oct27)

In its positive seasonal period from January 28 to May 5, Eastman Chemical during the period from 1994 to 2021, has produced an average 11.6% gain and has been positive 82% of the time.

In its short sell seasonal period from May 30 to October 27, in the same yearly period, Eastman Chemical has produced an average loss of 4.9% and has been positive 39% of the time.

17.4% growth

Eastman Chemical, in its 10-K report filed with regulators in 2013, outlines the seasonal trends in its business. "The Company's earnings are typically greater in second and third quarters." This is a bit different than many other cyclical companies, that tend to have weaker earnings over the summer months.

The net result is for Eastman Chemical to outperform into May and then underperform at the tail end of Q2, and Q3, as investors anticipate a weaker Q4 earnings report. In Q4, Eastman tends to perform at market.

2021/22 Performance Update.
In 2021, Eastman underperformed the S&P 500 for the full year. but managed to perform very well in its strong seasonal period and then underperform the S&P 500 in its weak seasonal period. The combination of trades worked well. In the first half of 2022, Eastman underperformed the S&P 500 in its strong seasonal period and underperformed the S&P 500 in June, when it typically performs poorly.

ⓘ *Eastman Chemical Company manufactures and sells chemicals, fibers, and plastics, globally. It trades on the NYSE, adjusted for splits.*

Eastman Chemical* vs. S&P 500 1994 to 2021

Positive Long ▢   Negative Short ▢

Year	Jan 28 to May 5 S&P 500	EMN	May 30 to Oct 27 S&P 500	EMN	Compound Growth S&P 500	EMN
1994	-5.4	7.8 %	1.9 %	8.7 %	-3.6 %	-1.6 %
1995	10.6	11.0	10.7	2.6	22.4	8.2
1996	3.2	7.1	4.9	-21.8	8.3	30.5
1997	8.5	-1.1	3.9	2.7	12.8	-3.8
1998	15.1	18.7	-2.3	-15.3	12.4	36.8
1999	8.4	32.1	-0.4	-24.5	8.0	64.4
2000	2.4	21.9	0.1	-19.3	2.6	45.3
2001	-6.5	22.7	-12.9	-33.1	-18.6	63.2
2002	-5.3	13.1	-15.9	-21.2	-20.4	37.0
2003	9.3	-11.4	8.6	-0.6	18.7	-10.9
2004	-2.0	16.4	0.4	-1.9	-1.6	18.6
2005	-0.2	10.5	-1.7	-15.7	-1.8	27.9
2006	3.3	17.3	7.6	5.5	11.1	10.9
2007	5.9	11.8	1.1	-0.1	7.1	11.9
2008	5.8	14.9	-39.3	-55.6	-35.8	78.8
2009	6.9	52.4	15.7	34.3	23.6	0.2
2010	6.2	12.4	8.5	33.0	15.3	-24.7
2011	2.7	9.2	-3.5	-23.1	-0.8	34.5
2012	4.0	0.6	6.0	21.6	10.2	-21.1
2013	7.4	-5.6	6.8	8.4	14.7	-13.5
2014	5.8	15.5	2.2	-15.6	8.1	33.4
2015	3.0	13.1	-2.0	-6.0	0.9	19.9
2016	8.9	21.5	1.6	-8.8	10.7	32.1
2017	4.6	2.5	6.8	16.4	11.7	-14.3
2018	-7.3	2.4	-1.2	-25.0	-8.4	28.0
2019	10.5	-1.6	8.6	12.7	20.1	-14.2
2020	-11.6	-13.9	11.4	21.1	-1.5	-32.1
2021	11.1	22.7	8.3	-15.8	20.3	42.1
Avg.	3.8 %	11.6 %	1.3 %	-4.9 %	5.2 %	17.4 %
Fq>0	75 %	82 %	68 %	39 %	68 %	68 %

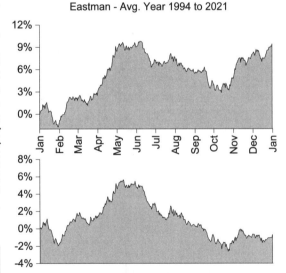

Eastman - Avg. Year 1994 to 2021

Eastman / S&P 500 Rel. Strength- Avg Yr. 1994-2021

Eastman Chemical Performance

EMN Monthly % Gain (1994-2021)

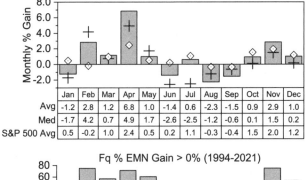

	Jan	Feb	Mar	Apr	May	Jun	Jul	Aug	Sep	Oct	Nov	Dec
Avg	-1.2	2.8	1.2	6.8	1.0	-1.4	0.6	-2.3	-1.5	0.9	2.9	1.0
Med	-1.7	4.2	0.7	4.9	1.7	-2.6	-2.5	-1.2	-0.6	0.1	1.5	0.2
S&P 500 Avg	0.5	-0.2	1.0	2.4	0.5	0.2	1.1	-0.3	-0.4	1.5	2.0	1.2

Fq % EMN Gain > 0% (1994-2021)

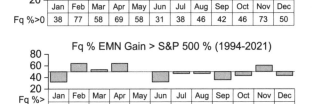

	Jan	Feb	Mar	Apr	May	Jun	Jul	Aug	Sep	Oct	Nov	Dec
Fq %>0	38	77	58	69	58	31	38	46	42	46	73	50

Fq % EMN Gain > S&P 500 % (1994-2021)

	Jan	Feb	Mar	Apr	May	Jun	Jul	Aug	Sep	Oct	Nov	Dec
Fq %> S&P 500	32	64	54	64	50	32	46	46	36	43	61	43

EMN % Gain 5 Year (2017-2021)

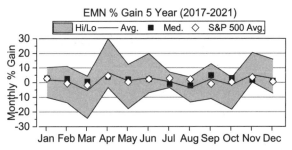

EMN Performance 2021-2022

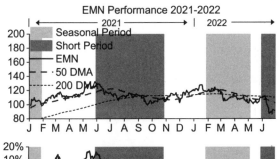

Relative Strength, % Gain vs. S&P 500

Market Indices & Rates
Weekly Values**

Stock Markets	2021	2022
Dow	31,494	34,079
S&P500	3,907	4,349
Nasdaq	13,874	13,548
TSX	18,384	21,008
FTSE	6,624	7,514
DAX	13,993	15,043
Nikkei	30,018	27,122
Hang Seng	30,645	24,328

Commodities	2021	2022
Oil	59.24	91.07
Gold	1786.2	1893.6

Bond Yields	2021	2022
USA 5 Yr Treasury	0.59	1.82
USA 10 Yr T	1.34	1.92
USA 20 Yr T	1.98	2.30
Moody's Aaa	2.76	3.29
Moody's Baa	3.48	4.05
CAN 5 Yr T	0.64	1.72
CAN 10 Yr T	1.21	1.88

Money Market	2021	2022
USA Fed Funds	0.25	0.25
USA 3 Mo T-B	0.04	0.35
CAN tgt overnight rate	0.25	0.25
CAN 3 Mo T-B	0.09	0.34

Foreign Exchange	2021	2022
EUR/USD	1.21	1.13
GBP/USD	1.40	1.36
USD/CAD	1.26	1.28
USD/JPY	105.45	115.01

FEBRUARY

M	T	W	T	F	S	S
		1	2	3	4	5
6	7	8	9	10	11	12
13	14	15	16	17	18	19
20	21	22	23	24	25	26
27	28					

MARCH

M	T	W	T	F	S	S
	1	2	3	4	5	
6	7	8	9	10	11	12
13	14	15	16	17	18	19
20	21	22	23	24	25	26
27	28	29	30	31		

APRIL

M	T	W	T	F	S	S
				1	2	3
4	5	6	7	8	9	10
11	13	13	14	15	16	17
18	20	20	21	22	23	24
25	27	27	28	29	30	

ADOBE
ADBE ① Feb 1 to May 23 ② Oct 10 to Nov 17

Adobe's strongest fiscal quarter is its first quarter which ends in February. Adobe tends to report on the quarter in late March. Investors tend to front run the quarter, helping to push Adobe stock price higher in February and March.

The trend continues on into May. This is a bit unusual for a seasonal trend, to last past the event that is being front run.

The trend fades fast in late May as Adobe gets ready to report its second fiscal quarter, which tends to be the weakest revenue quarter. From February 1 to May 23, in the period from 1990 to 2021, Adobe has produced an average gain of 22% and has been positive 89% of the time.

37% gain & 88% of the time positive

Adobe also tends to perform well leading up to its fourth fiscal quarter which ends in November and is typically reported in mid-December.

On average, its fourth fiscal quarter is its second best revenue generating quarter. From October 10 to November 17, in the period from 1990 to 2021, Adobe has produced an average gain of 12% and has been positive 75% of the time.

2021/22 Performance Update.
In 2021, Adobe was volatile, but the combination of long trades outperformed the S&P 500. In 2022, Adobe underperformed the S&P 500, including in its Feb 1 to May 23 strong seasonal period. At the end of June 2022, Adobe corrected back to its February 2020 pre-COVID high.

ⓘ *Adobe is a software company. It trades on the Nasdaq, adjusted for splits.*

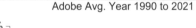
Adobe vs S&P 500 - 1990 to 2021   Positive

Year	Feb 1-May 23 S&P 500	Feb 1-May 23 Adobe	Oct 10-Nov 17 S&P 500	Oct 10-Nov 17 Adobe	Compound Growth S&P 500	Compound Growth Adobe
1990	9.2 %	108.5 %	3.9 %	38.7 %	13.5 %	189.1 %
1991	9.0	26.3	1.5	3.4	10.7	30.6
1992	1.3	-27.1	4.1	22.9	5.5	-10.4
1993	1.6	57.8	1.0	7.8	2.6	70.1
1994	-5.9	-2.9	1.9	-2.5	-4.1	-5.3
1995	12.4	96.1	3.8	26.3	16.6	147.8
1996	6.3	23.2	5.9	17.2	12.5	44.4
1997	7.7	22.4	-2.5	-5.3	5.0	15.9
1998	13.3	12.7	15.7	34.7	31.1	51.8
1999	4.0	66.0	5.6	30.9	9.8	117.2
2000	-1.5	97.8	-2.4	10.6	-3.9	118.7
2001	-5.6	1.8	7.8	10.6	1.7	12.6
2002	-2.9	10.1	17.1	59.3	13.7	75.5
2003	9.1	31.1	0.5	-3.6	9.6	26.3
2004	-3.3	16.0	5.3	17.8	1.8	36.7
2005	1.1	10.2	3.9	16.0	5.0	27.8
2006	-1.8	-27.0	3.7	10.9	1.8	-19.0
2007	5.8	11.2	-6.8	-6.2	-1.4	4.3
2008	-0.2	18.1	-6.5	-18.5	-6.7	-3.8
2009	7.4	37.1	3.6	6.5	11.3	46.1
2010	1.3	-0.4	1.2	7.1	2.5	6.7
2011	2.4	4.2	5.3	9.5	7.8	14.1
2012	0.5	4.0	-5.7	3.0	-5.2	7.1
2013	10.2	13.1	8.6	16.0	19.6	31.1
2014	6.6	8.6	5.9	6.6	12.9	15.8
2015	6.6	14.1	1.8	7.7	8.5	22.9
2016	5.6	8.4	1.6	-2.6	7.2	5.6
2017	5.2	23.1	1.3	20.3	6.7	48.0
2018	-3.2	22.1	-5.0	-6.0	-8.0	14.8
2019	4.4	10.7	6.9	8.5	11.6	20.0
2020	-8.4	9.7	3.8	-6.8	-4.9	2.2
2021	11.9	6.4	6.8	16.3	19.5	23.7
Avg.	3.4 %	22.3 %	3.1 %	11.5 %	6.7 %	37.1 %
Fq>0	72 %	89 %	81 %	75 %	78 %	88 %

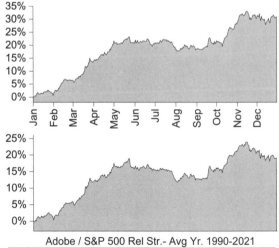
Adobe Avg. Year 1990 to 2021

Adobe / S&P 500 Rel Str.- Avg Yr. 1990-2021

Adobe Performance

ADBE Monthly % Gain (1990-2021)

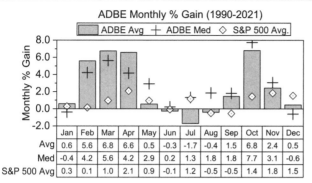

	Jan	Feb	Mar	Apr	May	Jun	Jul	Aug	Sep	Oct	Nov	Dec
Avg	0.6	5.6	6.8	6.6	0.5	-0.3	-1.7	-0.4	1.5	6.8	2.4	0.5
Med	-0.4	4.2	5.6	4.2	2.9	0.2	1.3	1.8	1.8	7.7	3.1	-0.6
S&P 500 Avg	0.3	0.1	1.0	2.1	0.9	-0.1	1.2	-0.5	-0.5	1.4	1.8	1.5

Fq % ADBE Gain > 0% (1990-2021)

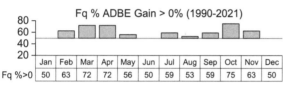

	Jan	Feb	Mar	Apr	May	Jun	Jul	Aug	Sep	Oct	Nov	Dec
Fq %>0	50	63	72	72	56	50	59	53	59	75	63	50

Fq % ADBE Gain > S&P 500 % (1990-2021)

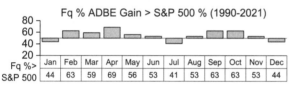

	Jan	Feb	Mar	Apr	May	Jun	Jul	Aug	Sep	Oct	Nov	Dec
Fq %> S&P 500	44	63	59	69	56	53	41	53	63	63	53	44

ADBE % Gain 5 Year (2017-2021)

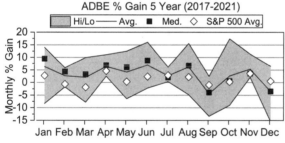

ADBE Performance 2021-2022

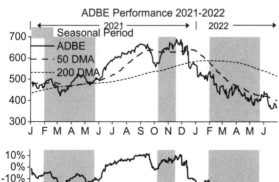

Relative Strength, % Gain vs. S&P 500

Market Indices & Rates
Weekly Values**

Stock Markets	2021	2022
Dow	30,932	34,059
S&P500	3,811	4,385
Nasdaq	13,192	13,695
TSX	18,060	21,106
FTSE	6,483	7,489
DAX	13,786	14,567
Nikkei	28,966	26,477
Hang Seng	28,980	22,767

Commodities	2021	2022
Oil	61.50	92.59
Gold	1742.9	1884.8

Bond Yields	2021	2022
USA 5 Yr Treasury	0.75	1.86
USA 10 Yr T	1.44	1.97
USA 20 Yr T	2.08	2.37
Moody's Aaa	2.86	3.37
Moody's Baa	3.56	4.17
CAN 5 Yr T	0.88	1.74
CAN 10 Yr T	1.36	1.90

Money Market	2021	2022
USA Fed Funds	0.25	0.25
USA 3 Mo T-B	0.04	0.33
CAN tgt overnight rate	0.25	0.25
CAN 3 Mo T-B	0.13	0.38

Foreign Exchange	2021	2022
EUR/USD	1.21	1.13
GBP/USD	1.39	1.34
USD/CAD	1.27	1.27
USD/JPY	106.57	115.55

FEBRUARY

M	T	W	T	F	S	S
		1	2	3	4	5
6	7	8	9	10	11	12
13	14	15	16	17	18	19
20	21	22	23	24	25	26
27	28					

MARCH

M	T	W	T	F	S	S
	1	2	3	4	5
6	7	8	9	10	11	12
13	14	15	16	17	18	19
20	21	22	23	24	25	26
27	28	29	30	31		

APRIL

M	T	W	T	F	S	S
					1	2	3
4	5	6	7	8	9	10
11	13	13	14	15	16	17
18	20	20	21	22	23	24
25	27	27	28	29	30	

OIL STOCKS
①LONG (Feb25-May9) ②SHORT (May10-Jun26)
③LONG (Jul24-Oct3)

Oil stocks have two seasonal periods largely based upon the supply and demand cycles of oil. The highest demand for oil on a seasonal basis occurs in May as the US driving season kicks off. This tends to drive the value of oil stocks higher in the months leading up to the US driving season.

As the driving season gets underway, investors become less interested in oil stocks and as a result, oil stocks tend to perform poorly from mid-May until late June.

9% gain & positive
79% of the time positive

In addition, oil stocks have another strong seasonal period from late July to early October. This is a minor seasonal period and is not as strong as the February to May seasonal period. This seasonal period is based upon the increased demand for oil in the winter heating season.

2021/22 Performance Update.

In 2021, the energy sector outperformed the S&P 500. At the beginning of 2022, the energy sector accelerated its outperformance and strongly outperformed the S&P 500 in the first half of the year.

NYSE Arca Oil Index (XOI): *An index designed to represent a cross section of widely held oil corporations involved in various phases of the oil industry.*
For more information on the XOI index, see www.cboe.com

XOI* vs. S&P 500 1984 to 2021
Negative Short □   Positive Long ▨

	Feb 25 to May 9		May 10 to Jun 26		Jul 24 to Oct 3		Compound Growth	
Year	S&P 500	XOI	S&P 500	XOI	S&P 500	XOI	S&P 500	XOI
1984	1.7 %	5.6 %	-4.6 %	-8.0 %	9.1 %	9.0 %	5.7 %	24.3 %
1985	1.4	4.9	4.5	-2.8	-4.3	6.7	1.5	15.1
1986	6.0	7.7	4.6	-3.2	-2.1	15.7	8.6	28.5
1987	3.7	25.5	4.7	1.3	6.6	-1.2	15.7	22.4
1988	-3.0	5.6	6.7	-1.8	3.0	-3.6	6.6	3.7
1989	6.3	8.1	7.0	1.9	5.6	5.7	20.1	12.0
1990	5.8	-0.6	2.7	-1.3	-12.4	-0.5	-4.8	0.2
1991	4.8	6.8	-3.0	-8.1	1.3	0.7	3.0	16.3
1992	0.9	5.8	-3.0	-1.5	-0.4	2.9	-2.5	10.6
1993	0.3	6.3	1.2	-2.5	3.2	7.8	4.7	17.5
1994	-4.7	3.2	0.1	-1.8	1.9	-3.6	-2.8	1.2
1995	7.3	10.3	3.9	-3.4	5.2	-2.2	17.3	11.6
1996	-2.1	2.2	2.9	1.8	10.5	7.7	11.4	8.1
1997	1.8	4.7	7.1	4.4	3.0	8.9	12.4	8.9
1998	7.5	9.8	2.3	-3.6	-12.0	1.4	-3.3	15.5
1999	7.3	35.4	-2.2	-4.4	-5.5	-2.1	-0.8	38.3
2000	4.3	22.2	3.1	3.3	-3.6	12.2	3.6	32.6
2001	0.8	10.2	-3.1	-2.5	-10.0	-5.1	-12.1	7.1
2002	-1.5	5.3	-9.3	-2.6	2.7	7.3	-8.3	15.9
2003	12.1	5.7	5.6	5.8	4.2	5.5	23.3	5.1
2004	-3.5	4.0	3.3	4.9	4.2	10.9	3.7	9.7
2005	-1.8	-1.0	1.1	7.0	-0.6	14.3	-1.3	5.4
2006	2.8	9.4	-5.6	-4.9	7.6	-8.5	4.3	4.9
2007	4.2	10.1	-1.3	6.5	-0.1	-4.2	2.7	-1.4
2008	2.6	7.6	-7.6	-1.7	-14.3	-18.1	-18.7	-10.4
2009	20.2	15.8	-1.1	-7.6	5.0	3.0	24.8	28.3
2010	0.5	-2.3	-3.1	-7.9	4.0	8.5	1.3	14.3
2011	3.1	-0.6	-5.8	-7.6	-18.3	-26.0	-20.6	-20.8
2012	-0.8	-13.4	-2.6	-4.9	7.4	6.1	3.8	-3.6
2013	7.3	3.8	-1.4	-4.0	-0.8	-0.8	4.9	7.2
2014	1.7	9.1	4.2	4.5	-1.0	-10.7	4.9	-7.1
2015	0.0	1.2	-0.7	-5.9	-7.2	-9.5	-7.8	-3.1
2016	6.7	11.1	-1.0	1.9	-0.6	2.1	4.9	11.4
2017	1.3	-4.0	1.8	-4.2	2.5	8.9	5.6	9.0
2018	-1.8	15.4	0.9	-2.3	4.2	7.4	3.3	26.8
2019	2.8	-2.6	1.5	0.6	-3.2	-7.9	1.0	-10.9
2020	-9.2	-25.2	2.7	-4.6	3.5	-24.0	-3.5	-40.5
2021	7.8	7.0	1.1	6.4	-1.2	13.2	7.7	13.4
Avg.	2.8 %	6.1 %	0.5 %	-1.4 %	-0.1 %	10.0 %	3.2 %	8.6 %
Fq>0	76 %	78 %	58	34 %	53 %	58 %	68 %	79 %

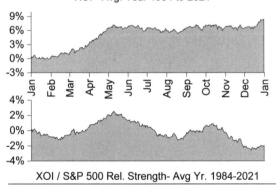

XOI - Avg. Year 1984 to 2021

XOI / S&P 500 Rel. Strength- Avg Yr. 1984-2021

NYSE Arca Oil Index (XOI) Performance

XOI Monthly % Gain (1984-2021)

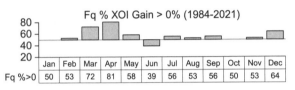

Legend: XOI Avg + XOI Med ◇ S&P 500 Avg.

	Jan	Feb	Mar	Apr	May	Jun	Jul	Aug	Sep	Oct	Nov	Dec
Avg	0.5	0.4	2.9	3.2	0.2	-0.5	0.5	0.3	0.3	-0.0	-0.4	1.7
Med	-0.7	0.4	2.5	2.4	0.5	-1.3	1.7	0.2	1.1	0.4	0.6	1.1
S&P 500 Avg	1.1	0.5	1.3	1.4	0.9	0.2	1.0	-0.2	-0.6	0.8	1.3	1.5

Fq % XOI Gain > 0% (1984-2021)

	Jan	Feb	Mar	Apr	May	Jun	Jul	Aug	Sep	Oct	Nov	Dec
Fq %>0	50	53	72	81	58	39	56	53	56	50	53	64

Fq % XOI Gain > S&P 500 % (1984-2021)

	Jan	Feb	Mar	Apr	May	Jun	Jul	Aug	Sep	Oct	Nov	Dec
Fq %> S&P 500	33	50	64	61	39	36	47	58	61	47	33	56

XOI % Gain 5 Year (2017-2021)

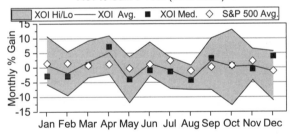

Legend: XOI Hi/Lo — XOI Avg. ■ XOI Med. ◇ S&P 500 Avg.

XOI Performance 2021-2022

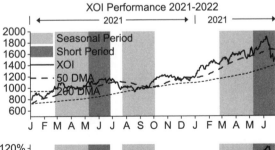

Relative Strength, % Gain vs. S&P 500

Market Indices & Rates
Weekly Values**

Stock Markets	2021	2022
Dow	31,496	33,615
S&P500	3,842	4,329
Nasdaq	12,920	13,313
TSX	18,381	21,402
FTSE	6,631	6,987
DAX	13,921	13,095
Nikkei	28,864	25,985
Hang Seng	29,098	21,905

Commodities	2021	2022
Oil	66.09	115.68
Gold	1696.3	1945.3

Bond Yields	2021	2022
USA 5 Yr Treasury	0.79	1.65
USA 10 Yr T	1.56	1.74
USA 20 Yr T	2.18	2.23
Moody's Aaa	2.97	3.24
Moody's Baa	3.69	4.05
CAN 5 Yr T	0.91	1.46
CAN 10 Yr T	1.50	1.67

Money Market	2021	2022
USA Fed Funds	0.25	0.25
USA 3 Mo T-B	0.04	0.34
CAN tgt overnight rate	0.25	0.50
CAN 3 Mo T-B	0.11	0.58

Foreign Exchange	2021	2022
EUR/USD	1.19	1.09
GBP/USD	1.38	1.32
USD/CAD	1.27	1.27
USD/JPY	108.31	114.82

FEBRUARY

M	T	W	T	F	S	S
	1	2	3	4	5
6	7	8	9	10	11	12
13	14	15	16	17	18	19
20	21	22	23	24	25	26
27	28					

MARCH

M	T	W	T	F	S	S
	1	2	3	4	5
6	7	8	9	10	11	12
13	14	15	16	17	18	19
20	21	22	23	24	25	26
27	28	29	30	31		

APRIL

M	T	W	T	F	S	S
				1	2	3
4	5	6	7	8	9	10
11	13	13	14	15	16	17
18	20	20	21	22	23	24
25	27	27	28	29	30	

MARCH

	MONDAY	TUESDAY	WEDNESDAY
WEEK 09	27	28	**1** 30
WEEK 10	**6** 25	**7** 24	**8** 23
WEEK 11	**13** 18	**14** 17	**15** 16
WEEK 12	**20** 11	**21** 10	**22** 9
WEEK 13	**27** 4	**28** 3	**29** 2

THURSDAY	FRIDAY
2 29	**3** 28
9 22	**10** 21
16 15	**17** 14
23 8	**24** 7
30 1	**31**

APRIL

M	T	W	T	F	S	S
					1	2
3	4	5	6	7	8	9
10	11	13	13	14	15	16
17	18	19	20	21	22	23
22	23	26	27	28	29	30

MAY

M	T	W	T	F	S	S
1	2	3	4	5	6	7
8	9	10	11	12	13	14
15	16	17	18	19	20	21
22	23	24	25	26	27	28
29	30	31				

JUNE

M	T	W	T	F	S	S
			1	2	3	4
5	6	7	8	9	10	11
12	13	14	15	16	17	18
19	20	21	22	23	24	25
26	27	28	29	30		

JULY

M	T	W	T	F	S	S
					1	2
3	4	5	6	7	8	9
10	11	12	13	14	15	16
17	18	19	20	21	22	23
24	25	26	27	28	29	30
31						

MARCH SUMMARY

	Dow Jones	S&P 500	Nasdaq	TSX Comp
Month Rank	6	6	9	8
# Up	46	46	31	22
# Down	26	26	19	15
% Pos	64	64	62	59
% Avg. Gain	0.9	1.0	0.6	0.6

Dow & S&P 1950-2020, Nasdaq 1972-2021, TSX 1985-2021

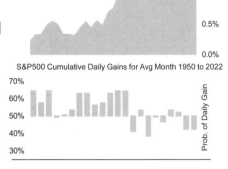

S&P500 Cumulative Daily Gains for Avg Month 1950 to 2022

Prob. of Daily Gain

♦ March tends to be a strong month for stocks. ♦ Typically, in March, it is the cyclical sectors that perform well and the defensive sectors that underperform. ♦ The energy, consumer discretionary and the financial sectors are typically strong performing sectors in March. ♦ Retail, also tends to perform well in March. ♦ The information technology sector tends to be a laggard in March.

BEST / WORST MARCH BROAD MKTS. 2013-2022

BEST MARCH MARKETS
♦ Russell 2000 (2016) 7.7%
♦ Nikkei 225 (2013) 7.3%
♦ Dow (2016) 7.1%

WORST MARCH MARKETS
♦ Russell 2000 (2020) -21.9%
♦ TSX Comp. (2020) -17.7%
♦ FTSE 100 (2020) -13.8%

Index Values End of Month

	2013	2014	2015	2016	2017	2018	2019	2020	2021	2022
Dow	14,579	16,458	17,776	17,685	20,663	24,103	25,929	21,917	32,982	34,678
S&P 500	1,569	1,872	2,068	2,060	2,363	2,641	2,834	2,585	3,973	4,530
Nasdaq	3,268	4,199	4,901	4,870	5,912	7,063	7,729	7,700	13,247	14,221
TSX	12,750	14,335	14,902	13,494	15,548	15,367	16,102	13,379	18,701	21,890
Russell 1000	872	1,046	1,157	1,139	1,310	1,465	1,570	1,416	2,238	2,501
Russell 2000	952	1,173	1,253	1,114	1,386	1,529	1,540	1,153	2,221	2,070
FTSE 100	6,412	6,598	6,773	6,175	7,323	7,057	7,279	5,672	6,714	7,516
Nikkei 225	12,398	14,828	19,207	16,759	18,909	21,454	21,206	18,917	29,179	27,821

Percent Gain for March

	2013	2014	2015	2016	2017	2018	2019	2020	2021	2022
Dow	3.7	0.8	-2.0	7.1	-0.7	-3.7	0.0	-13.7	6.6	2.3
S&P 500	3.6	0.7	-1.7	6.6	0.0	-2.7	1.8	-12.5	4.2	3.6
Nasdaq	3.4	-2.5	-1.3	6.8	1.5	-2.9	2.6	-10.1	0.4	3.4
TSX	-0.6	0.9	-2.2	4.9	1.0	-0.5	0.6	-17.7	3.5	3.6
Russell 1000	3.7	0.5	-1.4	6.8	-0.1	-2.4	1.6	-13.4	3.7	3.2
Russell 2000	4.4	-0.8	1.6	7.8	-0.1	1.1	-2.3	-21.9	0.9	1.1
FTSE 100	0.8	-3.1	-2.5	1.3	0.8	-2.4	2.9	-13.8	3.6	0.8
Nikkei 225	7.3	-0.1	2.2	4.6	-1.1	-2.8	-0.8	-10.5	0.7	4.9

March Market Avg. Performance 2013 to 2022[1]

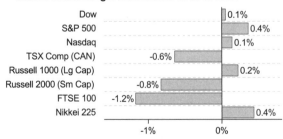

	Dow	0.1%
	S&P 500	0.4%
	Nasdaq	0.1%
	TSX Comp (CAN)	-0.6%
	Russell 1000 (Lg Cap)	0.2%
	Russell 2000 (Sm Cap)	-0.8%
	FTSE 100	-1.2%
	Nikkei 225	0.4%

Interest Corner Mar[2]

	Fed Funds % [3]	3 Mo. T-Bill % [4]	10 Yr % [5]	20 Yr % [6]
2022	0.50	0.52	2.32	2.59
2021	0.25	0.03	1.74	2.31
2020	0.25	0.11	0.70	1.15
2019	2.50	2.40	2.41	2.63
2018	1.75	1.73	2.74	2.85

(1) Russell Data provided by Russell (2) Federal Reserve Bank of St. Louis- end of month values (3) Target rate set by FOMC (4)(5)(6) Constant yield maturities.

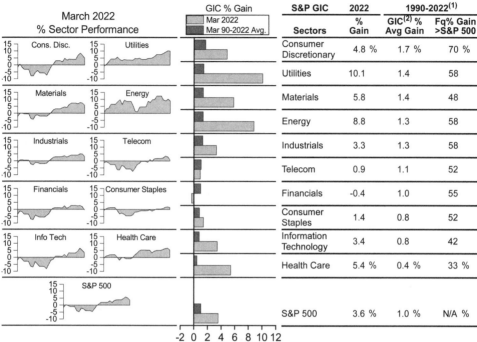

March 2022 % Sector Performance

S&P GIC Sectors	2022 % Gain	1990-2022[1] GIC[2] % Avg Gain	1990-2022[1] Fq% Gain >S&P 500
Consumer Discretionary	4.8 %	1.7 %	70 %
Utilities	10.1	1.4	58
Materials	5.8	1.4	48
Energy	8.8	1.3	58
Industrials	3.3	1.3	58
Telecom	0.9	1.1	52
Financials	-0.4	1.0	55
Consumer Staples	1.4	0.8	52
Information Technology	3.4	0.8	42
Health Care	5.4 %	0.4 %	33 %
S&P 500	3.6 %	1.0 %	N/A %

Sector Commentary

◆ In March 2022, all of the major sectors of the stock market were positive, except the financials sector. ◆ The top performing sector was utilities, gaining over 10%. Although the utilities sector on average performs well in March, the strength of the sector was surprising given that the yield on the US Treasury 10-Year Note rose during the month.

Sub-Sector Commentary

◆ In March 2022, the cyclical sub-sectors of the stock market performed well. ◆ From the selected sub-sectors, auto was at the top of the list, gaining over 17%. ◆ This was partly the result of a rebound after the sector's poor performance in February. ◆ The cyclical sub-sectors, steel and metals & mining both performed well, with returns greater than 12%. ◆ The resource sub-sectors generally benefited from the Russia-Ukraine war unfolding.

SELECTED SUB-SECTORS[3]

	2022 % Gain	Avg Gain	Fq% Gain
Steel	12.9 %	3.1 %	58 %
Retail	2.7	3.0	76
Railroads	10.9	1.8	55
Transportation	6.0	1.7	61
Chemicals	5.3	1.6	52
Metals & Mining	12.2	1.2	45
SOX (1995-2022)	0.0	1.2	50
Agriculture (1994-2022)	15.1	1.1	38
Pharma	8.1	0.7	36
Auto	17.9	0.6	48
Homebuilders	-11.7	0.3	52
Banks	-7.0	0.1	45
Biotech (1993-2022)	8.4	-0.2	35
Silver	1.9	-0.2	36
Gold	1.7	-0.9	33

DUK — DUKE ENERGY
① Mar 13 to Apr 30   ② Jul 17 to Oct 3

Duke Energy (Duke) operates an electric power and natural gas holding company. Duke tends to perform well from mid-March to the end of April. Both Duke and the S&P 500 tend to be positive at this time. Duke is an attractive holding at this time because it is considered a defensive stock with a lower beta than the S&P 500, and yet on average it has outperformed the S&P 500 when the S&P 500 has been positive.

8% gain & 78% of the time positive

Duke also has a strong seasonal period from mid-July to early October. This time period tends not to be as strong as the seasonal period from mid-March to late April.

Nevertheless, the mid-July to early October seasonal period is an attractive opportunity relative to the S&P 500. In the July 17 to October 3 time period, from 1990 to 2021, the S&P 500 has produced an average loss of 1.1%. In comparison, Duke has produced an average gain of 3.0% and has been positive 63% of the time.

2021/22 Performance Update.

In 2021, Duke outperformed the S&P 500 in its March 13 to April 30 seasonal period and underperformed in its seasonal period from July 17 to October 3.

In 2022, Duke started to outperform the S&P 500 early in the year as the stock market headed lower. For most of the first six months of the year, the S&P 500 moved lower, which helped to boost Duke's relative performance compared to the S&P 500.

* DUK- stock symbol for Duke Energy. which trades on the NYSE, adjusted for stock splits.

Duke vs S&P 500 - 1990 to 2021   Positive

Year	Mar 13-Apr 30 S&P 500	Mar 13-Apr 30 DUK	Jul 17-Oct 3 S&P 500	Jul 17-Oct 3 DUK	Compound Growth S&P 500	Compound Growth DUK
1990	-2.3 %	-3.0 %	-15.6 %	1.6 %	-17.6 %	-1.5 %
1991	1.4	1.4	0.8	15.6	2.2	17.1
1992	2.7	6.7	-1.7	-0.7	1.0	5.9
1993	-2.1	2.6	3.5	3.9	1.3	6.6
1994	-3.3	-4.6	1.7	5.1	-1.7	0.3
1995	5.1	1.9	4.0	6.0	9.4	8.1
1996	2.7	-1.6	10.3	-6.3	13.2	-7.7
1997	-0.4	0.0	3.0	0.4	2.7	0.4
1998	3.9	0.9	-15.3	17.0	-12.0	18.0
1999	3.1	-7.1	-9.6	0.6	-6.7	-6.5
2000	4.1	24.0	-5.5	41.6	-1.6	75.6
2001	5.9	14.9	-10.8	-4.9	-5.6	9.2
2002	-7.6	7.1	-9.1	-13.0	-16.0	-6.8
2003	14.0	32.8	3.6	-1.1	18.1	31.4
2004	-1.2	-2.9	2.7	9.5	1.5	6.3
2005	-3.6	6.3	-0.1	-2.9	-3.7	3.2
2006	2.3	3.6	7.9	6.2	10.4	10.0
2007	5.4	4.7	-0.6	6.6	4.7	11.7
2008	5.9	4.5	-11.7	1.6	-6.6	6.2
2009	16.3	9.2	9.0	4.1	26.7	13.7
2010	3.2	2.8	7.6	5.7	11.1	8.6
2011	4.5	1.2	-16.5	4.6	-12.7	5.8
2012	2.0	0.3	7.2	-2.9	9.3	-2.7
2013	2.9	8.1	0.1	-5.9	3.1	1.8
2014	0.8	5.9	-0.7	3.8	0.1	9.9
2015	0.9	3.0	-8.1	-3.8	-7.3	-0.9
2016	2.1	1.3	0.0	-6.9	2.1	-5.6
2017	0.5	2.3	3.1	0.0	3.6	2.3
2018	-4.9	4.7	4.5	-2.0	-0.5	2.7
2019	5.5	0.7	-3.1	6.8	2.2	7.5
2020	17.4	5.2	4.1	13.0	22.3	18.8
2021	6.0	10.2	0.7	-6.0	6.8	3.5
Avg.	2.9 %	4.6 %	-1.1 %	3.0 %	1.9 %	7.9 %
Fq>0	75 %	81 %	53 %	63 %	63 %	78 %

DUK Avg. Year 1990 to 2021

DUK / S&P 500 Rel Str.- Avg Yr. 1990-2021

Duke Energy Performance

DUK Monthly % Gain (1990-2021)

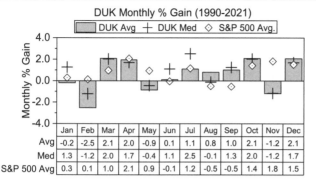

Legend: DUK Avg + DUK Med ◇ S&P 500 Avg.

	Jan	Feb	Mar	Apr	May	Jun	Jul	Aug	Sep	Oct	Nov	Dec
Avg	-0.2	-2.5	2.1	2.0	-0.9	0.1	1.1	0.8	1.0	2.1	-1.2	2.1
Med	1.3	-1.2	2.0	1.7	-0.4	1.1	2.5	-0.1	1.3	2.0	-1.2	1.7
S&P 500 Avg	0.3	0.1	1.0	2.1	0.9	-0.1	1.2	-0.5	-0.5	1.4	1.8	1.5

Fq % DUK Gain > 0% (1990-2021)

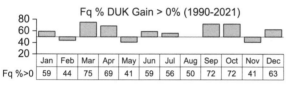

	Jan	Feb	Mar	Apr	May	Jun	Jul	Aug	Sep	Oct	Nov	Dec
Fq %>0	59	44	75	69	41	59	56	50	72	72	41	63

Fq % DUK Gain > S&P 500 % (1990-2021)

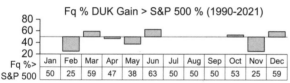

	Jan	Feb	Mar	Apr	May	Jun	Jul	Aug	Sep	Oct	Nov	Dec
Fq %> S&P 500	50	25	59	47	38	63	50	50	50	53	25	59

DUK % Gain 5 Year (2017-2021)

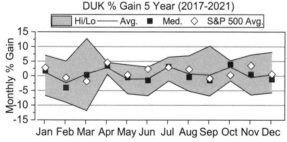

Legend: Hi/Lo —— Avg. ■ Med. ◇ S&P 500 Avg.

DUK Performance 2021-2022

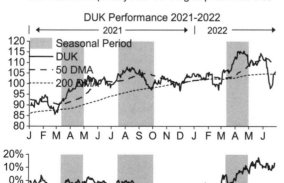

Seasonal Period — DUK — - 50 DMA ···· 200 DMA

Relative Strength, % Gain vs. S&P 500

WEEK 10

Market Indices & Rates
Weekly Values**

Stock Markets	2021	2022
Dow	32,779	32,944
S&P500	3,943	4,204
Nasdaq	13,320	12,844
TSX	18,851	21,462
FTSE	6,761	7,156
DAX	14,502	13,628
Nikkei	29,718	25,163
Hang Seng	28,740	20,554

Commodities	2021	2022
Oil	65.61	109.33
Gold	1704.8	1978.7

Bond Yields	2021	2022
USA 5 Yr Treasury	0.85	1.96
USA 10 Yr T	1.64	2.00
USA 20 Yr T	2.31	2.45
Moody's Aaa	3.13	3.47
Moody's Baa	3.83	4.35
CAN 5 Yr T	1.04	1.80
CAN 10 Yr T	1.59	1.99

Money Market	2021	2022
USA Fed Funds	0.25	0.25
USA 3 Mo T-B	0.04	0.40
CAN tgt overnight rate	0.25	0.50
CAN 3 Mo T-B	0.11	0.56

Foreign Exchange	2021	2022
EUR/USD	1.20	1.09
GBP/USD	1.39	1.30
USD/CAD	1.25	1.27
USD/JPY	109.03	117.29

MARCH

M	T	W	T	F	S	S
		1	2	3	4	5
6	7	8	9	10	11	12
13	14	15	16	17	18	19
20	21	22	23	24	25	26
27	28	29	30	31		

APRIL

M	T	W	T	F	S	S
					1	2
3	4	5	6	7	8	9
10	11	13	13	14	15	16
17	18	19	20	21	22	23
24	25	26	27	28	29	30

MAY

M	T	W	T	F	S	S
1	2	2	4	5	6	7
8	9	10	11	12	13	14
15	16	17	18	19	20	21
22	23	24	25	26	27	28
29	30	31				

DEO # DIAGEO PLC
March 14 to May 12

Diageo markets and sells alcoholic beverages. Diageo is considered a defensive stock and tends to perform well from March 14 to May 12. In this time period, from 1992 to 2022, Diageo has produced an average gain of 6.9% and has been positive 87% of the time. It has also outperformed the S&P 500, 68% of the time.

The strength of Diageo's seasonal trend is that it tends to perform well in the six-month seasonal period for the stock market, which lasts from late October until early May. Despite being considered a defensive stock, with a lower beta than the S&P 500, it manages to outperform S&P 500.

4% gain &
positive 68% of the time

The risk-reward profile of Diageo in its strong seasonal period is favorable. Diageo has produced returns of 10% or greater seven times in its strong seasonal period from 1992 to 2022. In comparison, the largest loss in this period was 4.8%. In addition, Diageo has only been negative three times in this time period.

Over the last five years, Diageo has generally followed its seasonal trend performing better well and outperforming the S&P 500 in its strong seasonal period.

DEO* vs. S&P 500 1992 to 2021			
			Positive
Mar 14 to May 12	S&P 500	DEO	Diff
1992	2.6%	17.0%	14.4%
1993	-1.1	-0.9	0.2
1994	-4.9	-4.8	0.1
1995	7.2	3.6	-3.6
1996	2.1	1.9	-0.2
1997	6.1	25.4	19.3
1998	4.4	6.3	1.9
1999	5.4	3.7	-1.7
2000	2.7	42.1	39.4
2001	4.0	3.8	-0.2
2002	-8.6	2.3	10.9
2003	13.6	4.7	-8.9
2004	-2.1	0.7	2.8
2005	-3.4	1.9	5.3
2006	0.6	6.7	6.2
2007	9.3	10.8	1.6
2008	6.7	0.0	-6.7
2009	20.1	24.0	4.0
2010	1.9	-1.4	-3.3
2011	3.4	10.3	6.9
2012	-3.0	2.1	5.1
2013	5.1	4.2	-0.9
2014	2.7	4.8	2.1
2015	2.2	0.1	-2.2
2016	2.1	1.5	-0.6
2017	0.7	6.3	5.6
2018	-1.4	7.0	8.4
2019	2.5	5.7	3.2
2020	5.9	9.9	4.0
2021	3.0	10.0	7.0
2022	-6.5	3.8	10.3
Avg	2.7%	6.9%	4.2%
Fq > 0	74%	87%	68%

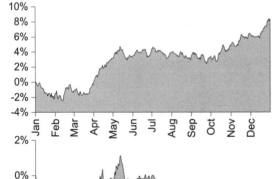

DEO - Avg. Year 1992 to 2021

DEO / S&P 500 Relative Strength - Avg Yr. 1992-2021

2021/22 Performance Update.
In 2021, Diageo was positive in its strong seasonal period. In contrast, the S&P 500 was negative. For the full year of 2021, Diageo was strongly positive and outperformed the S&P 500.

In 2022, Diageo was negative in the first six months of the year, following the stock market lower. However, Diageo managed to outperform the S&P 500 in its strong seasonal period and in the first six months of the year.

 * DEO- stock symbol for The Diageo PLC which trades on the NYSE, adjusted for stock splits.

Diageo PLC Performance

DEO Monthly % Gain (1992-2021)

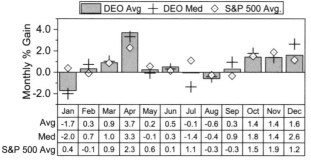

	Jan	Feb	Mar	Apr	May	Jun	Jul	Aug	Sep	Oct	Nov	Dec
Avg	-1.7	0.3	0.9	3.7	0.2	0.5	-0.1	-0.6	0.3	1.4	1.4	1.6
Med	-2.0	0.7	1.0	3.3	-0.1	0.3	-1.4	-0.4	0.9	1.8	1.4	2.6
S&P 500 Avg	0.4	-0.1	0.9	2.3	0.6	0.1	1.1	-0.3	-0.3	1.5	1.9	1.2

Fq % DEO Gain > 0% (1992-2021)

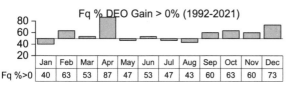

	Jan	Feb	Mar	Apr	May	Jun	Jul	Aug	Sep	Oct	Nov	Dec
Fq %>0	40	63	53	87	47	53	47	43	60	63	60	73

Fq % DEO Gain > S&P 500 % (1992-2021)

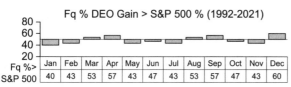

	Jan	Feb	Mar	Apr	May	Jun	Jul	Aug	Sep	Oct	Nov	Dec
Fq %> S&P 500	40	43	53	57	43	47	43	53	57	47	43	60

DEO % Gain 5 Year (2017-2021)

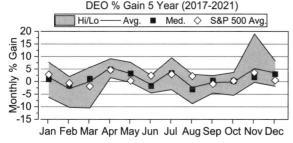

DEO Performance 2021-2022

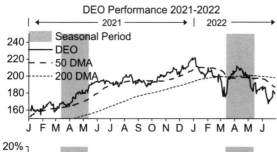

Relative Strength, % Gain vs. S&P 500

Stock Markets	2021	2022
Dow	32,628	34,755
S&P500	3,913	4,463
Nasdaq	13,215	13,894
TSX	18,854	21,818
FTSE	6,709	7,405
DAX	14,621	14,413
Nikkei	29,792	26,827
Hang Seng	28,991	21,412

Commodities	2021	2022
Oil	61.42	104.70
Gold	1735.2	1935.8

Bond Yields	2021	2022
USA 5 Yr Treasury	0.90	2.14
USA 10 Yr T	1.74	2.14
USA 20 Yr T	2.36	2.53
Moody's Aaa	3.13	3.28
Moody's Baa	3.84	4.28
CAN 5 Yr T	1.01	2.03
CAN 10 Yr T	1.59	2.19

Money Market	2021	2022
USA Fed Funds	0.25	0.50
USA 3 Mo T-B	0.01	0.42
CAN tgt overnight rate	0.25	0.50
CAN 3 Mo T-B	0.09	0.53

Foreign Exchange	2021	2022
EUR/USD	1.19	1.11
GBP/USD	1.39	1.32
USD/CAD	1.25	1.26
USD/JPY	108.88	119.17

MARCH

M	T	W	T	F	S	S
		1	2	3	4	5
6	7	8	9	10	11	12
13	14	15	16	17	18	19
20	21	22	23	24	25	26
27	28	29	30	31		

APRIL

M	T	W	T	F	S	S
					1	2
3	4	5	6	7	8	9
10	11	13	13	14	15	16
17	18	19	20	21	22	23
24	25	26	27	28	29	30

MAY

M	T	W	T	F	S	S
1	2	2	4	5	6	7
8	9	10	11	12	13	14
15	16	17	18	19	20	21
22	23	24	25	26	27	28
29	30	31				

NATURAL GAS – FIRES UP AND DOWN
①LONG (Mar22-Jun19) & ②LONG (Sep5-Dec21)
③SELL SHORT (Dec22-Dec31)

There are two high consumption times for natural gas: winter and summer. The colder it gets in winter, the more natural gas is consumed to keep the furnaces going. The warmer it gets in summer, the more natural gas is used to produce power for air conditioners.

On the supply side, weather plays a large factor in determining price. During the hurricane season in the Gulf of Mexico, the price of natural gas is affected by the number and severity of hurricanes.

Natural Gas (Cash) Henry Hub LA*
Seasonal Gains 1995 to 2021

Year %	Pos. Mar 22 to Jun 19	Pos. Sep 5 to Dec 21	Neg. (Short) Dec 22 to Dec 31	Pos. Compound Growth
1995	99.4	13.0 %	103.0 %	1.2 %	126.7 %
1996	-27.4	-6.6	170.4	-46.2	269.2
1997	-9.4	16.8	-13.1	-6.3	7.9
1998	-13.0	-2.6	20.9	-6.7	25.7
1999	18.6	28.9	5.3	-11.2	50.9
2000	356.5	57.1	121.9	0.7	246.3
2001	-74.3	-24.1	21.5	1.5	-9.2
2002	70.0	0.6	61.3	-9.1	77.1
2003	26.4	9.5	47.1	-16.3	87.4
2004	3.6	18.2	54.6	-11.6	103.9
2005	58.4	6.3	14.5	-29.6	57.7
2006	-42.2	-1.8	17.4	-9.5	26.3
2007	30.2	9.2	32.7	2.0	42.1
2008	-21.4	52.2	-21.4	-0.9	20.6
2009	3.6	1.5	208.0	0.7	210.4
2010	-27.4	28.6	10.4	2.4	38.6
2011	-29.6	10.0	-26.1	-1.7	-17.3
2012	15.4	18.7	21.7	0.6	43.7
2013	26.3	-1.4	18.2	-0.2	16.8
2014	-31.1	7.7	-11.8	-12.9	7.2
2015	-22.8	-0.5	-36.1	35.6	-59.0
2016	59.2	46.6	21.9	5.8	68.3
2017	-3.9	-6.6	-10.4	36.0	-46.4
2018	-9.9	9.1	16.7	-7.7	37.1
2019	-34.4	-13.2	-8.5	-7.9	-14.3
2020	14.4	-17.0	47.2	-9.8	34.1
2021	53.1	28.7	-17.8	-5.4	11.5
Avg.	18.2 %	10.7 %	32.2 %	-3.8 %	54.0 %

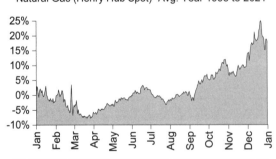

Natural Gas (Henry Hub Spot)- Avg. Year 1995 to 2021

Natural gas prices tend to rise from mid-March to mid-June ahead of the cooling season demands in the summer. From 1995 to 2021, during the period of March 22 to June 19, the spot price of natural gas has on average increased 10.7% and has been positive 67% of the time. The price of natural gas also tends to rise between September 5 and December 21, due to the demands of the heating season. In this period, from 1995 to 2021, natural gas has produced an average gain of 32% and has been positive 70% of the time.

54% Gain & Positive 81% of the time

Natural gas tends to fall in price from December 22 to December 31. Although this is a short time period, for the years from 1995 to 2021, natural gas has produced an average loss of 3.8% and has only been positive 37% of the time. Also, in this period, when gains did occur, they were relatively small. The poor performance of natural gas at this time is largely driven by southern U.S. refiners dumping inventory on the market to help mitigate year-end taxes on their inventory.

2021/22 Performance Update.
In the first three quarters of 2021, natural gas performed well, and then corrected in the fourth quarter. In its strong seasonal period from March 22 to June 19, natural gas was positive. In its September 5 to December 21 seasonal period, natural gas turned lower in November and as a result, natural gas was negative in its seasonal period.

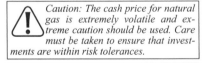

Caution: The cash price for natural gas is extremely volatile and extreme caution should be used. Care must be taken to ensure that investments are within risk tolerances.

Source: New York Mercantile Exchange. NYMX is an exchange provider of futures and options.

Natural Gas Performance

Natural Gas Monthly % Gain (1995-2021)

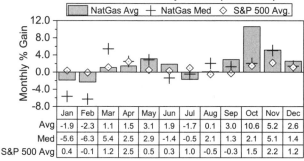

	Jan	Feb	Mar	Apr	May	Jun	Jul	Aug	Sep	Oct	Nov	Dec
Avg	-1.9	-2.3	1.1	1.5	3.1	1.9	-1.7	0.1	3.0	10.6	5.2	2.6
Med	-5.6	-6.3	5.4	2.5	2.9	-1.4	-0.5	2.1	1.3	2.1	5.1	1.4
S&P 500 Avg	0.4	-0.1	1.2	2.5	0.5	0.3	1.0	-0.5	-0.3	1.5	2.2	1.2

Fq % Natural Gas Gain > 0% (1995-2021)

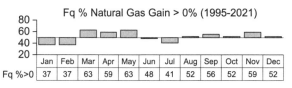

	Jan	Feb	Mar	Apr	May	Jun	Jul	Aug	Sep	Oct	Nov	Dec
Fq %>0	37	37	63	59	63	48	41	52	56	52	59	52

Fq % Natural Gas Gain > S&P 500 % (1995-2021)

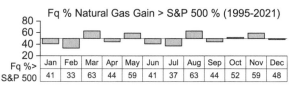

	Jan	Feb	Mar	Apr	May	Jun	Jul	Aug	Sep	Oct	Nov	Dec
Fq %> S&P 500	41	33	63	44	59	41	37	63	44	52	59	48

Natural Gas % Gain 5 Year (2017-2021)

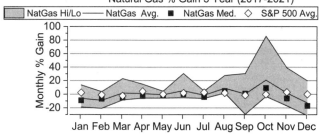

Natural Gas Performance 2021-2022

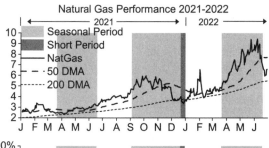

Relative Strength, % Gain vs. S&P 500

Stock Markets	2021	2022
Dow	33,073	34,861
S&P500	3,975	4,543
Nasdaq	13,139	14,169
TSX	18,753	22,006
FTSE	6,741	7,483
DAX	14,749	14,306
Nikkei	29,177	28,150
Hang Seng	28,336	21,405

Commodities	2021	2022
Oil	60.97	115.40
Gold	1731.8	1953.8

Bond Yields	2021	2022
USA 5 Yr Treasury	0.85	2.55
USA 10 Yr T	1.67	2.48
USA 20 Yr T	2.27	2.74
Moody's Aaa	3.06	3.54
Moody's Baa	3.76	4.44
CAN 5 Yr T	0.94	2.49
CAN 10 Yr T	1.50	2.55

Money Market	2021	2022
USA Fed Funds	0.25	0.50
USA 3 Mo T-B	0.02	0.55
CAN tgt overnight rate	0.25	0.50
CAN 3 Mo T-B	0.09	0.54

Foreign Exchange	2021	2022
EUR/USD	1.18	1.10
GBP/USD	1.38	1.32
USD/CAD	1.26	1.25
USD/JPY	109.64	122.05

MARCH
M	T	W	T	F	S	S
		1	2	3	4	5
6	7	8	9	10	11	12
13	14	15	16	17	18	19
20	21	22	23	24	25	26
27	28	29	30	31		

APRIL
M	T	W	T	F	S	S
					1	2
3	4	5	6	7	8	9
10	11	13	13	14	15	16
17	18	19	20	21	22	23
24	25	26	27	28	29	30

MAY
M	T	W	T	F	S	S
1	2	2	4	5	6	7
8	9	10	11	12	13	14
15	16	17	18	19	20	21
22	23	24	25	26	27	28
29	30	31				

CANADIANS GIVE 3 CHEERS FOR AMERICAN HOLIDAYS

When I used to work on the retail side of the investment business, I was always amazed at how often the Canadian stock market increased on U.S. holidays, when the US market was closed.

The Canadian stock market on U.S. holidays had light volume, tended to have small increases or decreases, but usually ended the day with a gain.

0.9% average gain

How the trade works

For the three big holidays in the United States that do not exist in Canada (Memorial, Independence and U.S. Thanksgiving Days), buy at the end of the market day before the holiday (TSX Composite) and sell at the end of the U.S. holiday when the U.S markets are closed.

For U.S. investors to take advantage of this trade, they must have access to the TSX Composite. Unfortunately, SEC regulations do not allow most Americans to purchase foreign ETFs.

Generally, markets perform well around most major U.S. holidays, hence the trading strategies for U.S holidays included in this book. The typical U.S. holiday trade is to get into the stock market the day before the holiday and then exit the day after the holiday. The main reason for the strong performance around these holidays is a lack of institutional involvement in the markets, allowing bullish retail investors to push up the markets.

On the actual American holidays, economic reports are not released in the U.S. and are very seldom released in Canada. During market hours on U.S. holidays, without any strong influences, the TSX Composite tends to float, as investors wait until the next day before making any significant moves. Despite this lackadaisical action during the day, the TSX Composite tends to end the day on a gain. This is true for the three major U.S. holidays: Memorial Day, Independence Day and U.S. Thanksgiving.

From a theoretical perspective, a lot of the gain that is captured on the U.S. holidays in the Canadian stock market is realized the next day when the U.S stock market is open. This does not invalidate the *Canadians Give 3 Cheers* trade – it presents more alternatives for the astute investor.

For example, an investor can allocate a portion of money to a standard U.S. holiday trade and another portion to the *Canadian Give 3 Cheers* version. By spreading out the exit days, the overall risk in the trade is reduced.

S&P/TSX Comp
Gain 1977-2021   Positive ▢

	Memorial	Independence	Thanksgiving	Compound Growth
1977	0.10 %	-0.08 %	0.61 %	0.63 %
1978	-0.05	-0.16	0.57	0.36
1979	1.11	0.23	0.58	1.93
1980	1.64	0.76	0.89	3.32
1981	0.51	-0.15	1.03	1.40
1982	-0.18	-0.01	0.35	0.17
1983	0.29	0.53	0.15	0.97
1984	0.86	-0.11	0.73	1.48
1985	0.61	0.31	0.31	1.24
1986	0.23	-0.02	0.22	0.44
1987	-0.11	1.08	1.57	2.55
1988	0.44	0.08	0.58	1.11
1989	0.10	-0.12	-0.11	-0.13
1990	0.11	0.43	0.02	0.57
1991	0.02	0.18	-0.09	0.11
1992	-0.06	0.35	0.36	0.65
1993	0.42	-0.18	0.14	0.38
1994	-0.19	0.70	0.91	1.43
1995	0.14	0.25	0.29	0.68
1996	0.11	0.25	0.54	0.90
1997	1.08	-0.04	-0.85	0.18
1998	0.56	0.18	0.51	1.25
1999	0.57	1.63	1.14	3.39
2000	0.43	1.04	0.91	2.40
2001	-0.02	-0.23	0.70	0.45
2002	-0.01	0.08	0.38	0.45
2003	0.03	0.03	0.26	0.31
2004	0.84	-0.02	0.55	1.39
2005	0.56	0.39	1.48	2.45
2006	0.70	1.04	0.70	2.46
2007	0.35	-0.03	0.76	1.08
2008	0.24	-0.94	1.28	0.56
2009	0.76	0.36	-1.29	-0.18
2010	0.78	-0.92	0.34	0.19
2011	0.23	0.64	-0.75	0.12
2012	-0.09	0.55	0.44	0.90
2013	0.23	0.17	0.07	0.47
2014	0.05	0.05	-0.77	-0.67
2015	-0.09	0.30	0.16	0.38
2016	-0.13	1.48	-0.04	1.21
2017	0.03	-0.34	0.00	-0.30
2018	-0.37	0.26	-0.02	-0.14
2019	0.72	0.08	0.08	0.88
2020	1.08	-0.16	0.22	1.14
2021	-0.80	0.26	0.34	-0.2
Avg	0.31 %	0.22 %	0.36 %	0.90 %
Fq > 0	73 %	64 %	82 %	87 %

Canadians Give 3 Cheers Performance

Market Indices & Rates
Weekly Values**

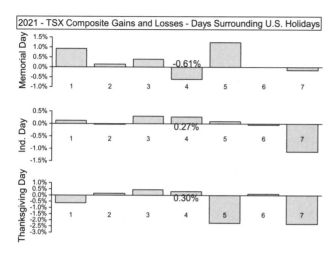

2021 - TSX Composite Gains and Losses - Days Surrounding U.S. Holidays

Stock Markets	2021	2022
Dow	33,153	34,818
S&P500	4,020	4,546
Nasdaq	13,480	14,262
TSX	18,990	21,953
FTSE	6,737	7,538
DAX	15,107	14,446
Nikkei	29,854	27,666
Hang Seng	28,939	22,040

Commodities	2021	2022
Oil	61.45	99.27
Gold	1726.1	1929.4

Bond Yields	2021	2022
USA 5 Yr Treasury	0.97	2.55
USA 10 Yr T	1.72	2.39
USA 20 Yr T	2.27	2.60
Moody's Aaa	2.91	3.32
Moody's Baa	3.67	4.20
CAN 5 Yr T	0.97	2.47
CAN 10 Yr T	1.51	2.43

Money Market	2021	2022
USA Fed Funds	0.25	0.50
USA 3 Mo T-B	0.02	0.53
CAN tgt overnight rate	0.25	0.50
CAN 3 Mo T-B	0.09	0.70

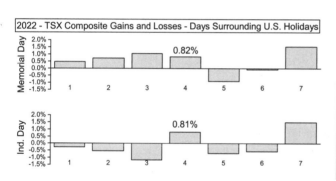

2022 - TSX Composite Gains and Losses - Days Surrounding U.S. Holidays

Foreign Exchange	2021	2022
EUR/USD	1.18	1.10
GBP/USD	1.38	1.31
USD/CAD	1.26	1.25
USD/JPY	110.69	122.52

MARCH

M	T	W	T	F	S	S
		1	2	3	4	5
6	7	8	9	10	11	12
13	14	15	16	17	18	19
20	21	22	23	24	25	26
27	28	29	30	31		

Canadians Give 3 Cheers Performance

APRIL

M	T	W	T	F	S	S
					1	2
3	4	5	6	7	8	9
10	11	13	13	14	15	16
17	18	19	20	21	22	23
24	25	26	27	28	29	30

In 2021, the TSX Composite produced a loss of 0.6% on Memorial Day. The day following Memorial Day produced a large gain. On Independence Day, the TSX Composite was positive, but the gain did not make up for the loss on Memorial Day. Thanksgiving Day was positive, but the day after produced a large loss.

In 2022, the TSX Composite produced a large gain on Memorial Day. On Independence Day, the TSX Composite was slightly negative. On Thanksgiving Day, the TSX produced a large gain. Overall, the combination of the two holidays produced a gain of more than 1.6%

MAY

M	T	W	T	F	S	S
1	2	2	4	5	6	7
8	9	10	11	12	13	14
15	16	17	18	19	20	21
22	23	24	25	26	27	28
29	30	31				

APRIL

	MONDAY	TUESDAY	WEDNESDAY
WEEK 13	27	28	29
WEEK 14	**3** 27	**4** 26	**5** 25
WEEK 15	**10** 20	**11** 19	**12** 18
WEEK 16	**17** 13	**18** 12	**19** 11
WEEK 17	**24** 6	**25** 5	**26** 4

THURSDAY	FRIDAY
30	31
6 24	**7** 23
	USA Market Closed- Good Friday CAN Market Closed- Good Friday
13 17	**14** 16
20 10	**21** 9
27 3	**28** 2

MAY

M	T	W	T	F	S	S
1	2	3	4	5	6	7
8	9	10	11	12	13	14
15	16	17	18	19	20	21
22	23	24	25	26	27	28
29	30	31				

JUNE

M	T	W	T	F	S	S
			1	2	3	4
5	6	7	8	9	10	11
12	13	14	15	16	17	18
19	20	21	22	23	24	25
26	27	28	29	30		

JULY

M	T	W	T	F	S	S
					1	2
3	4	5	6	7	8	9
10	11	12	13	14	15	16
17	18	19	20	21	22	23
24	25	26	27	28	29	30
31						

AUGUST

M	T	W	T	F	S	S
	1	2	3	4	5	6
7	8	9	10	11	12	13
14	15	16	17	18	19	20
21	22	23	24	25	26	27
29	30	31				

APRIL
S U M M A R Y

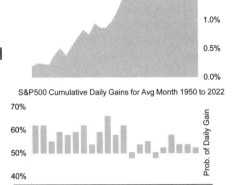

S&P500 Cumulative Daily Gains for Avg Month 1950 to 2022

	Dow Jones	S&P 500	Nasdaq	TSX Comp
Month Rank	1	2	3	3
# Up	50	51	33	24
# Down	22	21	17	13
% Pos	69	71	66	65
% Avg. Gain	2.1	1.7	1.7	1.2

Dow & S&P 1950-2021, Nasdaq 1972-2021, TSX 1985-2021

♦ The first part of April tends to be the strongest (see *18 Day Earnings Month Effect strategy*). ♦ The last part of April tends to be "flat." ♦ Overall, April tends to be a volatile month with the cyclical sectors outperforming. ♦ In 2022, all of the major sectors of the stock market were negative except the consumer staples sector. The stock market moved lower as investors became increasingly concerned that the economy was slowing and at the same time, inflation was increasing.

BEST / WORST APRIL BROAD MKTS. 2013-2022

BEST APRIL MARKETS
♦ Nasdaq (2020) 15.4%
♦ Russell 2000 (2020) 13.7%
♦ Russell 1000 (2020) 13.1%

WORST APRIL MARKETS
♦ Nasdaq (2022) -13.3%
♦ Russell 2000 (2022) -10.0%
♦ Russell 1000 (2022) -9.0%

Index Values End of Month

	2013	2014	2015	2016	2017	2018	2019	2020	2021	2022
Dow	14,840	16,581	17,841	17,774	20,941	24,163	26,593	24,346	33,875	32,977
S&P 500	1,598	1,884	2,086	2,065	2,384	2,648	2,946	2,912	4,181	4,132
Nasdaq	3,329	4,115	4,941	4,775	6,048	7,066	8,095	8,890	13,963	12,335
TSX	12,457	14,652	15,225	13,951	15,586	15,608	16,581	14,781	19,108	20,762
Russell 1000	887	1,050	1,164	1,144	1,322	1,468	1,632	1,602	2,357	2,276
Russell 2000	947	1,127	1,220	1,131	1,400	1,542	1,591	1,311	2,266	1,864
FTSE 100	6,430	6,780	6,961	6,242	7,204	7,509	7,418	5,901	6,970	7,545
Nikkei 225	13,861	14,304	19,520	16,666	19,197	22,468	22,259	20,194	28,813	26,848

Percent Gain for April

	2013	2014	2015	2016	2017	2018	2019	2020	2021	2022
Dow	1.8	0.7	0.4	0.5	1.3	0.2	2.6	11.1	2.7	-4.9
S&P 500	1.8	0.6	0.9	0.3	0.9	0.3	3.9	12.7	5.2	-8.8
Nasdaq	1.9	-2.0	0.8	-1.9	2.3	0.0	4.7	15.4	5.4	-13.3
TSX	-2.3	2.2	2.2	3.4	0.2	1.6	3.0	10.5	2.2	-5.2
Russell 1000	1.7	0.4	0.6	0.4	0.9	0.2	3.9	13.1	5.3	-9.0
Russell 2000	-0.4	-3.9	-2.6	1.5	1.0	0.8	3.3	13.7	2.1	-10.0
FTSE 100	0.3	2.8	2.8	1.1	-1.6	6.4	1.9	4.0	3.8	0.4
Nikkei 225	11.8	-3.5	1.6	-0.6	1.5	4.7	5.0	6.7	-1.3	-3.5

April Market Avg. Performance 2013 to 2022[1]

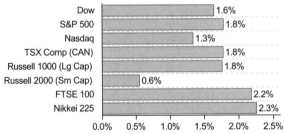

Dow	1.6%
S&P 500	1.8%
Nasdaq	1.3%
TSX Comp (CAN)	1.8%
Russell 1000 (Lg Cap)	1.8%
Russell 2000 (Sm Cap)	0.6%
FTSE 100	2.2%
Nikkei 225	2.3%

Interest Corner Apr[2]

	Fed Funds %[3]	3 Mo. T-Bill %[4]	10 Yr %[5]	20 Yr %[6]
2022	0.50	0.85	2.89	3.14
2021	0.25	0.01	1.65	2.19
2020	0.25	0.09	0.64	1.05
2019	2.50	2.43	2.51	2.75
2018	1.75	1.87	2.95	3.01

(1) Russell Data provided by Russell (2) Federal Reserve Bank of St. Louis- end of month values (3) Target rate set by FOMC (4)(5)(6) Constant yield maturities.

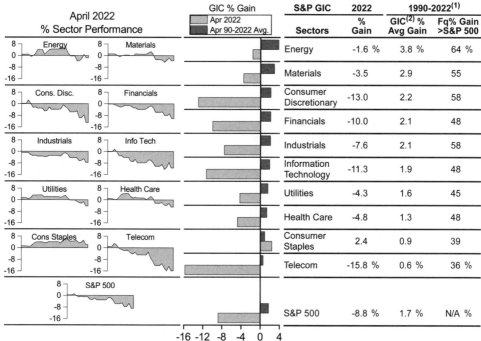

S&P GIC	2022	1990-2022[1]	
Sectors	% Gain	GIC[2] % Avg Gain	Fq% Gain >S&P 500
Energy	-1.6 %	3.8 %	64 %
Materials	-3.5	2.9	55
Consumer Discretionary	-13.0	2.2	58
Financials	-10.0	2.1	48
Industrials	-7.6	2.1	58
Information Technology	-11.3	1.9	48
Utilities	-4.3	1.6	45
Health Care	-4.8	1.3	48
Consumer Staples	2.4	0.9	39
Telecom	-15.8 %	0.6 %	36 %
S&P 500	-8.8 %	1.7 %	N/A %

Sector Commentary

♦ After a strong rally in March, the stock market corrected sharply in April 2022. ♦ All of the sectors were negative, except consumer staples. ♦ The worst performing sector was the telecom sector which was hit hard with rising interest rates and produced a loss of almost 16%. ♦ Growth sectors did not perform well in April, with the consumer discretionary sector and information technology sector losing 13% and 11% respectively.

Sub-Sector Commentary

♦ In April 2022, the auto sub-sector performed poorly with a loss of over 18%. Typically, the auto sub-sector is one of the better performing sub-sectors. ♦ The semiconductor sub-sector also performed poorly producing a loss of almost 15%. ♦ A divergence took place with the cyclical sub-sectors metals & mining and steel producing negative and positive returns respectively. The metals & mining sector produced a loss of almost 10%.

SELECTED SUB-SECTORS[3]			
Auto	-18.3 %	5.1 %	48 %
Railroads	-11.8	3.4	61
Chemicals	-2.1	3.4	73
SOX (1995-2022)	-14.9	2.7	46
Banks	-11.6	2.5	48
Metals & Mining	-9.7	2.4	42
Transportation	-10.3	2.1	58
Homebuilders	-4.5	2.1	48
Steel	4.1	2.0	52
Pharma	0.6	1.7	48
Retail	-13.9	1.6	52
Agriculture (1994-2022)	-0.8	1.1	55
Gold	-1.6	0.5	42
Silver	-5.5	0.4	36
Biotech (1993-2022)	-6.4	-0.1	35

(1) Sector data provided by Standard and Poors (2) GIC is short form for Global Industry Classification (3) Sub Sector data provided by Standard and Poors, except where marked by symbol.

18 DAY EARNINGS MONTH EFFECT
Markets Outperform 1st 18 Calendar Days of Earnings Months

Earnings season occurs the first month of every quarter. At this time, public companies report their financials for the previous quarter and give guidance on future expectations. As a result, investors tend to bid up stocks, anticipating good earnings. Earnings are a major driver of stock market prices as investors generally get in the stock market early, in anticipation of favorable results, which helps to run stock prices up in the first half of the month.

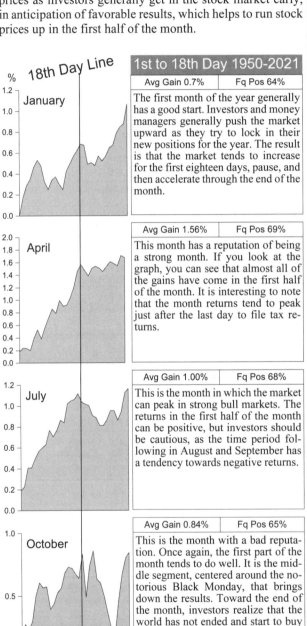

18th Day Line

January

1st to 18th Day 1950-2021

Avg Gain 0.7%	Fq Pos 64%

The first month of the year generally has a good start. Investors and money managers generally push the market upward as they try to lock in their new positions for the year. The result is that the market tends to increase for the first eighteen days, pause, and then accelerate through the end of the month.

April

Avg Gain 1.56%	Fq Pos 69%

This month has a reputation of being a strong month. If you look at the graph, you can see that almost all of the gains have come in the first half of the month. It is interesting to note that the month returns tend to peak just after the last day to file tax returns.

July

Avg Gain 1.00%	Fq Pos 68%

This is the month in which the market can peak in strong bull markets. The returns in the first half of the month can be positive, but investors should be cautious, as the time period following in August and September has a tendency towards negative returns.

October

Avg Gain 0.84%	Fq Pos 65%

This is the month with a bad reputation. Once again, the first part of the month tends to do well. It is the middle segment, centered around the notorious Black Monday, that brings down the results. Toward the end of the month, investors realize that the world has not ended and start to buy stocks again, providing a strong finish to the month.

1st to 18th Day Gain S&P500

	JAN	APR	JUL	OCT
1950	0.36 %	4.28 %	-3.56 %	2.88 %
1951	4.75	3.41	4.39	1.76
1952	2.02	-3.57	-0.44	-1.39
1953	-2.07	-2.65	0.87	3.38
1954	2.50	3.71	2.91	-1.49
1955	-3.28	4.62	3.24	-4.63
1956	-2.88	-1.53	4.96	2.18
1957	-4.35	2.95	2.45	-4.93
1958	2.78	1.45	1.17	2.80
1959	1.09	4.47	1.23	0.79
1960	-3.34	2.26	-2.14	1.55
1961	2.70	1.75	-0.36	2.22
1962	-4.42	-1.84	2.65	0.12
1963	3.30	3.49	-1.27	2.26
1964	2.05	1.99	2.84	0.77
1965	2.05	2.31	1.87	1.91
1966	1.64	2.63	2.66	2.77
1967	6.80	1.84	3.16	-1.51
1968	-0.94	7.63	1.87	2.09
1969	-1.76	-0.27	-2.82	3.37
1970	-1.24	-4.42	6.83	-0.02
1971	1.37	3.17	0.42	-1.01
1972	1.92	2.40	-1.22	-2.13
1973	0.68	0.02	2.00	1.46
1974	-2.04	0.85	-2.58	13.76
1975	3.50	3.53	-2.09	5.95
1976	7.55	-2.04	0.38	-3.58
1977	-3.85	2.15	0.47	-3.18
1978	-4.77	4.73	1.40	-2.00
1979	3.76	0.11	-1.19	-5.22
1980	2.90	-1.51	6.83	4.83
1981	-0.73	-0.96	-0.34	2.59
1982	-4.35	4.33	1.33	13.54
1983	4.10	4.43	-2.20	1.05
1984	1.59	-0.80	-1.16	1.20
1985	2.44	0.10	1.32	2.72
1986	-1.35	1.46	-5.77	3.25
1987	9.96	-1.64	3.48	-12.16
1988	1.94	0.12	-1.09	2.75
1989	3.17	3.78	4.20	-2.12
1990	-4.30	0.23	1.73	-0.10
1991	0.61	3.53	3.83	1.20
1992	0.42	3.06	1.83	-1.45
1993	0.26	-0.60	-1.06	2.07
1994	1.67	-0.74	2.46	1.07
1995	2.27	0.93	2.52	0.52
1996	-1.25	-0.29	-4.04	3.42
1997	4.78	1.22	3.41	-0.33
1998	-0.92	1.90	4.67	3.88
1999	1.14	2.54	3.36	-2.23
2000	-0.96	-3.80	2.69	-6.57
2001	2.10	6.71	-1.36	2.66
2002	-1.79	-2.00	-10.94	8.48
2003	2.50	5.35	1.93	4.35
2004	2.51	0.75	-3.46	-0.05
2005	-1.32	-2.93	2.50	-4.12
2006	2.55	1.22	0.51	3.15
2007	1.41	4.33	-3.20	1.48
2008	-9.75	5.11	-1.51	-19.36
2009	-5.88	8.99	2.29	2.89
2010	1.88	1.94	3.32	3.81
2011	2.97	-1.56	-1.15	8.30
2012	4.01	-1.66	0.78	1.16
2013	4.2	-1.76	5.17	3.74
2014	-0.52	-0.4	0.92	-4.34
2015	-1.92	0.64	3.08	5.89
2016	-8.0	1.68	3.21	-1.32
2017	1.48	-0.87	1.54	1.66
2018	4.65	2.57	3.58	-4.98
2019	6.54	2.49	1.81	0.32
2020	3.06	11.21	4.01	3.59
2021	0.32	5.35	0.69	4.15
Avg	0.70 %	1.56 %	1.00 %	0.84 %

Earnings Month Effect Performance

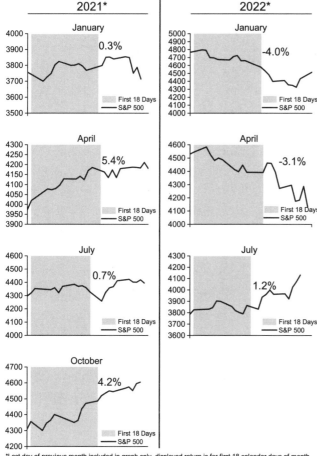

*Last day of previous month included in graph only, displayed return is for first 18 calendar days of month

Market Indices & Rates
Weekly Values**

Stock Markets	2021	2022
Dow	33,801	34,721
S&P500	4,129	4,488
Nasdaq	13,900	13,711
TSX	19,228	21,874
FTSE	6,916	7,670
DAX	15,234	14,284
Nikkei	29,768	26,986
Hang Seng	28,699	21,872

Commodities	2021	2022
Oil	59.32	98.26
Gold	1741.2	1941.4

Bond Yields	2021	2022
USA 5 Yr Treasury	0.87	2.76
USA 10 Yr T	1.67	2.72
USA 20 Yr T	2.23	2.94
Moody's Aaa	2.92	3.60
Moody's Baa	3.63	4.50
CAN 5 Yr T	0.96	2.60
CAN 10 Yr T	1.50	2.64

Money Market	2021	2022
USA Fed Funds	0.25	0.50
USA 3 Mo T-B	0.02	0.70
CAN tgt overnight rate	0.25	0.50
CAN 3 Mo T-B	0.09	0.91

Foreign Exchange	2021	2022
EUR/USD	1.19	1.09
GBP/USD	1.37	1.30
USD/CAD	1.25	1.26
USD/JPY	109.67	124.34

APRIL

M	T	W	T	F	S	S
					1	2
3	4	5	6	7	8	9
10	11	13	13	14	15	16
17	18	19	20	21	22	23
24	25	26	27	28	29	30

MAY

M	T	W	T	F	S	S
1	2	2	4	5	6	7
8	9	10	11	12	13	14
15	16	17	18	19	20	21
22	23	24	25	26	27	28
29	30	31				

JUNE

M	T	W	T	F	S	S
			1	2	3	4
5	6	7	8	9	10	11
12	13	14	15	16	17	18
19	20	21	22	23	24	25
26	27	28	29	30		

Earnings Month Effect Performance

In 2021, the *Earnings Month Effect* was positive in the first three earnings months. The biggest performance gain was made in April with the first eighteen calendar days producing a gain of 5.4% in the S&P 500. The gain in this period was larger than the gain for the month of 5.2%.

In 2022, the *Earnings Month Effect* in January was not successful as the stock market started a substantial correction at the beginning of January. In April, the stock market also faltered in its *Earnings Month Effect* period. In July, the S&P 500, was positive in its *Earnings Month Effect* period, but the main gains for the market were made later in July.

CONSUMER STAPLES
① Apr 25 to May 31 ② Sep 25 to Oct 27

The consumer staples sector is not an attractive sector for most investors as it is typically not a fast moving sector. Nevertheless, it can play an important part in an investment portfolio.

There are two times of the year when the consumer staples sector tends to perform well relative to the S&P 500. The first period overlaps the transition period out of the favorable six-month period for the stock market, which takes place in early May. The second period leads into the favorable six-month period for the stock market in late October.

75% of the time positive

From April 25 to May 31, in the period from 1990 to 2021, the consumer staples sector has produced an average gain of 2.0% and has been positive 75% of the time. This is by no means a huge gain, but it is better than the average 1.3% that the S&P 500 has produced in the same time period. In the same yearly period, from September 25 to October 27, the consumer staples sector has produced an average gain of 1.6% compared to a gain of 0.5% for the S&P 500. The gain in the consumer staples sector is fairly moderate, but can provide a more defensive profile than many sectors of the S&P 500.

2021/22 Performance Update.

In 2021, the consumer staples sector underperformed the S&P 500 as the market was in a risk-on mode. In 2022, the situation flipped in the first six months of the year.

Cons. Staples vs S&P 500 - 1990 to 2021   Positive ▭

Year	Apr 25 to May 31		Sep 25 Oct 27		Compound Growth	
	S&P 500	Cons. Staples	S&P 500	Cons. Staples	S&P 500	Cons. Staples
1990	9.3 %	10.9 %	0.0 %	7.6 %	9.4 %	19.3 %
1991	1.8	1.5	-0.9	-2.1	0.9	-0.6
1992	1.5	2.6	0.0	-0.5	1.6	2.0
1993	3.0	3.7	1.5	4.4	4.6	8.2
1994	2.0	-0.1	1.3	4.9	3.4	4.8
1995	4.0	3.9	-0.3	2.7	3.6	6.7
1996	2.9	7.5	2.2	0.6	5.2	8.2
1997	10.0	7.8	-7.1	-5.7	2.1	1.6
1998	-1.5	1.5	2.2	11.2	0.6	12.8
1999	-4.1	1.1	1.5	-0.2	-2.6	1.0
2000	-0.6	3.8	-4.8	11.7	-5.4	15.9
2001	3.8	5.0	10.1	4.1	14.3	9.3
2002	-2.4	0.5	9.6	4.2	7.0	4.7
2003	5.7	4.7	2.2	2.2	8.0	6.9
2004	-1.7	-1.9	1.4	1.0	-0.4	-0.9
2005	3.4	2.7	-3.0	-0.1	0.3	2.6
2006	-2.9	1.8	4.8	1.7	1.7	3.5
2007	3.4	0.5	1.2	2.8	4.6	3.3
2008	0.8	0.9	-28.4	-19.2	-27.8	-18.5
2009	6.1	7.3	1.2	2.3	7.4	9.7
2010	-10.5	-6.1	2.9	1.7	-7.9	-4.5
2011	0.6	4.2	13.0	6.4	13.7	10.8
2012	-4.5	-0.3	-3.1	-2.3	-7.4	-2.7
2013	3.3	-1.9	3.7	3.4	7.1	1.4
2014	2.4	3.0	-1.8	0.9	0.5	3.9
2015	-0.5	-0.9	6.9	7.4	6.4	6.5
2016	0.3	1.4	-1.5	-1.9	-1.2	-0.5
2017	1.6	2.0	3.2	-1.6	4.8	0.4
2018	2.7	-1.1	-8.9	-0.7	-6.5	-1.8
2019	-6.0	-2.6	1.9	0.7	-4.2	-1.9
2020	7.3	0.6	4.4	2.5	12.1	3.1
2021	0.8	1.6	2.2	0.5	2.7	2.0
Avg.	1.3 %	2.0 %	0.5 %	1.6 %	1.8 %	3.7 %
Fq>0	69 %	75 %	69 %	69 %	72 %	75 %

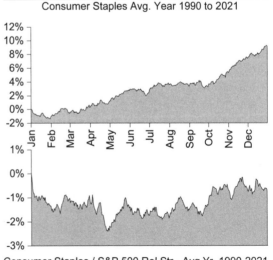

Consumer Staples Avg. Year 1990 to 2021

Consumer Staples / S&P 500 Rel Str.- Avg Yr. 1990-2021

Consumer Staples Performance

Cons. Staples Monthly % Gain (1990-2021)

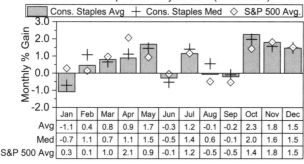

	Jan	Feb	Mar	Apr	May	Jun	Jul	Aug	Sep	Oct	Nov	Dec
Avg	-1.1	0.4	0.8	0.9	1.7	-0.3	1.2	-0.1	-0.2	2.3	1.8	1.5
Med	-0.7	1.1	0.7	1.1	1.5	-0.5	1.4	0.6	-0.1	2.0	1.6	1.5
S&P 500 Avg	0.3	0.1	1.0	2.1	0.9	-0.1	1.2	-0.5	-0.5	1.4	1.8	1.5

Fq % Cons. Staples Gain > 0% (1990-2021)

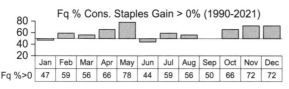

	Jan	Feb	Mar	Apr	May	Jun	Jul	Aug	Sep	Oct	Nov	Dec
Fq %>0	47	59	56	66	78	44	59	56	50	66	72	72

Fq % Cons. Staples Gain > S&P 500 % (1990-2021)

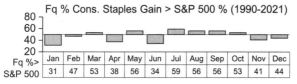

	Jan	Feb	Mar	Apr	May	Jun	Jul	Aug	Sep	Oct	Nov	Dec
Fq %> S&P 500	31	47	53	38	56	34	59	56	56	53	41	44

Cons. Staples % Gain 5 Year (2017-2021)

Cons. Staples Performance 2021-2022

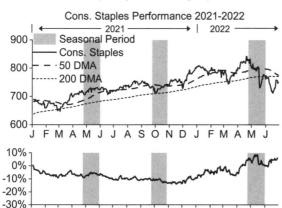

Relative Strength, % Gain vs. S&P 500

Market Indices & Rates
Weekly Values**

Stock Markets	2021	2022
Dow	34,201	34,451
S&P500	4,185	4,393
Nasdaq	14,052	13,351
TSX	19,351	21,856
FTSE	7,020	7,616
DAX	15,460	14,164
Nikkei	29,683	27,093
Hang Seng	28,970	21,518

Commodities	2021	2022
Oil	63.13	106.95
Gold	1774.5	1963.3

Bond Yields	2021	2022
USA 5 Yr Treasury	0.84	2.79
USA 10 Yr T	1.59	2.83
USA 20 Yr T	2.15	3.09
Moody's Aaa	2.85	3.88
Moody's Baa	3.56	4.76
CAN 5 Yr T	0.96	2.64
CAN 10 Yr T	1.54	2.76

Money Market	2021	2022
USA Fed Funds	0.25	0.50
USA 3 Mo T-B	0.02	0.79
CAN tgt overnight rate	0.25	1.00
CAN 3 Mo T-B	0.09	0.97

Foreign Exchange	2021	2022
EUR/USD	1.20	1.08
GBP/USD	1.38	1.31
USD/CAD	1.25	1.26
USD/JPY	108.80	126.46

APRIL

M	T	W	T	F	S	S
					1	2
3	4	5	6	7	8	9
10	11	13	13	14	15	16
17	18	19	20	21	22	23
24	25	26	27	28	29	30

MAY

M	T	W	T	F	S	S
1	2	2	4	5	6	7
8	9	10	11	12	13	14
15	16	17	18	19	20	21
22	23	24	25	26	27	28
29	30	31				

JUNE

M	T	W	T	F	S	S
		1	2	3	4	
5	6	7	8	9	10	11
12	13	14	15	16	17	18
19	20	21	22	23	24	25
26	27	28	29	30		

U.S. GOVERNMENT BONDS (7-10 YEARS)
May 6 to October 3

The following government bond seasonal period analysis has been broken down into two contiguous periods in order to demonstrate the relative strength of the first part of the trade compared with the second part. Although both the May 6 to August 8 and the August 9 to October 3 periods provide value, the sweet spot to the government bond trade is in the latter period from August 9 to October 3.

Bonds tend to outperform from late spring into autumn for three reasons. First, governments and companies tend to raise more money through bond issuance at the beginning of the year to meet their needs for the rest of the year. With more bonds competing in the market for money, bond prices tend to decrease. Less bonds tend to be issued in late spring and early summer during their seasonal period, helping to support bond prices.

Positive 79% of the time

Second, optimistic forecasts at the beginning of the year for stronger GDP growth tend to increase inflation expectations and as a result interest rates respond by increasing. As economic growth expectations tend to decrease in the summer, interest rates respond by retreating.

Third, the stock market often peaks in May and investors rotate their money into bonds. As the demand for bonds increases, interest rates decrease and bonds increase in value. For seasonal investors looking to put their money to work in the unfavorable six months of the year for the stock market, buying bonds in the summer months fits perfectly with their strategy.

(i) *Source: Barclays Capital Inc.*
The U.S. Treasury: 7-10 Year is a total return index.

U.S. Gov. Bonds* vs. S&P 500 1998 to 2021   Positive ☐

Year	May 6 to Aug 8 S&P 500	May 6 to Aug 8 Gov. Bonds	Aug 9 to Oct 3 S&P 500	Aug 9 to Oct 3 Gov. Bonds	Total Growth S&P 500	Total Growth Gov. Bonds
1998	-2.3 %	3.3 %	-8.0 %	8.3 %	-10.1 %	11.9 %
1999	-3.5	-3.0	-1.3	0.9	-4.8	-2.1
2000	3.5	5.8	-3.8	0.9	-0.4	6.7
2001	-6.6	2.6	-9.4	4.4	-15.3	7.1
2002	-15.7	6.5	-9.6	5.0	-23.7	11.9
2003	5.5	-1.3	5.4	1.3	11.2	0.0
2004	-5.1	3.6	6.4	0.8	0.9	4.4
2005	4.3	-0.9	0.3	0.7	4.6	-0.2
2006	-4.1	2.6	4.9	2.7	0.6	5.3
2007	-0.5	-0.3	2.8	3.3	2.3	3.0
2008	-7.9	0.9	-15.2	2.4	-21.9	3.4
2009	11.8	-4.0	1.5	5.4	13.4	1.1
2010	-3.8	7.1	2.2	2.6	-1.7	9.8
2011	-16.2	7.6	-1.8	4.6	-17.7	12.6
2012	2.4	2.3	3.5	0.9	6.0	3.3
2013	5.1	-5.2	-1.1	0.3	4.0	-4.9
2014	2.5	2.3	1.9	0.1	4.4	2.4
2015	-0.6	0.6	-6.1	2.1	-6.6	2.6
2016	6.4	1.6	-0.9	-0.1	5.4	1.6
2017	3.2	1.3	2.4	-0.1	5.6	1.2
2018	7.3	0.6	2.4	-1.0	9.8	-0.4
2019	-0.2	7.1	-0.9	1.5	-1.2	8.7
2020	16.8	1.1	0.0	-0.6	16.7	0.6
2021	6.5	2.5	-1.8	-1.1	4.5	1.4
Avg.	3.7 %	1.9 %	-1.1 %	1.9 %	-0.6 %	3.8 %
Fq>0	50 %	75 %	46 %	79 %	58 %	79 %

In periods when the stock market rallies in the early summer months, positive bond performance can be delayed until later in the summer, typically early August, which coincides with the bond seasonal period sweet spot, from August 9 to October 3.

2021/22 Performance Update.

In 2021, government bonds were negative as the economy was showing signs of solid growth. In 2022, government bonds performed very poorly in the first six months of the year. From the start of its strong seasonal period on May 6 to the end of June (first part of seasonal period), government bonds started to stabilize.

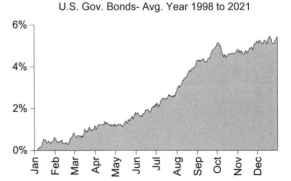

U.S. Gov. Bonds- Avg. Year 1998 to 2021

U.S. Government Bond Performance

UST 7-10YR Monthly % Gain (1998-2021)

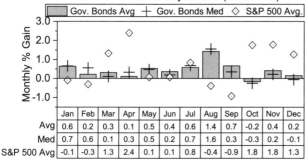

	Jan	Feb	Mar	Apr	May	Jun	Jul	Aug	Sep	Oct	Nov	Dec
Avg	0.6	0.2	0.3	0.1	0.5	0.4	0.6	1.4	0.7	-0.2	0.4	0.2
Med	0.7	0.6	0.1	0.3	0.5	0.2	0.7	1.6	0.3	-0.3	0.2	-0.1
S&P 500 Avg	-0.1	-0.3	1.3	2.4	0.1	0.1	0.8	-0.4	-0.9	1.8	1.8	1.3

Fq % UST 7-10YR Gain > 0% (1998-2021)

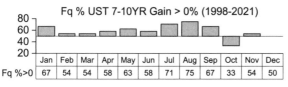

	Jan	Feb	Mar	Apr	May	Jun	Jul	Aug	Sep	Oct	Nov	Dec
Fq %>0	67	54	54	58	63	58	71	75	67	33	54	50

Fq % UST 7-10YR Gain > S&P 500 % (1998-2021)

	Jan	Feb	Mar	Apr	May	Jun	Jul	Aug	Sep	Oct	Nov	Dec
Fq %> S&P 500	54	50	42	29	42	42	50	58	50	38	25	38

UST 7-10YR % Gain 5 Year (2017-2021)

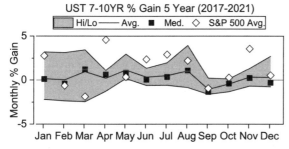

UST 10YR Performance 2021-2022

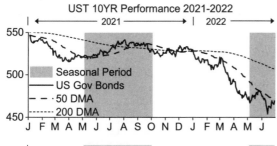

Relative Strength, % Gain vs. S&P 500

Market Indices & Rates Weekly Values**

Stock Markets	2021	2022
Dow	34,043	33,811
S&P500	4,180	4,272
Nasdaq	14,017	12,839
TSX	19,102	21,186
FTSE	6,939	7,522
DAX	15,280	14,142
Nikkei	29,021	27,105
Hang Seng	29,079	20,639

Commodities	2021	2022
Oil	62.18	103.07
Gold	1781.8	1941.6

Bond Yields	2021	2022
USA 5 Yr Treasury	0.83	2.94
USA 10 Yr T	1.58	2.90
USA 20 Yr T	2.14	3.14
Moody's Aaa	2.88	3.96
Moody's Baa	3.57	4.86
CAN 5 Yr T	0.94	2.79
CAN 10 Yr T	1.52	2.87

Money Market	2021	2022
USA Fed Funds	0.25	0.50
USA 3 Mo T-B	0.03	0.83
CAN tgt overnight rate	0.25	1.00
CAN 3 Mo T-B	0.09	1.32

Foreign Exchange	2021	2022
EUR/USD	1.21	1.08
GBP/USD	1.39	1.28
USD/CAD	1.25	1.27
USD/JPY	107.88	128.50

APRIL

M	T	W	T	F	S	S
					1	2
3	4	5	6	7	8	9
10	11	13	13	14	15	16
17	18	19	20	21	22	23
24	25	26	27	28	29	30

MAY

M	T	W	T	F	S	S
1	2	2	4	5	6	7
8	9	10	11	12	13	14
15	16	17	18	19	20	21
22	23	24	25	26	27	28
29	30	31				

JUNE

M	T	W	T	F	S	S
		1	2	3	4	
5	6	7	8	9	10	11
12	13	14	15	16	17	18
19	20	21	22	23	24	25
26	27	28	29	30		

AXP AMERICAN EXPRESS
April 1 to April 30

(NEW)

Financial stocks tend perform well in April. American Express is no exception.

If there was only one month of the year that you could invest in American Express, on a seasonal basis, April would be the month. April is the strongest month of the year for American Express on an average, median and frequency basis, since 1990.

American Express also tends to perform well in March, with an average and median positive performance and outperformance of the S&P 500. It is possible to enter into a position in American Express before April, particularly if American Express is showing strong signs of positive momentum.

From 1990 to 2022, American Express has produced an average gain of 6.1% in April and has been positive 76% of the time. In this time period, it has also outperformed the S&P 500, 67% of the time.

> ### *6% gain &*
> ### *positive 76% of the time*

In the five year period from 2017 to 2021, the best month of the year for American Express on an average and median basis has been April. In the same time period, March has been one of the weaker months of the year.

AXP* vs. S&P 500
1990 to 2022

Apr 1 to Apr 30	S&P 500	AXP	Diff (Positive)
1990	-2.7%	5.3%	8.0%
1991	0.0	-13.4	-13.5
1992	2.8	-1.6	-4.4
1993	-2.5	3.2	5.8
1994	1.2	6.8	5.6
1995	2.8	-0.4	-3.2
1996	1.3	-1.8	-3.1
1997	5.8	9.8	4.0
1998	0.9	11.3	10.4
1999	3.8	11.0	7.2
2000	-3.1	0.4	3.5
2001	7.7	2.8	-4.9
2002	-6.1	0.1	6.3
2003	8.1	13.9	5.8
2004	-1.7	-5.6	-3.9
2005	-2.0	2.6	4.6
2006	1.2	2.4	1.2
2007	4.3	7.6	3.2
2008	4.8	9.8	5.1
2009	9.4	85.0	75.6
2010	1.5	11.8	10.3
2011	2.9	8.6	5.7
2012	-0.8	4.1	4.8
2013	1.8	1.4	-0.4
2014	0.6	-2.9	-3.5
2015	0.9	-0.9	-1.7
2016	0.3	6.6	6.3
2017	0.9	0.2	-0.7
2018	0.3	5.9	5.6
2019	3.9	7.3	3.3
2020	12.7	6.6	-6.1
2021	5.2	8.4	3.2
2022	-8.8	-6.6	2.2
Avg	1.7%	6.1%	4.3%
Fq > 0	76%	76%	67%

AXP- Avg. Year 1990 to 2021

AXP / S&P 500 Relative Strength - Avg. Yr. 1990-2021

2021/22 Performance Update.
In 2021, American Express performed particularly well and outperformed the S&P 500. In its strong seasonal period it was positive and outperformed the S&P 500.

In 2022, American Express performed very well in January and February, and strongly outperformed the S&P 500. American Express was negative in its seasonal period, but managed to outperform the S&P 500.

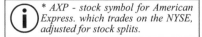

(i) *AXP - stock symbol for American Express. which trades on the NYSE, adjusted for stock splits.*

American Express Performance

AXP Monthly % Gain (1990-2021)

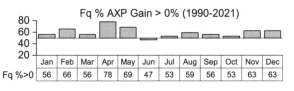

	AXP Avg	+ AXP Med	◇ S&P 500 Avg.

	Jan	Feb	Mar	Apr	May	Jun	Jul	Aug	Sep	Oct	Nov	Dec
Avg	-1.3	-0.2	2.2	6.4	1.6	-0.6	2.1	-0.5	-0.2	-0.1	3.2	0.8
Med	0.4	1.7	2.7	4.7	2.3	-0.4	1.0	0.9	0.4	1.4	2.6	1.4
S&P 500 Avg	0.3	0.1	1.0	2.1	0.9	-0.1	1.2	-0.5	-0.5	1.4	1.8	1.5

Fq % AXP Gain > 0% (1990-2021)

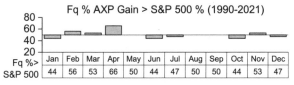

	Jan	Feb	Mar	Apr	May	Jun	Jul	Aug	Sep	Oct	Nov	Dec
Fq %>0	56	66	56	78	69	47	53	59	56	53	63	63

Fq % AXP Gain > S&P 500 % (1990-2021)

	Jan	Feb	Mar	Apr	May	Jun	Jul	Aug	Sep	Oct	Nov	Dec
Fq %> S&P 500	44	56	53	66	50	44	47	50	50	44	53	47

AXP % Gain 5 Year (2017-2021)

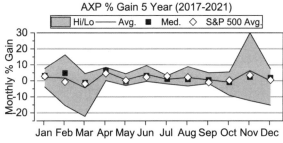

	Hi/Lo	— Avg.	■ Med.	◇ S&P 500 Avg.

Jan Feb Mar Apr May Jun Jul Aug Sep Oct Nov Dec

AXP Performance 2021-2022

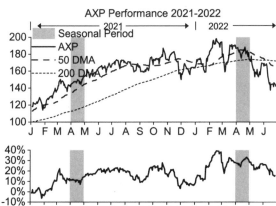

Relative Strength, % Gain vs. S&P 500

Stock Markets	2021	2022
Dow	33,875	32,977
S&P500	4,181	4,132
Nasdaq	13,963	12,335
TSX	19,108	20,762
FTSE	6,970	7,545
DAX	15,136	14,098
Nikkei	28,813	26,848
Hang Seng	28,725	21,089

Commodities	2021	2022
Oil	63.58	104.69
Gold	1767.7	1911.3

Bond Yields	2021	2022
USA 5 Yr Treasury	0.86	2.92
USA 10 Yr T	1.65	2.89
USA 20 Yr T	2.19	3.14
Moody's Aaa	2.94	4.01
Moody's Baa	3.61	4.94
CAN 5 Yr T	0.93	2.75
CAN 10 Yr T	1.55	2.87

Money Market	2021	2022
USA Fed Funds	0.25	0.50
USA 3 Mo T-B	0.01	0.85
CAN tgt overnight rate	0.25	1.00
CAN 3 Mo T-B	0.11	1.39

Foreign Exchange	2021	2022
EUR/USD	1.20	1.05
GBP/USD	1.38	1.26
USD/CAD	1.23	1.28
USD/JPY	109.31	129.70

APRIL

M	T	W	T	F	S	S
					1	2
3	4	5	6	7	8	9
10	11	13	13	14	15	16
17	18	19	20	21	22	23
24	25	26	27	28	29	30

MAY

M	T	W	T	F	S	S
1	2	2	4	5	6	7
8	9	10	11	12	13	14
15	16	17	18	19	20	21
22	23	24	25	26	27	28
29	30	31				

JUNE

M	T	W	T	F	S	S
		1	2	3	4	
5	6	7	8	9	10	11
12	13	14	15	16	17	18
19	20	21	22	23	24	25
26	27	28	29	30		

MAY

	MONDAY		TUESDAY		WEDNESDAY
WEEK 18	**1** 30		**2** 29		**3** 28
WEEK 19	**8** 23		**9** 22		**10** 21
WEEK 20	**15** 16		**16** 15		**17** 14
WEEK 21	**22** 9 CAN Market Closed- Victoria Day		**23** 8		**24** 7
WEEK 22	**29** 2 USA Market Closed- Memorial Day		**30** 1		**31**

THURSDAY		FRIDAY	
4	27	**5**	26
11	29	**12**	19
18	13	**19**	12
25	6	**26**	5
1		2	

JUNE

M	T	W	T	F	S	S
			1	2	3	4
5	6	7	8	9	10	11
12	13	14	15	16	17	18
19	20	21	22	23	24	25
26	27	28	29	30		

JULY

M	T	W	T	F	S	S
					1	2
3	4	5	6	7	8	9
10	11	12	13	14	15	16
17	18	19	20	21	22	23
24	25	26	27	28	29	30
31						

AUGUST

M	T	W	T	F	S	S
	1	2	3	4	5	6
7	8	9	10	11	12	13
14	15	16	17	18	19	20
21	22	23	24	25	26	27
28	29	30	31			

SEPTEMBER

M	T	W	T	F	S	S
				1	2	3
4	5	6	7	8	9	10
11	12	13	14	15	16	17
18	19	20	21	22	23	24
25	26	27	28	29	30	

MAY
SUMMARY

	Dow Jones	S&P 500	Nasdaq	TSX Comp
Month Rank	9	8	5	2
# Up	39	43	31	23
# Down	33	29	19	14
% Pos	54	60	62	62
% Avg. Gain	0.0	0.2	1.0	1.3

Dow & S&P 1950-2021, Nasdaq 1972-2021 TSX 1985-2021

S&P500 Cumulative Daily Gains for Avg Month 1950 to 2022

Prob. of Daily Gain

♦ The first few days and the last few days in May tend to be strong and the period in between tends to be negative. ♦ A lot of the cyclical sectors finish their seasonal periods at the beginning of May. Some of the defensive sectors start their strong seasonal period in May. ♦ Government bonds start their strong seasonal period in May. ♦ In May 2022, the S&P 500 increased in volatility, and only managed to end the month with no change in value.

BEST / WORST MAY BROAD MKTS. 2013-2022

BEST MAY MARKETS
- Nikkei 225 (2020) 8.3%
- Nasdaq (2020) 6.8%
- Russell 2000 (2020) 6.4%

WORST MAY MARKETS
- Nikkei 225 (2012) -10.3%
- Nasdaq (2019) -7.9%
- Russell 2000 (2019) -7.9%

Index Values End of Month

	2013	2014	2015	2016	2017	2018	2019	2020	2021	2022
Dow	15,116	16,717	18,011	17,787	21,009	24,416	24,815	25,383	34,529	32,990
S&P 500	1,631	1,924	2,107	2,097	2,412	2,663	2,752	3,044	4,204	4,132
Nasdaq	3,456	4,243	5,070	4,948	6,199	7,442	7,453	9,490	13,749	12,081
TSX Comp.	12,650	14,604	15,014	14,066	15,350	16,062	16,037	15,193	19,731	20,729
Russell 1000	904	1,072	1,177	1,161	1,336	1,502	1,524	1,683	2,365	2,269
Russell 2000	984	1,135	1,247	1,155	1,370	1,634	1,465	1,394	2,269	1,864
FTSE 100	6,583	6,845	6,984	6,231	7,520	7,678	7,162	6,077	7,023	7,608
Nikkei 225	13,775	14,632	20,563	17,235	19,651	22,202	20,601	21,878	28,860	27,280

Percent Gain for May

	2013	2014	2015	2016	2017	2018	2019	2020	2021	2022
Dow	1.9	0.8	1.0	0.1	0.3	1.0	-6.7	4.3	1.9	0.0
S&P 500	2.1	2.1	1.0	1.5	1.2	0.6	-6.6	4.5	0.5	0.0
Nasdaq	3.8	3.1	2.6	3.6	2.5	5.3	-7.9	6.8	-1.5	-2.1
TSX Comp.	1.6	-0.3	-1.4	0.8	-1.5	2.9	-3.3	2.8	3.3	-0.2
Russell 1000	2.0	2.1	1.1	1.5	1.0	2.3	-6.6	5.1	0.3	-0.3
Russell 2000	3.9	0.7	2.2	2.1	-2.2	5.9	-7.9	6.4	0.1	0.0
FTSE 100	2.4	1.0	0.3	-0.2	4.4	2.2	-3.5	3.0	0.8	0.8
Nikkei 225	-0.6	2.3	5.3	3.4	2.4	-1.2	-7.4	8.3	0.2	1.6

May Market Avg. Performance 2013 to 2022[1]

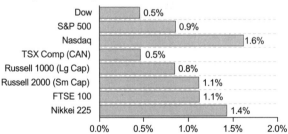

Dow	0.5%
S&P 500	0.9%
Nasdaq	1.6%
TSX Comp (CAN)	0.5%
Russell 1000 (Lg Cap)	0.8%
Russell 2000 (Sm Cap)	1.1%
FTSE 100	1.1%
Nikkei 225	1.4%

Interest Corner May[2]

	Fed Funds % [3]	3 Mo. T-Bill % [4]	10 Yr % [5]	20 Yr % [6]
2022	1.00	1.16	2.85	3.28
2021	0.25	0.01	1.58	2.18
2020	0.25	0.14	0.65	1.18
2019	2.50	2.35	2.14	2.39
2018	1.75	1.93	2.83	2.91

(1) Russell Data provided by Russell (2) Federal Reserve Bank of St. Louis- end of month values (3) Target rate set by FOMC (4)(5)(6) Constant yield maturities.

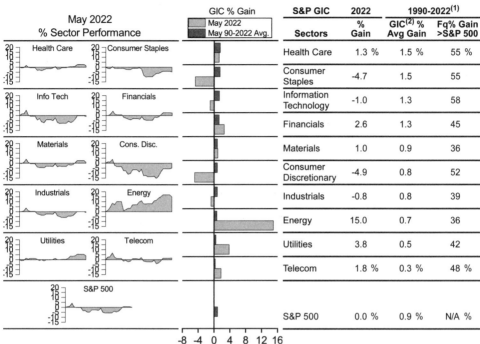

S&P GIC Sectors	2022 % Gain	1990-2022[1] GIC[2] % Avg Gain	Fq% Gain >S&P 500
Health Care	1.3 %	1.5 %	55 %
Consumer Staples	-4.7	1.5	55
Information Technology	-1.0	1.3	58
Financials	2.6	1.3	45
Materials	1.0	0.9	36
Consumer Discretionary	-4.9	0.8	52
Industrials	-0.8	0.8	39
Energy	15.0	0.7	36
Utilities	3.8	0.5	42
Telecom	1.8 %	0.3 %	48 %
S&P 500	0.0 %	0.9 %	N/A %

Sector Commentary

♦ In May 2022, the S&P 500 was flat. ♦ The sector with the biggest gain was the energy sector, with a gain of 15%. ♦ The utilities sector also performed well with a gain of almost 4%. The sector was helped with interest rates falling during the month. ♦ The growth sectors, consumer discretionary and information technology performed poorly, with losses of 4.9% and 1.0% respectively.

Sub-Sector Commentary

♦ In May 2022, the cyclical sub-sectors in the list performed poorly. ♦ The steel sub-sector lost 14.4% and the metals and mining sub-sector lost 7.6.♦ Gold, which is usually a mediocre performer in May, lost 3.8%. ♦ Silver, which is typically also a mediocre performer in May, produced a loss of 7.1%. ♦ The auto sector lost 10.7%. ♦ The homebuilders sub-sector, which typically produces a loss in May, went against its trend with a gain of almost 6%.

SELECTED SUB-SECTORS[3]

	2022 %	GIC % Avg	Fq% >S&P
Biotech (1993-2022)	3.4 %	2.0 %	68 %
Banks	6.7	1.7	48
Agriculture (1994-2022)	1.4	1.6	55
SOX (1995-2022)	6.1	1.3	61
Retail	-3.6	1.2	55
Railroads	-6.7	1.2	61
Pharma	3.3	1.2	48
Chemicals	4.0	1.0	48
Transportation	-2.4	0.5	52
Metals & Mining	-7.6	0.4	42
Steel	-14.4	0.4	45
Silver	-7.1	0.3	45
Gold	-3.8	0.2	48
Auto	-10.7	-0.1	27
Homebuilders	5.8	-0.4	48

DISNEY–TIME TO STAY AWAY & TIME TO VISIT
①SELL SHORT (Jun5-Sep30) ②LONG(Oct1-Feb15)

Disney has two seasonal periods, one positive and one negative. The positive (strong) seasonal period for Disney, from October 1 to February 15, is stronger in magnitude than its weak seasonal period which takes place from June 5 to September 30.

Gain of 26%

According to Disney's Form 10-K filed with the Securities and Exchange Commission for the year ended September 29, 2012: "Revenues in our Media Networks segment are subject to seasonal advertising patterns... these commitments are typically satisfied during the second half of the Company's fiscal year." The media segment is the biggest driver of revenue for Disney. In addition, their other business segments are skewed towards revenue generation in the summer.

Disney's year-end occurs at the end of September and it typically reports its results in the first week of November. Investors start to increase their positions at the beginning of October in anticipation of positive year-end news.

Do not "visit" the Disney stock from June 5 to September 30. For the period from 1990 to 2021, Disney has produced an average loss of 6.7% and has only beaten the S&P 500, 31% of the time.

2021/22 Performance Update.
In 2021, Disney ended the year lower on an absolute basis. This was partly due to increased competition in its streaming services and lower subscription levels than expected.

ⓘ *DIS - stock symbol for Walt Disney Company which trades on the NYSE. is a diversified worldwide entertainment company. Price is adjusted for stock splits.*

Disney vs. S&P 500 1990/91 to 2021/22

Negative Short [ ]　　　　　　Positive Long [ ]

Year	Jun 5 to Sep 30 S&P 500	Jun 5 to Sep 30 Dis-ney	Oct 1 to Feb 15 S&P 500	Oct 1 to Feb 15 Dis-ney	Compound Growth S&P 500	Compound Growth Dis-ney
1990/91	-16.7 %	-29.7 %	20.6 %	30.1 %	0.5 %	68.2 %
1991/92	0.0	-3.0	6.4	25.4	6.4	29.2
1992/93	1.1	-2.7	6.4	29.7	7.6	33.1
1993/94	2.0	-14.7	3.0	23.9	5.0	42.0
1994/95	0.6	-13.2	4.7	38.5	5.3	56.6
1995/96	9.8	2.7	11.5	11.3	22.3	8.3
1996/97	2.2	5.2	17.6	23.6	20.2	17.1
1997/98	12.8	0.9	7.7	38.2	21.4	36.9
1998/99	-7.1	-30.4	21.0	39.6	12.4	82.3
1999/00	-3.4	-15.1	9.3	41.9	5.6	63.2
2001/01	-2.8	-5.4	-7.7	-15.3	-10.2	-10.7
2001/02	-17.9	-41.1	6.1	28.4	-12.9	81.1
2002/03	-21.7	-31.9	2.4	10.5	-19.8	45.8
2003/04	1.0	-2.7	15.0	33.5	16.2	37.1
2004/05	-0.7	-6.3	8.6	31.2	7.8	39.4
2005/06	2.7	-11.7	4.2	11.4	7.0	24.4
2006/07	3.7	1.0	9.1	12.2	13.1	11.1
2007/08	-0.8	-3.7	-11.6	-5.5	-12.3	-2.1
2008/09	-15.3	-10.7	-29.1	-39.7	-40.0	-33.2
2009/10	12.2	9.2	1.7	9.5	14.1	0.6
2010/11	7.2	-1.8	16.4	30.2	24.7	32.5
2011/12	-13.0	-23.4	18.7	36.8	3.3	68.8
2012/13	12.7	17.7	5.5	6.4	18.9	-12.5
2013/14	3.1	0.2	9.3	22.9	12.7	22.6
2014/15	2.3	5.7	6.3	17.0	8.8	10.4
2015/16	-8.4	-7.3	-2.9	-10.8	-11.0	-4.3
2016/17	3.3	-6.0	8.4	18.7	11.9	25.7
2017/18	3.3	-8.0	8.4	6.7	12.0	15.3
2018/19	6.1	16.7	-4.8	-3.7	1.0	-19.8
2019/20	6.2	-3.3	13.6	7.1	20.6	10.6
2020/21	8.1	3.2	17.0	51.2	26.4	50.8
2021/22	1.8	-4.5	3.8	-8.5	5.7	-4.4
Avg.	-0.2 %	-6.7 %	6.5 %	17.2 %	6.4 %	25.7 %
Fq>0	66 %	31 %	84 %	81 %	81 %	75 %

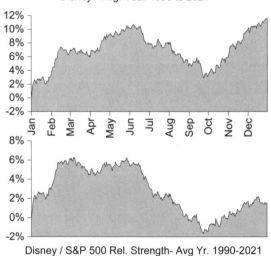

Disney - Avg. Year 1990 to 2021

Disney / S&P 500 Rel. Strength- Avg Yr. 1990-2021

Disney Performance

DIS Monthly % Gain (1990-2021)

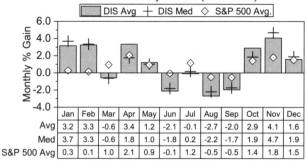

Legend: DIS Avg ☐ | DIS Med + | S&P 500 Avg. ◇

	Jan	Feb	Mar	Apr	May	Jun	Jul	Aug	Sep	Oct	Nov	Dec
Avg	3.2	3.3	-0.6	3.4	1.2	-2.1	-0.1	-2.7	-2.0	2.9	4.1	1.6
Med	3.7	3.3	-0.6	1.8	1.0	-1.8	0.2	-2.2	-1.7	1.9	4.7	1.9
S&P 500 Avg	0.3	0.1	1.0	2.1	0.9	-0.1	1.2	-0.5	-0.5	1.4	1.8	1.5

Fq % DIS Gain > 0% (1990-2021)

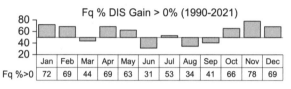

	Jan	Feb	Mar	Apr	May	Jun	Jul	Aug	Sep	Oct	Nov	Dec
Fq %>0	72	69	44	69	63	31	53	34	41	66	78	69

Fq % DIS Gain > S&P 500 % (1990-2021)

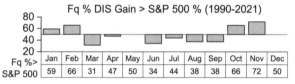

	Jan	Feb	Mar	Apr	May	Jun	Jul	Aug	Sep	Oct	Nov	Dec
Fq %> S&P 500	59	66	31	47	50	34	44	38	38	66	72	50

DIS % Gain 5 Year (2017-2021)

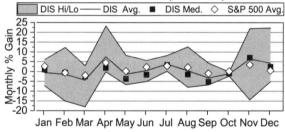

Legend: DIS Hi/Lo ☐ | DIS Avg. — | DIS Med. ■ | S&P 500 Avg. ◇

DIS Performance 2021-2022

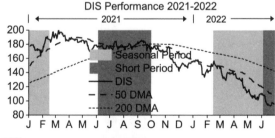

Seasonal Period
Short Period
DIS
50 DMA
200 DMA

Relative Strength, % Gain vs. S&P 500

Stock Markets	2021	2022
Dow	34,778	32,899
S&P500	4,233	4,123
Nasdaq	13,752	12,145
TSX	19,473	20,633
FTSE	7,130	7,388
DAX	15,400	13,674
Nikkei	29,358	27,004
Hang Seng	28,611	20,002

Commodities	2021	2022
Oil	64.90	109.77
Gold	1836.6	1882.4

Bond Yields	2021	2022
USA 5 Yr Treasury	0.77	3.06
USA 10 Yr T	1.60	3.12
USA 20 Yr T	2.17	3.43
Moody's Aaa	2.91	4.28
Moody's Baa	3.57	5.21
CAN 5 Yr T	0.88	2.92
CAN 10 Yr T	1.50	3.13

Money Market	2021	2022
USA Fed Funds	0.25	1.00
USA 3 Mo T-B	0.02	0.85
CAN tgt overnight rate	0.25	1.00
CAN 3 Mo T-B	0.11	1.41

Foreign Exchange	2021	2022
EUR/USD	1.22	1.06
GBP/USD	1.40	1.23
USD/CAD	1.21	1.29
USD/JPY	108.60	130.56

MAY

M	T	W	T	F	S	S
1	2	2	4	5	6	7
8	9	10	11	12	13	14
15	16	17	18	19	20	21
22	23	24	25	26	27	28
29	30	31				

JUNE

M	T	W	T	F	S	S
			1	2	3	4
5	6	7	8	9	10	11
12	13	14	15	16	17	18
19	20	21	22	23	24	25
26	27	28	29	30		

JULY

M	T	W	T	F	S	S
					1	2
3	4	5	6	7	8	9
10	11	12	13	14	15	16
17	18	19	20	21	22	23
24	25	26	27	28	29	30
31						

The six-month cycle is the result of several factors but is mainly driven by the investor liquidity preference cycle (investors tending to decrease risk in the summer months).

Most pundits do not grasp the full value of the favorable six month period for stocks from October 28 to May 5, compared with the other six months: the unfavorable six month period.

Not only does the favorable period on average have bigger gains more frequently and smaller losses, but also on a yearly basis, outperforms the unfavorable period 69% of the time (last column in the table with YES values). There is no question which six month period seasonal investors should favor.

$1,993,569 gain on $10,000

The accompanying table uses the S&P 500 to compare the returns made from Oct 28 to May 5, to the returns made during the remainder of the year.

Starting with $10,000 and investing from October 28 to May 5 every year (October 28, 1950, to May 5, 2022) has produced a gain of $1,993,569. On the flip side, being invested from May 6 to October 27, an initial investment of $10,000 has gained $1,360 over the same time period.

S&P 500 Unfavorable 6 Month Avg. Gain vs Favorable 6 Month Avg. Gain (1950-2022)

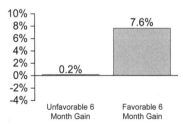

	Unfavorable 6 Month Gain	Favorable 6 Month Gain
	0.2%	7.6%

ⓘ *The above growth rates are geometric averages in order to represent the cumulative growth of a dollar investment over time. These figures differ from the arithmetic mean calculations used in the Six 'N' Six Take a Break Strategy, which are used to represent an average year.*

	S&P 500 % May 6 to Oct 27	$10,000 Start	S&P 500 % Oct 28 to May 5	$10,000 Start	Oct28-May5 > May6-Oct27
1950/51	8.5%	10,851	15.2%	11,517	YES
1951/52	0.2	10,870	3.7	11,947	YES
1952/53	1.8	11,067	3.9	12,413	YES
1953/54	-3.1	10,727	16.6	14,475	YES
1954/55	13.2	12,141	18.1	17,097	YES
1955/56	11.4	13,528	15.1	19,681	YES
1956/57	-4.6	12,903	0.2	19,711	YES
1957/58	-12.4	11,302	7.9	21,265	YES
1958/59	15.1	13,013	14.5	24,356	
1959/60	-0.6	12,939	-4.5	23,270	
1960/61	-2.3	12,647	24.1	28,869	YES
1961/62	2.7	12,993	-3.1	27,982	
1962/63	-17.7	10,698	28.4	35,929	YES
1963/64	5.7	11,306	9.3	39,264	YES
1964/65	5.1	11,882	5.5	41,440	YES
1965/66	3.1	12,253	-5.0	39,388	
1966/67	-8.8	11,180	17.7	46,364	YES
1967/68	0.6	11,241	3.9	48,171	YES
1968/69	5.6	11,872	0.2	48,249	
1969/70	-6.2	11,141	-19.7	38,722	
1970/71	5.8	11,782	24.9	48,346	YES
1971/72	-9.6	10,647	13.7	54,965	YES
1972/73	3.7	11,046	0.3	55,154	
1973/74	0.3	11,084	-18.0	45,205	
1974/75	-23.2	8,513	28.5	58,073	YES
1975/76	-0.4	8,480	12.4	65,290	YES
1976/77	0.9	8,554	-1.6	64,231	
1977/78	-7.8	7,890	4.5	67,146	YES
1978/79	-2.0	7,732	6.4	71,476	YES
1979/80	-0.1	7,723	5.8	75,605	YES
1980/81	20.2	9,283	1.9	77,047	
1981/82	-8.5	8,498	-1.4	76,001	YES
1982/83	15.0	9,769	21.4	92,293	YES
1983/84	0.3	9,803	-3.5	89,085	
1984/85	3.9	10,183	8.9	97,057	YES
1985/86	4.1	10,604	26.8	123,044	YES
1986/87	0.4	10,651	23.7	152,196	YES
1987/88	-21.0	8,409	11.0	168,904	YES
1988/89	7.1	9,010	10.9	187,380	YES
1989/90	8.9	9,814	1.0	189,242	
1990/91	-10.0	8,837	25.0	236,498	YES
1991/92	0.9	8,916	8.5	256,590	YES
1992/93	0.4	8,952	6.2	272,550	YES
1993/94	4.5	9,356	-2.8	264,789	
1994/95	3.2	9,656	11.6	295,636	YES
1995/96	11.5	10,762	10.7	327,219	
1996/97	9.2	11,757	18.5	387,591	YES
1997/98	5.6	12,419	27.2	493,003	YES
1998/99	-4.5	11,860	26.5	623,489	YES
1999/00	-3.8	11,415	10.5	688,842	YES
2000/01	-3.7	10,992	-8.2	632,435	
2001/02	-12.8	9,586	-2.8	614,583	YES
2002/03	-16.4	8,016	3.2	634,369	YES
2003/04	11.3	8,921	8.8	689,985	
2004/05	0.3	8,952	4.2	718,942	YES
2005/06	0.5	9,000	12.5	808,503	YES
2006/07	3.9	9,350	9.3	883,804	YES
2007/08	2.0	9,534	-8.3	810,240	
2008/09	-39.7	5,750	6.5	862,619	YES
2009/10	17.7	6,766	9.6	934,470	
2010/11	1.4	6,862	12.9	1,067,851	YES
2011/12	-3.8	6,602	6.6	1,138,103	YES
2012/13	3.1	6,809	14.3	1,301,313	YES
2013/14	9.0	7,422	7.1	1,393,667	
2014/15	4.1	7,725	6.5	1,484,478	YES
2015/16	-1.1	7,638	-0.7	1,473,513	YES
2016/17	4.0	7,985	12.5	1,649,048	YES
2017/18	7.6	8,591	3.2	1,701,662	
2018/19	-0.2	8,575	10.8	1,885,321	YES
2019/20	2.6	8,799	-5.1	1,789,194	
2020/21	18.2	10,401	22.9	2,199,154	YES
2021/22	9.2	11,360	-8.9	2,003,569	
Total Gain (Loss)		**$1,360**		**$1,993,569**	

6 'n' 6 Strategy Performance

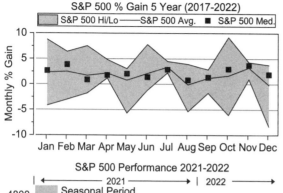

S&P 500 % Gain 5 Year (2017-2022)

Legend: S&P 500 Hi/Lo — S&P 500 Avg. ■ S&P 500 Med.

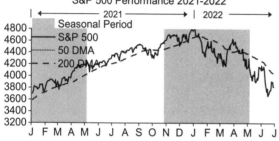

S&P 500 Performance 2021-2022

Seasonal Period — S&P 500 ···· 50 DMA –·– 200 DMA

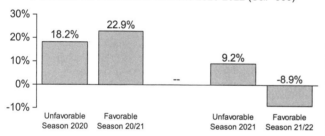

Favorable vs. Unfavorable Seasons 2020-2022 (S&P 500)

- Unfavorable Season 2020: 18.2%
- Favorable Season 20/21: 22.9%
- Unfavorable Season 2021: 9.2%
- Favorable Season 21/22: -8.9%

Over the last five years, the six month seasonal strategy for the stock market generally has followed its seasonal pattern. The months in the six month favorable seasonal period have generally been better than the other six months of the year. The outperformance in the favorable period has been weaker than its long-term average.

In 2020/21, the S&P 500 in its favorable six month period produced a large gain, larger than the gain in the unfavorable period. In 2021/22, the S&P 500 in its favorable six month period produced a loss of 8.9%. In comparison the S&P 500 produced a gain of 9.2%.

Market Indices & Rates
Weekly Values**

Stock Markets	2021	2022
Dow	34,382	32,197
S&P500	4,174	4,024
Nasdaq	13,430	11,805
TSX	19,367	20,100
FTSE	7,044	7,418
DAX	15,417	14,028
Nikkei	28,084	26,428
Hang Seng	28,028	19,899

Commodities	2021	2022
Oil	65.37	110.49
Gold	1838.1	1811.6

Bond Yields	2021	2022
USA 5 Yr Treasury	0.82	2.89
USA 10 Yr T	1.63	2.93
USA 20 Yr T	2.25	3.32
Moody's Aaa	3.00	4.19
Moody's Baa	3.66	5.17
CAN 5 Yr T	0.95	2.78
CAN 10 Yr T	1.56	2.96

Money Market	2021	2022
USA Fed Funds	0.25	1.00
USA 3 Mo T-B	0.01	1.03
CAN tgt overnight rate	0.25	1.00
CAN 3 Mo T-B	0.09	1.31

Foreign Exchange	2021	2022
EUR/USD	1.21	1.04
GBP/USD	1.41	1.23
USD/CAD	1.21	1.29
USD/JPY	109.35	129.22

MAY

M	T	W	T	F	S	S
1	2	2	4	5	6	7
8	9	10	11	12	13	14
15	16	17	18	19	20	21
22	23	24	25	26	27	28
29	30	31				

JUNE

M	T	W	T	F	S	S
			1	2	3	4
5	6	7	8	9	10	11
12	13	14	15	16	17	18
19	20	21	22	23	24	25
26	27	28	29	30		

JULY

M	T	W	T	F	S	S
					1	2
3	4	5	6	7	8	9
10	11	12	13	14	15	16
17	18	19	20	21	22	23
24	25	26	27	28	29	30
31						

In analyzing long-term trends for the broad markets such as the S&P 500 or the TSX Composite, a large data set is preferable because it incorporates various economic cycles. The daily data set for the TSX Composite starts in 1977.

Over this time period, investors have been rewarded for following the six month cycle of investing from October 28 to May 5, versus the unfavorable six month period, May 6 to October 27.

Starting with an investment of $10,000 in 1977, investing in the unfavorable six months has produced a loss of $2,448, versus investing in the favorable six month period which has produced a gain of $262,942.

$262,942 gain on $10,000 since 1977

The TSX Composite Average Year 1977 to 2021 graph (below), indicates that the market tended to peak in mid-July or the end of August. In our book *Time In Time Out, Outsmart the Stock Market Using Calendar Investment Strategies*, Bruce Lindsay and I analyzed a number of market trends and peaks over different decades.

What we found was that the markets tend to peak at the beginning of May or mid-July. The mid-July peak was usually the result of a strong bull market in place that had a lot of momentum.

The main reason that the TSX Composite data shows a peak occurring in July-August is that the data is primarily from the biggest bull market in history, starting in 1982.

intervals, the period from October to May is far superior compared with the other half of the year. The table below illustrates the superiority of the best six months over the worst six months. Going down the table year by year, the period from October 28 to May 5 outperforms the period from May 6 to October 27 on a regular basis. In a strong bull market, investors always have the choice of using a stop loss or technical indicators to help extend the exit point past the May date.

	TSX Comp May 6 to Oct 27	$10,000 Start	TSX Comp Oct 28 to May 5	$10,000 Start
1977/78	-3.9 %	9,608	13.1 %	11,313
1978/79	12.1	10,775	21.3	13,728
1979/80	2.9	11,084	23.0	16,883
1980/81	22.5	13,579	-2.4	16,479
1981/82	-17.0	11,272	-18.2	13,488
1982/83	16.6	13,138	34.6	18,150
1983/84	-0.9	13,015	-1.9	17,811
1984/85	1.6	13,226	10.7	19,718
1985/86	0.5	13,299	16.5	22,978
1986/87	-1.9	13,045	24.8	28,666
1987/88	-23.4	9,992	15.3	33,050
1988/89	2.7	10,260	5.7	34,939
1989/90	7.9	11,072	-13.3	30,294
1990/91	-8.4	10,148	13.1	34,266
1991/92	-1.6	9,982	-2.0	33,571
1992/93	-2.3	9,750	15.3	38,704
1993/94	10.8	10,801	1.7	39,365
1994/95	-0.1	10,792	0.3	39,483
1995/96	1.3	10,936	18.2	46,671
1996/97	8.3	11,843	10.8	51,725
1997/98	7.3	12,707	17.0	60,510
1998/99	-22.3	9,870	17.1	70,871
1999/00	-0.2	9,853	36.9	97,009
2000/01	-2.9	9,570	-14.4	83,062
2001/02	-12.2	8,399	9.4	90,875
2002/03	-16.4	7,020	4.0	94,476
2003/04	15.1	8,079	10.3	104,252
2004/05	3.9	8,398	7.8	112,379
2005/06	8.1	9,080	19.8	134,587
2006/07	0.0	9,079	12.2	151,053
2007/08	3.8	9,426	-0.2	150,820
2008/09	-40.2	5,638	15.7	174,551
2009/10	11.9	6,307	7.4	187,526
2010/11	5.8	6,674	7.1	200,778
2011/12	-7.4	6,183	-4.8	191,207
2012/13	3.6	6,407	1.1	193,348
2013/14	7.7	6,902	9.7	212,072
2014/15	-1.6	6,795	4.9	222,404
2015/16	-9.7	6,135	-4.9	221,307
2016/17	8.8	6,676	5.0	232,470
2017/18	2.4	6,835	-1.4	229,205
2018/19	-5.3	6,733	10.8	253,932
2019/20	-0.5	6,696	-9.7	229,275
2020/21	8.2	6,959	20.5	276,355
2021/22	8.5	7,552	-1.2	272,942
Total Gain (Loss)	**$(2,448)**		**$262,942**	

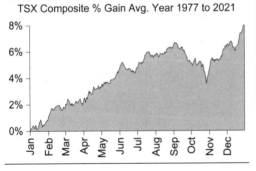

TSX Composite % Gain Avg. Year 1977 to 2021

Does a later average peak in the stock market mean that the best six month cycle does not work? No. Dividing the year up into six month

Costco Performance

COST Monthly % Gain (1994-2021)

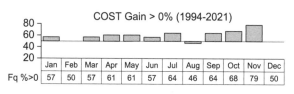

Legend: COST Avg · COST Med · S&P 500 Avg.

Monthly % Gain

	Jan	Feb	Mar	Apr	May	Jun	Jul	Aug	Sep	Oct	Nov	Dec
Avg	1.2	0.7	2.3	0.7	-0.2	2.9	1.4	-1.2	1.4	4.0	4.0	0.5
Med	1.6	0.5	3.9	1.4	0.5	3.5	2.1	-0.2	1.5	2.8	2.9	-0.1
S&P 500 Avg	0.5	-0.2	1.0	2.4	0.5	0.2	1.1	-0.3	-0.4	1.5	2.0	1.2

COST Gain > 0% (1994-2021)

	Jan	Feb	Mar	Apr	May	Jun	Jul	Aug	Sep	Oct	Nov	Dec
Fq %>0	57	50	57	61	61	57	64	46	64	68	79	50

Fq % COST Gain > S&P 500 % (1994-2021)

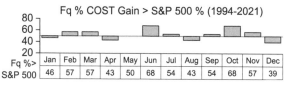

	Jan	Feb	Mar	Apr	May	Jun	Jul	Aug	Sep	Oct	Nov	Dec
Fq %> S&P 500	46	57	57	43	50	68	54	43	54	68	57	39

COST % Gain 5 Year (2017-2021)

Legend: Hi/Lo — Avg. ■ Med. ◇ S&P 500 Avg.

Monthly % Gain

Jan Feb Mar Apr May Jun Jul Aug Sep Oct Nov Dec

COST Performance 2021-2022

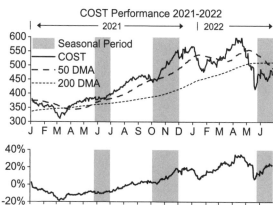

|← 2021 →| |2022 →|

Seasonal Period
COST
50 DMA
200 DMA

J F M A M J J A S O N D J F M A M J

J F M A M J J A S O N D J F M A M J

Relative Strength, % Gain vs. S&P 500

Market Indices & Rates
Weekly Values**

Stock Markets	2021	2022
Dow	34,529	33,213
S&P500	4,204	4,158
Nasdaq	13,749	12,131
TSX	19,852	20,749
FTSE	7,023	7,585
DAX	15,520	14,462
Nikkei	29,149	26,782
Hang Seng	29,124	20,697

Commodities	2021	2022
Oil	66.32	115.07
Gold	1900.0	1851.8

Bond Yields	2021	2022
USA 5 Yr Treasury	0.79	2.71
USA 10 Yr T	1.58	2.74
USA 20 Yr T	2.18	3.16
Moody's Aaa	2.90	3.95
Moody's Baa	3.57	5.00
CAN 5 Yr T	0.92	2.64
CAN 10 Yr T	1.50	2.79

Money Market	2021	2022
USA Fed Funds	0.25	1.00
USA 3 Mo T-B	0.01	1.08
CAN tgt overnight rate	0.25	1.00
CAN 3 Mo T-B	0.11	1.41

Foreign Exchange	2021	2022
EUR/USD	1.22	1.07
GBP/USD	1.42	1.26
USD/CAD	1.21	1.27
USD/JPY	109.85	127.11

MAY

M	T	W	T	F	S	S
1	2	2	4	5	6	7
8	9	10	11	12	13	14
15	16	17	18	19	20	21
22	23	24	25	26	27	28
29	30	31				

JUNE

M	T	W	T	F	S	S
				1	2	3	4
5	6	7	8	9	10	11
12	13	14	15	16	17	18
19	20	21	22	23	24	25
26	27	28	29	30		

JULY

M	T	W	T	F	S	S
					1	2
3	4	5	6	7	8	9
10	11	12	13	14	15	16
17	18	19	20	21	22	23
24	25	26	27	28	29	30
31						

COSTCO – BUY AT A DISCOUNT
COST ① May 26 to Jun 30   ② Oct 4 to Dec 1

Shoppers are attracted to Costco because of its consistently low prices. They take comfort in the fact that although the prices may not always be the lowest, they are consistently in the lower range.

Costco performs well in late spring into early summer, and in autumn into early winter. These two periods are considered to be transition periods where the stock market is moving to and from its unfavorable and favorable seasons. Companies such as Costco that have stable earnings are desirable at these times.

There are two times when Costco is a seasonal bargain: May 26 to June 30 and October 4 to December 1.

13% gain & positive 96% of the time

Putting both seasonal periods together has produced a 96% positive success rate and an average gain of 13.4%. Although the earlier strong years in the 1990's skews the data to the high-side, Costco has still maintained its strong seasonal performances in both the May to June and the October to December time periods.

2021/22 Performance Update.
In 2021, Costco strongly outperformed the S&P 500 as investors were attracted to the stability of its earnings. In the first half of 2022, up until April, Costco outperformed the S&P 500, underperformed for most of May and started to outperform the S&P 500 in late May as its strong seasonal period started.

ⓘ *COST - stock symbol for Costco which trades on the Nasdaq exchange. Stock data adjusted for stock splits.*

Costco* vs. S&P 500 1994 to 2021 Positive

Year	May 26 to Jun 30 S&P 500	COST	Oct 4 to Dec 1 S&P 500	COST	Compound Growth S&P 500	COST
1994	-2.6 %	10.7 %	-2.8	-6.3 %	-5.3	3.7 %
1995	3.1	19.3	4.2	-2.2	7.4	16.7
1996	-1.2	9.5	9.3	15.5	8.0	26.5
1997	4.5	3.1	1.0	16.5	5.6	20.2
1998	2.1	17.6	17.2	41.1	19.7	66.0
1999	6.9	8.1	9.0	30.7	16.5	41.3
2000	5.3	10.0	-7.8	-3.6	-2.9	6.1
2001	-4.2	9.3	6.3	12.3	1.8	22.6
2002	-8.7	-0.8	14.3	4.6	4.4	3.8
2003	4.4	5.3	3.9	13.5	8.5	19.4
2004	2.5	10.3	5.3	17.4	7.9	29.4
2005	0.1	-1.5	3.1	13.9	3.2	12.2
2006	-0.2	5.0	4.7	6.0	4.5	11.3
2007	-0.8	3.8	-3.8	8.9	-4.6	12.9
2008	-7.0	-1.7	-25.8	-23.5	-30.9	-24.7
2009	3.6	-5.2	8.2	7.5	12.1	1.9
2010	-4.0	-3.0	5.2	5.0	1.0	1.9
2011	0.0	1.2	13.2	6.7	13.2	7.9
2012	3.4	12.5	-2.4	4.3	0.9	17.3
2013	-2.6	-3.3	7.6	9.6	4.7	6.0
2014	3.1	0.2	4.4	11.7	7.6	11.9
2015	-3.0	-6.0	7.8	10.6	4.6	3.9
2016	0.4	8.7	1.4	0.5	1.8	9.2
2017	0.4	-8.5	4.3	12.1	4.6	2.7
2018	-0.1	5.4	-5.7	-0.8	-5.8	4.5
2019	4.1	6.9	7.9	3.7	12.3	10.9
2020	4.9	0.3	9.4	9.2	14.7	9.5
2021	2.6	2.7	3.6	18.2	6.3	21.3
Avg.	6.1 %	4.3 %	3.8 %	8.7 %	4.4 %	13.4 %
Fq>0	61 %	71 %	79 %	82 %	82 %	96 %

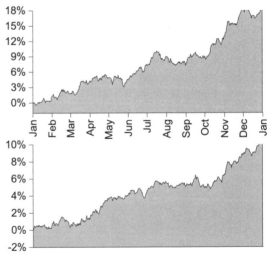

Costco - Avg. Year 1994 to 2021

18%
15%
12%
9%
6%
3%
0%
Jan Feb Mar Apr May Jun Jul Aug Sep Oct Nov Dec Jan

10%
8%
6%
4%
2%
0%
-2%

Costco / S&P 500 Rel. Strength- Avg Yr. 1994-2021

CADUSD Strategy Performance

CADUSD Monthly % Gain (1990-2021)

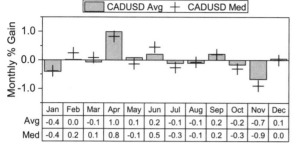

	Jan	Feb	Mar	Apr	May	Jun	Jul	Aug	Sep	Oct	Nov	Dec
Avg	-0.4	0.0	-0.1	1.0	0.1	0.2	-0.1	-0.1	0.2	-0.2	-0.7	0.1
Med	-0.4	0.2	0.1	0.8	-0.1	0.5	-0.3	-0.1	0.2	-0.3	-0.9	0.0

Fq % CADUSD Gain > 0% (1990-2021)

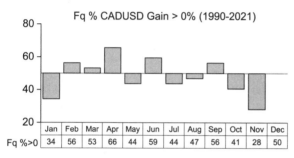

	Jan	Feb	Mar	Apr	May	Jun	Jul	Aug	Sep	Oct	Nov	Dec
Fq %>0	34	56	53	66	44	59	44	47	56	41	28	50

CADUSD % Gain 5 Year (2017-2021)

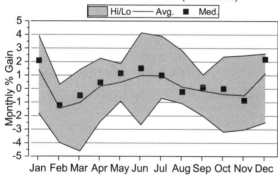

CADUSD Performance 2021-2022

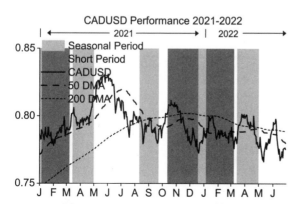

Market Indices & Rates
Weekly Values**

Stock Markets	2021	2022
Dow	34,756	32,900
S&P500	4,230	4,109
Nasdaq	13,814	12,013
TSX	20,029	20,791
FTSE	7,069	7,533
DAX	15,693	14,460
Nikkei	28,942	27,762
Hang Seng	28,918	21,082

Commodities	2021	2022
Oil	69.62	118.87
Gold	1890.6	1844.9

Bond Yields	2021	2022
USA 5 Yr Treasury	0.78	2.95
USA 10 Yr T	1.56	2.96
USA 20 Yr T	2.16	3.33
Moody's Aaa	2.88	4.06
Moody's Baa	3.54	5.05
CAN 5 Yr T	0.86	2.97
CAN 10 Yr T	1.46	3.06

Money Market	2021	2022
USA Fed Funds	0.25	1.00
USA 3 Mo T-B	0.02	1.21
CAN tgt overnight rate	0.25	1.50
CAN 3 Mo T-B	0.12	1.56

Foreign Exchange	2021	2022
EUR/USD	1.22	1.07
GBP/USD	1.42	1.25
USD/CAD	1.21	1.26
USD/JPY	109.52	130.88

MAY

M	T	W	T	F	S	S
1	2	2	4	5	6	7
8	9	10	11	12	13	14
15	16	17	18	19	20	21
22	23	24	25	26	27	28
29	30	31				

JUNE

M	T	W	T	F	S	S
			1	2	3	4
5	6	7	8	9	10	11
12	13	14	15	16	17	18
19	20	21	22	23	24	25
26	27	28	29	30		

JULY

M	T	W	T	F	S	S
					1	2
3	4	5	6	7	8	9
10	11	12	13	14	15	16
17	18	19	20	21	22	23
24	25	26	27	28	29	30
31						

CAD VS US DOLLAR ①SELL SHORT (Jan6-Mar7)

CAD ②LONG (Mar15-Apr30) ③LONG(Aug12-Sep22)
④SELL SHORT (Oct13-Dec18) ⑤LONG(Dec19-Jan5)

The Canadian dollar versus the US dollar has many drivers of valuation, but two of the bigger drivers are the price of oil and the spread on the two year differential government bonds between the two countries.

Although the energy sector seasonal period does not line up exactly with the seasonality for the Canadian dollar, there is an overlap. The energy sector tends to perform well from late February into early May. Correspondingly, the Canadian dollar tends to perform well from mid-March to the end of April. In addition, the energy sector tends to perform well from late July to early October, and the Canadian dollar tends to perform well from early August to late September.

The Canadian dollar also performs well from mid-December to early January. The US dollar tends to perform poorly against most currencies in late December.

The US dollar's strongest period relative to the Canadian dollar is from mid-October to mid-December. Overall, this is one of the weaker seasonal periods for oil.

The US dollar also tends to perform well relative to the Canadian dollar from early January to early March. The US dollar tends to perform well against most major world currencies at this time.

2021/22 Performance Update.
In 2021, the Canadian dollar lost ground to the US dollar, but generally managed to perform according to its seasonal trends. In the first half of 2022, the Canadian dollar underperformed the US dollar in a cyclical range. In 2022, the Canadian dollar was one of the better performing currencies in the world.

Canadian Dollar vs. US Dollar 1990/91 to 2021/22

Negative Short ☐   Positive Long ▨

Year	Jan6 Mar7	Mar15 Apr30	Aug12 Sep22	Oct13 Dec18	Dec19 Jan5	Compound
1990/91	-2.1 %	0.8 %	-0.5 %	-0.9 %	0.5 %	3.9 %
1991/92	-0.8	0.2	1.0	-1.5	0.0	3.4
1992/93	-3.5	0.3	-4.1	-2.8	0.1	2.4
1993/94	2.5	-2.1	-1.0	-0.8	1.4	-3.4
1994/95	-2.7	-1.5	2.8	-3.3	-0.6	6.8
1995/96	-1.0	4.3	0.8	-2.9	1.5	10.9
1996/97	-1.0	0.5	0.2	-1.1	-0.2	2.6
1997/98	0.1	-2.3	0.3	-3.4	0.2	1.5
1998/99	0.3	-1.3	-0.4	-0.2	2.1	0.3
1999/00	-0.4	4.6	1.0	-0.2	1.9	8.4
2001/01	-0.4	-1.0	-0.3	-0.6	1.7	1.4
2001/02	-3.3	1.4	-2.1	-0.7	-1.3	2.0
2002/03	0.8	1.5	0.0	2.1	-0.7	-2.0
2003/04	6.7	3.0	2.3	-0.6	3.7	2.6
2004/05	-3.0	-2.8	3.4	2.1	0.3	1.6
2005/06	-0.3	-4.1	2.5	1.0	-0.3	-2.7
2006/07	1.0	3.6	0.7	-2.0	-1.4	3.9
2007/08	-0.5	6.0	5.2	-3.4	0.3	16.2
2008/09	1.2	-1.8	3.2	-2.6	1.3	4.1
2009/10	-7.6	6.7	3.0	-3.0	2.6	25.0
2010/11	1.0	0.1	1.5	-0.4	1.8	2.9
2011/12	2.3	3.0	-4.3	-2.0	1.8	0.1
2012/13	2.2	0.5	1.5	-0.6	-0.2	0.2
2013/14	-4.1	1.5	-0.1	-3.3	0.6	9.7
2014/15	-4.1	1.3	-1.1	-3.3	-1.6	5.9
2015/16	-6.8	5.8	-1.2	-6.9	-0.3	19.1
2016/17	5.4	5.6	-0.4	-0.5	0.8	0.8
2017/18	-1.4	-1.3	2.7	-3.0	3.6	9.8
2018/19	-3.9	0.9	1.7	-3.3	0.7	10.9
2019/20	-0.6	-0.4	-0.3	0.7	0.9	0.1
2020/21	-3.1	-0.9	0.0	2.5	0.9	0.4
2021/22	0.1	1.5	-2.1	-3.3	1.0	3.6
Avg.	-0.8 %	1.1 %	0.5 %	-1.5 %	0.7 %	4.8 %
Fq>0	38 %	66 %	53 %	16 %	69 %	91 %

CAD vs USD - Avg. Year 1990 to 2021

6 'n' 6 Canada Strategy Performance

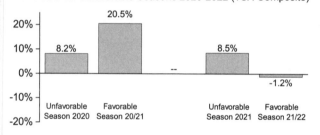

TSX Comp. Gain 5 Year (2017-2021)

TSX Comp. Hi/Lo — TSX Comp. Avg. ■ TSX Comp. Med.

Monthly % Gain — Jan Feb Mar Apr May Jun Jul Aug Sep Oct Nov Dec

TSX Comp. Performance 2021-2022

← 2021 → | 2022 →

- Seasonal Period
- TSX Comp
- 50 DMA
- 200 DMA

J F M A M J J A S O N D J F M A M J J

Favorable vs. Unfavorable Seasons 2020-2022 (TSX Composite)

8.2%	20.5%	
Unfavorable Season 2020	Favorable Season 20/21	--
	8.5%	-1.2%
	Unfavorable Season 2021	Favorable Season 21/22

Market Indices & Rates
Weekly Values

Stock Markets	2021	2022
Dow	34,208	31,262
S&P500	4,156	3,901
Nasdaq	13,471	11,355
TSX	19,527	20,198
FTSE	7,018	7,390
DAX	15,438	13,982
Nikkei	28,318	26,739
Hang Seng	28,458	20,717

Commodities	2021	2022
Oil	63.70	113.23
Gold	1875.9	1834.2

Bond Yields	2021	2022
USA 5 Yr Treasury	0.84	2.80
USA 10 Yr T	1.63	2.78
USA 20 Yr T	2.24	3.17
Moody's Aaa	2.97	4.11
Moody's Baa	3.64	5.14
CAN 5 Yr T	0.93	2.73
CAN 10 Yr T	1.54	2.84

Money Market	2021	2022
USA Fed Funds	0.25	1.00
USA 3 Mo T-B	0.01	1.03
CAN tgt overnight rate	0.25	1.00
CAN 3 Mo T-B	0.09	1.36

Foreign Exchange	2021	2022
EUR/USD	1.22	1.06
GBP/USD	1.42	1.25
USD/CAD	1.21	1.28
USD/JPY	108.96	127.88

Over the last five years, the TSX Composite generally followed its six month favorable/unfavorable cycle.

In 2020/21, the unfavorable period produced a gain of 8.2% for the TSX Composite, which was lower than the gain of 20.5% in the 2020/21 favorable period. Overall, between the two years, the favorable period produced a better gain profile.

In 2021/22, the unfavorable six month period produced a gain of 8.5% for the TSX Composite. The following six month favorable period produced a loss of 1.2%.

MAY

M	T	W	T	F	S	S
1	2	2	4	5	6	7
8	9	10	11	12	13	14
15	16	17	18	19	20	21
22	23	24	25	26	27	28
29	30	31				

JUNE

M	T	W	T	F	S	S
			1	2	3	4
5	6	7	8	9	10	11
12	13	14	15	16	17	18
19	20	21	22	23	24	25
26	27	28	29	30		

JULY

M	T	W	T	F	S	S
					1	2
3	4	5	6	7	8	9
10	11	12	13	14	15	16
17	18	19	20	21	22	23
24	25	26	27	28	29	30
31						

JUNE

	MONDAY	TUESDAY	WEDNESDAY
WEEK 22	29	30	31
WEEK 23	**5** 25	**6** 24	**7** 23
WEEK 24	**12** 18	**13** 17	**14** 16
WEEK 25	**19** 11 USA Market Closed- Juneteenth National Independence Day	**20** 10	**21** 9
WEEK 26	**26** 4	**27** 3	**28** 2

THURSDAY		FRIDAY	
1	29	**2**	28
8	22	**9**	21
15	15	**16**	14
22	8	**23**	7
29	1	**30**	

JULY

M	T	W	T	F	S	S
					1	2
3	4	5	6	7	8	9
10	11	12	13	14	15	16
17	18	19	20	21	22	23
24	25	26	27	28	29	30
31						

AUGUST

M	T	W	T	F	S	S
	1	2	3	4	5	6
7	8	9	10	11	12	13
14	15	16	17	18	19	20
21	22	23	24	25	26	27
28	29	30	31			

SEPTEMBER

M	T	W	T	F	S	S
				1	2	3
4	5	6	7	8	9	10
11	12	13	14	15	16	17
18	19	20	21	22	23	24
25	26	27	28	29	30	

OCTOBER

M	T	W	T	F	S	S
						1
2	3	4	5	6	7	8
9	10	11	12	13	14	15
16	17	18	19	20	21	22
23	24	25	26	27	28	29
30	31					

JUNE SUMMARY

	Dow Jones	S&P 500	Nasdaq	TSX Comp
Month Rank	11	9	6	11
# Up	34	40	29	18
# Down	38	32	21	19
% Pos	47	56	58	49
% Avg. Gain	-0.1	0.1	1.0	-0.2

Dow & S&P 1950-2021, Nasdaq 1972-2021 TSX 1985-2021

S&P500 Cumulative Daily Gains for Avg Month 1950 to 2022

♦ On average, June is not a strong month for the S&P 500. From 1950 to 2021, it was the fourth worst month of the year, producing a nominal gain of 0.1%. ♦ From year to year, different sectors of the market tend to lead in June as there is not a strong consistent outperforming major sector. ♦ The last few days of June, the start of the successful *Summer Sizzler Trade,* tend to be positive. ♦ In 2022, the S&P 500 dropped significantly, but managed to rally in late June into the period for the *Summer Sizzler Trade.*

BEST / WORST JUNE BROAD MKTS. 2013-2022

BEST JUNE MARKETS
- ♦ Nasdaq (2019) 7.4%
- ♦ Dow (2019) 7.2%
- ♦ Russell 2000 (2019) 6.9%

WORST JUNE MARKETS
- ♦ Nikkei 225 (2016) -9.6%
- ♦ TSX Comp (2022) -9.0%
- ♦ Nasdaq (2022) -8.7%

Index Values End of Month

	2013	2014	2015	2016	2017	2018	2019	2020	2021	2022
Dow	14,910	16,827	17,620	17,930	21,350	24,271	26,600	25,813	34,503	30,775
S&P 500	1,606	1,960	2,063	2,099	2,423	2,663	2,942	3,100	4,298	3,785
Nasdaq	3,403	4,408	4,987	4,843	6,140	7,510	8,006	10,059	14,504	11,029
TSX Comp.	12,129	15,146	14,553	14,065	15,182	16,278	16,382	15,515	20,166	18,861
Russell 1000	891	1,095	1,153	1,162	1,344	1,510	1,629	1,717	2,421	2,076
Russell 2000	977	1,193	1,254	1,152	1,415	1,643	1,567	1,441	2,311	1,708
FTSE 100	6,215	6,744	6,521	6,504	7,313	7,637	7,426	6,170	7,037	7,169
Nikkei 225	13,677	15,162	20,236	15,576	20,033	22,305	21,276	22,288	28,792	26,393

Percent Gain for June

	2013	2014	2015	2016	2017	2018	2019	2020	2021	2022
Dow	-1.4	0.7	-2.2	0.8	1.6	-0.6	7.2	1.7	-0.1	-6.7
S&P 500	-1.5	1.9	-2.1	0.1	0.5	0.0	6.9	1.8	2.2	-8.4
Nasdaq	-1.5	3.9	-1.6	-2.1	-0.9	0.9	7.4	6.0	5.5	-8.7
TSX Comp.	-4.1	3.7	-3.1	0.0	-1.1	1.3	2.1	2.1	2.2	-9.0
Russell 1000	-1.5	2.1	-2.0	0.1	0.5	0.5	6.9	2.1	2.4	-8.5
Russell 2000	-0.7	5.2	0.6	-0.2	3.3	0.6	6.9	3.4	1.8	-8.4
FTSE 100	-5.6	-1.5	-6.6	4.4	-2.8	-0.5	3.7	1.5	0.2	-5.8
Nikkei 225	-0.7	3.6	-1.6	-9.6	1.9	0.5	3.3	1.9	-0.2	-3.3

June Market Avg. Performance 2013 to 2022[1]

Dow	0.1%
S&P 500	0.2%
Nasdaq	0.9%
TSX Comp (CAN)	-0.6%
Russell 1000 (Lg Cap)	0.2%
Russell 2000 (Sm Cap)	1.2%
FTSE 100	-1.3%
Nikkei 225	-0.4%

-1.5% -1.0% -0.5% 0.0% 0.5% 1.0% 1.5%

Interest Corner Jun[2]

	Fed Funds %[3]	3 Mo. T-Bill %[4]	10 Yr %[5]	20 Yr %[6]
2022	1.75	1.72	2.98	3.38
2021	0.25	0.05	1.45	2.00
2020	0.25	0.16	0.66	1.18
2019	2.50	2.12	2.00	2.31
2018	2.00	1.93	2.85	2.91

(1) Russell Data provided by Russell (2) Federal Reserve Bank of St. Louis- end of month values (3) Target rate set by FOMC (4)(5)(6) Constant yield maturities.

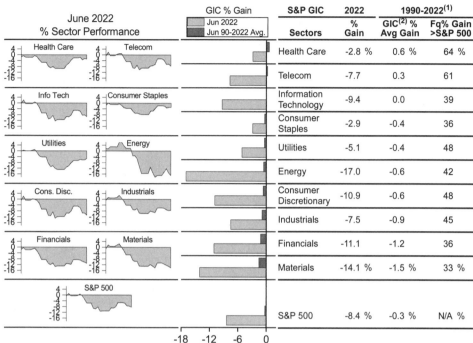

S&P GIC Sectors	2022 % Gain	1990-2022[1] GIC[2] % Avg Gain	Fq% Gain >S&P 500
Health Care	-2.8 %	0.6 %	64 %
Telecom	-7.7	0.3	61
Information Technology	-9.4	0.0	39
Consumer Staples	-2.9	-0.4	36
Utilities	-5.1	-0.4	48
Energy	-17.0	-0.6	42
Consumer Discretionary	-10.9	-0.6	48
Industrials	-7.5	-0.9	45
Financials	-11.1	-1.2	36
Materials	-14.1 %	-1.5 %	33 %
S&P 500	-8.4 %	-0.3 %	N/A %

Sector Commentary

♦ In June 2022, the S&P 500 performed poorly in the first half of the month and rallied in the second half. Overall, the S&P 500 lost 8.4% in June. ♦ All of the major sectors of the market produced losses. ♦ The defensive sectors, utilities, health care and consumer staples all performed better than the market. ♦ The energy sector corrected sharply, producing a loss of 17%. The main reason for this loss was investor's concern of a slowing economy. ♦ The concern of a slowing economy also showed up in the poor performance of the materials sector, which lost over 14%.

Sub-Sector Commentary

♦ In June 2022, the cyclical sub-sectors performed poorly, with the metals & mining sub-sector producing a loss of over 19% and the steel sub-sector producing a loss of over 20%. ♦ Gold performed relatively well, and only produced a loss of 1.2% despite a stronger US dollar and rising interest rates.

SELECTED SUB-SECTORS[3]

Pharma	-0.1 %	0.7 %	67 %
Retail	-10.0	-0.1	58
Gold	-1.2	-0.2	52
Biotech (1993-2022)	-0.8	-0.2	52
SOX (1995-2022)	-17.5	-0.8	39
Metals & Mining	-19.4	-0.9	52
Railroads	-4.9	-1.1	36
Transportation	-6.3	-1.2	33
Homebuilders	-11.7	-1.3	39
Auto	-12.4	-1.3	48
Steel	-21.2	-1.5	39
Chemicals	-13.9	-1.6	33
Agriculture (1994-2022)	-14.6	-1.7	31
Banks	-13.9	-2.1	30
Silver	-6.2	-3.0	32

(1) Sector data provided by Standard and Poors (2) GIC is short form for Global Industry Classification (3) Sub Sector data provided by Standard and Poors, except where marked by symbol.

The *Biotech Summer Solstice* trade starts on June 23 and lasts until September 13. The trade is aptly named as its outperformance starts approximately when summer solstice starts– the longest day of the year.

There are two main drivers of the trade: biotech is a good substitute for technology stocks in the summer, and investors want to take a position in the biotech sector before the autumn conferences.

Positive 83% of the time

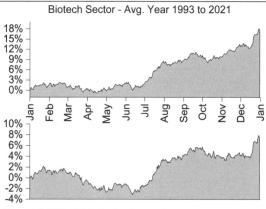

Biotech Sector - Avg. Year 1993 to 2021

Biotech / S&P 500 Relative Strength - Avg Yr. 1993-2021

Biotech* vs. S&P 500 1992 to 2021			
		Positive	
Jun 23 to Sep 13	S&P 500	Biotech	Diff
1992	4.0 %	17.9 %	13.8 %
1993	3.6	3.6	0.0
1994	3.2	24.2	21.0
1995	5.0	31.5	26.5
1996	2.1	7.0	4.9
1997	2.8	-18.9	-21.7
1998	-8.5	20.6	29.1
1999	0.6	64.3	63.7
2000	2.3	7.6	5.4
2001	-10.8	-3.6	7.2
2002	-10.0	8.1	18.2
2003	2.3	6.4	4.1
2004	-0.8	8.9	9.6
2005	1.4	26.0	24.5
2006	5.8	7.4	1.6
2007	-1.2	6.0	7.2
2008	-5.0	11.4	16.5
2009	16.8	7.7	-9.1
2010	2.4	2.8	0.4
2011	-8.9	-3.7	5.2
2012	9.4	15.6	6.2
2013	6.0	24.9	18.9
2014	1.2	14.8	13.6
2015	-7.6	-7.2	0.5
2016	2.0	7.3	5.3
2017	2.6	11.1	8.5
2018	5.4	7.5	2.1
2019	1.9	-4.5	-6.4
2020	7.2	-6.9	-14.1
2021	5.2	1.8	-3.4
Avg	1.3 %	10.0 %	9.0 %
Fq>0	73 %	80 %	83 %

The biotechnology sector is often considered the cousin of the technology sector, a good place for speculative investments. The sectors are similar as both include concept companies (companies without a product, but with good potential).

Despite their similarity, investors view the sectors differently. The technology sector is viewed as being much more dependent on the economy compared with the biotech sector. The end product of biotechnology companies is mainly medicine, which is not economically sensitive.

As a result, in the summer months when investors tend to be more cautious, they are more willing to commit speculative money into the biotech sector, compared with the technology sector.

The biotech sector is one of the few sectors that starts its outperformance in June. This is in part because of the biotech conferences that occur in autumn and with the possibility of positive announcements, the price of biotech companies can increase dramatically. As a re-

sult, investors try to lock in positions early.

2021/22 Performance Update.
In 2021, the biotech sector underperformed the S&P 500 for the full year and in its strong seasonal period. In the first half of the year, the biotech sector started the year underperforming. In May, the biotech sector started to improve its relative performance and as the strong seasonal period for the biotech sector started in June, the biotech sector improved its relative performance.

(i) *Biotech SP GIC Sector # 352010: Companies primarily engaged in the research, development, manufacturing and/or marketing of products based on genetic analysis and genetic engineering.*

Biotech Performance

Biotech Monthly % Gain (1993-2021)

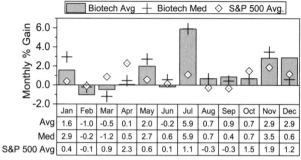

	Jan	Feb	Mar	Apr	May	Jun	Jul	Aug	Sep	Oct	Nov	Dec
Avg	1.6	-1.0	-0.5	0.1	2.0	-0.2	5.9	0.7	0.9	0.7	2.9	2.9
Med	2.9	-0.2	-1.2	0.5	2.7	0.6	5.9	0.7	0.4	0.7	3.5	0.6
S&P 500 Avg	0.4	-0.1	0.9	2.3	0.6	0.1	1.1	-0.3	-0.3	1.5	1.9	1.2

Fq % Biotech Gain > 0% (1993-2021)

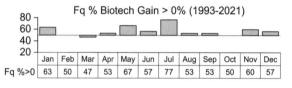

	Jan	Feb	Mar	Apr	May	Jun	Jul	Aug	Sep	Oct	Nov	Dec
Fq %>0	63	50	47	53	67	57	77	53	53	50	60	57

Fq % Biotech Gain > S&P 500 % (1993-2021)

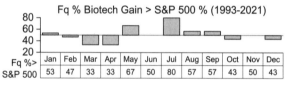

	Jan	Feb	Mar	Apr	May	Jun	Jul	Aug	Sep	Oct	Nov	Dec
Fq %> S&P 500	53	47	33	33	67	50	80	57	57	43	50	43

Biotech % Gain 5 Year (2017-2021)

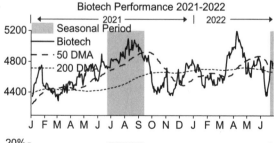

Jan Feb Mar Apr May Jun Jul Aug Sep Oct Nov Dec

Biotech Performance 2021-2022

J F M A M J J A S O N D J F M A M J

J F M A M J J A S O N D J F M A M J

Relative Strength, % Gain vs. S&P 500

Market Indices & Rates
Weekly Values**

Stock Markets	2021	2022
Dow	34,480	31,393
S&P500	4,247	3,901
Nasdaq	14,069	11,340
TSX	20,138	20,275
FTSE	7,134	7,318
DAX	15,693	13,762
Nikkei	28,949	27,824
Hang Seng	28,842	21,806

Commodities	2021	2022
Oil	70.91	120.67
Gold	1881.1	1830.0

Bond Yields	2021	2022
USA 5 Yr Treasury	0.76	3.25
USA 10 Yr T	1.47	3.15
USA 20 Yr T	2.08	3.45
Moody's Aaa	2.80	4.20
Moody's Baa	3.44	5.19
CAN 5 Yr T	0.82	3.33
CAN 10 Yr T	1.37	3.35

Money Market	2021	2022
USA Fed Funds	0.25	1.00
USA 3 Mo T-B	0.03	1.39
CAN tgt overnight rate	0.25	1.50
CAN 3 Mo T-B	0.11	1.73

Foreign Exchange	2021	2022
EUR/USD	1.21	1.05
GBP/USD	1.41	1.23
USD/CAD	1.22	1.28
USD/JPY	109.66	134.41

JUNE

M	T	W	T	F	S	S
			1	2	3	4
5	6	7	8	9	10	11
12	13	14	15	16	17	18
19	20	21	22	23	24	25
26	27	28	29	30		

JULY

M	T	W	T	F	S	S
				1	2	
3	4	5	6	7	8	9
10	11	12	13	14	15	16
17	18	19	20	21	22	23
24	25	26	27	28	29	30
31						

AUGUST

M	T	W	T	F	S	S
	1	2	3	4	5	6
7	8	9	10	11	12	13
14	15	16	17	18	19	20
21	22	23	24	25	26	27
28	29	30	31			

CAMECO – CHARGES DOWN AND UP

①SELL SHORT (Jun5-Aug7)
②LONG (Oct4-Jan24)

Cameco is the world's largest publicly traded uranium company. It trades on both the NYSE stock exchange (ticker: CCJ) and the Toronto Stock Exchange (ticker: CCO).

Cameco has a very narrow market for its product: countries that need uranium to power their nuclear reactors. Mining operations do not vary much throughout the year, so supply is fairly constant. In addition actual usage of uranium does not change much throughout the year as nuclear reactors are run most efficiently at one constant level over time. Yet, there is a seasonal tendency for Cameco to perform well from October 4 to January 24.

> *21% growth &
> positive 85% of the time*

The seasonal trend for Cameco can be partly explained by the overall tendency of the stock market to perform well during Cameco's strong seasonal period, and poorly during Cameco's weak seasonal period.

The seasonal trend for Cameco can also be explained somewhat with buyer behavior. The World Nuclear Association (WNA) has an annual conference that takes place in the middle of September of each year. As a result of the conference, buyers tend to be reassured of the future demand of uranium, helping to give Cameco a boost starting in October. Likewise, investors often have a low interest level in Cameco in the summer months ahead of the WNA conference in mid-September.

> ⓘ *Cameco Corporation is in the materials sector. Its stock symbol is CCO, which trades on the Toronto Stock Exchange, adjusted for splits.*

Cameco vs. TSX Composite Index - 1995/96 to 2021/22

Negative Short ▭　　　　Positive Long ▨

Year	Jun 5 to Aug 7 TSX	Jun 5 to Aug 7 CCO	Oct 4 to Jan 24 TSX	Oct 4 to Jan 24 CCO	Compound Growth TSX	Compound Growth CCO
1995/96	3.7 %	0.6 %	8.1	42.7 %	12.1 %	41.8 %
1996/97	-3.7	-6.1	12.2	-16.5	8.0	-11.5
1997/98	8.0	1.1	-8.5	-22.6	-1.1	-23.4
1998/99	-11.3	-23.2	19.5	44.4	6.0	77.9
1999/00	-0.9	-16.9	22.0	-24.8	21.0	-12.1
2000/01	8.4	-13.7	-11.0	25.0	-3.5	42.1
2001/02	-6.4	-20.3	10.9	14.6	3.9	37.9
2002/03	-14.3	-28.6	10.6	27.9	-5.2	64.5
2003/04	2.6	4.9	14.4	35.7	17.4	29.1
2004/05	-2.1	8.9	3.8	30.6	1.7	19.0
2005/06	9.1	5.7	5.5	38.3	15.1	30.4
2006/07	0.3	-9.1	12.9	18.6	13.2	29.4
2007/08	-4.1	-30.2	-7.9	-15.7	-11.8	9.8
2008/09	-8.9	-15.0	-20.1	-6.5	-27.2	7.5
2009/10	3.9	0.5	3.5	6.2	7.5	5.6
2010/11	2.0	11.2	8.0	35.6	10.1	20.4
2011/12	-10.0	-13.7	10.2	29.0	-0.9	45.0
2012/13	4.7	9.0	3.8	12.6	8.6	2.4
2013/14	-1.4	-10.3	7.7	29.6	6.2	42.9
2014/15	2.2	-3.1	-0.1	-8.9	2.1	-6.0
2015/16	-4.8	-6.2	-7.1	-0.9	-11.6	5.3
2016/17	3.0	-17.3	6.3	54.0	9.4	80.7
2017/18	-1.2	3.7	3.5	8.0	2.3	4.0
2018/19	1.5	1.7	-4.9	4.0	-3.5	2.3
2019/20	0.6	-16.1	7.3	-11.5	8.0	2.9
2020/21	6.5	-0.3	10.2	21.5	17.4	21.9
2021/22	2.2	-16.1	2.1	-9.3	4.4	5.4
Avg.	-0.4 %	-7.3 %	4.5	13.4 %	4.1 %	21.3 %
Fq>0	56 %	37 %	74 %	67 %	70 %	85 %

2021/22 Performance Update.

In 2021, Cameco was volatile, but strongly outperformed the S&P/TSX Composite Index. In the first half of the year, Cameco performed very well into April, at which time it started to correct into June.

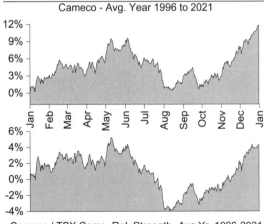

Cameco - Avg. Year 1996 to 2021

Cameco / TSX Comp. Rel. Strength- Avg Yr. 1996-2021

Cameco Performance

CCO Monthly % Gain (1996-2021)

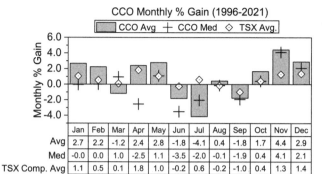

	Jan	Feb	Mar	Apr	May	Jun	Jul	Aug	Sep	Oct	Nov	Dec
Avg	2.7	2.2	-1.2	2.4	2.8	-1.8	-4.1	0.4	-1.8	1.7	4.4	2.9
Med	-0.0	0.0	1.0	-2.5	1.1	-3.5	-2.0	-0.1	-1.9	0.4	4.1	2.1
TSX Comp. Avg	1.1	0.5	0.1	1.8	1.0	-0.2	0.6	-0.2	-1.0	0.4	1.3	1.4

Fq % CCO Gain > 0% (1996-2021)

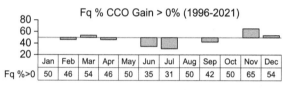

	Jan	Feb	Mar	Apr	May	Jun	Jul	Aug	Sep	Oct	Nov	Dec
Fq %>0	50	46	54	46	50	35	31	50	42	50	65	54

Fq % CCO Gain > TSX Comp. % (1996-2021)

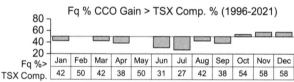

	Jan	Feb	Mar	Apr	May	Jun	Jul	Aug	Sep	Oct	Nov	Dec
Fq %> TSX Comp.	42	50	42	38	50	31	27	42	38	54	58	58

CCO % Gain 5 Year (2017-2021)

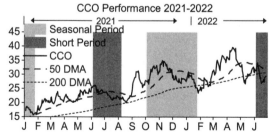

CCO Performance 2021-2022

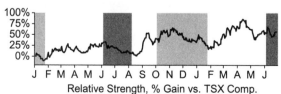

Relative Strength, % Gain vs. TSX Comp.

WEEK 24

Market Indices & Rates
Weekly Values**

Stock Markets	2021	2022
Dow	33,290	29,889
S&P500	4,166	3,675
Nasdaq	14,030	10,798
TSX	20,000	18,930
FTSE	7,017	7,016
DAX	15,448	13,126
Nikkei	28,964	25,963
Hang Seng	28,801	21,075

Commodities	2021	2022
Oil	71.64	109.56
Gold	1773.1	1841.6

Bond Yields	2021	2022
USA 5 Yr Treasury	0.89	3.34
USA 10 Yr T	1.45	3.25
USA 20 Yr T	1.97	3.55
Moody's Aaa	2.64	4.32
Moody's Baa	3.30	5.38
CAN 5 Yr T	0.96	3.34
CAN 10 Yr T	1.37	3.41

Money Market	2021	2022
USA Fed Funds	0.25	1.75
USA 3 Mo T-B	0.05	1.63
CAN tgt overnight rate	0.25	1.50
CAN 3 Mo T-B	0.13	1.96

Foreign Exchange	2021	2022
EUR/USD	1.19	1.05
GBP/USD	1.38	1.22
USD/CAD	1.25	1.30
USD/JPY	110.21	135.02

JUNE

M	T	W	T	F	S	S
			1	2	3	4
5	6	7	8	9	10	11
12	13	14	15	16	17	18
19	20	21	22	23	24	25
26	27	28	29	30		

JULY

M	T	W	T	F	S	S
				1	2	
3	4	5	6	7	8	9
10	11	12	13	14	15	16
17	18	19	20	21	22	23
24	25	26	27	28	29	30
31						

AUGUST

M	T	W	T	F	S	S
	1	2	3	4	5	6
7	8	9	10	11	12	13
14	15	16	17	18	19	20
21	22	23	24	25	26	27
28	29	30	31			

SUMMER SIZZLER – THE FULL TRADE
PROFIT BEFORE & AFTER FIREWORKS
Two Market Days Before June Month End
To 5 Market Days After Independence Day

The beginning of July is a time for celebration and the markets tend to agree.

Based on previous market data, the best way to take advantage of this trend is to be invested for the two market days prior to June month end and hold until five market days after Independence Day. This time period has produced above average returns on a fairly consistent basis.

Since 1950, 1% avg. gain

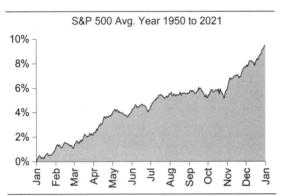

S&P 500 Avg. Year 1950 to 2021

The typical strategy to take advantage of the tendency of positive performance around Independence Day has been to invest one or two days before the holiday and take profits one or two days after the holiday.

Although this strategy has produced profits, it has left a lot of money on the table. This strategy misses out on the positive days at the end of June and on the full slate of positive days after Independence Day.

The beginning part of the *Summer Sizzler Trade's* positive trend is driven by portfolio managers who "window dress" their portfolios, buying stocks at month end that have a favorable perception in the market in order to make their portfolios look good on month and quarter end statements. This is particularly true at quarter ends. The result is typically increased buying pressure that lifts the stock market.

Depending on market conditions at the time, investors should consider extending the exit date of the *Summer Sizzler Trade* until eighteen calendar days into July. With July being an earnings month, the market can continue to rally until mid-month (see *18 Day Earnings Month Strategy*).

2021/22 Performance Update.
In 2021, the S&P 500 moved higher for most of the year. The *Summer Sizzler*, produced a large return in the rallying market. In 2022, the S&P 500 produced a gain in its *Summer Sizzler* period despite a high degree of volatility at the time.

S&P 500, 2 Market Days Before June Month End To 5 Market Days after Independence Day % Gain 1950 to 2022 — Positive

1950	-4.4	1960	-0.1	1970	1.5	1980	1.4	1990	1.7	2000	1.8	2010	0.4	2020	5.5
1951	1.5	1961	1.7	1971	3.2	1981	-2.4	1991	1.4	2001	-2.6	2011	1.8	2021	2.2
1952	0.9	1962	9.8	1972	0.3	1982	-0.6	1992	2.8	2002	-4.7	2012	0.7	2022	0.9
1953	0.8	1963	0.5	1973	2.1	1983	1.5	1993	-0.6	2003	1.2	2013	4.5		
1954	2.9	1964	2.3	1974	-8.8	1984	-0.7	1994	0.4	2004	-1.7	2014	0.5		
1955	4.9	1965	5.0	1975	-0.2	1985	1.5	1995	1.8	2005	1.5	2015	-1.2		
1956	3.4	1966	2.1	1976	2.4	1986	-2.6	1996	-2.8	2006	2.1	2016	5.0		
1957	3.8	1967	1.3	1977	-0.6	1987	0.4	1997	3.7	2007	0.8	2017	0.2		
1958	2.0	1968	2.3	1978	0.6	1988	-0.6	1998	2.7	2008	-3.4	2018	2.8		
1959	3.3	1969	-1.5	1979	1.3	1989	0.9	1999	5.1	2009	-4.3	2019	3.0		
Avg.	1.9		2.3		0.2		-0.1		1.8		-0.9		1.8		2.9

Summer Sizzler Strategy (S&P 500) Performance

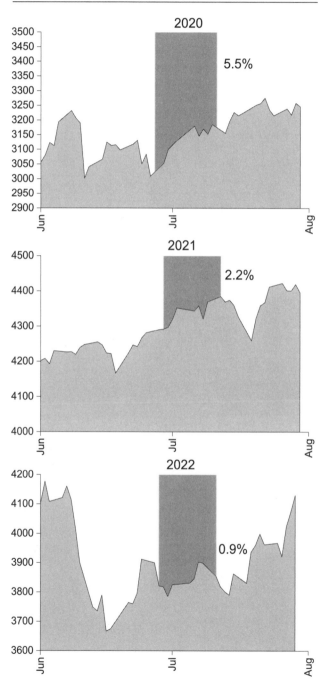

Summer Sizzler Trade

2020 — 5.5%

2021 — 2.2%

2022 — 0.9%

Market Indices & Rates
Weekly Values**

Stock Markets	2021	2022
Dow	34,434	31,501
S&P500	4,281	3,912
Nasdaq	14,360	11,608
TSX	20,230	19,063
FTSE	7,136	7,209
DAX	15,608	13,118
Nikkei	29,066	26,492
Hang Seng	29,288	21,719

Commodities	2021	2022
Oil	74.25	109.47
Gold	1786.7	1825.5

Bond Yields	2021	2022
USA 5 Yr Treasury	0.92	3.18
USA 10 Yr T	1.54	3.13
USA 20 Yr T	2.09	3.51
Moody's Aaa	2.77	4.25
Moody's Baa	3.44	5.35
CAN 5 Yr T	1.01	3.21
CAN 10 Yr T	1.45	3.33

Money Market	2021	2022
USA Fed Funds	0.25	1.75
USA 3 Mo T-B	0.06	1.73
CAN tgt overnight rate	0.25	1.50
CAN 3 Mo T-B	0.14	2.01

Foreign Exchange	2021	2022
EUR/USD	1.19	1.06
GBP/USD	1.39	1.23
USD/CAD	1.23	1.29
USD/JPY	110.75	135.23

JUNE

M	T	W	T	F	S	S
			1	2	3	4
5	6	7	8	9	10	11
12	13	14	15	16	17	18
19	20	21	22	23	24	25
26	27	28	29	30		

JULY

M	T	W	T	F	S	S
					1	2
3	4	5	6	7	8	9
10	11	12	13	14	15	16
17	18	19	20	21	22	23
24	25	26	27	28	29	30
31						

AUGUST

M	T	W	T	F	S	S
	1	2	3	4	5	6
7	8	9	10	11	12	13
14	15	16	17	18	19	20
21	22	23	24	25	26	27
28	29	30	31			

ORCL ORACLE
June 1 to July 1

Oracle's stock price performance exhibits a positive seasonal trend in the run-up to and after reporting on its fiscal year-end. Oracle's year-end is on May 31 and it typically reports its full-year earnings in mid-to-late June.

Selling software is instantly scalable, which provides an incentive to increase sales at year-end without disrupting operations. Oracle places a lot of emphasis on providing its sales force with incentives to increase sales before its year-end closes.

Oracle's May 31, 2020 SEC Filing 10-K Annual Report states: "Our quarterly revenues have historically been affected by a variety of seasonal factors, including the structure of our sales force incentive compensation plans, which are common in the technology industry. In each fiscal year, our total revenues and operating margins are typically highest in our fourth fiscal quarter and lowest in our first fiscal quarter."

7% gain & positive 73% of the time

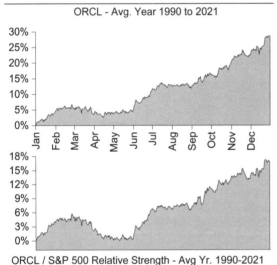

ORCL - Avg. Year 1990 to 2021

ORCL / S&P 500 Relative Strength - Avg Yr. 1990-2021

Jun 1 to Jul 1	S&P 500	ORCL	Diff
			Positive
1990	-0.9	17.1	18.0%
1991	-3.1	13.3	16.4
1992	-0.6	16.8	17.4
1993	-0.3	19.8	20.0
1994	-2.3	10.9	13.2
1995	2.1	11.2	9.0
1996	1.0	18.1	17.1
1997	5.0	4.2	-0.9
1998	5.3	1.9	-3.4
1999	6.1	52.1	46.1
2000	2.4	17.0	14.6
2001	-2.5	24.2	26.7
2002	-9.2	13.6	22.9
2003	1.9	-5.2	-7.2
2004	0.7	3.6	2.9
2005	0.2	3.8	3.6
2006	0.0	1.9	1.9
2007	-1.8	1.7	3.5
2008	-8.2	-6.7	1.5
2009	0.5	11.0	10.5
2010	-5.7	-4.5	1.2
2011	-0.4	-3.4	-3.0
2012	4.0	12.2	8.2
2013	-1.0	-10.9	-9.9
2014	2.6	-3.0	-5.6
2015	-1.4	-7.5	-6.1
2016	0.3	1.6	1.4
2017	0.5	10.5	10.0
2018	0.5	-5.7	-6.2
2019	7.7	14.6	6.9
2020	2.4	3.2	0.8
2021	2.8	1.0	-1.8
2022	-7.4	-1.5	6.0
Avg	0.0%	7.2%	7.1%
Fq > 0	57%	73%	73%

ORCL* vs. S&P 500 - 1990 to 2022

2021/22 Performance Update.
In 2021, Oracle performed very well and outperformed the S&P 500. Like many technology stocks, it corrected late in the year.

In the first half of 2022, Oracle performed at approximately equal to the S&P 500. In its strong seasonal period in June, Oracle managed to outperform the S&P 500.

Investors tend to front-run Oracle's full-year earnings report pushing up Oracle's stock price. Oracle tends to be conservative in managing financial analyst expectations around year-end. The result is that its period of seasonal strength tends to last past the earnings report and finish at the beginning of July

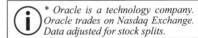

*(i) * Oracle is a technology company. Oracle trades on Nasdaq Exchange. Data adjusted for stock splits.*

Oracle Performance

ORCL Monthly % Gain (1990-2021)

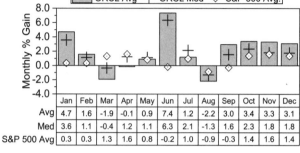

Legend: ORCL Avg | + ORCL Med | ◇ S&P 500 Avg.

	Jan	Feb	Mar	Apr	May	Jun	Jul	Aug	Sep	Oct	Nov	Dec
Avg	4.7	1.6	-1.9	-0.1	0.9	7.4	1.2	-2.2	3.0	3.4	3.3	3.1
Med	3.6	1.1	-0.4	1.2	1.1	6.3	2.1	-1.3	1.6	2.3	1.8	1.8
S&P 500 Avg	0.3	0.3	1.3	1.6	0.8	-0.2	1.0	-0.9	-0.3	1.4	1.6	1.4

Fq % ORCL Gain > 0% (1990-2021)

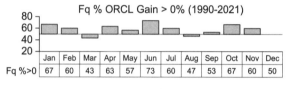

	Jan	Feb	Mar	Apr	May	Jun	Jul	Aug	Sep	Oct	Nov	Dec
Fq %>0	67	60	43	63	57	73	60	47	53	67	60	50

Fq % ORCL Gain > S&P 500 % (1990-2021)

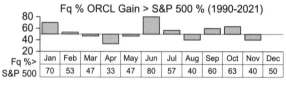

	Jan	Feb	Mar	Apr	May	Jun	Jul	Aug	Sep	Oct	Nov	Dec
Fq %> S&P 500	70	53	47	33	47	80	57	40	60	63	40	50

ORCL % Gain 5 Year (2017-2021)

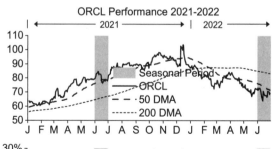

Legend: Hi/Lo — Avg. ■ Med. ◇ S&P 500 Avg.

ORCL Performance 2021-2022

2021 → | 2022 →

Legend: Seasonal Period | ORCL | — 50 DMA | ···· 200 DMA

Relative Strength, % Gain vs. S&P 500

Market Indices & Rates
Weekly Values**

Stock Markets	2021	2022
Dow	34,786	30,775
S&P500	4,352	3,785
Nasdaq	14,639	11,029
TSX	20,226	18,861
FTSE	7,123	7,169
DAX	15,650	12,784
Nikkei	28,783	26,393
Hang Seng	28,310	21,860

Commodities	2021	2022
Oil	75.16	105.76
Gold	1786.2	1817.0

Bond Yields	2021	2022
USA 5 Yr Treasury	0.86	3.01
USA 10 Yr T	1.44	2.98
USA 20 Yr T	1.98	3.38
Moody's Aaa	2.62	4.19
Moody's Baa	3.31	5.29
CAN 5 Yr T	0.97	3.11
CAN 10 Yr T	1.37	3.22

Money Market	2021	2022
USA Fed Funds	0.25	1.75
USA 3 Mo T-B	0.05	1.73
CAN tgt overnight rate	0.25	1.50
CAN 3 Mo T-B	0.14	2.08

Foreign Exchange	2021	2022
EUR/USD	1.19	1.05
GBP/USD	1.38	1.22
USD/CAD	1.23	1.29
USD/JPY	111.05	135.72

JUNE

M	T	W	T	F	S	S
			1	2	3	4
5	6	7	8	9	10	11
12	13	14	15	16	17	18
19	20	21	22	23	24	25
26	27	28	29	30		

JULY

M	T	W	T	F	S	S
					1	2
3	4	5	6	7	8	9
10	11	12	13	14	15	16
17	18	19	20	21	22	23
24	25	26	27	28	29	30
31						

AUGUST

M	T	W	T	F	S	S
	1	2	3	4	5	6
7	8	9	10	11	12	13
14	15	16	17	18	19	20
21	22	23	24	25	26	27
28	29	30	31			

JULY

	MONDAY	TUESDAY	WEDNESDAY
WEEK 27	**3** 28 USA Market Early Close 1:00pm-Independence Day	**4** 27 USA Market Closed - Independence Day	**5** 26
WEEK 28	**10** 21	**11** 20	**12** 19
WEEK 29	**17** 14	**18** 13	**19** 12
WEEK 30	**24** 7	**25** 6	**26** 5
WEEK 31	**31**	1	2

THURSDAY		FRIDAY	
6	25	**7**	24
		CAN Market Closed- Canada Day	
13	18	**14**	17
20	11	**21**	10
27	4	**28**	3
3		4	

AUGUST

M	T	W	T	F	S	S
	1	2	3	4	5	6
7	8	9	10	11	12	13
14	15	16	17	18	19	20
21	22	23	24	25	26	27
28	29	30	31			

SEPTEMBER

M	T	W	T	F	S	S
				1	2	3
4	5	6	7	8	9	10
11	12	13	14	15	16	17
18	19	20	21	22	23	24
25	26	27	28	29	30	

OCTOBER

M	T	W	T	F	S	S
						1
2	3	4	5	6	7	8
9	10	11	12	13	14	15
16	17	18	19	20	21	22
23	24	25	26	27	28	29
30	31					

NOVEMBER

M	T	W	T	F	S	S
		1	2	3	4	5
6	7	8	9	10	11	12
13	14	15	16	17	18	19
20	21	22	23	24	25	26
27	28	29	30			

JULY
S U M M A R Y

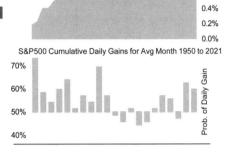

	Dow Jones	S&P 500	Nasdaq	TSX Comp
Month Rank	4	4	8	5
# Up	47	42	29	25
# Down	25	30	21	12
% Pos	65	58	57	68
% Avg. Gain	1.3	1.1	0.7	0.9

Dow & S&P 1950-2021, Nasdaq 1972-2021, TSX 1985-2021

S&P500 Cumulative Daily Gains for Avg Month 1950 to 2021

Prob. of Daily Gain

♦ When a summer rally occurs in the stock market, the gains are usually made in July. ♦ Typically, it is the first part of July that produces the gains as the market tends to rally before Independence Day and into the first eighteen calendar days (see the *18 Days Earnings Month Effect*). ♦ On average, volatility starts to increase in July and continues this trend into October, with August and September being two of the weaker seasonal months of the year.

BEST / WORST JULY BROAD MKTS. 2012-2021

BEST JULY MARKETS
- ♦ Russell 2000 (2013) 6.9%
- ♦ Nasdaq (2020) 6.8%
- ♦ Nasdaq (2016) 6.6%

WORST JULY MARKETS
- ♦ Russell 2000 (2014) -6.1%
- ♦ Nikkei 225 (2021) -5.2%
- ♦ FTSE 100 (2020) -4.4%

Index Values End of Month

	2012	2013	2014	2015	2016	2017	2018	2019	2020	2021
Dow	13,009	15,500	16,563	17,690	18,432	21,891	25,415	26,864	26,428	34,935
S&P 500	1,379	1,686	1,931	2,104	2,174	2,470	2,816	2,980	3,271	4,395
Nasdaq	2,940	3,626	4,370	5,128	5,162	6,348	7,672	8,175	10,745	14,673
TSX Comp.	11,665	12,487	15,331	14,468	14,583	15,144	16,434	16,407	16,169	20,288
Russell 1000	759	937	1,076	1,174	1,204	1,369	1,560	1,652	1,816	2,469
Russell 2000	787	1,045	1,120	1,239	1,220	1,425	1,671	1,575	1,480	2,226
FTSE 100	5,635	6,621	6,730	6,696	6,724	7,372	7,749	7,587	5,898	7,032
Nikkei 225	8,695	13,668	15,621	20,585	16,569	19,925	22,554	21,522	21,710	27,284

Percent Gain for July

	2012	2013	2014	2015	2016	2017	2018	2019	2020	2021
Dow	1.0	4.0	-1.6	0.4	2.8	2.5	4.7	1.0	2.4	1.3
S&P 500	1.3	4.9	-1.5	2.0	3.6	1.9	3.6	1.3	5.5	2.3
Nasdaq	0.2	6.6	-0.9	2.8	6.6	3.4	2.2	2.1	6.8	1.2
TSX Comp.	0.6	2.9	1.2	-0.6	3.7	-0.3	1.0	0.1	4.2	0.6
Russell 1000	1.1	5.2	-1.7	1.8	3.7	1.9	3.3	1.4	5.7	2.0
Russell 2000	-1.4	6.9	-6.1	-1.2	5.9	0.7	1.7	0.5	2.7	-3.6
FTSE 100	1.2	6.5	-0.2	2.7	3.4	0.8	1.5	2.2	-4.4	-0.1
Nikkei 225	-3.5	-0.1	3.0	1.7	6.4	-0.5	1.1	1.2	-2.6	-5.2

July Market Avg. Performance 2012 to 2021[1]

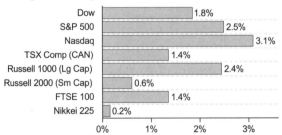

Dow	1.8%
S&P 500	2.5%
Nasdaq	3.1%
TSX Comp (CAN)	1.4%
Russell 1000 (Lg Cap)	2.4%
Russell 2000 (Sm Cap)	0.6%
FTSE 100	1.4%
Nikkei 225	0.2%

Interest Corner Jul[2]

	Fed Funds %[3]	3 Mo. T-Bill %[4]	10 Yr %[5]	20 Yr %[6]
2021	0.25	0.06	1.24	1.81
2020	0.25	0.09	0.55	0.98
2019	2.25	2.08	2.02	2.31
2018	2.00	2.03	2.96	3.03
2017	1.25	1.07	2.30	2.66

(1) Russell Data provided by Russell (2) Federal Reserve Bank of St. Louis- end of month values (3) Target rate set by FOMC (4)(5)(6) Constant yield maturities.

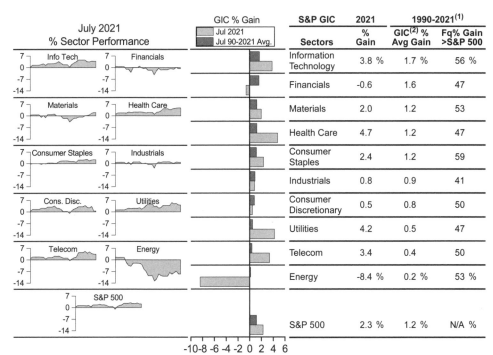

July 2021 % Sector Performance

GIC % Gain
- Jul 2021
- Jul 90-2021 Avg.

S&P GIC Sectors	2021 % Gain	1990-2021[1] GIC[2] % Avg Gain	1990-2021[1] Fq% Gain >S&P 500
Information Technology	3.8 %	1.7 %	56 %
Financials	-0.6	1.6	47
Materials	2.0	1.2	53
Health Care	4.7	1.2	47
Consumer Staples	2.4	1.2	59
Industrials	0.8	0.9	41
Consumer Discretionary	0.5	0.8	50
Utilities	4.2	0.5	47
Telecom	3.4	0.4	50
Energy	-8.4 %	0.2 %	53 %
S&P 500	2.3 %	1.2 %	N/A %

-10 -8 -6 -4 -2 0 2 4 6

Sector Commentary

♦ July is an earnings month and the S&P 500 was positive as the earnings season started mid-July 2021, and continued to perform well into the end of the month. ♦ Performance across the sectors of the market was broad based. ♦ The only sectors that were an anomaly, were the energy sector, producing a loss of 8.4% and the financials sector, producing a loss of 0.6%.

Sub-Sector Commentary

♦ In July 2021, the homebuilders sector was the top performing sub-sector from the selected list. It produced a gain of 4.7%. ♦ The biotech sub-sector is typically one of the better performing sub-sectors, but only managed to produce a gain of 2.3%, which was equal to the S&P 500. ♦ The steel sub-sector tends to one of the weaker sub-sectors in July, but the sub-sector managed to produce a gain of 8.4%. ♦ Declining interest rates managed to boost the performance in gold, which produced a gain of 3.6%.

SELECTED SUB-SECTORS[3]

Biotech (1993-2021)	2.3 %	5.9 %	80 %
Silver	-1.1	3.8	62
Railroads	-1.1	2.3	56
Homebuilders	4.7	1.6	50
Banks	-3.2	1.6	63
Chemicals	2.5	1.5	56
Transportation	-3.5	1.5	50
Retail	-0.8	1.4	56
Auto	0.3	1.2	44
SOX (1995-2021)	0.3	1.2	48
Metals & Mining	2.6	0.7	50
Gold	3.6	0.7	53
Pharma	4.6	0.7	50
Steel	8.4	0.3	47
Agriculture (1994-2021)	-1.5	-0.2	46

(1) Sector data provided by Standard and Poors (2) GIC is short form for Global Industry Classification (3) Sub Sector data provided by Standard and Poors, except where marked by symbol.

GOLD SHINES

(Metal) ① Jul 12 to Oct 9 ② Dec 27 to Jan 26

Most of the gold produced each year is consumed in jewelery fabrication. The time of the year with the highest demand for gold is in the fourth quarter, particularly around Indian Diwali, the festival of lights. The demand for gold bullion takes place in previous months as gold fabricators purchase gold bullion to fashion into jewelery for Diwali.

6% gain & 66% of the time positive

The result is that gold bullion tends to rise from July 12 to October 9. In this period, from 1984 to 2021, gold bullion has increased on average 3.2% and has been positive 63% of the time.

In more recent years, the Chinese have become large consumers of gold and have vied with India for the top gold consuming country. The Chinese consume most of their gold around the Chinese New Year, which takes place early in the calendar year. In the yearly period from 1985 to 2022, from December 27 to January 26, gold bullion has produced an average gain of 2.3% and has been positive 61% of the time. Gains in this period have been more frequent in recent years as the Chinese population has increased its consumption of gold.

2021/22 Performance Update.
In 2021 gold was negative as rising interest rates and US dollar pushed the price of gold lower.
In the first half of 2022, gold performed well in the first quarter as Russia invaded Ukraine. Starting in March, gold retreated as interest rates and the US dollar continued to climb.

ⓘ *Source: Bank of England- London PM represents the close value of gold in afternoon trading in London.*

Gold* vs. S&P 500 - 1984/85 to 2021/22   Positive ☐

Year	Jul 12 to Oct 9 S&P 500	Jul 12 to Oct 9 Gold	Dec 27 to Jan 26 S&P 500	Dec 27 to Jan 26 Gold	Compound Growth S&P 500	Compound Growth Gold
1984/85	7.4 %	0.5 %	6.5 %	-3.9 %	14.4 %	-3.4 %
1985/86	-5.4	4.2	-0.4	9.0	-5.7	13.5
1986/87	-2.6	25.2	9.2	4.3	6.3	30.6
1987/88	0.9	3.9	-1.0	-2.4	-0.1	1.4
1988/89	2.8	-7.5	5.0	-2.6	7.9	-10.0
1989/90	9.4	-4.2	-6.1	1.3	2.8	-3.0
1990/91	-15.5	12.1	1.6	-2.5	-14.2	9.3
1991/92	-0.1	-2.9	2.6	-1.8	2.6	-4.6
1992/93	-2.9	0.4	0.0	-0.6	-2.8	-0.2
1993/94	2.7	-8.8	1.3	-0.5	4.0	-9.3
1994/95	1.6	1.6	1.9	-0.1	3.4	1.6
1995/96	4.3	-0.1	1.2	4.8	5.5	4.7
1996/97	7.9	-0.4	1.9	-4.4	10.0	-4.7
1997/98	5.9	4.4	2.2	3.5	8.2	8.0
1998/99	-15.5	2.8	2.1	0.5	-13.7	3.3
1999/00	-4.8	25.6	-3.7	-0.5	-8.3	25.0
2000/01	-5.3	-4.5	3.0	-3.5	-2.5	-7.9
2001/02	-10.5	8.4	-1.4	0.5	-11.7	9.0
2002/03	-16.2	1.7	-3.2	6.4	-18.9	8.2
2003/04	4.1	7.8	5.4	-0.3	9.7	7.5
2004/05	0.8	3.8	-3.0	-3.5	-2.2	0.1
2005/06	-1.9	11.4	0.4	11.3	-1.5	24.0
2006/07	6.1	-8.8	0.4	4.0	6.5	-5.1
2007/08	3.1	11.0	-11.2	13.3	-8.4	25.8
2008/09	-26.6	-8.2	-4.2	7.9	-29.6	-1.0
2009/10	21.9	15.2	-3.1	0.7	18.2	16.0
2010/11	8.1	11.0	3.2	-3.3	11.5	7.3
2011/12	-12.4	6.2	4.2	7.5	-8.8	14.2
2012/13	7.5	12.5	5.9	0.5	13.7	13.1
2013/14	-1.1	1.5	-2.8	5.7	-3.9	7.2
2014/15	-2.0	-8.1	-1.5	9.0	-3.5	0.1
2015/16	-3.0	-0.7	-7.6	4.3	-10.4	3.6
2016/17	0.8	-7.3	1.5	5.2	2.2	-2.5
2017/18	4.9	5.6	7.2	7.0	12.4	13.0
2018/19	3.8	-5.3	8.0	2.8	12.1	-2.6
2019/20	-2.6	6.6	1.7	5.5	-1.1	12.5
2020/21	9.2	6.7	4.0	-1.0	13.5	5.6
2021/22	0.5	-1.8	-8.0	1.7	-7.5	-0.1
Avg.	-0.4 %	3.2 %	0.6 %	2.3 %	0.3 %	5.5 %
Fq>0	55 %	63 %	63 %	61 %	50 %	66 %

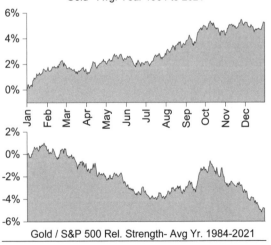

Gold - Avg. Year 1984 to 2021

Gold / S&P 500 Rel. Strength- Avg Yr. 1984-2021

Gold Performance

Gold Monthly % Gain (1984-2021)

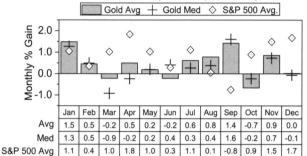

Legend: Gold Avg + Gold Med ◇ S&P 500 Avg.

	Jan	Feb	Mar	Apr	May	Jun	Jul	Aug	Sep	Oct	Nov	Dec
Avg	1.5	0.5	-0.2	0.5	0.2	-0.2	0.6	0.8	1.4	-0.7	0.9	0.0
Med	1.3	0.5	-0.9	-0.2	0.2	0.4	0.3	0.4	1.6	-0.2	0.7	-0.1
S&P 500 Avg	1.1	0.4	1.0	1.8	1.0	0.3	1.1	0.1	-0.8	0.9	1.5	1.7

Fq % Gold Gain > 0% (1984-2021)

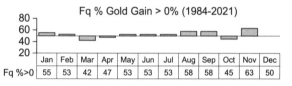

	Jan	Feb	Mar	Apr	May	Jun	Jul	Aug	Sep	Oct	Nov	Dec
Fq %>0	55	53	42	47	53	53	53	58	58	45	63	50

Fq % Gold Gain > S&P 500 % (1984-2021)

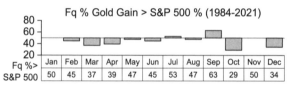

	Jan	Feb	Mar	Apr	May	Jun	Jul	Aug	Sep	Oct	Nov	Dec
Fq %> S&P 500	50	45	37	39	47	45	53	47	63	29	50	34

Gold % Gain 5 Year (2017-2021)

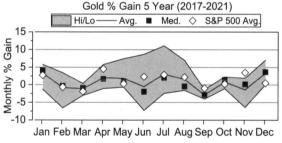

Legend: Hi/Lo — Avg. ■ Med. ◇ S&P 500 Avg.

Gold Performance 2021-2022

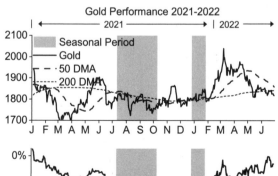

Relative Strength, % Gain vs. S&P 500

Market Indices & Rates
Weekly Values**

Stock Markets	2020	2021
Dow	25,827	34,870
S&P500	3,130	4,370
Nasdaq	10,208	14,702
TSX	15,597	20,258
FTSE	6,157	7,122
DAX	12,528	15,688
Nikkei	22,306	27,940
Hang Seng	25,373	27,345

Commodities	2020	2021
Oil	40.65	74.56
Gold	1772.9	1806.0

Bond Yields	2020	2021
USA 5 Yr Treasury	0.29	0.79
USA 10 Yr T	0.68	1.37
USA 20 Yr T	1.20	1.91
Moody's Aaa	2.37	2.62
Moody's Baa	3.55	3.28
CAN 5 Yr T	0.38	0.94
CAN 10 Yr T	0.56	1.33

Money Market	2020	2021
USA Fed Funds	0.25	0.25
USA 3 Mo T-B	0.14	0.06
CAN tgt overnight rate	0.25	0.25
CAN 3 Mo T-B	0.20	0.14

Foreign Exchange	2020	2021
EUR/USD	1.12	1.19
GBP/USD	1.25	1.39
USD/CAD	1.35	1.24
USD/JPY	107.51	110.14

JULY

M	T	W	T	F	S	S
					1	2
3	4	5	6	7	8	9
10	11	12	13	14	15	16
17	18	19	20	21	22	23
24	25	26	27	28	29	30
31						

AUGUST

M	T	W	T	F	S	S
	1	2	3	4	5	6
7	8	9	10	11	12	13
14	15	16	17	18	19	20
21	22	23	24	25	26	27
28	29	30	31			

SEPTEMBER

M	T	W	T	F	S	S
			1	2	3	
4	5	6	7	8	9	10
12	12	13	14	15	16	17
20	20	20	21	22	23	24
26	26	27	28	29	30	

GOLD MINERS – DIG GAINS
① Jul 27 to Sep 25 ② Dec 23 to Feb 14

The gold miners sector tends to perform well at approximately the same time of the year that gold bullion performs well. As gold bullion moves higher in price, gold miners benefit from their gold in the ground increasing in value.

Gold miners have their main seasonal period of strength from July 27 to September 25. Gold miners tend to perform well as gold bullion tends to increase at this time due to increased demand to make gold jewelery for fourth quarter consumption.

9% gain & 61% of the time positive

Gold miners also tend to perform well at the beginning of the year as Chinese New Year approaches. The Chinese buy a large amount of their gold in the period leading up to Chinese New Year.

Over the years, this trend has become more predominant as the wealth of Chinese citizens has increased.

2021/22 Performance Update.
In 2021, gold miners underperformed the S&P 500 as lower gold prices put downward pressure on gold miners.

In the first half of 2022, gold miners performed well into April as gold prices rose, but then corrected in the remainder of the first half of the year.

XAU vs. S&P 500 - 1984/85 to 2021/22*   Positive ▢

Year	Jul 27 to Sep 25 S&P 500	Jul 27 to Sep 25 XAU	Dec 23 to Feb 14 S&P 500	Dec 23 to Feb 14 XAU	Compound Growth S&P 500	Compound Growth XAU
1984/85	10.4 %	20.8 %	10.2 %	10.6 %	21.6 %	33.6 %
1985/86	-6.1	-5.5	4.2	-2.0	-2.2	-7.2
1986/87	-3.5	36.9	12.4	14.4	8.5	56.6
1987/88	3.5	23.0	3.1	-15.9	6.7	3.4
1988/89	1.7	-11.9	5.4	12.1	7.2	-1.3
1989/90	1.8	10.5	-4.4	6.8	-2.7	18.1
1990/91	-13.4	3.8	9.8	-0.8	-4.9	3.1
1991/92	1.6	-11.9	6.6	9.8	8.2	-3.3
1992/93	0.7	-3.8	1.0	8.9	1.6	4.8
1993/94	1.9	-7.3	0.6	-1.4	2.5	-8.6
1994/95	1.4	18.2	5.0	-4.4	6.4	13.0
1995/96	3.6	-1.0	7.1	20.8	11.0	19.6
1996/97	7.9	-1.0	8.0	-2.2	16.4	-3.2
1997/98	-0.1	8.7	7.0	6.9	6.9	16.2
1998/99	-8.4	12.0	2.2	8.8	-6.4	21.9
1999/00	-5.2	16.9	-3.2	-1.3	-8.3	15.3
2000/01	-0.9	-2.8	0.8	-12.5	-0.2	-15.0
2001/02	-15.9	3.2	-2.5	23.7	-17.9	27.6
2002/03	-1.6	29.8	-6.8	-3.7	-8.2	25.1
2003/04	0.5	11.0	4.8	-0.8	5.3	10.1
2004/05	2.4	16.5	-0.3	-3.8	2.1	12.1
2005/06	-1.3	20.6	0.6	10.0	-0.7	32.6
2006/07	4.6	-11.8	3.2	3.7	7.9	-8.5
2007/08	2.3	14.0	-9.1	5.3	-7.0	20.1
2008/09	-3.9	-18.5	-5.1	19.2	-8.8	-2.8
2009/10	6.7	6.0	-3.8	-3.8	2.6	2.0
2010/11	3.0	14.7	5.8	-5.0	9.0	8.9
2011/12	-14.7	-13.7	7.7	3.8	-8.1	-10.4
2012/13	6.0	24.0	6.4	-7.2	12.8	15.1
2013/14	0.1	-5.6	1.1	26.8	1.2	19.8
2014/15	-0.6	-16.4	0.9	18.0	0.3	-1.3
2015/16	-7.1	-2.6	-8.5	33.7	-15.1	30.2
2016/17	-0.2	-7.0	3.4	29.1	3.2	20.0
2017/18	0.8	1.5	0.6	1.8	1.3	3.3
2018/19	2.8	-13.5	13.6	8.5	16.7	-6.0
2019/20	-1.4	4.3	4.9	4.6	3.5	9.0
2020/21	2.6	-7.1	6.7	0.8	9.5	-6.3
2021/22	0.8	-13.3	-6.3	5.8	-5.6	-8.2
Avg.	-0.5 %	3.7 %	2.4 %	6.0 %	2.0 %	9.4 %
Fq>0	58 %	53 %	74 %	63 %	63 %	61 %

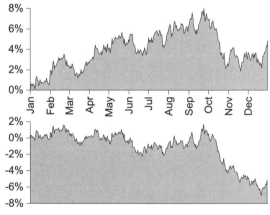

XAU - Avg. Year 1984 to 2021

XAU / S&P 500 Rel. Strength- Avg Yr. 1984-2021

ⓘ *XAU- PHLX Gold Silver Index consists of 12 precious metal mining companies.*

Gold Miners Performance

XAU Monthly % Gain (1984-2021)

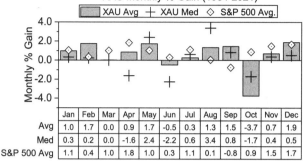

	Jan	Feb	Mar	Apr	May	Jun	Jul	Aug	Sep	Oct	Nov	Dec
Avg	1.0	1.7	0.0	0.9	1.7	-0.5	0.3	1.3	1.5	-3.7	0.7	1.9
Med	0.3	0.2	0.0	-1.6	2.4	-2.2	0.6	3.4	0.8	-1.7	0.4	0.5
S&P 500 Avg	1.1	0.4	1.0	1.8	1.0	0.3	1.1	0.1	-0.8	0.9	1.5	1.7

Fq % XAU Gain > 0% (1984-2021)

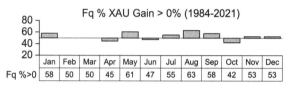

	Jan	Feb	Mar	Apr	May	Jun	Jul	Aug	Sep	Oct	Nov	Dec
Fq %>0	58	50	50	45	61	47	55	63	58	42	53	53

Fq % XAU Gain > S&P 500 % (1984-2021)

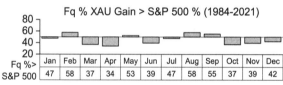

	Jan	Feb	Mar	Apr	May	Jun	Jul	Aug	Sep	Oct	Nov	Dec
Fq %> S&P 500	47	58	37	34	53	39	47	58	55	37	39	42

XAU % Gain 5 Year (2015-2021)

XAU Performance 2021-2022

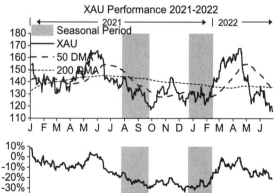

Relative Strength, % Gain vs. S&P 500

Stock Markets	2020	2021
Dow	26,075	34,688
S&P500	3,185	4,327
Nasdaq	10,617	14,427
TSX	15,714	19,986
FTSE	6,095	7,008
DAX	12,634	15,540
Nikkei	22,291	28,003
Hang Seng	25,727	28,005

Commodities	2020	2021
Oil	40.55	71.81
Gold	1803.1	1824.3

Bond Yields	2020	2021
USA 5 Yr Treasury	0.30	0.79
USA 10 Yr T	0.65	1.31
USA 20 Yr T	1.12	1.86
Moody's Aaa	2.19	2.56
Moody's Baa	3.39	3.24
CAN 5 Yr T	0.36	0.87
CAN 10 Yr T	0.55	1.24

Money Market	2020	2021
USA Fed Funds	0.25	0.25
USA 3 Mo T-B	0.13	0.05
CAN tgt overnight rate	0.25	0.25
CAN 3 Mo T-B	0.18	0.17

Foreign Exchange	2020	2021
EUR/USD	1.13	1.18
GBP/USD	1.26	1.38
USD/CAD	1.36	1.26
USD/JPY	106.93	110.07

JULY

M	T	W	T	F	S	S
					1	2
3	4	5	6	7	8	9
10	11	12	13	14	15	16
17	18	19	20	21	22	23
24	25	26	27	28	29	30
31						

AUGUST

M	T	W	T	F	S	S
	1	2	3	4	5	6
7	8	9	10	11	12	13
14	15	16	17	18	19	20
21	22	23	24	25	26	27
28	29	30	31			

SEPTEMBER

M	T	W	T	F	S	S
			1	2	3
4	5	6	7	8	9	10
12	12	13	14	15	16	17
20	20	20	21	22	23	24
26	26	27	28	29	30	

VOLATILITY INDEX
July 3 to October 9

The Chicago Board Options Exchange Market Volatility Index (VIX) is often referred to as a fear index as it measures investors' expectations of market volatility over the next thirty day period. The higher the VIX value, the greater the expectation of volatility and vice versa.

From 1990 to June 2022, the long-term average of the VIX is 19.5. In this time period, the VIX has bottomed at approximately 10 in the mid-90's, and the mid-2000's. In both cases, the VIX dropped below 10 for a few days.

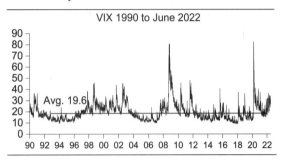

VIX 1990 to June 2022

Avg. 19.6

VIX - Avg. Year 1990 to 2021

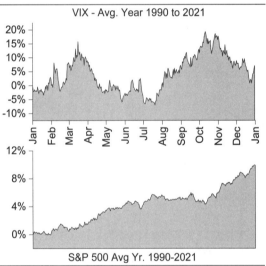

S&P 500 Avg Yr. 1990-2021

Levels below 15 are often associated with investor complacency, as investors are expecting very little volatility. Very often when a stock market correction occurs in this state, it can be sharp and severe. Knowing the trends of the VIX can be useful in adjusting the amount of risk in a portfolio.

From 1990 to 2021, during the period of July 3 to October 9, the VIX has increased 72% of the time. On

VIX* vs. S&P 500 1990 to 2021		
		Positive
July 3 to Oct 9	S&P 500	VIX %Gain
1990	-15.1%	88.9%
1991	-0.2	5.2
1992	-2.2	47.8
1993	3.3	6.3
1994	2.0	3.9
1995	6.2	30.5
1996	3.4	13.4
1997	7.4	13.3
1998	-14.1	138.8
1999	-4.0	9.8
2000	-3.6	22.9
2001	-14.6	85.7
2002	-18.1	45.5
2003	4.5	-1.1
2004	-0.3	-0.2
2005	0.1	28.0
2006	6.3	-10.7
2007	3.0	4.7
2008	-27.9	146.6
2009	19.5	-17.3
2010	13.9	-31.2
2011	-13.8	128.1
2012	5.6	-2.6
2013	2.6	19.2
2014	-2.4	73.4
2015	-2.9	1.7
2016	2.4	-8.7
2017	5.0	-7.6
2018	5.6	2.2
2019	-1.8	44.2
2020	11.1	-9.7
2021	0.9	24.6
Avg	-0.6%	27.8%
Fq > 0	56%	72%

average, the VIX tends to start increasing in July, particularly after the earnings season gets underway. After mid-July, without the expectation of strong earnings ahead, investors tend to focus on economic forecasts that often become more dire in the second half of the year.

In addition, stock market analysts tend to reduce their earnings forecasts at this time. Both of these effects tend to add volatility in the markets, increasing the VIX. The VIX tends to peak in October as the stock market often starts to establishing a rising trend at this time.

ⓘ *VIX - ticker symbol for the Chicago Board Options Exchange Market Volatility Index, measure implied volatility of S&P 500 index options*

VIX Performance

2021

Market Indices & Rates Weekly Values**		
Stock Markets	**2020**	**2021**
Dow	26,672	35,062
S&P500	3,225	4,412
Nasdaq	10,503	14,837
TSX	16,123	20,188
FTSE	6,290	7,028
DAX	12,920	15,669
Nikkei	22,696	27,548
Hang Seng	25,089	27,322
Commodities	**2020**	**2021**
Oil	40.59	72.27
Gold	1807.4	1799.6
Bond Yields	**2020**	**2021**
USA 5 Yr Treasury	0.29	0.72
USA 10 Yr T	0.64	1.30
USA 20 Yr T	1.11	1.85
Moody's Aaa	2.13	2.57
Moody's Baa	3.32	3.23
CAN 5 Yr T	0.35	0.80
CAN 10 Yr T	0.53	1.21
Money Market	**2020**	**2021**
USA Fed Funds	0.25	0.25
USA 3 Mo T-B	0.11	0.05
CAN tgt overnight rate	0.25	0.25
CAN 3 Mo T-B	0.17	0.17
Foreign Exchange	**2020**	**2021**
EUR/USD	1.14	1.18
GBP/USD	1.26	1.37
USD/CAD	1.36	1.26
USD/JPY	107.02	110.55

2022

JULY

M	T	W	T	F	S	S
					1	2
3	4	5	6	7	8	9
10	11	12	13	14	15	16
17	18	19	20	21	22	23
24	25	26	27	28	29	30
31						

AUGUST

M	T	W	T	F	S	S
	1	2	3	4	5	6
7	8	9	10	11	12	13
14	15	16	17	18	19	20
21	22	23	24	25	26	27
28	29	30	31			

In 2021, the VIX peaked in February and moved lower into the summer months. It increased during its seasonal period. While the VIX was rising, it was one of the weaker periods for the S&P 500 during 2021, despite the S&P 500 rallying for most of the year.

In 2022, the VIX rose in the first six months of the year as the S&P 500 headed lower.

SEPTEMBER

M	T	W	T	F	S	S
			1	2	3	
			1	2	3	
4	5	6	7	8	9	10
12	12	13	14	15	16	17
20	20	20	21	22	23	24
26	26	27	28	29	30	

VERIZON

VZ ①SHORT (Dec30-Mar12) ②SHORT (May2-May25)
③LONG (Aug24-Oct3)

Verizon pays a much higher dividend than the average company in the stock market. When the stock market heads lower, higher dividend paying companies tend to be more attractive.

One of the weakest months of the year for the stock market is September. It is also a time period when interest rates tend to decline on a seasonal basis, benefiting high dividend paying companies.

9% gain

Both of these factors help to drive Verizon higher from August 24 to October 3. In addition, Verizon's busiest quarter for revenue generation is the fourth quarter of the year. Investors try to front run this trend, which helps to push Verizon higher in its strong seasonal period.

Verizon has weak seasonal periods from December 30 to March 12 and from May 2 to May 25.

2021/22 Performance Update.
In 2021, Verizon underperformed the S&P 500, but overall outperformed in its seasonal period.

In the first half of 2022, Verizon was volatile, but managed to outperform the S&P 500.

ⓘ *VZ - stock symbol for Verizon, which trades on the NYSE, adjusted for stock splits.*

Verizon vs. S&P 500 1990 to 2021

Negative Short ☐   Positive Long ▨

Year	Dec 30 to Mar 12 S&P 500	VZ	May 2 to May 25 S&P 500	VZ	Aug 24 to Oct 3 S&P 500	VZ	Compound Growth S&P 500	VZ
1990	-4.2 %	-16.4 %	6.7 %	7.9 %	1.4 %	16.0 %	3.7 %	24.3 %
1991	12.6	-12.5	-0.7	-8.7	-2.5	-8.9	9.0	11.5
1992	-0.6	-10.6	0.4	-2.0	-1.1	-2.5	-1.3	9.9
1993	2.7	0.2	2.0	4.9	1.3	11.7	6.1	6.0
1994	-0.9	-13.6	1.2	1.0	-0.6	-3.2	-0.3	8.9
1995	6.2	5.2	2.8	-1.4	4.5	6.7	14.1	2.5
1996	3.4	-6.4	3.7	-1.4	3.9	5.3	11.4	13.6
1997	6.3	-3.9	6.1	2.2	4.5	12.1	17.8	13.9
1998	12.2	5.4	-0.9	-4.4	-7.3	18.8	3.1	17.3
1999	4.3	-7.6	-3.8	-4.2	-5.7	6.8	-5.4	19.9
2000	-4.7	-7.2	-5.9	-12.7	-5.3	17.6	-15.0	42.1
2001	-10.6	-5.3	0.9	-4.8	-7.7	5.5	-16.8	16.4
2002	0.4	-1.7	-0.2	4.7	-13.0	4.0	-12.8	0.7
2003	-8.1	-14.0	1.8	-1.8	3.7	-4.2	-3.0	11.2
2004	1.0	10.5	0.5	-6.1	3.3	1.5	4.8	-3.6
2005	-1.1	-11.7	2.9	-1.1	0.7	-2.5	2.5	10.1
2006	2.2	13.0	-2.5	-5.0	3.2	9.0	2.8	-0.4
2007	-0.8	-1.8	2.0	10.4	5.3	7.3	6.5	-2.1
2008	-11.5	-22.5	-2.4	-5.7	-14.9	-11.5	-26.5	14.6
2009	-13.7	-15.1	1.1	-5.7	-0.1	-4.7	-12.8	15.9
2010	2.1	-11.1	-9.5	-5.2	7.4	11.8	-0.8	30.7
2011	3.5	0.8	-3.2	-3.7	-5.4	1.1	-5.2	4.0
2012	8.6	-1.8	-6.3	2.2	3.5	9.5	5.3	9.1
2013	10.7	12.7	4.2	-1.9	0.9	-1.3	16.4	-12.2
2014	1.5	-5.7	0.9	5.3	-1.0	2.2	1.3	2.3
2015	-1.2	2.5	0.8	-1.6	-1.0	-7.1	-1.3	-7.9
2016	-2.7	11.3	1.2	-2.1	-1.2	-1.4	-2.7	-10.7
2017	5.5	-8.2	1.1	-1.2	3.7	3.3	10.6	13.1
2018	4.1	-7.8	2.5	-0.6	2.4	0.0	9.3	8.5
2019	12.3	3.9	-3.3	5.0	2.2	5.5	11.0	-3.6
2020	-23.4	-16.8	4.4	-4.8	-1.4	0.4	-21.2	22.9
2021	5.8	-5.4	0.2	-2.3	-2.7	-2.0	3.1	5.6
Avg.	0.7 %	-4.4 %	0.3 %	-1.4 %	-0.6 %	3.3 %	0.4 %	9.2 %
Fq>0	59 %	31 %	66 %	28 %	50 %	66 %	56 %	78 %

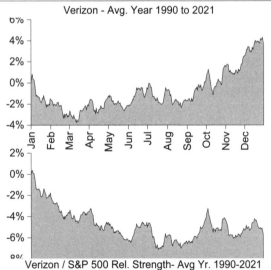

Verizon - Avg. Year 1990 to 2021

Verizon / S&P 500 Rel. Strength- Avg Yr. 1990-2021

Verizon Performance

VZ Monthly % Gain (1990-2021)

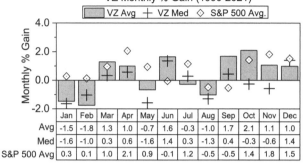

	Jan	Feb	Mar	Apr	May	Jun	Jul	Aug	Sep	Oct	Nov	Dec
Avg	-1.5	-1.8	1.3	1.0	-0.7	1.6	-0.3	-1.0	1.7	2.1	1.1	1.0
Med	-1.6	-1.0	0.3	0.6	-1.6	1.4	0.3	-1.3	0.4	-0.3	-0.6	1.4
S&P 500 Avg	0.3	0.1	1.0	2.1	0.9	-0.1	1.2	-0.5	-0.5	1.4	1.8	1.5

Fq % VZ Gain > 0% (1990-2021)

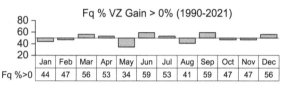

	Jan	Feb	Mar	Apr	May	Jun	Jul	Aug	Sep	Oct	Nov	Dec
Fq %>0	44	47	56	53	34	59	53	41	59	47	47	56

Fq % VZ Gain > S&P 500 % (1990-2021)

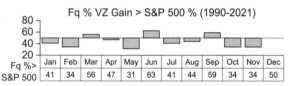

	Jan	Feb	Mar	Apr	May	Jun	Jul	Aug	Sep	Oct	Nov	Dec
Fq %> S&P 500	41	34	56	47	31	63	41	44	59	34	34	50

VZ % Gain 5 Year (2017-2021)

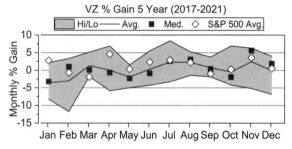

VZ Performance 2021-2022

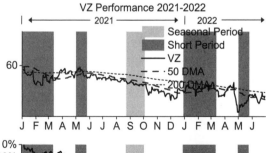

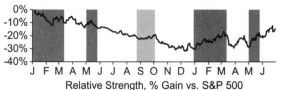

Relative Strength, % Gain vs. S&P 500

Market Indices & Rates
Weekly Values**

Stock Markets	2020	2021
Dow	26,470	34,935
S&P500	3,216	4,395
Nasdaq	10,363	14,673
TSX	15,997	20,288
FTSE	6,124	7,032
DAX	12,838	15,544
Nikkei	22,752	27,284
Hang Seng	24,705	25,961

Commodities	2020	2021
Oil	41.14	73.95
Gold	1902.1	1825.8

Bond Yields	2020	2021
USA 5 Yr Treasury	0.27	0.69
USA 10 Yr T	0.59	1.24
USA 20 Yr T	1.03	1.81
Moody's Aaa	2.01	2.51
Moody's Baa	3.17	3.19
CAN 5 Yr T	0.35	0.82
CAN 10 Yr T	0.50	1.20

Money Market	2020	2021
USA Fed Funds	0.25	0.25
USA 3 Mo T-B	0.11	0.06
CAN tgt overnight rate	0.25	0.25
CAN 3 Mo T-B	0.17	0.17

Foreign Exchange	2020	2021
EUR/USD	1.17	1.19
GBP/USD	1.28	1.39
USD/CAD	1.34	1.25
USD/JPY	106.14	109.72

JULY

M	T	W	T	F	S	S
					1	2
3	4	5	6	7	8	9
10	11	12	13	14	15	16
17	18	19	20	21	22	23
24	25	26	27	28	29	30
31						

AUGUST

M	T	W	T	F	S	S
	1	2	3	4	5	6
7	8	9	10	11	12	13
14	15	16	17	18	19	20
21	22	23	24	25	26	27
28	29	30	31			

SEPTEMBER

M	T	W	T	F	S	S
			1	2	3	
4	5	6	7	8	9	10
12	12	13	14	15	16	17
20	20	20	21	22	23	24
26	26	27	28	29	30	

Seasonal Investment Timeline[1]

Investment	Season		2022	2023

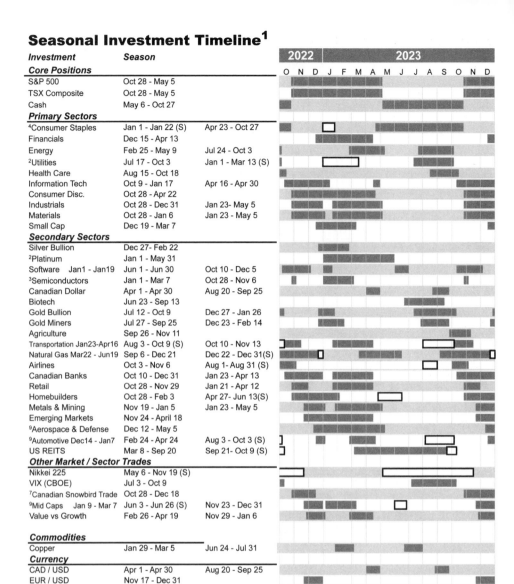

Investment	Season	
Core Positions		
S&P 500	Oct 28 - May 5	
TSX Composite	Oct 28 - May 5	
Cash	May 6 - Oct 27	
Primary Sectors		
[4]Consumer Staples	Jan 1 - Jan 22 (S)	Apr 23 - Oct 27
Financials	Dec 15 - Apr 13	
Energy	Feb 25 - May 9	Jul 24 - Oct 3
[2]Utilities	Jul 17 - Oct 3	Jan 1 - Mar 13 (S)
Health Care	Aug 15 - Oct 18	
Information Tech	Oct 9 - Jan 17	Apr 16 - Apr 30
Consumer Disc.	Oct 28 - Apr 22	
Industrials	Oct 28 - Dec 31	Jan 23- May 5
Materials	Oct 28 - Jan 6	Jan 23 - May 5
Small Cap	Dec 19 - Mar 7	
Secondary Sectors		
Silver Bullion	Dec 27- Feb 22	
[2]Platinum	Jan 1 - May 31	
Software Jan1 - Jan19	Jun 1 - Jun 30	Oct 10 - Dec 5
[3]Semiconductors	Jan 1 - Mar 7	Oct 28 - Nov 6
Canadian Dollar	Apr 1 - Apr 30	Aug 20 - Sep 25
Biotech	Jun 23 - Sep 13	
Gold Bullion	Jul 12 - Oct 9	Dec 27 - Jan 26
Gold Miners	Jul 27 - Sep 25	Dec 23 - Feb 14
Agriculture	Sep 26 - Nov 11	
Transportation Jan23-Apr16	Aug 3 - Oct 9 (S)	Oct 10 - Nov 13
Natural Gas Mar22 - Jun19	Sep 6 - Dec 21	Dec 22 - Dec 31(S)
Airlines	Oct 3 - Nov 6	Aug 1- Aug 31 (S)
Canadian Banks	Oct 10 - Dec 31	Jan 23 - Apr 13
Retail	Oct 28 - Nov 29	Jan 21 - Apr 12
Homebuilders	Oct 28 - Feb 3	Apr 27- Jun 13(S)
Metals & Mining	Nov 19 - Jan 5	Jan 23 - May 5
Emerging Markets	Nov 24 - April 18	
[9]Aerospace & Defense	Dec 12 - May 5	
[9]Automotive Dec14 - Jan7	Feb 24 - Apr 24	Aug 3 - Oct 3 (S)
US REITS	Mar 8 - Sep 20	Sep 21- Oct 9 (S)
Other Market / Sector Trades		
Nikkei 225	May 6 - Nov 19 (S)	
VIX (CBOE)	Jul 3 - Oct 9	
[7]Canadian Snowbird Trade	Oct 28 - Dec 18	
[9]Mid Caps Jan 9 - Mar 7	Jun 3 - Jun 26 (S)	Nov 23 - Dec 31
Value vs Growth	Feb 26 - Apr 19	Nov 29 - Jan 6
Commodities		
Copper	Jan 29 - Mar 5	Jun 24 - Jul 31
Currency		
CAD / USD	Apr 1 - Apr 30	Aug 20 - Sep 25
EUR / USD	Nov 17 - Dec 31	
USD / EUR	Jan 1 - Feb 7	
Fixed Income		
[3]U.S. Gov. Bonds	May 9 - Oct 3	
[3]U.S. High Yield	Nov 24 - Jan 8	
10YR Inflation Break-Even	Dec 20 - Mar 7	

Long Investment ▬▬▬   Short Investment (S) ▭   [1] Holiday, End of Month, Witches' Hangover, - et al not included.

[2]Thackray's 2012 Investor's Guide [3]Thackray's 2013 Investor's Guide [4]Thackray's 2014 Investor's Guide [5]Thackray's 2015 Investor's Guide
[6]Thackray's 2016 Investor's Guide [7]Thackray's 2017 Investor's Guide [8]Thackray's 2018 Investor's Guide[9]Thackray's 2019 Investor's Guide

Seasonal Investment Timeline[1]

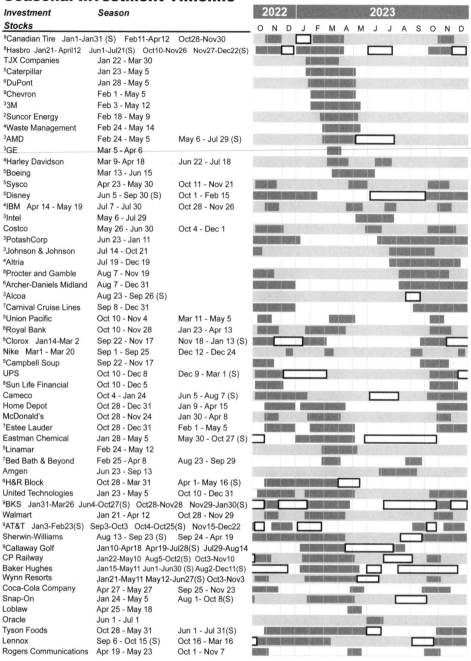

Investment	*Season*	
Stocks		
[9]Canadian Tire	Jan1-Jan31 (S) Feb11-Apr12	Oct28-Nov30
[8]Hasbro	Jan21- April12 Jun1-Jul21(S)	Oct10-Nov26 Nov27-Dec22(S)
TJX Companies	Jan 22 - Mar 30	
[5]Caterpillar	Jan 23 - May 5	
[6]DuPont	Jan 28 - May 5	
[9]Chevron	Feb 1 - May 5	
[3]3M	Feb 3 - May 12	
[2]Suncor Energy	Feb 18 - May 9	
[4]Waste Management	Feb 24 - May 14	
[3]AMD	Feb 24 - May 5	May 6 - Jul 29 (S)
[3]GE	Mar 5 - Apr 6	
[4]Harley Davidson	Mar 9- Apr 18	Jun 22 - Jul 18
[5]Boeing	Mar 13 - Jun 15	
[5]Sysco	Apr 23 - May 30	Oct 11 - Nov 21
[5]Disney	Jun 5 - Sep 30 (S)	Oct 1 - Feb 15
[4]IBM Apr 14 - May 19	Jul 7 - Jul 30	Oct 28 - Nov 26
[3]Intel	May 6 - Jul 29	
Costco	May 26 - Jun 30	Oct 4 - Dec 1
[3]PotashCorp	Jun 23 - Jan 11	
[3]Johnson & Johnson	Jul 14 - Oct 21	
[4]Altria	Jul 19 - Dec 19	
[8]Procter and Gamble	Aug 7 - Nov 19	
[6]Archer-Daniels Midland	Aug 7 - Dec 31	
[3]Alcoa	Aug 23 - Sep 26 (S)	
[7]Carnival Cruise Lines	Sep 8 - Dec 31	
[5]Union Pacific	Oct 10 - Nov 4	Mar 11 - May 5
[6]Royal Bank	Oct 10 - Nov 28	Jan 23 - Apr 13
[6]Clorox Jan14-Mar 2	Sep 22 - Nov 17	Nov 18 - Jan 13 (S)
Nike Mar1 - Mar 20	Sep 1 - Sep 25	Dec 12 - Dec 24
[5]Campbell Soup	Sep 22 - Nov 17	
UPS	Oct 10 - Dec 8	Dec 9 - Mar 1 (S)
[8]Sun Life Financial	Oct 10 - Dec 5	
Cameco	Oct 4 - Jan 24	Jun 5 - Aug 7 (S)
Home Depot	Oct 28 - Dec 31	Jan 9 - Apr 15
McDonald's	Oct 28 - Nov 24	Jan 30 - Apr 8
[7]Estee Lauder	Oct 28 - Dec 31	Feb 1 - May 5
Eastman Chemical	Jan 28 - May 5	May 30 - Oct 27 (S)
[5]Linamar	Feb 24 - May 12	
[7]Bed Bath & Beyond	Feb 25 - Apr 8	Aug 23 - Sep 29
Amgen	Jun 23 - Sep 13	
[6]H&R Block	Oct 28 - Mar 31	Apr 1- May 16 (S)
United Technologies	Jan 23 - May 5	Oct 10 - Dec 31
[9]BKS Jan31-Mar26	Jun4-Oct27(S) Oct28-Nov28	Nov29-Jan30(S)
Walmart	Jan 21 - Apr 12	Oct 28 - Nov 29
[9]AT&T Jan3-Feb23(S)	Sep3-Oct3 Oct4-Oct25(S)	Nov15-Dec22
Sherwin-Williams	Aug 13 - Sep 23 (S)	Sep 24 - Apr 19
[9]Callaway Golf	Jan10-Apr18 Apr19-Jul28(S)	Jul29-Aug14
CP Railway	Jan22-May10 Aug5-Oct2(S)	Oct3-Nov10
Baker Hughes	Jan15-May11 Jun1-Jun30 (S)	Aug2-Dec11(S)
Wynn Resorts	Jan21-May11 May12-Jun27(S)	Oct3-Nov3
Coca-Cola Company	Apr 27 - May 27	Sep 25 - Nov 23
Snap-On	Jan 24 - May 5	Aug 1- Oct 8(S)
Loblaw	Apr 25 - May 18	
Oracle	Jun 1 - Jul 1	
Tyson Foods	Oct 28 - May 31	Jun 1 - Jul 31(S)
Lennox	Sep 6 - Oct 15 (S)	Oct 16 - Mar 16
Rogers Communications	Apr 19 - May 23	Oct 1 - Nov 7

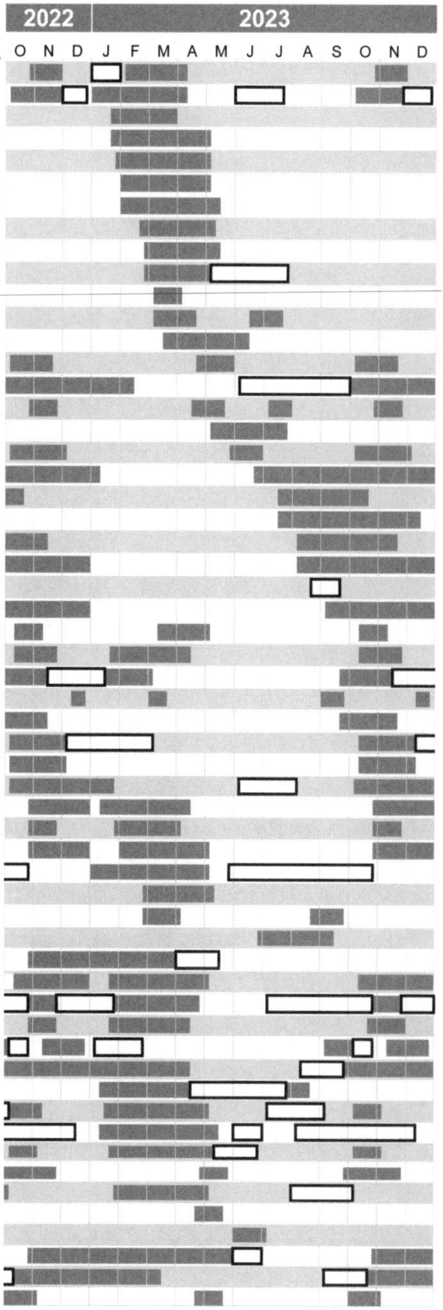

2022
2023
O N D J F M A M J J A S O N D

Long Investment ▬ Short Investment (S) ▭

[1] Holiday, End of Month, Witches' Hangover, - et al not included.

[2]Thackray's 2012 Investor's Guide [3]Thackray's 2013 Investor's Guide [4]Thackray's 2014 Investor's Guide [5]Thackray's 2015 Investor's Guide
[6]Thackray's 2016 Investor's Guide [7]Thackray's 2017 Investor's Guide [8]Thackray's 2018 Investor's Guide [9]Thackray's 2018 Investor's Guide

AUGUST

	MONDAY	TUESDAY	WEDNESDAY
WEEK 31	31	**1** 30	**2** 29
WEEK 32	**7** 24 CAN Market Closed- Civic Day	**8** 23	**9** 22
WEEK 33	**14** 17	**15** 16	**16** 15
WEEK 34	**21** 10	**22** 9	**23** 8
WEEK 35	**28** 3	**29** 2	**30** 1

THURSDAY		FRIDAY	
3	28	**4**	27
10	21	**11**	20
17	14	**18**	13
24	7	**25**	6
31		1	

SEPTEMBER

M	T	W	T	F	S	S
				1	2	3
4	5	6	7	8	9	10
11	12	13	14	15	16	17
18	19	20	21	22	23	24
25	26	27	28	29	30	

OCTOBER

M	T	W	T	F	S	S
						1
2	3	4	5	6	7	8
9	10	11	12	13	14	15
16	17	18	19	20	21	22
23	24	25	26	27	28	29
30	31					

NOVEMBER

M	T	W	T	F	S	S
		1	2	3	4	5
6	7	8	9	10	11	12
13	14	15	16	17	18	19
20	21	22	23	24	25	26
27	28	29	30			

DECEMBER

M	T	W	T	F	S	S
				1	2	3
4	5	6	7	8	9	10
11	12	13	14	15	16	17
18	19	20	21	22	23	24
25	26	27	28	29	30	31

AUGUST
S U M M A R Y

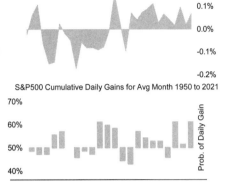

S&P500 Cumulative Daily Gains for Avg Month 1950 to 2021

	Dow Jones	S&P 500	Nasdaq	TSX Comp
Month Rank	10	10	11	10
# Up	41	40	28	22
# Down	31	32	22	15
% Pos	57	56	56	59
% Avg. Gain	0.0	0.1	0.4	-0.1

Dow & S&P 1950-2021, Nasdaq 1972-2021, TSX 1985-2021

♦ August is typically a marginal month and it has been the third worst month on average for the S&P 500 from 1950 to 2021. ♦ If there is a summer rally in July, it is often in jeopardy in August. ♦ In 2021, the S&P 500 performed well with all of the major sectors of the stock market being positive, except the energy sector. ♦ The TSX Composite is usually one of the better performing markets in August, but its strength is largely dependent on oil and gold stocks. In 2021, the TSX Composite underperformed the S&P 500 in August.

BEST / WORST AUGUST BROAD MKTS. 2012-2021

BEST AUGUST MARKETS
♦ Nasdaq (2020) 9.6%
♦ Dow (2020) 7.6%
♦ Russell 1000 (2020) 7.2%

WORST AUGUST MARKETS
♦ Nikkei 225 (2015) - 8.2%
♦ Nasdaq (2015) -6.9%
♦ FTSE 100 (2015) -6.7%

Index Values End of Month

	2012	2013	2014	2015	2016	2017	2018	2019	2020	2021
Dow	13,091	14,810	17,098	16,528	18,401	21,948	25,965	26,403	28,430	35,361
S&P 500	1,407	1,633	2,003	1,972	2,171	2,472	2,902	2,926	3,500	4,523
Nasdaq	3,067	3,590	4,580	4,777	5,213	6,429	8,110	7,963	11,775	15,259
TSX Comp.	11,949	12,654	15,626	13,859	14,598	15,212	16,263	16,442	16,514	20,583
Russell 1000	775	909	1,118	1,101	1,203	1,370	1,611	1,619	1,946	2,537
Russell 2000	812	1,011	1,174	1,159	1,240	1,405	1,741	1,495	1,562	2,274
FTSE 100	5,711	6,413	6,820	6,248	6,782	7,431	7,432	7,207	5,964	7,120
Nikkei 225	8,840	13,389	15,425	18,890	16,887	19,646	22,865	20,704	23,140	28,090

Percent Gain for August

	2012	2013	2014	2015	2016	2017	2018	2019	2020	2021
Dow	0.6	-4.4	3.2	-6.6	-0.2	0.3	2.2	-1.7	7.6	1.2
S&P 500	2.0	-3.1	3.8	-6.3	-0.1	0.1	3.0	-1.8	7.0	2.9
Nasdaq	4.3	-1.0	4.8	-6.9	1.0	1.3	5.7	-2.6	9.6	4.0
TSX Comp.	2.4	1.3	1.9	-4.2	0.1	0.4	-1.0	0.2	2.1	1.5
Russell 1000	2.2	-3.0	3.9	-6.2	-0.1	0.1	3.2	-2.0	7.2	2.8
Russell 2000	3.2	-3.3	4.8	-6.4	1.6	-1.4	4.2	-5.1	5.5	2.1
FTSE 100	1.4	-3.1	1.3	-6.7	0.8	0.8	-4.1	-5.0	1.1	1.2
Nikkei 225	1.7	-2.0	-1.3	-8.2	1.9	-1.4	1.4	-3.8	6.6	3.0

August Market Avg. Performance 2012 to 2021[1]

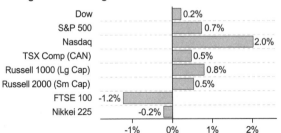

- Dow 0.2%
- S&P 500 0.7%
- Nasdaq 2.0%
- TSX Comp (CAN) 0.5%
- Russell 1000 (Lg Cap) 0.8%
- Russell 2000 (Sm Cap) 0.5%
- FTSE 100 -1.2%
- Nikkei 225 -0.2%

Interest Corner Aug[2]

	Fed Funds %[3]	3 Mo. T-Bill %[4]	10 Yr %[5]	20 Yr %[6]
2021	0.25	0.04	1.30	1.85
2020	0.25	0.05	0.72	1.26
2019	2.25	1.99	1.50	1.78
2018	2.00	2.11	2.86	2.95
2017	1.25	1.01	2.12	2.47

(1) Russell Data provided by Russell (2) Federal Reserve Bank of St. Louis- end of month values (3) Target rate set by FOMC (4)(5)(6) Constant yield maturities.

AUGUST SECTOR PERFORMANCE

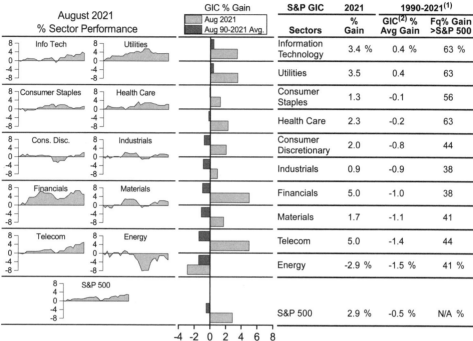

S&P GIC Sectors	2021 % Gain	1990-2021[1] GIC[2] % Avg Gain	Fq% Gain >S&P 500
Information Technology	3.4 %	0.4 %	63 %
Utilities	3.5	0.4	63
Consumer Staples	1.3	-0.1	56
Health Care	2.3	-0.2	63
Consumer Discretionary	2.0	-0.8	44
Industrials	0.9	-0.9	38
Financials	5.0	-1.0	38
Materials	1.7	-1.1	41
Telecom	5.0	-1.4	44
Energy	-2.9 %	-1.5 %	41 %
S&P 500	2.9 %	-0.5 %	N/A %

Sector Commentary

♦ In August 2021, the S&P 500 performed well, with a gain of 2.9%. This is in comparison to the seasonal trend of average negative performance. ♦ The top performing sectors were the financial and telecom sectors which both produced a gain of 5%. ♦ The only negative performing sector was the energy sector with a loss of 2.9%.

Sub-Sector Commentary

♦ In August 2021, the steel sub-sector produced a gain of 13%. Typically, the sub-sector performs poorly in August. ♦ In contrast, silver is typically one of the better assets in August. However, in 2021, silver lost 5.7%. ♦ The biotech sub-sector, after performing poorly in July, managed to outperform the S&P 500 with a gain of 3.2%. August is the last full month for the biotech's strong seasonal period that finishes in mid-September.

SELECTED SUB-SECTORS[3]

Silver	-5.7 %	1.3 %	57 %
Gold	-0.6	0.8	47
Biotech (1993-2021)	3.2	0.7	57
Home-builders	0.3	0.5	53
Agriculture (1994-2021)	0.5	0.2	46
SOX (1995-2021)	1.8	0.1	48
Retail	2.8	0.1	59
Pharma	2.3	-0.4	53
Banks	5.2	-1.0	34
Chemicals	0.9	-1.2	41
Metals & Mining	-1.7	-1.8	41
Railroads	-0.2	-1.8	44
Transportation	0.1	-2.0	34
Auto	2.6	-2.7	34
Steel	13.0	-3.0	47

(1) Sector data provided by Standard and Poors (2) GIC is short form for Global Industry Classification (3) Sub Sector data provided by Standard and Poors, except where marked by symbol.

CORNING

GLW

①SELL SHORT (Jul23-Aug12)
②LONG (Oct28-Mar26)

Corning is an industrial company and as such has a similar seasonal cycle as the industrial sector.

The two strongest months of the year for Corning since 1990 have been November and March. Both of these months are the bookends of the strong seasonal period for Corning, which lasts from October 28 to March 26. In this period, from 1990 to 2021, Corning has produced an average gain of 23% and has been positive 74%.

It should be noted that Corning's performance slips in April and May, underperforming the S&P 500 in both of these months. In general, Corning tends not to perform well in the summer months.

32% gain & 75% of the time positive

The weakest seasonal period for Corning from 1990 to 2021 has been from July 23 to August 12. In this period, Corning has produced an average loss of 4.5% and has only been positive 31% of the time.

2021/22 Performance Update.

In 2021, Corning performed well in its strong seasonal period and poorly in its weak seasonal period. Overall, Corning underperformed the S&P 500 in 2021.

In the first half of 2022, Corning performed well in its strong seasonal period and corrected sharply as the seasonal period ended.

GLW - stock symbol for Corning, which trades on the NYSE, adjusted for stock splits.

Corning vs. S&P 500 1990 to 2021

Positive Long   Negative Short

Year	Jul 23 to Aug 12 S&P 500	GLW	Oct 28 to Mar 26 S&P 500	GLW	Compound Growth S&P 500	GLW
1990	-7.2 %	-10.7 %	23.5 %	48.8 %	14.6 %	64.7 %
1991	1.3	1.3	6.2	-16.0	7.6	-17.1
1992	1.7	-2.7	7.0	-12.1	8.8	-9.7
1993	1.0	-2.3	-0.9	24.1	0.1	26.9
1994	1.9	-3.9	7.5	8.6	9.6	12.8
1995	0.3	-2.4	12.6	34.6	12.9	37.7
1996	5.0	6.0	12.8	20.7	18.5	13.4
1997	-0.8	3.7	25.5	3.3	24.5	-0.5
1998	-6.9	-8.7	20.4	63.8	12.2	78.0
1999	-4.6	-16.0	17.8	206.0	12.4	254.9
2000	-0.6	-2.9	-16.4	-68.3	-16.9	-67.4
2001	-1.7	18.8	3.1	-16.0	1.3	-31.8
2002	10.2	-51.5	-3.1	204.6	6.8	361.5
2003	0.2	-7.3	7.5	2.7	7.7	10.2
2004	-3.1	-20.2	4.1	-4.6	0.9	14.7
2005	-0.3	9.4	10.5	45.3	10.2	31.7
2006	2.1	-13.5	4.4	11.2	6.6	26.2
2007	-5.2	-11.6	-12.6	2.6	-17.2	14.5
2008	1.0	6.7	-1.9	40.2	-0.9	30.9
2009	5.4	-1.3	9.7	31.1	15.7	32.8
2010	-0.9	-3.3	11.1	16.4	10.1	20.3
2011	-12.4	-16.0	10.3	-6.6	-3.4	8.4
2012	3.2	-5.7	10.8	10.9	14.3	17.2
2013	-0.4	0.8	5.3	17.8	4.9	16.8
2014	-2.5	-8.9	4.8	19.2	2.2	29.9
2015	-1.3	-4.5	-1.5	10.9	-2.8	15.9
2016	0.4	5.6	9.9	19.6	10.3	12.9
2017	-1.3	-9.0	3.0	-10.2	1.7	-2.1
2018	1.1	12.4	6.0	9.5	7.2	-4.1
2019	-3.4	-16.8	-13.0	-28.5	-16.0	-16.5
2020	3.2	10.6	17.2	32.1	21.0	18.2
2021	2.1	-0.2	4.7	5.2	7.0	5.4
Avg.	-0.4 %	-4.5 %	6.4 %	22.7 %	6.0 %	31.5 %
Fq>0	50 %	31 %	78 %	75 %	81 %	75 %

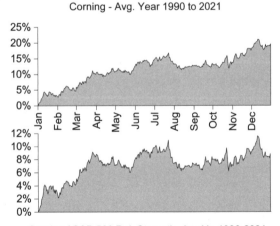

Corning - Avg. Year 1990 to 2021

Corning / S&P 500 Rel. Strength- Avg Yr. 1990-2021

Corning Performance

GLW Monthly % Gain (1990-2021)

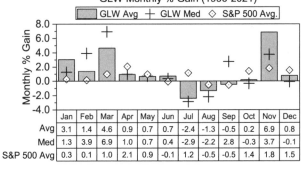

Legend: GLW Avg | + GLW Med | ◇ S&P 500 Avg.

	Jan	Feb	Mar	Apr	May	Jun	Jul	Aug	Sep	Oct	Nov	Dec
Avg	3.1	1.4	4.6	0.9	0.7	0.7	-2.4	-1.3	-0.5	0.2	6.9	0.8
Med	1.3	3.9	6.9	1.0	0.7	0.4	-2.9	-2.2	2.8	-0.3	3.7	-0.1
S&P 500 Avg	0.3	0.1	1.0	2.1	0.9	-0.1	1.2	-0.5	-0.5	1.4	1.8	1.5

Fq % GLW Gain > 0% (1990-2021)

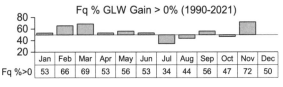

	Jan	Feb	Mar	Apr	May	Jun	Jul	Aug	Sep	Oct	Nov	Dec
Fq %>0	53	66	69	53	56	53	34	44	56	47	72	50

Fq % GLW Gain > S&P 500 % (1990-2021)

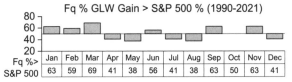

	Jan	Feb	Mar	Apr	May	Jun	Jul	Aug	Sep	Oct	Nov	Dec
Fq %> S&P 500	63	59	69	41	38	56	41	38	63	50	63	41

GLW % Gain 5 Year (2017-2021)

Legend: Hi/Lo — Avg. ■ Med. ◇ S&P 500 Avg.

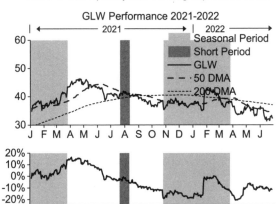

GLW Performance 2021-2022

Legend: Seasonal Period | Short Period | GLW | 50 DMA | 200 DMA

Relative Strength, % Gain vs. S&P 500

WEEK 31

Market Indices & Rates
Weekly Values**

Stock Markets	2020	2021
Dow	26,428	35,209
S&P500	3,271	4,437
Nasdaq	10,745	14,836
TSX	16,169	20,475
FTSE	5,898	7,123
DAX	12,313	15,761
Nikkei	21,710	27,820
Hang Seng	24,595	26,179

Commodities	2020	2021
Oil	40.27	68.28
Gold	1964.9	1762.9

Bond Yields	2020	2021
USA 5 Yr Treasury	0.21	0.77
USA 10 Yr T	0.55	1.31
USA 20 Yr T	0.98	1.85
Moody's Aaa	2.03	2.58
Moody's Baa	3.15	3.25
CAN 5 Yr T	0.32	0.89
CAN 10 Yr T	0.47	1.24

Money Market	2020	2021
USA Fed Funds	0.25	0.25
USA 3 Mo T-B	0.09	0.06
CAN tgt overnight rate	0.25	0.25
CAN 3 Mo T-B	0.17	0.17

Foreign Exchange	2020	2021
EUR/USD	1.18	1.18
GBP/USD	1.31	1.39
USD/CAD	1.34	1.26
USD/JPY	105.83	110.25

AUGUST

M	T	W	T	F	S	S
	1	2	3	4	5	6
7	8	9	10	11	12	13
14	15	16	17	18	19	20
21	22	23	24	25	26	27
28	29	30	31			

SEPTEMBER

M	T	W	T	F	S	S
			1	2	3	
4	5	6	7	8	9	10
12	12	13	14	15	16	17
20	20	20	21	22	23	24
26	26	27	28	29	30	

OCTOBER

M	T	W	T	F	S	S
						1
2	3	4	5	6	7	8
9	10	11	12	13	14	15
16	17	18	19	20	21	22
23	24	25	26	27	28	29
30	31					

TRANSPORTATION – ON A ROLL
①LONG (Jan23-Apr16) ②SELL SHORT (Aug1-Oct9)
③LONG (Oct10-Nov13)

The transportation sector can provide a "hilly" ride as the seasonal trends rise and fall throughout the year.

Activity in the transportation sub-sectors; railroads, airlines and freight, tends to bottom in February.

13% gain

Increased transportation activity in the spring, coupled with a typically positive economic outlook in the first part of the year, creates a positive seasonal trend, starting January 23 and lasting until April 16.

The next seasonal period is a weak period, giving investors an opportunity to sell short the sector and profit from its decline lasts from August 1 to October 9.

The third seasonal period is positive and occurs from October 10 to November 13. This trend is the result of a generally improved economic outlook at this time of the year.

2021/22 Performance Update.
In 2021, the transportation sector performed well in all of its seasonal periods, both long and short.

ⓘ *The SP GICS Transportation Sector encompasses a wide range transportation based companies. For more information, see www.standardandpoors.com*

Transportation Sector* vs. S&P 500 1990 to 2021
Negative Short ☐   Positive Long ▨

Year	Jan 23 to Apr 16 S&P 500	Jan 23 to Apr 16 Trans port	Aug 1 to Oct 9 S&P 500	Aug 1 to Oct 9 Trans port	Oct 10 to Nov 13 S&P 500	Oct 10 to Nov 13 Trans port	Compound Growth S&P 500	Compound Growth Trans port
1990	4.4 %	4.1 %	-14.3 %	-19.2 %	4.1 %	3.3 %	-6.9 %	28.1 %
1991	18.1	11.4	-2.8	0.5	5.5	9.6	21.0	21.5
1992	-0.5	3.7	-5.1	-9.1	4.9	14.1	-0.9	29.1
1993	2.9	9.1	2.7	-0.3	1.1	6.4	6.9	16.5
1994	-6.0	-10.7	-0.7	-9.3	1.6	0.8	-5.2	-1.6
1995	9.6	10.5	2.9	-1.3	2.4	5.0	15.5	17.6
1996	5.2	9.4	8.9	4.9	4.9	6.1	20.1	10.4
1997	-2.9	-2.0	1.7	0.9	-5.6	-5.4	-6.7	-8.2
1998	15.1	12.2	-12.2	-16.5	14.4	12.5	15.6	47.0
1999	7.7	17.7	0.6	-11.0	4.5	4.0	13.1	35.8
2000	-5.9	-2.7	-2.0	-6.0	-3.6	13.0	-11.1	16.6
2001	12.2	0.1	-12.8	-20.0	7.8	14.1	-17.4	37.0
2002	0.8	6.9	-14.8	-11.2	13.6	8.2	-2.4	28.6
2003	0.2	0.6	4.9	4.9	1.9	8.0	7.1	3.3
2004	-0.8	-2.9	1.9	6.6	5.5	11.1	6.6	0.7
2005	-2.2	-5.1	-3.1	-0.5	3.3	9.0	-2.1	3.9
2006	2.2	13.2	5.8	6.4	2.5	3.8	10.8	9.9
2007	3.2	4.8	7.6	-0.2	-5.4	-2.9	5.0	1.9
2008	4.1	19.1	-28.2	-23.5	0.2	4.0	-25.1	52.9
2009	4.6	7.2	8.5	6.7	2.1	5.9	15.8	5.9
2010	9.2	17.4	5.8	7.9	2.9	2.5	18.9	10.9
2011	2.8	2.2	-10.6	-11.8	9.4	11.4	0.6	26.9
2012	4.1	-2.0	4.5	-3.5	-4.6	-1.1	3.8	0.3
2013	5.5	3.5	-1.7	1.8	7.6	10.9	11.5	12.7
2014	1.0	1.7	-0.1	2.6	5.8	14.9	6.6	13.8
2015	2.0	-10.0	-4.2	-0.7	0.4	-2.0	-1.9	-11.2
2016	9.1	16.4	-0.9	4.3	0.5	6.4	8.7	18.6
2017	2.5	-4.0	3.0	6.5	1.6	-2.8	7.3	-12.7
2018	-5.5	-9.0	2.3	1.2	-5.5	-4.6	-8.6	-14.2
2019	10.4	10.7	-2.0	-9.0	6.0	10.0	14.6	32.7
2020	-15.7	-25.0	6.3	20.7	3.1	1.4	-7.6	-39.7
2021	9.0	14.0	-0.1	-1.8	6.6	9.7	16.1	27.3
Avg.	2.6 %	3.8 %	-1.5 %	-2.5 %	3.1 %	5.8 %	4.0 %	13.2 %
Fq>0	72 %	69 %	47 %	44 %	84 %	81 %	63 %	81 %

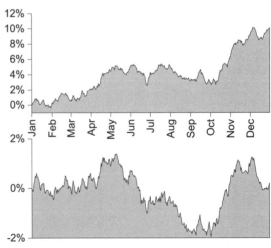

Transportation Sector - Avg. Year 1990 to 2021

Transportation / S&P 500 Rel. Strength- Avg Yr. 1990-2021

Transportation Performance

Transportation Monthly % Gain (1990-2021)

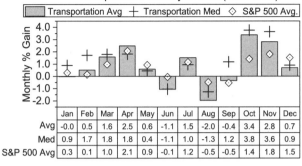

Transportation Avg + Transportation Med ◇ S&P 500 Avg.

	Jan	Feb	Mar	Apr	May	Jun	Jul	Aug	Sep	Oct	Nov	Dec
Avg	-0.0	0.5	1.6	2.5	0.6	-1.1	1.5	-2.0	-0.4	3.4	2.8	0.7
Med	0.9	1.7	1.8	1.8	0.4	-1.1	1.0	-1.3	1.2	3.8	3.6	0.9
S&P 500 Avg	0.3	0.1	1.0	2.1	0.9	-0.1	1.2	-0.5	-0.5	1.4	1.8	1.5

Fq % Transportation Gain > 0% (1990-2021)

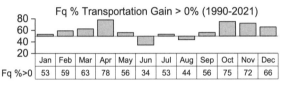

	Jan	Feb	Mar	Apr	May	Jun	Jul	Aug	Sep	Oct	Nov	Dec
Fq %>0	53	59	63	78	56	34	53	44	56	75	72	66

Fq % Transportation Gain > S&P 500 % (1990-2021)

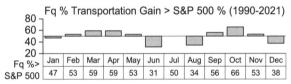

	Jan	Feb	Mar	Apr	May	Jun	Jul	Aug	Sep	Oct	Nov	Dec
Fq %> S&P 500	47	53	59	59	53	31	50	34	56	66	53	38

Transportation % Gain 5 Year (2017-2021)

Hi/Lo —— Avg. ■ Med. ◇ S&P 500 Avg.

Jan Feb Mar Apr May Jun Jul Aug Sep Oct Nov Dec

Transportation Performance 2021-2022

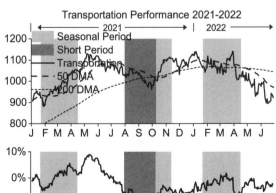

2021 | 2022

Seasonal Period
Short Period
Transportation
50 DMA
200 DMA

J F M A M J J A S O N D J F M A M J

Relative Strength, % Gain vs. S&P 500

Market Indices & Rates
Weekly Values**

Stock Markets	2020	2021
Dow	27,433	35,515
S&P500	3,351	4,468
Nasdaq	11,011	14,823
TSX	16,544	20,518
FTSE	6,032	7,219
DAX	12,675	15,977
Nikkei	22,330	27,977
Hang Seng	24,532	26,392

Commodities	2020	2021
Oil	41.22	68.44
Gold	2031.2	1773.9

Bond Yields	2020	2021
USA 5 Yr Treasury	0.23	0.79
USA 10 Yr T	0.57	1.29
USA 20 Yr T	1.01	1.85
Moody's Aaa	2.03	2.58
Moody's Baa	3.14	3.27
CAN 5 Yr T	0.32	0.84
CAN 10 Yr T	0.48	1.19

Money Market	2020	2021
USA Fed Funds	0.25	0.25
USA 3 Mo T-B	0.10	0.06
CAN tgt overnight rate	0.25	0.25
CAN 3 Mo T-B	0.16	0.16

Foreign Exchange	2020	2021
EUR/USD	1.18	1.18
GBP/USD	1.31	1.39
USD/CAD	1.34	1.25
USD/JPY	105.92	109.59

AUGUST

M	T	W	T	F	S	S
	1	2	3	4	5	6
7	8	9	10	11	12	13
14	15	16	17	18	19	20
21	22	23	24	25	26	27
28	29	30	31			

SEPTEMBER

M	T	W	T	F	S	S
				1	2	3
4	5	6	7	8	9	10
12	12	13	14	15	16	17
20	20	20	21	22	23	24
26	26	27	28	29	30	

OCTOBER

M	T	W	T	F	S	S
						1
2	3	4	5	6	7	8
9	10	11	12	13	14	15
16	17	18	19	20	21	22
23	24	25	26	27	28	29
30	31					

AGRICULTURE MOOOVES
September 26 to November 11

The agriculture seasonal trade is the result of the major summer growing season in the northern hemisphere producing cash for growers and subsequently, increasing sales for farming suppliers typically in the fourth quarter of the year. The seasonal period for the agriculture sector occurs towards the beginning of the fourth quarter.

> ### 64% of the time
> ### better than the S&P 500

Although this sector can represent a good opportunity, investors should be wary of the wide performance swings. Out of the twenty-eight cycles from 1994 to 2021, during its seasonal period, the agriculture sector has had eleven years of returns greater than +10%.

Agriculture* vs. S&P 500 1994 to 2021

Sep 26 to Nov 11	S&P 500	Positive	
		Agri	Diff
1994	0.6 %	5.7 %	5.1 %
1995	1.9	12.0	10.2
1996	6.7	24.7	18.0
1997	-1.5	-6.9	-5.4
1998	7.3	-1.7	-9.0
1999	8.2	1.4	-6.8
2000	-5.1	35.3	40.4
2001	10.7	18.1	7.5
2002	4.4	13.7	9.3
2003	4.3	9.8	5.5
2004	5.7	25.0	19.2
2005	1.6	7.2	5.6
2006	4.1	-5.7	-9.9
2007	-4.2	12.6	16.8
2008	-25.7	2.3	28.0
2009	5.2	17.8	12.6
2010	5.7	-4.9	-10.6
2011	11.2	17.9	6.7
2012	-4.3	-8.2	-3.9
2013	4.7	12.2	7.5
2014	3.8	1.3	-2.5
2015	7.4	-4.7	-12.1
2016	0.0	-1.7	-1.7
2017	3.4	-8.4	-11.8
2018	-4.6	-2.8	1.8
2019	3.4	7.5	4.1
2020	8.3	8.7	3.9
2021	4.3	10.7	6.3
Avg.	2.4 %	7.1 %	4.7 %
Fq > 0	75 %	68 %	64 %

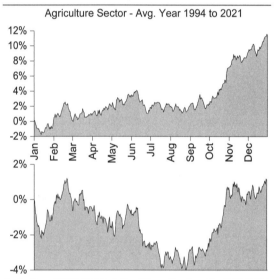

Agriculture Sector - Avg. Year 1994 to 2021

Agriculture / S&P 500 Relative Strength - Avg Yr. 1994-2021

The world population is still increasing and imbalances in food supply and demand will continue to exist in the future, helping to support the agriculture seasonal trade.

On a year by year basis, the agriculture sector has on average produced its biggest gains during its seasonally strong period. In 2000, the agriculture sector produced a gain of 35.3%. It is interesting to note that this is the same year that the technology sector's bubble burst.

In the 2000's, after realizing that technology stocks were not going to grow to the sky, investors started to have an epiphany– that the world might be running out of food, and as a result interest in the agriculture sector started to pick up.

2021/22 Performance Update.
In 2021, the agriculture sector started to underperform the S&P 500 in May and continued its underperformance for most of the year.

Starting in early 2022, the agriculture sector started to outperform the S&P 500. When Russia invaded Ukraine in late February 2022, the fear of reduced agriculture products continued to push the agriculture higher relative to the S&P 500.

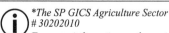

*The SP GICS Agriculture Sector # 30202010
For more information on the agriculture sector, see www.standardandpoors.com*

Agriculture Performance

Agriculture Monthly % Gain (1994-2021)

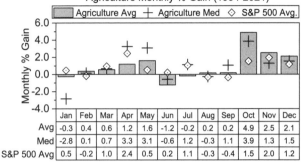

	Jan	Feb	Mar	Apr	May	Jun	Jul	Aug	Sep	Oct	Nov	Dec
Avg	-0.3	0.4	0.6	1.2	1.6	-1.2	-0.2	0.2	0.2	4.9	2.5	2.1
Med	-2.8	0.1	0.7	3.3	3.1	-0.6	1.2	-0.3	1.1	3.9	1.3	1.5
S&P 500 Avg	0.5	-0.2	1.0	2.4	0.5	0.2	1.1	-0.3	-0.4	1.5	2.0	1.2

Fq % Agriculture Gain > 0% (1994-2021)

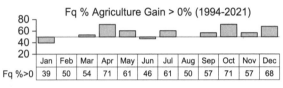

	Jan	Feb	Mar	Apr	May	Jun	Jul	Aug	Sep	Oct	Nov	Dec
Fq %>0	39	50	54	71	61	46	61	50	57	71	57	68

Fq % Agriculture Gain > S&P 500 % (1994-2021)

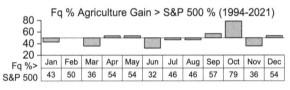

	Jan	Feb	Mar	Apr	May	Jun	Jul	Aug	Sep	Oct	Nov	Dec
Fq %> S&P 500	43	50	36	54	54	32	46	46	57	79	36	54

Agriculture % Gain 5 Year (2017-2021)

Hi/Lo —— Avg. ■ Med. ◇ S&P 500 Avg.

Agriculture Performance 2021-2022

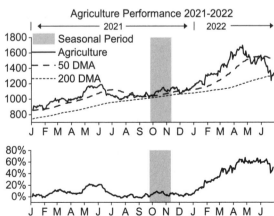

Relative Strength, % Gain vs. S&P 500

Stock Markets	2020	2021
Dow	27,931	35,120
S&P500	3,373	4,442
Nasdaq	11,019	14,715
TSX	16,515	20,339
FTSE	6,090	7,088
DAX	12,901	15,808
Nikkei	23,289	27,013
Hang Seng	25,183	24,850

Commodities	2020	2021
Oil	42.01	62.32
Gold	1944.8	1779.1

Bond Yields	2020	2021
USA 5 Yr Treasury	0.29	0.80
USA 10 Yr T	0.71	1.26
USA 20 Yr T	1.21	1.79
Moody's Aaa	2.30	2.51
Moody's Baa	3.32	3.22
CAN 5 Yr T	0.42	0.82
CAN 10 Yr T	0.61	1.14

Money Market	2020	2021
USA Fed Funds	0.25	0.25
USA 3 Mo T-B	0.10	0.05
CAN tgt overnight rate	0.25	0.25
CAN 3 Mo T-B	0.16	0.18

Foreign Exchange	2020	2021
EUR/USD	1.18	1.17
GBP/USD	1.31	1.36
USD/CAD	1.33	1.28
USD/JPY	106.60	109.78

AUGUST

M	T	W	T	F	S	S
	1	2	3	4	5	6
7	8	9	10	11	12	13
14	15	16	17	18	19	20
21	22	23	24	25	26	27
28	29	30	31			

SEPTEMBER

M	T	W	T	F	S	S
				1	2	3
4	5	6	7	8	9	10
12	12	13	14	15	16	17
20	20	20	21	22	23	24
26	26	27	28	29	30	

OCTOBER

M	T	W	T	F	S	S
						1
2	3	4	5	6	7	8
9	10	11	12	13	14	15
16	17	18	19	20	21	22
23	24	25	26	27	28	29
30	31					

MSFT MICROSOFT
October 1 to October 31

If there is only one month of the year that an investor could invest in Microsoft, October is the leader on a seasonal basis.

According to Microsoft's 10-K filling for the period ended June 30, 2021, the company has seasonal revenue trends.

"Our revenue fluctuates quarterly and is generally higher in the second and fourth quarters of our fiscal year. Second quarter revenue is driven by corporate year-end spending trends in our major markets and holiday season spending by consumers, and fourth quarter revenue is driven by the volume of multi-year on-premises contracts executed during the period."

5.3% gain & 72% of the time better than the S&P 500

The fourth quarter of the calendar year tends to be the strongest of the year. Microsoft has its fiscal year end on June 30, so its second quarter matches up with the fourth quarter of the calendar year. Microsoft tends to report its second quarter earnings in late October. Investors are attracted to Microsoft during the month of October, ahead of its earnings report, helping to push the stock price higher during the month.

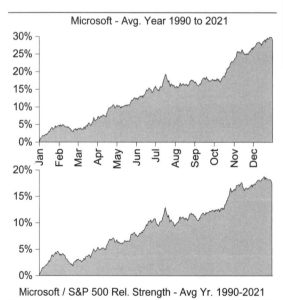

Microsoft - Avg. Year 1990 to 2021

Microsoft / S&P 500 Rel. Strength - Avg Yr. 1990-2021

As Microsoft has grown over the decades, its strong performance in October has been fairly consistent.

Oct 1 to Oct 31	S&P 500	Positive	
		MSFT	Diff
1990	-0.7 %	1.2 %	1.9 %
1991	1.2	5.5	4.3
1992	0.2	10.2	10.0
1993	1.9	-2.9	-4.8
1994	2.1	12.2	10.2
1995	-0.5	10.5	11.0
1996	2.6	4.1	1.5
1997	-3.4	-1.7	1.7
1998	8.0	-3.8	-11.8
1999	6.3	2.2	-4.0
2000	-0.5	14.2	14.7
2001	1.8	13.6	11.8
2002	8.6	22.2	13.6
2003	5.5	-6.0	-11.5
2004	1.4	1.2	-0.2
2005	-1.8	-0.1	1.7
2006	3.2	5.0	1.8
2007	1.5	24.9	23.5
2008	-16.9	-16.3	0.6
2009	-2.0	7.8	9.8
2010	3.7	8.9	5.2
2011	10.8	7.0	-3.8
2012	-2.0	-4.1	-2.1
2013	4.5	6.4	1.9
2014	2.3	1.3	-1.0
2015	8.3	18.9	10.6
2016	-1.9	4.0	6.0
2017	2.2	11.7	9.4
2018	-6.9	-6.6	0.3
2019	2.0	3.1	1.1
2020	-2.8	-3.7	-1.0
2021	6.9	17.6	10.7
Avg.	1.4 %	5.3 %	3.8 %
Fq > 0	66 %	72 %	72 %

Microsoft vs. S&P 500 1990 to 2021

Relative to the S&P 500, it has only suffered one double digit underperformance (a relative loss of greater than 10%) in October, but has had nine double digit out performances.

2021/22 Performance Update.
Microsoft outperformed the S&P 500 in 2021. It strongly outperformed in October (its strong seasonal period) and then underperformed in November and December. In the first half of 2022 Microsoft moderately underperformed the S&P 500, but managed to outperform the technology sector.

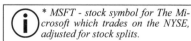

* MSFT - stock symbol for The Microsoft which trades on the NYSE, adjusted for stock splits.

Microsoft Performance

MSFT Monthly % Gain (1990-2021)

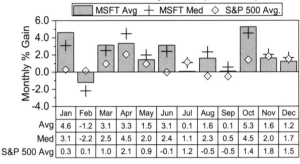

Legend: MSFT Avg + MSFT Med ◇ S&P 500 Avg.

	Jan	Feb	Mar	Apr	May	Jun	Jul	Aug	Sep	Oct	Nov	Dec
Avg	4.6	-1.2	3.1	3.3	1.5	3.1	0.1	1.6	0.1	5.3	1.6	1.2
Med	3.1	-2.2	2.5	4.5	2.0	2.4	1.1	2.3	0.5	4.5	2.0	1.7
S&P 500 Avg	0.3	0.1	1.0	2.1	0.9	-0.1	1.2	-0.5	-0.5	1.4	1.8	1.5

Fq % MSFT Gain > 0% (1990-2021)

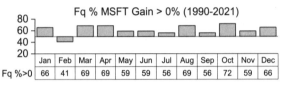

	Jan	Feb	Mar	Apr	May	Jun	Jul	Aug	Sep	Oct	Nov	Dec
Fq %>0	66	41	69	69	59	59	56	69	56	72	59	66

Fq % MSFT Gain > S&P 500 % (1990-2021)

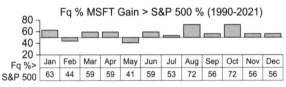

	Jan	Feb	Mar	Apr	May	Jun	Jul	Aug	Sep	Oct	Nov	Dec
Fq %> S&P 500	63	44	59	59	41	59	53	72	56	72	56	56

MSFT % Gain 5 Year (2017-2021)

Legend: Hi/Lo — Avg. ■ Med. ◇ S&P 500 Avg.

Jan Feb Mar Apr May Jun Jul Aug Sep Oct Nov Dec

MSFT Performance 2021-2022

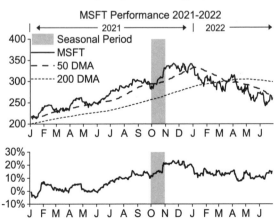

← 2021 → | 2022 →

Legend: Seasonal Period, MSFT, 50 DMA, 200 DMA

J F M A M J J A S O N D J F M A M J

Relative Strength, % Gain vs. S&P 500

Stock Markets	2020	2021
Dow	27,930	35,456
S&P500	3,397	4,509
Nasdaq	11,312	15,130
TSX	16,518	20,645
FTSE	6,002	7,148
DAX	12,765	15,852
Nikkei	22,920	27,641
Hang Seng	25,114	25,408

Commodities	2020	2021
Oil	42.19	68.74
Gold	1924.4	1798.5

Bond Yields	2020	2021
USA 5 Yr Treasury	0.27	0.79
USA 10 Yr T	0.64	1.31
USA 20 Yr T	1.13	1.84
Moody's Aaa	2.30	2.54
Moody's Baa	3.28	3.23
CAN 5 Yr T	0.36	0.84
CAN 10 Yr T	0.54	1.20

Money Market	2020	2021
USA Fed Funds	0.25	0.25
USA 3 Mo T-B	0.10	0.05
CAN tgt overnight rate	0.25	0.25
CAN 3 Mo T-B	0.15	0.18

Foreign Exchange	2020	2021
EUR/USD	1.18	1.18
GBP/USD	1.31	1.38
USD/CAD	1.32	1.26
USD/JPY	105.80	109.84

AUGUST

M	T	W	T	F	S	S
	1	2	3	4	5	6
7	8	9	10	11	12	13
14	15	16	17	18	19	20
21	22	23	24	25	26	27
28	29	30	31			

SEPTEMBER

M	T	W	T	F	S	S
				1	2	3
4	5	6	7	8	9	10
12	12	13	14	15	16	17
20	20	20	21	22	23	24
26	26	27	28	29	30	

OCTOBER

M	T	W	T	F	S	S
						1
2	3	4	5	6	7	8
9	10	11	12	13	14	15
16	17	18	19	20	21	22
23	24	25	26	27	28	29
30	31					

HEALTH CARE – PRESCRIPTION RENEWAL
①LONG (May1-Aug2) ②SELL SHORT (Aug3-Aug11)
③LONG (Aug12-Oct24)

Health care stocks have traditionally been classified as defensive stocks because of their stable earnings. Pharmaceutical and other health care companies typically still perform relatively well in an economic downturn.

7% gain & positive 75% of the time

The health care sector has on average been one of the top performing sectors in the month of May. Although the returns tend to be lower in June and July, there is value investing in the health care sector at this time. The sector does take a pause in early August, when the stock market tends to perform poorly.

The period from August 12 to October 24 tends to be positive for the health care sector as investor interest increases ahead of the many health care conferences that take place in autumn.

2021/22 Performance Update.
In 2021, the health care sector underperformed the S&P 500 for the year, but outperformed in its strong seasonal period from early May to early August, and then underperformed in its next strong seasonal period from mid-August to early October.

*Health Care SP GIC Sector# 35: An index designed to represent a cross section of health care companies. For more information see www.standardandpoors.com.

Health Care* vs. S&P 500 1990 to 2021
Negative Short ☐   Positive Long ▨

Year	May 1 to Aug 2		Aug 3 to Aug 11		Aug 12 to Oct 24		Compound Growth	
	S&P 500	Health Care	S&P 500	Health Care	S&P 500	Health Care	S&P 500	Health Care
1990	6.3 %	18.4 %	-4.5 %	-4.5 %	-6.8 %	2.8 %	-5.5 %	27.2 %
1991	3.2	7.9	0.0	-0.1	-0.5	1.8	2.6	9.9
1992	2.2	1.0	-1.3	-0.2	-1.2	-9.6	-0.2	-8.5
1993	2.3	-9.3	0.1	-4.2	2.8	12.2	5.2	6.0
1994	2.1	5.5	-0.4	3.6	0.4	7.4	2.2	9.2
1995	8.6	10.5	-0.7	-0.9	5.7	15.3	14.0	28.5
1996	1.3	4.7	-0.1	0.8	6.1	8.7	7.4	12.9
1997	18.2	16.3	-1.1	-3.9	0.5	6.1	17.5	28.0
1998	0.8	5.3	-4.6	-4.2	0.2	4.6	-3.7	14.8
1999	-0.5	-3.7	-2.0	-5.8	0.0	10.2	-2.5	12.2
2000	-1.0	13.0	2.3	-4.2	-5.0	7.1	-3.7	26.1
2001	-2.3	-0.1	-2.5	0.3	-8.8	0.9	-13.2	0.4
2002	-19.8	-16.1	5.1	4.8	-2.9	-1.1	-18.1	-20.9
2003	6.9	2.8	0.0	0.4	4.9	-2.3	12.2	0.0
2004	-0.1	-6.1	-2.8	-1.1	1.9	-5.5	-1.1	-10.3
2005	7.5	3.7	-0.5	-0.4	-3.1	-4.6	3.7	-0.7
2006	-2.5	3.8	-0.9	-1.8	8.7	7.3	5.1	13.2
2007	-0.7	-5.2	-1.3	-0.6	4.3	4.2	2.3	-0.6
2008	-9.0	0.7	3.6	5.2	-32.8	-23.4	-36.7	-26.9
2009	13.1	15.5	0.7	-0.5	8.6	3.4	23.7	20.0
2010	-5.1	-5.8	-3.2	-0.2	8.6	7.6	-0.3	1.6
2011	-8.0	-7.0	-6.5	-4.4	7.0	7.1	-8.0	4.0
2012	-2.4	1.4	3.0	1.8	0.2	3.7	0.8	3.3
2013	7.0	8.4	-1.1	-0.9	3.6	3.5	9.7	13.2
2014	2.2	4.6	0.6	-0.6	1.4	7.8	4.3	13.4
2015	0.9	6.7	-0.9	-1.7	-0.4	-8.0	-0.5	-0.1
2016	4.4	8.1	1.3	-0.6	-1.6	-7.1	4.2	1.0
2017	3.9	5.4	-1.5	-1.2	5.2	5.9	7.8	12.9
2018	6.8	8.5	0.2	0.4	-6.3	-2.5	0.3	5.3
2019	-0.4	1.9	-0.5	0.4	3.1	0.6	2.2	2.0
2020	12.3	5.7	1.9	-0.1	4.0	2.4	19.0	8.4
2021	4.9	9.1	1.4	-0.3	2.2	-0.1	8.7	9.3
Avg.	2.0 %	3.6 %	-0.5 %	-0.8 %	0.3 %	2.1 %	1.8 %	6.7 %
Fq>0	63 %	75 %	38	28 %	63 %	69 %	63 %	75 %

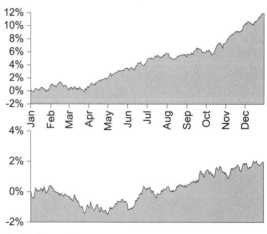

Health Care Sector - Avg. Year 1990 to 2021

Health Care / S&P 500 Rel. Strength- Avg Yr. 1990-2021

Health Care Performance

Health Care Monthly % Gain (1990-2021)

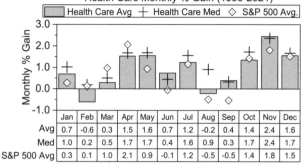

Legend: Health Care Avg + Health Care Med ◇ S&P 500 Avg.

	Jan	Feb	Mar	Apr	May	Jun	Jul	Aug	Sep	Oct	Nov	Dec
Avg	0.7	-0.6	0.3	1.5	1.6	0.7	1.2	-0.2	0.4	1.4	2.4	1.6
Med	1.0	0.2	0.5	1.7	1.7	0.4	1.6	0.9	0.3	1.7	2.4	1.7
S&P 500 Avg	0.3	0.1	1.0	2.1	0.9	-0.1	1.2	-0.5	-0.5	1.4	1.8	1.5

Fq % Health Care Gain > 0% (1990-2021)

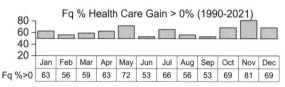

	Jan	Feb	Mar	Apr	May	Jun	Jul	Aug	Sep	Oct	Nov	Dec
Fq %>0	63	56	59	63	72	53	66	56	53	69	81	69

Fq % Health Care Gain > S&P 500 % (1990-2021)

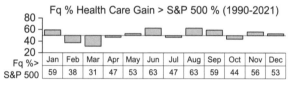

	Jan	Feb	Mar	Apr	May	Jun	Jul	Aug	Sep	Oct	Nov	Dec
Fq %> S&P 500	59	38	31	47	53	63	47	63	59	44	56	53

Health Care % Gain 5 Year (2017-2021)

Legend: Hi/Lo — Avg. ■ Med. ◇ S&P 500 Avg.

Health Care Performance 2021-2022

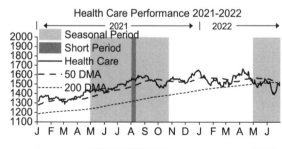

Legend: Seasonal Period, Short Period, Health Care, 50 DMA, 200 DMA

Relative Strength, % Gain vs. S&P 500

WEEK 35

Market Indices & Rates
Weekly Values**

Stock Markets	2020	2021
Dow	28,654	35,369
S&P500	3,508	4,535
Nasdaq	11,696	15,364
TSX	16,706	20,821
FTSE	5,964	7,138
DAX	13,033	15,781
Nikkei	22,883	29,128
Hang Seng	25,422	25,902

Commodities	2020	2021
Oil	42.97	69.29
Gold	1957.4	1823.7

Bond Yields	2020	2021
USA 5 Yr Treasury	0.28	0.78
USA 10 Yr T	0.74	1.33
USA 20 Yr T	1.29	1.87
Moody's Aaa	2.40	2.54
Moody's Baa	3.45	3.24
CAN 5 Yr T	0.40	0.79
CAN 10 Yr T	0.63	1.19

Money Market	2020	2021
USA Fed Funds	0.25	0.25
USA 3 Mo T-B	0.10	0.05
CAN tgt overnight rate	0.25	0.25
CAN 3 Mo T-B	0.15	0.15

Foreign Exchange	2020	2021
EUR/USD	1.19	1.19
GBP/USD	1.34	1.39
USD/CAD	1.31	1.25
USD/JPY	105.37	109.71

AUGUST

M	T	W	T	F	S	S
	1	2	3	4	5	6
7	8	9	10	11	12	13
14	15	16	17	18	19	20
21	22	23	24	25	26	27
28	29	30	31			

SEPTEMBER

M	T	W	T	F	S	S
					1	2	3
4	5	6	7	8	9	10
12	12	13	14	15	16	17
20	20	20	21	22	23	24
26	26	27	28	29	30	

OCTOBER

M	T	W	T	F	S	S
						1
2	3	4	5	6	7	8
9	10	11	12	13	14	15
16	17	18	19	20	21	22
23	24	25	26	27	28	29
30	31					

SEPTEMBER

	MONDAY	TUESDAY	WEDNESDAY
WEEK 35	28	29	30
WEEK 36	**4** 26 USA Market Closed- Labor Day CAN Market Closed- Labor Day	**5** 25	**6** 24
WEEK 37	**11** 19	**12** 18	**13** 17
WEEK 38	**18** 12	**19** 11	**20** 10
WEEK 39	**25** 5	**26** 4	**27** 3

THURSDAY	FRIDAY
31 29	**1** 29
7 23	**8** 22
14 16	**15** 15
21 9	**22** 8
28 2	**29** 1

OCTOBER

M	T	W	T	F	S	S
						1
2	3	4	5	6	7	8
9	10	11	12	13	14	15
16	17	18	19	20	21	22
23	24	25	26	27	28	29
30	31					

NOVEMBER

M	T	W	T	F	S	S
		1	2	3	4	5
6	7	8	9	10	11	12
13	14	15	16	17	18	19
20	21	22	23	24	25	26
27	28	29	30			

DECEMBER

M	T	W	T	F	S	S
				1	2	3
4	5	6	7	8	9	10
11	12	13	14	15	16	17
18	19	20	21	22	23	24
25	26	27	28	29	30	31

JANUARY

M	T	W	T	F	S	S
1	2	3	4	5	6	7
8	9	10	11	12	13	14
15	16	17	18	19	20	21
22	23	24	25	26	27	28
29	30	31				

SEPTEMBER
S U M M A R Y

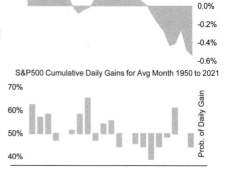

	Dow Jones	S&P 500	Nasdaq	TSX Comp
Month Rank	12	12	12	12
# Up	29	32	26	15
# Down	43	40	24	22
% Pos	40	44	52	41
% Avg. Gain	-0.8	-0.5	-0.7	-1.4

Dow & S&P 1950-2021, Nasdaq 1972-2021, TSX 1985-2021

S&P500 Cumulative Daily Gains for Avg Month 1950 to 2021

◆ September has the reputation of being the worst month of the year for the S&P 500. From 1950 to 2021, September has produced an average loss of 0.5% and has only been positive 44% of the time. ◆ In particular, the last part of September tends to be negative. ◆ The defensive sectors are typically the favored sectors in September as investors seek more stable earnings in a month that is often volatile ◆ The materials sector on average performs poorly in September and has outperformed the S&P 500 only 28% of the time from 1990 to 2021.

BEST / WORST SEPTEMBER BROAD MKTS. 2012-2021

BEST SEPTEMBER MARKETS
◆ Nikkei 225 (2013) 8.0%
◆ Russell 2000 (2013) 6.2%
◆ Russell 2000 (2017) 6.1%

WORST SEPTEMBER MARKETS
◆ Nikkei 225 (2015) -8.0%
◆ Russell 2000 (2014) -6.2%
◆ Nasdaq (2021) -5.3%

Index Values End of Month

	2012	2013	2014	2015	2016	2017	2018	2019	2020	2021
Dow	13,437	15,130	17,043	16,285	18,308	22,405	26,458	26,917	27,782	33,844
S&P 500	1,441	1,682	1,972	1,920	2,168	2,519	2,914	2,977	3,363	4,308
Nasdaq	3,116	3,771	4,493	4,620	5,312	6,496	8,046	7,999	11,168	14,449
TSX Comp.	12,317	12,787	14,961	13,307	14,726	15,635	16,073	16,659	16,121	20,070
Russell 1000	794	940	1,096	1,068	1,202	1,397	1,615	1,644	1,873	2,418
Russell 2000	837	1,074	1,102	1,101	1,252	1,491	1,697	1,523	1,508	2,204
FTSE 100	5,742	6,462	6,623	6,062	6,899	7,373	7,510	7,408	5,866	7,086
Nikkei 225	8,870	14,456	16,174	17,388	16,450	20,356	24,120	21,756	23,185	29,453

Percent Gain for September

	2012	2013	2014	2015	2016	2017	2018	2019	2020	2021
Dow	2.6	2.2	-0.3	-1.5	-0.5	2.1	1.9	1.9	-2.3	-4.3
S&P 500	2.4	3.0	-1.6	-2.6	-0.1	1.9	0.4	1.7	-3.9	-4.8
Nasdaq	1.6	5.1	-1.9	-3.3	1.9	1.0	-0.8	0.5	-5.2	-5.3
TSX Comp.	3.1	1.1	-4.3	-4.0	0.9	2.8	-1.2	1.3	-2.4	-2.5
Russell 1000	2.4	3.3	-1.9	-2.9	-0.1	2.0	0.2	1.6	-3.8	-4.7
Russell 2000	3.1	6.2	-6.2	-5.1	0.9	6.1	-2.5	1.9	-3.5	-3.1
FTSE 100	0.5	0.8	-2.9	-3.0	1.7	-0.8	1.0	2.8	-1.6	-0.5
Nikkei 225	0.3	8.0	4.9	-8.0	-2.6	3.6	5.5	5.1	0.2	4.9

September Market Avg. Performance 2012 to 2021[1]

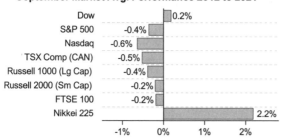

Dow	0.2%
S&P 500	-0.4%
Nasdaq	-0.6%
TSX Comp (CAN)	-0.5%
Russell 1000 (Lg Cap)	-0.4%
Russell 2000 (Sm Cap)	-0.2%
FTSE 100	-0.2%
Nikkei 225	2.2%

Interest Corner Sep[2]

	Fed Funds %[3]	3 Mo. T-Bill %[4]	10 Yr %[5]	20 Yr %[6]
2021	0.25	0.09	1.52	2.02
2020	0.25	0.10	0.69	1.23
2019	2.00	1.88	1.68	1.94
2018	2.25	2.19	3.05	3.13
2017	1.25	1.06	2.33	2.63

(1) Russell Data provided by Russell (2) Federal Reserve Bank of St. Louis- end of month values (3) Target rate set by FOMC (4)(5)(6) Constant yield maturities.

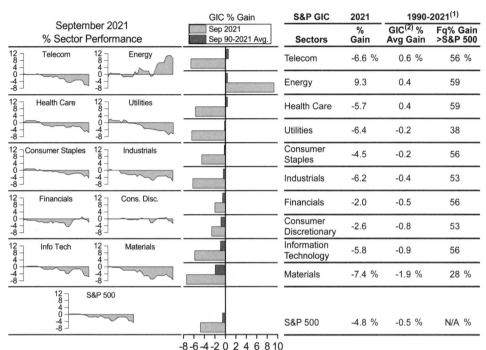

| S&P GIC | 2021 | 1990-2021[1] | |
Sectors	% Gain	GIC[2] % Avg Gain	Fq% Gain >S&P 500
Telecom	-6.6 %	0.6 %	56 %
Energy	9.3	0.4	59
Health Care	-5.7	0.4	59
Utilities	-6.4	-0.2	38
Consumer Staples	-4.5	-0.2	56
Industrials	-6.2	-0.4	53
Financials	-2.0	-0.5	56
Consumer Discretionary	-2.6	-0.8	53
Information Technology	-5.8	-0.9	56
Materials	-7.4 %	-1.9 %	28 %
S&P 500	-4.8 %	-0.5 %	N/A %

Sector Commentary

♦ In September 2021, the S&P 500 corrected sharply, with a loss of 4.8%. ♦ All of the major sectors of the stock market were negative, except the energy sector, which produced a gain of 9.3%. The energy sector's strong performance was in large part the result of the realization that oil was in short supply. ♦ Typically, the materials sector is the worst performing sector of the market in August. In 2021, the materials sector followed its seasonal trend and was the worst performing sector of the market.

Sub-Sector Commentary

♦ September is typically the month when precious metals tend to perform well. ♦ In September 2021, both gold and silver performed poorly. ♦ The top performing sub-sector from the list of selected sub-sectors was the auto sub-sector, which had no change in value in August. ♦ The steel sub-sector typically performs poorly in September and in 2021 steel followed its seasonal trend with a loss of 16.2%.

SELECTED SUB-SECTORS[3]			
Gold	-4.0 %	1.6 %	63 %
Biotech (1993-2021)	-7.4	0.9	57
Pharma	-6.7	0.5	56
Agriculture (1994-2021)	0.0	0.2	57
Railroads	-8.0	-0.2	47
Transportation	-6.6	-0.4	56
Retail	-4.1	-0.7	50
Silver	-10.5	-0.7	52
Banks	2.3	-0.7	53
Home-builders	-11.8	-0.9	56
Chemicals	-6.6	-1.7	34
Auto	5.3	-1.7	44
SOX (1995-2021)	-4.7	-2.1	52
Metals & Mining	-10.6	-2.1	41
Steel	-16.2	-3.4	47

(1) Sector data provided by Standard and Poors (2) GIC is short form for Global Industry Classification (3) Sub Sector data provided by Standard and Poors, except where marked by symbol.

EMA EMERA
September 13 to October 27

Emera is a Canadian highly regulated utility and is considered a defensive stock with a lower beta than the overall Canadian stock market.

It can be considered a transition stock as it tends to perform well in the shoulder season for the stock market. Emera tends to perform well, as the stock market moves from its weak six month period (early May to late October) to its strong seasonal period (late October to early May).

From September 13 to October 27, in the period from 1996 to 2021, Emera has produced an average gain of 3.8% and has been positive 69% of the time. Emera has also outperformed the S&P/TSX Composite Index 73% of the time.

73% of the time better than the S&P/TSX Composite Index

On average, Emera has also performed well in November and December, outperforming the stock market in both months. Despite having a stronger average gain than the stock market in November, Emera has only outperformed the stock market slightly over one-third of the time.

EMA vs. TSX Comp. 1996 to 2021			
Sep 13 to Oct 27	TSX Comp	Positive EMA	Diff
1996	6.9 %	11.3 %	4.4 %
1997	-2.5	5.6	8.1
1998	1.8	13.9	12.1
1999	-2.1	-1.9	0.3
2000	-11.7	-1.6	10.1
2001	-0.6	9.3	10.0
2002	-1.7	1.4	3.1
2003	1.1	1.6	0.5
2004	5.0	0.4	-4.6
2005	-5.9	6.5	12.4
2006	5.1	6.2	1.1
2007	3.9	1.9	-2.0
2008	-33.1	-10.4	22.8
2009	-1.8	9.7	11.5
2010	3.9	9.4	5.5
2011	2.6	9.0	6.4
2012	0.6	-0.2	-0.8
2013	5.5	8.4	2.9
2014	-6.8	11.0	17.8
2015	1.8	6.0	4.2
2016	1.6	-0.3	-2.0
2017	5.4	4.0	-1.4
2018	-7.2	-1.4	5.8
2019	-1.4	-2.7	-1.3
2020	-1.2	2.9	4.1
2021	1.6	-1.6	-3.2
Avg.	-1.1 %	3.8 %	4.9 %
Fq > 0	54 %	69 %	73 %

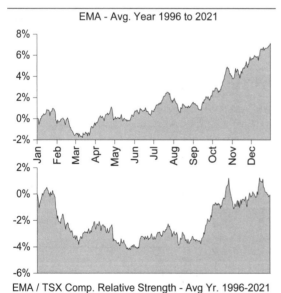

EMA - Avg. Year 1996 to 2021

EMA / TSX Comp. Relative Strength - Avg Yr. 1996-2021

2021/22 Performance Update.
In 2021, Emera slightly outperformed the S&P/TSX Composite Index for the entire year. In its strong seasonal period it was negative and underperformed the S&P/TSX Composite Index as interest rates were increasing at the time, putting downward pressure on utility stocks.

In the first six months of 2022, Emera was slightly negative, but managed to strongly outperform the S&P/TSX Composite Index. At the time, investors were moving away from growth stocks and investing in defensive companies, such as Emera.

Over the last five years, Emera has been positive in November and December and on average has outperformed the stock market.

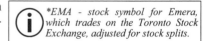

EMA - stock symbol for Emera, which trades on the Toronto Stock Exchange, adjusted for stock splits.

Emera Performance

EMA Monthly % Gain (1996-2021)

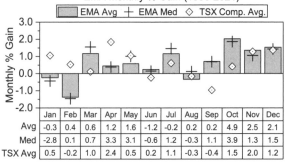

	Jan	Feb	Mar	Apr	May	Jun	Jul	Aug	Sep	Oct	Nov	Dec
Avg	-0.3	0.4	0.6	1.2	1.6	-1.2	-0.2	0.2	0.2	4.9	2.5	2.1
Med	-2.8	0.1	0.7	3.3	3.1	-0.6	1.2	-0.3	1.1	3.9	1.3	1.5
TSX Avg	0.5	-0.2	1.0	2.4	0.5	0.2	1.1	-0.3	-0.4	1.5	2.0	1.2

Fq % EMA Gain > 0% (1996-2021)

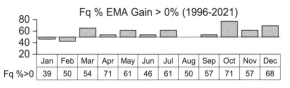

	Jan	Feb	Mar	Apr	May	Jun	Jul	Aug	Sep	Oct	Nov	Dec
Fq %>0	39	50	54	71	61	46	61	50	57	71	57	68

Fq % EMA Gain > TSX Comp. % (1996-2021)

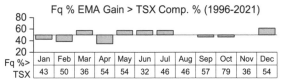

	Jan	Feb	Mar	Apr	May	Jun	Jul	Aug	Sep	Oct	Nov	Dec
Fq %> TSX	43	50	36	54	54	32	46	46	57	79	36	54

EMA % Gain 5 Year (2017-2021)

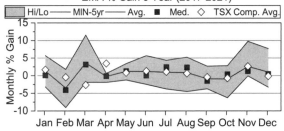

EMA Performance 2021-2022

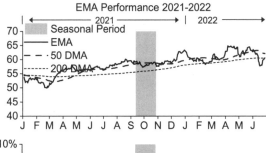

Relative Strength, % Gain vs. TSX Comp.

WEEK 36

Market Indices & Rates
Weekly Values**

Stock Markets	2020	2021
Dow	28,133	34,608
S&P500	3,427	4,459
Nasdaq	11,313	15,115
TSX	16,218	20,633
FTSE	5,799	7,029
DAX	12,843	15,610
Nikkei	23,205	30,382
Hang Seng	24,695	26,206

Commodities	2020	2021
Oil	39.77	69.72
Gold	1926.3	1794.6

Bond Yields	2020	2021
USA 5 Yr Treasury	0.30	0.82
USA 10 Yr T	0.72	1.35
USA 20 Yr T	1.25	1.86
Moody's Aaa	2.34	2.51
Moody's Baa	3.40	3.23
CAN 5 Yr T	0.39	0.83
CAN 10 Yr T	0.60	1.24

Money Market	2020	2021
USA Fed Funds	0.25	0.25
USA 3 Mo T-B	0.11	0.05
CAN tgt overnight rate	0.25	0.25
CAN 3 Mo T-B	0.15	0.14

Foreign Exchange	2020	2021
EUR/USD	1.18	1.18
GBP/USD	1.33	1.38
USD/CAD	1.31	1.27
USD/JPY	106.24	109.94

SEPTEMBER

M	T	W	T	F	S	S
				1	2	3
4	5	6	7	8	9	10
11	12	13	14	15	16	17
18	19	20	21	22	23	24
25	26	27	28	29	30	

OCTOBER

M	T	W	T	F	S	S
						1
2	3	4	5	6	7	8
9	10	11	12	13	14	15
16	17	18	19	20	21	22
23	24	25	26	27	28	29
30	31					

NOVEMBER

M	T	W	T	F	S	S
	1	2	3	4	5	
6	7	8	9	10	11	12
13	14	15	16	17	18	19
20	21	22	23	24	25	26
27	28	28	30			

LOCKHEED MARTIN
September 1 to September 30

Lockheed Martin has a few months when it tends to outperform the S&P 500, but if there were only one month to invest in Lockheed Martin vs the S&P 500, on a seasonal basis it is September.

April is also a strong month for Lockheed. From 1990 to 2021, the average gain is higher than in September, but its frequency of outperformance compared to the S&P 500 is lower than September.

69% of the time
better than the S&P 500

Lockheed is an aerospace company and by definition is part of the industrial sector. Most industrial companies start their strong seasonal period in late October. Although Lockheed is an industrial company, the nature of its business with government defense contracts tends to be less sensitive to economic conditions than the average industrial company.

LMT vs. S&P 500 1990 to 2021

Sep 1 to Sep 30	S&P 500	Positive LMT	Diff
1990	-5.1 %	2.0 %	7.1 %
1991	-1.9	-6.7	-4.8
1992	0.9	1.6	0.7
1993	-1.0	0.4	1.4
1994	-2.7	-11.6	-8.9
1995	4.0	10.3	6.3
1996	5.4	7.1	1.7
1997	5.3	2.8	-2.5
1998	6.2	15.1	8.9
1999	-2.9	-11.7	-8.8
2000	-5.3	16.1	21.4
2001	-8.2	9.8	17.9
2002	-11.0	2.1	13.1
2003	-1.2	-9.9	-8.7
2004	0.9	3.7	2.8
2005	0.7	-1.9	-2.6
2006	2.5	4.2	1.7
2007	3.6	9.4	5.9
2008	-9.1	-5.8	3.3
2009	3.6	4.1	0.6
2010	8.8	2.5	-6.2
2011	-7.2	-2.1	5.1
2012	2.4	2.5	0.0
2013	3.0	4.2	1.2
2014	-1.6	5.0	6.6
2015	-2.6	3.0	5.7
2016	-0.1	-1.3	-1.2
2017	1.9	1.6	-0.3
2018	0.4	8.0	7.5
2019	1.7	1.5	-0.2
2020	-3.9	-1.8	2.1
2021	-4.8	-4.1	0.7
Avg.	-0.5 %	1.9 %	2.4 %
Fq > 0	50 %	69 %	69 %

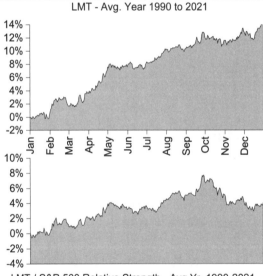

LMT - Avg. Year 1990 to 2021

LMT / S&P 500 Relative Strength - Avg Yr. 1990-2021

tends to perform poorly in October, leading up to its third quarter earnings report.

2021/22 Performance Update.
In 2021, Lockheed Martin underperformed the S&P 500, but managed to outperform in its strong seasonal period in September. In late 2021, Lockheed Martin started to ramp up its outperformance and in 2022 it benefited from the Russia-Ukraine war.

During the summer months investors generally take on less risk in their equity portfolios. As autumn approaches investors are looking to transition back to more of a risk portfolio. The process is not typically a binary event. For investors looking to increase their industrial sector exposure, Lockheed can provide a good stepping stone in the month of September, before investors shift to increased equity holdings in October. Investors should be careful as Lockheed

 LMT - stock symbol for Lockheed Martin, which trades on the NYSE, adjusted for stock splits.

Lockheed Martin Performance

LMT Monthly % Gain (1990-2021)

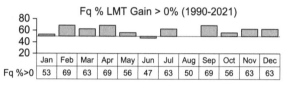

Legend: LMT Avg + LMT Med ◇ S&P 500 Avg.

	Jan	Feb	Mar	Apr	May	Jun	Jul	Aug	Sep	Oct	Nov	Dec
Avg	0.3	1.2	2.1	3.6	0.7	0.3	1.9	0.3	1.9	-1.5	1.4	1.5
Med	0.6	2.5	1.5	2.8	0.8	-0.5	2.2	0.0	2.3	0.4	0.8	0.9
S&P 500 Avg	0.3	0.1	1.0	2.1	0.9	-0.1	1.2	-0.5	-0.5	1.4	1.8	1.5

Fq % LMT Gain > 0% (1990-2021)

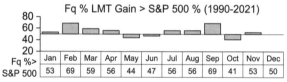

	Jan	Feb	Mar	Apr	May	Jun	Jul	Aug	Sep	Oct	Nov	Dec
Fq %>0	53	69	63	69	56	47	63	50	69	56	63	63

Fq % LMT Gain > S&P 500 % (1990-2021)

	Jan	Feb	Mar	Apr	May	Jun	Jul	Aug	Sep	Oct	Nov	Dec
Fq %> S&P 500	53	69	59	56	44	47	56	56	69	41	53	50

LMT % Gain 5 Year (2017-2021)

Legend: Hi/Lo — Avg. ■ Med. ◇ S&P 500 Avg.

LMT Performance 2021-2022

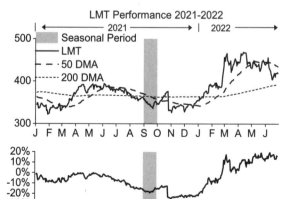

Legend: Seasonal Period, LMT, 50 DMA, 200 DMA

Relative Strength, % Gain vs. S&P 500

Market Indices & Rates
Weekly Values**

Stock Markets	2020	2021
Dow	27,666	34,585
S&P500	3,341	4,433
Nasdaq	10,854	15,044
TSX	16,222	20,490
FTSE	6,032	6,964
DAX	13,203	15,490
Nikkei	23,406	30,500
Hang Seng	24,503	24,921

Commodities	2020	2021
Oil	37.33	71.97
Gold	1947.4	1756.0

Bond Yields	2020	2021
USA 5 Yr Treasury	0.26	0.88
USA 10 Yr T	0.67	1.37
USA 20 Yr T	1.21	1.85
Moody's Aaa	2.32	2.48
Moody's Baa	3.36	3.20
CAN 5 Yr T	0.36	0.90
CAN 10 Yr T	0.55	1.28

Money Market	2020	2021
USA Fed Funds	0.25	0.25
USA 3 Mo T-B	0.11	0.04
CAN tgt overnight rate	0.25	0.25
CAN 3 Mo T-B	0.15	0.12

Foreign Exchange	2020	2021
EUR/USD	1.18	1.17
GBP/USD	1.28	1.37
USD/CAD	1.32	1.28
USD/JPY	106.16	109.93

SEPTEMBER

M	T	W	T	F	S	S
			1	2	3	
4	5	6	7	8	9	10
11	12	13	14	15	16	17
18	19	20	21	22	23	24
25	26	27	28	29	30	

OCTOBER

M	T	W	T	F	S	S
						1
2	3	4	5	6	7	8
9	10	11	12	13	14	15
16	17	18	19	20	21	22
23	24	25	26	27	28	29
30	31					

NOVEMBER

M	T	W	T	F	S	S
	1	2	3	4	5	
6	7	8	9	10	11	12
13	14	15	16	17	18	19
20	21	22	23	24	25	26
27	28	28	30			

INFORMATION TECHNOLOGY
①LONG (Oct9-Dec5) ②LONG (Dec15-Jan17)
③LONG (Apr16-Jun15) ④LONG (Jun28-Jul17)

Over the long-term, since 1990, the technology sector has performed better at certain times of the year compared to other sectors.

The technology sector performs well from October 9 to December 5 and then from December 15 to January 17. The interim period in between these two periods tends to be negative.

20% gain

The technology sector also tends to perform well from April 16 to June 5 and then from June 28 to Jul 17. The interim period in between these two periods tends to be negative.

If the technology sector has strong momentum in the first leg of its seasonal period from either October 9 to December 5, or from April 16 to June 5, it is possible to hold a position in the technology sector during the interim period that starts either December 15 or June 28.

Info Tech vs. S&P 500 1990 to 2021   Positive Long

Year	Oct 9 to Dec 5 S&P 500	Info Tech	Dec 15 to Jan 17 S&P 500	Info Tech	Apr 16 to Jun 5 S&P 500	Info Tech	Jun 28 to Jul 17 S&P 500	Info Tech	Compound Growth S&P 500	Info Tech
1989/90	-2.6 %	-5.7 %	-3.9 %	3.8 %	6.5 %	10.8 %	3.5 %	2.8 %	3.2 %	11.5 %
1990/91	5.2	11.2	0.4	5.5	1.0	-1.8	1.8	1.0	8.6	16.2
1991/92	-0.9	-1.4	8.9	17.6	-0.7	-3.6	3.0	2.6	10.5	14.7
1992/93	6.0	6.8	1.0	7.4	0.4	9.5	-0.4	-7.0	7.0	16.8
1993/94	1.0	6.9	2.2	8.8	3.1	6.9	1.5	-0.3	8.1	23.9
1994/95	-0.4	8.5	3.3	9.6	5.2	11.9	3.7	14.1	12.3	51.8
1995/96	6.0	3.2	-1.7	-8.0	5.6	11.6	-5.2	-7.2	4.4	-1.6
1996/97	6.2	14.4	6.5	7.3	11.8	16.6	5.0	17.5	32.8	68.2
1997/98	1.0	-8.1	0.9	4.0	-0.5	-0.8	4.7	10.3	6.2	4.6
1998/99	22.6	46.8	8.9	18.7	0.4	1.6	7.9	15.8	44.7	105.0
1999/00	7.3	18.7	4.4	9.7	8.2	13.4	4.1	8.1	26.2	59.8
2001/01	-2.3	-12.8	-0.9	-3.3	8.5	9.7	0.3	-0.4	5.3	-7.9
2001/02	10.2	31.9	1.4	2.3	-4.8	-7.4	-8.5	-0.4	-2.7	24.4
2002/03	13.5	37.2	1.4	-0.6	11.2	16.7	0.6	4.0	28.7	65.6
2003/04	2.7	2.3	6.1	11.1	-0.6	-1.2	-2.9	-8.7	5.2	2.5
2004/05	6.2	11.7	-1.6	-4.1	4.7	10.4	3.1	6.5	12.8	26.0
2005/06	5.5	8.4	0.8	1.5	-1.8	-8.9	-0.4	-3.9	4.0	-3.7
2006/07	4.8	6.5	0.4	0.8	5.4	7.0	2.9	5.2	14.0	20.9
2007/08	-4.4	-2.6	-9.2	-12.7	5.2	13.5	-1.4	-0.9	-9.9	-4.3
2008/09	-11.1	-14.2	-3.4	-1.9	10.3	13.0	2.3	5.7	-3.0	0.6
2009/10	3.8	6.3	2.0	2.7	-12.1	-11.7	-1.1	-0.3	-8.0	-3.9
2010/11	5.1	7.0	4.2	4.9	-1.5	-0.9	2.8	5.0	10.9	16.8
2011/12	8.8	7.6	6.8	4.9	-6.2	-9.3	2.4	0.0	11.6	2.3
2012/13	-3.2	-6.4	4.8	4.0	3.6	6.6	4.2	4.8	9.5	8.8
2013/14	7.8	10.2	3.6	5.5	5.3	6.8	-0.1	1.6	17.4	26.1
2014/15	5.4	6.8	0.9	-0.7	-0.7	1.8	1.2	3.1	6.9	11.4
2015/16	3.9	8.2	-7.0	-9.4	0.9	-1.4	8.1	9.1	5.3	5.5
2016/17	2.4	-1.5	0.6	1.5	4.6	10.3	1.6	3.7	9.5	14.4
2017/18	3.1	4.6	5.7	6.3	3.5	9.1	4.1	6.3	17.4	29.0
2018/19	-6.4	-8.5	1.4	0.0	-2.7	-3.9	2.0	3.0	-5.8	-9.5
2019/20	7.8	10.0	5.1	8.9	14.8	16.4	7.2	5.2	39.2	46.6
2020/21	7.3	6.3	3.3	2.3	1.4	-2.5	1.1	4.5	13.7	10.8
Avg.	3.8 %	6.9 %	1.8 %	3.4 %	2.8 %	4.7 %	1.8 %	3.5 %	10.8 %	20.4 %
Fq>0	75 %	72 %	78 %	75 %	69 %	63 %	75 %	69 %	84 %	81 %

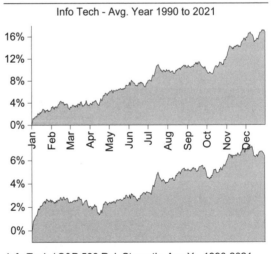

Info Tech - Avg. Year 1990 to 2021

Info Tech / S&P 500 Rel. Strength- Avg Yr. 1990-2021

Information Technology Performance

Information Technology Monthly % Gain (1990-2021)

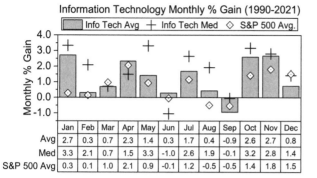

Legend: Info Tech Avg | + Info Tech Med | ◇ S&P 500 Avg.

	Jan	Feb	Mar	Apr	May	Jun	Jul	Aug	Sep	Oct	Nov	Dec
Avg	2.7	0.3	0.7	2.3	1.4	0.3	1.7	0.4	-0.9	2.6	2.7	0.8
Med	3.3	2.1	0.7	1.5	3.3	-1.0	2.6	1.9	-0.1	3.2	2.8	1.4
S&P 500 Avg	0.3	0.1	1.0	2.1	0.9	-0.1	1.2	-0.5	-0.5	1.4	1.8	1.5

Fq % Information Technology Gain > 0% (1990-2021)

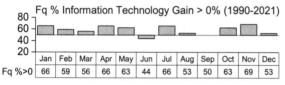

	Jan	Feb	Mar	Apr	May	Jun	Jul	Aug	Sep	Oct	Nov	Dec
Fq %>0	66	59	56	66	63	44	66	53	50	63	69	53

Fq % Information Technology Gain > S&P 500 % (1990-2021)

	Jan	Feb	Mar	Apr	May	Jun	Jul	Aug	Sep	Oct	Nov	Dec
Fq %> S&P 500	75	56	44	50	59	41	56	63	56	56	63	38

Information Technology % Gain 5 Year (2017-2021)

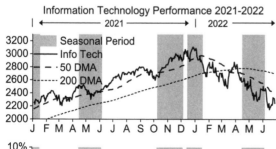

Legend: Hi/Lo — Avg. ■ Med. ◇ S&P 500 Avg.

Information Technology Performance 2021-2022

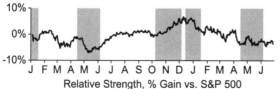

Seasonal Period — Info Tech — · 50 DMA ···· 200 DMA

Relative Strength, % Gain vs. S&P 500

Market Indices & Rates
Weekly Values

Stock Markets	2020	2021
Dow	27,657	34,798
S&P500	3,319	4,455
Nasdaq	10,793	15,048
TSX	16,199	20,403
FTSE	6,007	7,051
DAX	13,116	15,532
Nikkei	23,360	30,249
Hang Seng	24,455	24,192

Commodities	2020	2021
Oil	41.11	74.13
Gold	1950.9	1746.8

Bond Yields	2020	2021
USA 5 Yr Treasury	0.29	0.97
USA 10 Yr T	0.70	1.47
USA 20 Yr T	1.24	1.94
Moody's Aaa	2.30	2.59
Moody's Baa	3.36	3.27
CAN 5 Yr T	0.37	1.03
CAN 10 Yr T	0.58	1.38

Money Market	2020	2021
USA Fed Funds	0.25	0.25
USA 3 Mo T-B	0.10	0.03
CAN tgt overnight rate	0.25	0.25
CAN 3 Mo T-B	0.15	0.12

Foreign Exchange	2020	2021
EUR/USD	1.18	1.17
GBP/USD	1.29	1.37
USD/CAD	1.32	1.27
USD/JPY	104.57	110.73

SEPTEMBER

M	T	W	T	F	S	S
				1	2	3
4	5	6	7	8	9	10
11	12	13	14	15	16	17
18	19	20	21	22	23	24
25	26	27	28	29	30	

OCTOBER

M	T	W	T	F	S	S
						1
2	3	4	5	6	7	8
9	10	11	12	13	14	15
16	17	18	19	20	21	22
23	24	25	26	27	28	29
30	31					

NOVEMBER

M	T	W	T	F	S	S
		1	2	3	4	5
6	7	8	9	10	11	12
13	14	15	16	17	18	19
20	21	22	23	24	25	26
27	28	28	30			

The Canadian bank sector, has a strong seasonal period from October 10 to December 31 and then from January 23 to April 13.

Canadian banks have their year-end on October 31st. Why does this matter? In the past Canadian banks have announced most of their dividend increases and stock splits when they announce their typically optimistic full year fiscal reports at the end of November and beginning of December. Investors tend to push up bank stocks ahead of their earnings announcement. Canadian banks also tend to perform well early in the year as economic reports at this time tend to be favorable.

In the following table, Canadian bank returns in December have been separated out from their autumn seasonal period to show the impact of bank earnings on returns. In December, Canadian banks have provided gains 73% of the time, but they have underperformed the TSX Composite. If Canadian banks have performed well leading into their earnings, they often pause in December.

2021/22 Performance Update.

In 2021, Canadian banks outperformed the S&P/TSX Composite and then at the start of 2022, the Canadian banks outperformed in January.

(i) * Banks SP GIC Canadian Bank Sector Level 2 Represents a cross section of Canadian banking companies.

Canadian Banks* vs. S&P 500 1989/90 to 2021/22

Positive [ ] | 1989 to 2021

Year	Oct 10 to Dec 31 TSX-Comp	Oct 10 to Dec 31 Cdn. Banks	Jan 23 to Apr 13 TSX-Comp	Jan 23 to Apr 13 Cdn. Banks	Compound Growth TSX-Comp	Compound Growth Cdn. Banks	Dec 1 Dec 31 TSX-Comp	Dec 1 Dec 31 Cdn. Banks
89/90	-1.7 %	-1.8 %	-6.3 %	-9.1 %	-7.9	-10.8 %	0.7 %	-1.4 %
90/91	3.7	8.9	9.8	14.6	13.9	24.8	3.4	5.5
91/92	5.2	10.2	-6.8	-11.6	-2.0	-2.6	1.9	4.6
92/93	4.1	2.5	10.7	14.4	15.2	17.3	2.1	1.8
93/94	6.3	6.8	-5.6	-13.3	0.3	-7.4	3.4	5.1
94/95	-1.8	3.4	5.0	10.0	3.1	13.8	2.9	0.9
95/96	4.9	3.5	3.6	-3.2	8.6	0.1	1.1	1.5
96/97	9.0	15.1	-6.2	0.7	2.3	15.9	-1.5	-1.9
97/98	-6.1	7.6	19.9	38.8	12.6	49.4	2.9	4.2
98/99	18.3	28.0	4.8	13.0	24.0	44.6	2.2	3.0
99/00	18.2	5.1	3.8	22.1	22.8	28.3	11.8	0.7
00/01	-14.4	1.7	-14.1	-6.7	-26.4	-5.1	1.3	9.6
01/02	11.9	6.5	2.3	8.2	14.5	15.1	3.5	3.4
02/03	16.1	21.3	-4.3	2.6	11.1	24.4	0.7	2.6
03/04	8.1	5.1	2.0	2.1	10.3	7.4	4.6	2.0
04/05	4.9	6.2	4.5	6.9	9.6	13.5	2.4	4.7
05/06	6.2	8.4	5.5	2.7	12.1	11.3	4.1	2.1
06/07	10.4	8.4	6.9	3.2	18.0	11.8	1.2	3.7
07/08	-3.0	-10.4	8.2	-3.5	5.0	-13.5	1.1	-7.7
08/09	-6.4	-14.8	9.4	24.4	2.4	6.1	-3.1	-11.2
09/10	2.7	2.4	6.7	15.2	9.6	18.0	2.6	0.1
10/11	7.2	-0.2	4.3	9.1	11.9	8.9	3.8	-0.5
11/12	3.2	3.1	-2.9	1.1	0.2	4.2	-2.0	2.7
12/13	1.3	4.4	-3.8	-2.0	-2.5	2.3	1.6	1.5
13/14	7.0	9.0	1.9	1.6	9.1	10.7	1.7	0.9
14/15	1.2	-0.9	4.2	4.4	5.4	3.5	-0.8	-4.3
15/16	-6.8	-1.5	10.4	11.0	2.8	9.4	-3.4	-3.6
16/17	5.0	11.8	-0.1	-1.5	4.9	10.2	1.4	4.3
17/18	3.1	4.4	-6.6	-8.8	-3.7	-4.8	0.9	1.1
18/19	-9.7	-11.1	8.2	2.5	-2.3	-8.8	-5.8	-6.8
19/20	4.2	0.0	-20.0	-22.8	-16.7	-22.9	0.1	-4.0
20/21	5.3	13.3	7.6	12.1	13.3	27.1	1.4	2.3
21/22	4.0	7.0	5.9	-5.6	10.1	1.0	2.7	6.1
Avg.	3.7 %	5.0 %	2.1 %	4.0 %	5.8 %	9.2 %	1.5 %	1.0 %
Fq>0	76 %	76 %	67 %	67 %	79 %	76 %	82 %	73 %

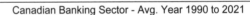

Canadian Banking Sector - Avg. Year 1990 to 2021

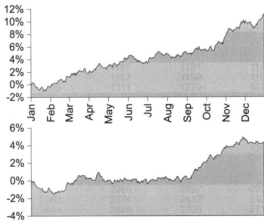

Cdn. Banking / TSX Comp Rel. Strength- Avg Yr. 1990-2021

Canadian Banks Performance

CDN Banks Monthly % Gain (1990-2021)

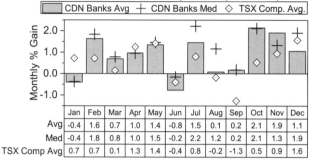

Legend: CDN Banks Avg | + CDN Banks Med | ◇ TSX Comp. Avg.

	Jan	Feb	Mar	Apr	May	Jun	Jul	Aug	Sep	Oct	Nov	Dec
Avg	-0.4	1.6	0.7	1.0	1.4	-0.8	1.5	0.1	0.2	2.1	1.9	1.1
Med	-0.4	1.8	0.8	1.0	1.5	-0.2	2.2	1.2	0.2	2.1	1.3	1.9
TSX Comp Avg	0.7	0.7	0.1	1.3	1.4	-0.4	0.8	-0.2	-1.3	0.5	0.9	1.6

Fq % CDN Banks Gain > 0% (1990-2021)

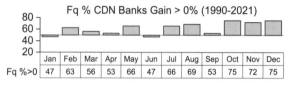

	Jan	Feb	Mar	Apr	May	Jun	Jul	Aug	Sep	Oct	Nov	Dec
Fq %>0	47	63	56	53	66	47	66	69	53	75	72	75

Fq % CDN Banks Gain > S&P 500 % (1990-2021)

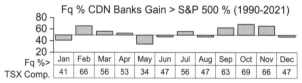

	Jan	Feb	Mar	Apr	May	Jun	Jul	Aug	Sep	Oct	Nov	Dec
Fq %> TSX Comp.	41	66	56	53	34	47	56	47	63	69	66	47

CDN Banks % Gain 5 Year (2017-2021)

Legend: Hi/Lo — Avg. ■ Med. ◇ S&P 500 Avg.

CDN Banks Performance 2021-2022

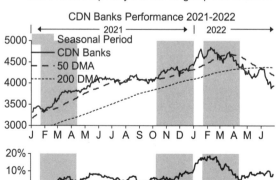

Seasonal Period — CDN Banks — 50 DMA -- 200 DMA

Relative Strength, % Gain vs. TSX Comp.

Market Indices & Rates
Weekly Values**

Stock Markets	2020	2021
Dow	27,174	34,326
S&P500	3,298	4,357
Nasdaq	10,914	14,567
TSX	16,065	20,151
FTSE	5,843	7,027
DAX	12,469	15,156
Nikkei	23,205	28,771
Hang Seng	23,235	24,576

Commodities	2020	2021
Oil	40.10	75.88
Gold	1859.7	1757.1

Bond Yields	2020	2021
USA 5 Yr Treasury	0.26	0.93
USA 10 Yr T	0.66	1.48
USA 20 Yr T	1.19	1.99
Moody's Aaa	2.31	2.65
Moody's Baa	3.40	3.33
CAN 5 Yr T	0.35	1.07
CAN 10 Yr T	0.54	1.47

Money Market	2020	2021
USA Fed Funds	0.25	0.25
USA 3 Mo T-B	0.10	0.04
CAN tgt overnight rate	0.25	0.25
CAN 3 Mo T-B	0.14	0.12

Foreign Exchange	2020	2021
EUR/USD	1.16	1.16
GBP/USD	1.27	1.35
USD/CAD	1.34	1.26
USD/JPY	105.58	111.05

SEPTEMBER

M	T	W	T	F	S	S
				1	2	3
4	5	6	7	8	9	10
11	12	13	14	15	16	17
18	19	20	21	22	23	24
25	26	27	28	29	30	

OCTOBER

M	T	W	T	F	S	S
						1
2	3	4	5	6	7	8
9	10	11	12	13	14	15
16	17	18	19	20	21	22
23	24	25	26	27	28	29
30	31					

NOVEMBER

M	T	W	T	F	S	S
	1	2	3	4	5
6	7	8	9	10	11	12
13	14	15	16	17	18	19
20	21	22	23	24	25	26
27	28	28	30			

OCTOBER

	MONDAY	TUESDAY	WEDNESDAY
WEEK 40	**2** 29	**3** 28	**4** 27
WEEK 41	**9** 22 USA Bond Market Closed-Columbus Day CAN Market Closed-Thanksgiving Day	**10** 21	**11** 20
WEEK 42	**16** 15	**17** 14	**18** 13
WEEK 43	**23** 8	**24** 7	**25** 6
WEEK 44	**30** 1	**31**	1

THURSDAY		FRIDAY	
5	26	**6**	25
12	19	**13**	18
19	12	**20**	11
26	5	**27**	4
2		3	

NOVEMBER

M	T	W	T	F	S	S
		1	2	3	4	5
6	7	8	9	10	11	12
13	14	15	16	17	18	19
20	21	22	23	24	25	26
27	28	29	30			

DECEMBER

M	T	W	T	F	S	S
				1	2	3
4	5	6	7	8	9	10
11	12	13	14	15	16	17
18	19	20	21	22	23	24
25	26	27	28	29	30	31

JANUARY

M	T	W	T	F	S	S
1	2	3	4	5	6	7
8	9	10	11	12	13	14
15	16	17	18	19	20	21
22	23	24	25	26	27	28
29	30	31				

FEBRUARY

M	T	W	T	F	S	S
			1	2	3	4
5	6	7	8	9	10	11
12	13	14	15	16	17	18
19	20	21	22	23	24	25
26	27	28				

OCTOBER
S U M M A R Y

S&P500 Cumulative Daily Gains for Avg Month 1950 to 2021

	Dow Jones	S&P 500	Nasdaq	TSX Comp
Month Rank	7	7	7	9
# Up	43	43	28	23
# Down	29	29	22	14
% Pos	59	60	56	62
% Avg. Gain	0.5	0.9	0.8	0.0

Dow & S&P 1950-2020, Nasdaq 1972-2021, TSX 1985-2021

♦ October, on average, is the most volatile month of the year for the stock market and often provides opportunities for short-term traders. The first half of October tends to be positive. ♦ The second half of the month, leading up to the last four days, tends to be negative, and prone to large drops. ♦ Seasonal opportunities in mid-October include Canadian banks, technology and transportation sectors. ♦ In late October, a lot of sectors start their seasonal period, including the materials, industrials, consumer discretionary and retail sectors.

BEST / WORST OCTOBER BROAD MKTS. 2012-2021

BEST OCTOBER MARKETS
- ♦ Nikkei 225 (2015) 9.7%
- ♦ Nasdaq (2015) 9.4%
- ♦ Dow (2015) 8.5%

WORST OCTOBER MARKETS
- ♦ Russell 2000 (2018) -10.9%
- ♦ Nasdaq (2018) -9.2%
- ♦ Nikkei 225 (2018) -9.1%

Index Values End of Month

	2012	2013	2014	2015	2016	2017	2018	2019	2020	2021
Dow	13,096	15,546	17,391	17,664	18,142	23,377	25,116	27,046	26,502	35,820
S&P 500	1,412	1,757	2,018	2,079	2,126	2,575	2,712	3,038	3,270	4,605
Nasdaq	2,977	3,920	4,631	5,054	5,189	6,728	7,306	8,292	10,912	15,498
TSX Comp.	12,423	13,361	14,613	13,529	14,787	16,026	15,027	16,483	15,581	21,037
Russell 1000	779	980	1,122	1,154	1,177	1,427	1,499	1,677	1,826	2,584
Russell 2000	819	1,100	1,174	1,162	1,191	1,503	1,511	1,562	1,538	2,297
FTSE 100	5,783	6,731	6,546	6,361	6,954	7,493	7,128	7,248	5,577	7,238
Nikkei 225	8,928	14,328	16,414	19,083	17,425	22,012	21,920	22,927	22,977	28,893

Percent Gain for October

	2012	2013	2014	2015	2016	2017	2018	2019	2020	2021
Dow	-2.5	2.8	2.0	8.5	-0.9	4.3	-5.1	0.5	-4.6	5.8
S&P 500	-2.0	4.5	2.3	8.3	-1.9	2.2	-6.9	2.0	-2.8	6.9
Nasdaq	-4.5	3.9	3.1	9.4	-2.3	3.6	-9.2	3.7	-2.3	7.3
TSX Comp.	0.9	4.5	-2.3	1.7	0.4	2.5	-6.5	-1.1	-3.4	4.8
Russell 1000	-1.8	4.3	2.3	8.0	-2.1	2.2	-7.2	2.0	-2.5	6.9
Russell 2000	-2.2	2.5	6.5	5.6	-4.8	0.8	-10.9	2.6	2.0	4.2
FTSE 100	0.7	4.2	-1.2	4.9	0.8	1.6	-5.1	-2.2	-4.9	2.1
Nikkei 225	0.7	-0.9	1.5	9.7	5.9	8.1	-9.1	5.4	-0.9	-1.9

October Market Avg. Performance 2012 to 2021[1]

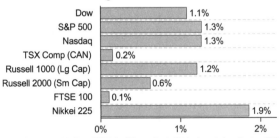

	Dow	1.1%
	S&P 500	1.3%
	Nasdaq	1.3%
	TSX Comp (CAN)	0.2%
	Russell 1000 (Lg Cap)	1.2%
	Russell 2000 (Sm Cap)	0.6%
	FTSE 100	0.1%
	Nikkei 225	1.9%

Interest Corner Oct[2]

	Fed Funds %[3]	3 Mo. T-Bill %[4]	10 Yr %[5]	20 Yr %[6]
2021	0.25	0.05	1.55	1.98
2020	0.25	0.09	0.88	1.43
2019	1.75	1.54	1.69	2.00
2018	2.25	2.34	3.15	3.30
2017	1.25	1.15	2.38	2.66

(1) Russell Data provided by Russell (2) Federal Reserve Bank of St. Louis- end of month values (3) Target rate set by FOMC (4)(5)(6) Constant yield maturities.

OCTOBER SECTOR PERFORMANCE

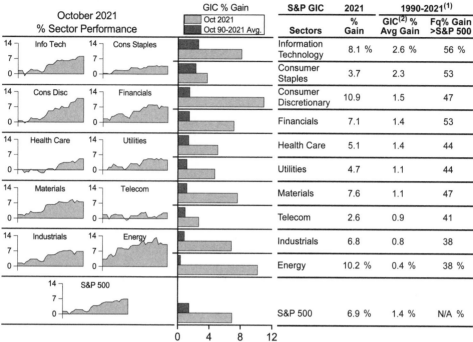

S&P GIC Sectors	2021 % Gain	1990-2021[1] GIC[2] % Avg Gain	Fq% Gain >S&P 500
Information Technology	8.1 %	2.6 %	56 %
Consumer Staples	3.7	2.3	53
Consumer Discretionary	10.9	1.5	47
Financials	7.1	1.4	53
Health Care	5.1	1.4	44
Utilities	4.7	1.1	44
Materials	7.6	1.1	47
Telecom	2.6	0.9	41
Industrials	6.8	0.8	38
Energy	10.2 %	0.4 %	38 %
S&P 500	6.9 %	1.4 %	N/A %

Sector Commentary

♦ At the beginning of October 2021, the S&P 500 put in a short-term bottom and then rallied for the remainder of the month. The S&P 500 produced a gain of 6.9% for the month. ♦ Energy is on average over the long-term, the weakest sector of the market in October. In 2021, the energy sector was the second best performing sector with a gain of 10.2%. ♦ The sectors with the weakest performance were generally the defensive sectors.

Sub-Sector Commentary

♦ In October 2021, the auto sub-sector produced a large gain of 36.4%. Generally, the cyclical sub-sectors produced strong gains. ♦ Silver produced a strong gain of 11.5%. In contrast, gold only managed to produce a gain of 1.5%. The performance of silver was largely the result industrial metals performing well. ♦ The biotech sub-sector, which finished its strong seasonal period in mid-September lost 1.4% in October.

SELECTED SUB-SECTORS[3]

Agriculture (1994-2021)	7.1 %	4.9 %	79 %
Railroads	21.9	3.5	59
Transportation	14.4	3.4	66
Steel	13.4	2.7	53
Auto	36.4	2.1	47
SOX (1995-2021)	5.9	2.0	48
Chemicals	8.1	1.8	53
Pharma	5.3	1.8	53
Retail	6.1	1.4	53
Banks	6.4	1.3	44
Biotech (1993-2021)	-1.4	0.7	43
Homebuilders	5.4	0.7	38
Metals & Mining	9.4	0.5	41
Silver	11.5	0.5	52
Gold	1.5	-0.8	25

VALERO

VLO ①LONG (Dec12-Apr1) ②SELL SHORT (May11-Jun26) ②LONG (Oct19-Nov2)

Valero acknowledges the seasonality of its business in its 10k report as of December 31, 2020.

"Demand for gasoline, diesel, and asphalt is higher during the spring and summer months than during the winter months in most of our markets, primarily due to seasonal increases in highway traffic and construction."

26% gain

The time to be in a stock is typically well before the seasonal event. With Valero, this has been from December 12 until April 1. This provides an exit before the driving season starts in May. One of the better times to short sell the stock has been from May 11 to June 26 as the driving season gets underway. Valero also performs well from October 19 to November 2.

2021/22 Performance Update.
In 2021, Valero slightly outperformed the S&P 500, but managed to strongly outperform the S&P 500 in its strong seasonal period in early 2021. Overall, the combination of seasonal trades worked well in 2021. In 2022, Valero outperformed in its strong seasonal period from mid-December to early April.

ⓘ *VLO - stock symbol for Valero, which trades on the NYSE, adjusted for stock splits.*

Valero vs. S&P 500 1990 to 2021
Negative Short ☐   Positive Long ▦

Year	Dec 12 to Apr 1		May 11 to Jun 26		Oct 19 to Nov 2		Compound Growth	
	S&P 500	VLO	S&P 500	VLO	S&P 500	VLO	S&P 500	VLO
1990	-2.5 %	5.3 %	2.4 %	8.5 %	2.0 %	9.4 %	1.9 %	5.4 %
1991	13.7	37.2	-1.1	-11.7	-0.3	3.3	12.1	58.4
1992	7.0	18.1	-3.0	-22.7	2.7	3.4	6.6	49.8
1993	3.8	9.4	1.1	-8.3	0.0	-6.8	4.9	10.4
1994	-3.9	-0.6	-0.7	-19.8	-0.2	4.8	-4.8	24.8
1995	12.0	-0.7	3.8	-5.9	0.4	2.7	16.7	8.0
1996	5.5	-4.9	1.9	-10.2	-1.0	3.8	6.4	8.9
1997	2.6	24.9	7.1	-1.4	-3.1	-4.7	6.4	20.6
1998	16.0	12.9	2.3	-5.3	5.2	35.0	24.9	60.4
1999	10.9	29.4	-1.9	-6.5	7.5	-0.3	17.0	37.3
2000	5.8	58.9	5.2	0.4	6.4	-1.5	18.4	55.9
2001	-15.9	7.2	-3.1	-23.6	1.7	5.6	-17.1	39.8
2002	0.9	30.7	-7.7	-10.9	1.9	12.3	-5.2	62.8
2003	-5.1	23.5	5.6	2.7	1.1	7.3	1.3	29.0
2004	5.7	31.6	4.4	16.9	1.5	4.2	11.9	14.0
2005	-1.3	80.8	2.2	17.2	3.1	8.2	4.0	62.0
2006	2.8	13.4	-5.5	-4.2	0.1	-3.2	-2.7	14.3
2007	0.6	15.7	0.1	2.9	-2.0	-2.2	-1.3	10.0
2008	-7.3	-20.1	-7.6	-7.4	3.0	13.6	-11.7	-2.5
2009	-7.2	-5.5	-1.1	-29.3	-4.1	-10.1	-12.0	9.8
2010	6.5	20.5	-7.2	-4.9	0.7	-2.4	-0.4	23.3
2011	7.4	38.9	-6.5	-18.6	1.0	7.5	1.4	77.1
2012	12.2	21.8	-2.8	3.5	-3.0	-4.9	5.8	11.9
2013	9.4	37.7	-1.9	-8.8	1.0	4.9	8.4	57.0
2014	5.8	20.6	4.2	-6.5	7.0	10.9	17.9	42.5
2015	1.2	35.5	-0.7	3.1	3.5	6.7	4.0	40.2
2016	3.0	-6.8	-2.3	-6.1	-1.9	5.4	-1.3	4.2
2017	4.6	-2.5	1.6	-1.0	0.7	5.1	7.1	3.5
2018	-0.7	6.4	0.0	-3.7	-1.7	-11.2	-2.4	-2.0
2019	8.7	18.0	1.1	1.4	2.7	9.7	12.9	27.5
2020	-21.4	-55.9	2.7	-14.6	-5.0	-0.8	-23.3	-49.8
2021	9.7	27.6	2.2	3.1	3.2	-2.9	15.8	20.0
Avg.	2.8 %	16.5 %	-0.2 %	-5.4 %	1.1 %	3.5 %	3.9 %	26.1 %
Fq>0	72 %	75 %	50	31 %	66 %	63 %	66 %	91 %

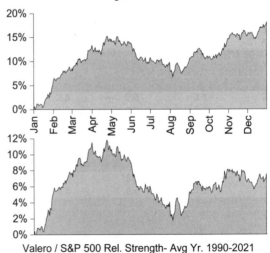

Valero - Avg. Year 1990 to 2021

Valero / S&P 500 Rel. Strength- Avg Yr. 1990-2021

Valero Performance

VLO Monthly % Gain (1990-2021)

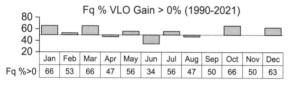

	Jan	Feb	Mar	Apr	May	Jun	Jul	Aug	Sep	Oct	Nov	Dec
Avg	5.5	2.5	3.9	2.7	-0.3	-3.1	-0.8	0.3	-0.6	4.1	0.6	3.0
Med	5.3	2.1	3.0	-0.5	0.8	-4.6	1.4	-0.5	-0.4	4.9	-0.3	4.1
S&P 500 Avg	0.3	0.1	1.0	2.1	0.9	-0.1	1.2	-0.5	-0.5	1.4	1.8	1.5

Fq % VLO Gain > 0% (1990-2021)

	Jan	Feb	Mar	Apr	May	Jun	Jul	Aug	Sep	Oct	Nov	Dec
Fq %>0	66	53	66	47	56	34	56	47	50	66	50	63

Fq % VLO Gain > S&P 500 % (1990-2021)

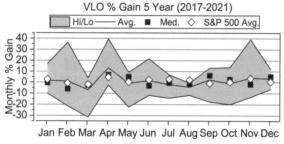

	Jan	Feb	Mar	Apr	May	Jun	Jul	Aug	Sep	Oct	Nov	Dec
Fq %> S&P 500	66	50	72	44	47	38	50	53	41	59	50	59

VLO % Gain 5 Year (2017-2021)

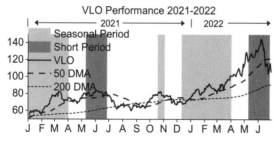

VLO Performance 2021-2022

Relative Strength, % Gain vs. S&P 500

WEEK 40

Market Indices & Rates
Weekly Values**

Stock Markets	2020	2021
Dow	27,683	34,746
S&P500	3,348	4,391
Nasdaq	11,075	14,580
TSX	16,199	20,416
FTSE	5,902	7,096
DAX	12,689	15,206
Nikkei	23,030	28,049
Hang Seng	23,459	24,838

Commodities	2020	2021
Oil	37.05	79.35
Gold	1903.1	1773.3

Bond Yields	2020	2021
USA 5 Yr Treasury	0.28	1.05
USA 10 Yr T	0.70	1.61
USA 20 Yr T	1.25	2.11
Moody's Aaa	2.37	2.77
Moody's Baa	3.46	3.45
CAN 5 Yr T	0.36	1.21
CAN 10 Yr T	0.57	1.63

Money Market	2020	2021
USA Fed Funds	0.25	0.25
USA 3 Mo T-B	0.09	0.05
CAN tgt overnight rate	0.25	0.25
CAN 3 Mo T-B	0.12	0.12

Foreign Exchange	2020	2021
EUR/USD	1.17	1.16
GBP/USD	1.29	1.36
USD/CAD	1.33	1.25
USD/JPY	105.29	112.24

OCTOBER

M	T	W	T	F	S	S
						1
2	3	4	5	6	7	8
9	10	11	12	13	14	15
16	17	18	19	20	21	22
23	24	25	26	27	28	29
30	31					

NOVEMBER

M	T	W	T	F	S	S
	1	2	3	4	5
6	7	8	9	10	11	12
13	14	15	16	17	18	19
20	21	22	23	24	25	26
27	28	29	30			

DECEMBER

M	T	W	T	F	S	S
				1	2	3
4	5	6	7	8	9	10
11	13	13	14	15	16	17
18	19	20	21	22	23	24
25	26	27	28	29	30	31

HOMEBUILDERS –
TIME TO BREAK & TIME TO BUILD
①SELL SHORT (Apr27-Jun13) ②LONG (Oct28-Feb3)

Historically, the best time to be in the homebuilders sector has been from October 28 to February 3. This period is the lead up to the spring build season. Investors strive to be in the sector well before the spring season takes place, which helps to push up the price of homebuilding stocks.

18% gain & positive 75% of the time

Generally, the time period outside of the strong seasonal period for homebuilders should be avoided by investors, as not only has the average performance relative to the S&P 500 been negative, but the sector has produced both large gains and losses. In other words, the risk is substantially higher that a large draw-down could occur. This is particularly true for the time period from April 27 to June 13. The weak seasonal period takes place when the spring home building season and house sales season gets underway. At this point, the sector has generally priced in expected gains.

2021/22 Performance Update.
In 2021, the homebuilders sector outperformed the S&P 500, but performed poorly in its weak seasonal period from late April to mid-June. It started its strong seasonal period from late October to early February, but started to underperform the S&P 500 in mid-December. In the first half of 2022, the homebuilders sector underperformed the S&P 500 as investors became concerned about rising mortgage rates.

> (i) *Homebuilders: SP GIC Sector: An index designed to represent a cross section of homebuilding companies.*
> *For more information, see www.standardandpoors.com.*

Homebuilders (HB)* vs. S&P 500 1990/91 to 2021/22
Negative Short [ ]   Positive Long [ ]

Year	SHORT Apr 27 to Jun 13 S&P 500	HB.	LONG Oct 28 to Feb 3 S&P 500	HB.	Compound Growth S&P 500	HB.
1990/91	9.6 %	7.9 %	12.6 %	58.0 %	23.4 %	45.5 %
1991/92	-0.4	-4.8	6.6	41.2	6.2	48.0
1992/93	0.2	-11.5	6.9	26.7	7.1	41.2
1993/94	3.2	12.6	3.5	8.6	6.7	-5.1
1994/95	1.6	-4.0	2.8	-4.0	4.4	-0.2
1995/96	4.6	11.1	9.7	16.7	14.7	3.7
1996/97	2.2	10.6	12.2	6.3	14.7	-4.9
1997/98	16.7	22.6	14.7	24.8	33.9	-3.4
1998/99	-0.8	-10.6	19.4	12.4	18.4	24.2
1999/00	-4.9	-7.1	9.9	-3.9	4.5	2.9
2000/01	0.6	-3.8	-2.2	18.6	-1.6	23.1
2001/02	0.6	-17.5	1.6	43.1	2.2	68.1
2002/03	-6.2	-5.3	-4.2	6.7	-10.1	12.3
2003/04	10.0	31.5	10.2	7.6	21.2	-26.3
2004/05	0.1	-2.6	5.7	23.7	5.8	26.9
2005/06	4.3	11.9	7.2	14.8	11.8	1.1
2006/07	-6.3	-27.1	5.2	16.8	-1.4	48.4
2007/08	1.4	-7.9	-9.1	8.8	-7.8	17.4
2008/09	-2.7	-25.3	-1.2	27.7	-3.9	60.0
2009/10	9.2	-25.1	3.2	15.5	12.7	44.4
2010/11	-9.9	-22.9	10.5	12.9	-0.4	38.7
2011/12	-5.6	-11.2	4.7	35.0	-1.2	50.1
2012/13	-6.1	-9.3	7.2	13.7	0.7	24.3
2013/14	3.4	-7.2	-1.0	10.1	2.4	18.1
2014/15	3.9	4.5	4.5	7.8	8.6	3.0
2015/16	-1.1	-0.8	-7.4	-15.3	-8.5	-14.6
2016/17	-0.6	-2.3	7.7	10.9	7.1	13.5
2017/18	2.2	4.6	7.0	4.2	9.4	-0.6
2018/19	4.1	-3.6	1.8	10.2	5.9	14.2
2019/20	-1.6	2.8	7.5	7.5	5.7	4.5
2020/21	7.2	29.0	13.0	13.4	21.1	-19.4
2021/22	1.4	-8.5	-1.6	2.2	-0.2	10.9
Avg.	1.3 %	-2.2 %	5.3 %	15.1 %	6.7 %	17.8 %
Fq>0	63 %	34 %	78 %	91 %	72 %	75 %

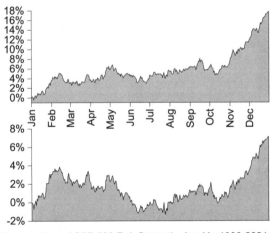

Homebuilders - Avg. Year 1990 to 2021

Homebuilders / S&P 500 Rel. Strength- Avg Yr. 1990-2021

Homebuilders Performance

Homebuilders Monthly % Gain (1990-2021)

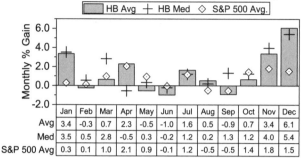

Legend: HB Avg + HB Med ◇ S&P 500 Avg.

	Jan	Feb	Mar	Apr	May	Jun	Jul	Aug	Sep	Oct	Nov	Dec
Avg	3.4	-0.3	0.7	2.3	-0.5	-1.0	1.6	0.5	-0.9	0.7	3.4	6.1
Med	3.5	0.5	2.8	-0.5	0.3	-0.2	1.2	0.2	1.3	1.2	4.0	5.4
S&P 500 Avg	0.3	0.1	1.0	2.1	0.9	-0.1	1.2	-0.5	-0.5	1.4	1.8	1.5

Fq % Homebuilders Gain > 0% (1990-2021)

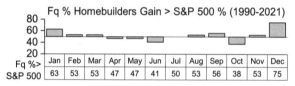

	Jan	Feb	Mar	Apr	May	Jun	Jul	Aug	Sep	Oct	Nov	Dec
Fq %>0	69	53	53	50	53	47	53	53	56	59	69	66

Fq % Homebuilders Gain > S&P 500 % (1990-2021)

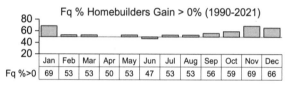

	Jan	Feb	Mar	Apr	May	Jun	Jul	Aug	Sep	Oct	Nov	Dec
Fq %> S&P 500	63	53	53	47	47	41	50	53	56	38	53	75

Homebuilders % Gain 5 Year (2017-2021)

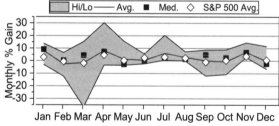

Legend: Hi/Lo — Avg. ■ Med. ◇ S&P 500 Avg.

Homebuilders Performance 2021-2022

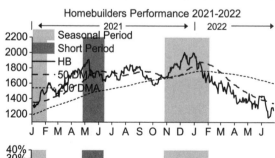

Relative Strength, % Gain vs. S&P 500

WEEK 41

Market Indices & Rates
Weekly Values**

Stock Markets	2020	2021
Dow	28,587	35,295
S&P500	3,477	4,471
Nasdaq	11,580	14,897
TSX	16,563	20,928
FTSE	6,017	7,234
DAX	13,051	15,587
Nikkei	23,620	29,069
Hang Seng	24,119	25,331

Commodities	2020	2021
Oil	40.60	82.28
Gold	1923.3	1772.7

Bond Yields	2020	2021
USA 5 Yr Treasury	0.34	1.13
USA 10 Yr T	0.79	1.59
USA 20 Yr T	1.34	2.02
Moody's Aaa	2.34	2.66
Moody's Baa	3.46	3.35
CAN 5 Yr T	0.38	1.24
CAN 10 Yr T	0.63	1.59

Money Market	2020	2021
USA Fed Funds	0.25	0.25
USA 3 Mo T-B	0.10	0.05
CAN tgt overnight rate	0.25	0.25
CAN 3 Mo T-B	0.09	0.12

Foreign Exchange	2020	2021
EUR/USD	1.18	1.16
GBP/USD	1.30	1.38
USD/CAD	1.31	1.24
USD/JPY	105.62	114.22

OCTOBER

M	T	W	T	F	S	S
						1
2	3	4	5	6	7	8
9	10	11	12	13	14	15
16	17	18	19	20	21	22
23	24	25	26	27	28	29
30	31					

NOVEMBER

M	T	W	T	F	S	S
		1	2	3	4	5
6	7	8	9	10	11	12
13	14	15	16	17	18	19
20	21	22	23	24	25	26
27	28	29	30			

DECEMBER

M	T	W	T	F	S	S
				1	2	3
4	5	6	7	8	9	10
11	13	13	14	15	16	17
18	19	20	21	22	23	24
25	26	27	28	29	30	31

Emerson Electric (Emerson) is a technology and engineering company that provides solutions for customers in the industrial, commercial and residential markets.

Emerson has a strong track record of outperforming the S&P 500 from October 11 to December 31. In this period, from 1990 to 2021, Emerson has produced an average gain of 7.8% and has been positive 88% of the time. In addition, Emerson has outperformed the S&P 500, 69% of the time.

69% of the time
better than the S&P 500

On average, Emerson also performs well in April. However, its median performance is less than the S&P 500. In addition, Emerson has only outperformed the S&P 500, 53% of the time.

It should also be noted that if there is one month of the year that should be avoided on a seasonal basis, it is June. From 1990 to 2021, Emerson has had an average loss of 1.8% in June, has only been positive 41% of the time and only outperformed the S&P 500, 28% of the time.

EMR vs. S&P 500 1990 to 2021

Oct 11 to Dec 31	S&P 500	Positive EMR	Diff
1990	9.9 %	15.3 %	5.3 %
1991	9.6	15.8	6.2
1992	8.2	6.0	-2.2
1993	1.3	5.9	4.6
1994	0.1	6.4	6.3
1995	6.7	16.6	9.9
1996	6.6	8.4	1.8
1997	0.4	1.7	1.3
1998	24.9	-1.1	-26.0
1999	10.0	-6.1	-16.1
2000	-4.8	22.3	27.1
2001	6.2	20.7	14.5
2002	9.4	14.7	5.2
2003	7.1	18.0	10.9
2004	8.0	11.4	3.4
2005	5.1	7.7	2.6
2006	4.8	4.4	-0.4
2007	-6.0	3.8	9.9
2008	0.4	9.7	9.2
2009	4.1	9.0	4.9
2010	7.9	7.0	-0.9
2011	5.2	2.6	-2.6
2012	-0.4	9.7	10.1
2013	9.2	8.0	-1.2
2014	8.0	3.9	-4.1
2015	1.4	1.4	0.0
2016	3.5	7.7	4.2
2017	4.8	9.9	5.1
2018	-10.0	-18.5	-8.5
2019	10.0	17.2	7.3
2020	8.0	14.9	6.9
2021	8.5	-3.8	-12.3
Avg.	5.3 %	7.8 %	2.6 %
Fq > 0	88 %	88 %	69 %

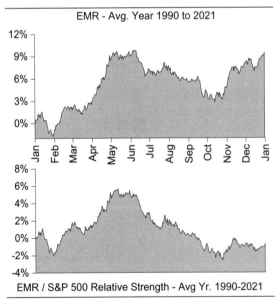

EMR - Avg. Year 1990 to 2021

EMR / S&P 500 Relative Strength - Avg Yr. 1990-2021

and outperformed in December. The net result has been that Emerson on average slightly underperformed the S&P 500 in its strong seasonal period.

2021/22 Performance Update.
In 2021, Emerson started the year strongly outperforming the S&P 500. It started to underperform in September and then underperformed in its seasonal period.

In 2022, Emerson outperformed the S&P 500 in the first six months of the year.

Over the last five years, Emerson outperformed the S&P 500 in October, underperformed in November

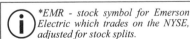

EMR - stock symbol for Emerson Electric which trades on the NYSE, adjusted for stock splits.

Emerson Electric Performance

EMR Monthly % Gain (1990-2021)

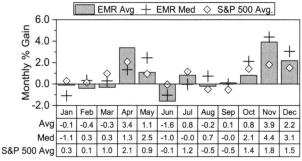

	Jan	Feb	Mar	Apr	May	Jun	Jul	Aug	Sep	Oct	Nov	Dec
Avg	-0.1	-0.4	-0.3	3.4	1.1	-1.6	0.8	-0.2	0.1	0.8	3.9	2.2
Med	-1.1	0.3	0.3	1.3	2.5	-1.0	-0.0	0.7	-0.0	2.1	4.4	3.1
S&P 500 Avg	0.3	0.1	1.0	2.1	0.9	-0.1	1.2	-0.5	-0.5	1.4	1.8	1.5

Fq % EMR Gain > 0% (1990-2021)

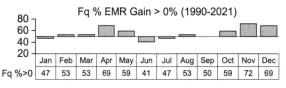

	Jan	Feb	Mar	Apr	May	Jun	Jul	Aug	Sep	Oct	Nov	Dec
Fq %>0	47	53	53	69	59	41	47	53	50	59	72	69

Fq % EMR Gain > S&P 500 % (1990-2021)

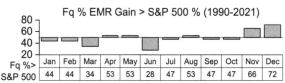

	Jan	Feb	Mar	Apr	May	Jun	Jul	Aug	Sep	Oct	Nov	Dec
Fq %> S&P 500	44	44	34	53	53	28	47	53	47	47	66	72

EMR % Gain 5 Year (2017-2021)

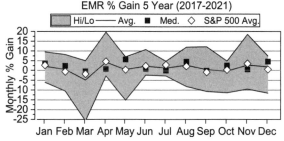

EMR Performance 2021-2022

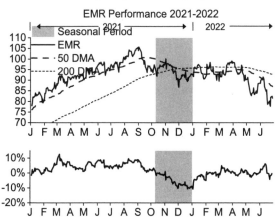

Relative Strength, % Gain vs. S&P 500

Market Indices & Rates
Weekly Values**

Stock Markets	2020	2021
Dow	28,606	35,677
S&P500	3,484	4,545
Nasdaq	11,672	15,090
TSX	16,439	21,216
FTSE	5,920	7,205
DAX	12,909	15,543
Nikkei	23,411	28,805
Hang Seng	24,387	26,127

Commodities	2020	2021
Oil	40.88	84.61
Gold	1905.1	1808.3

Bond Yields	2020	2021
USA 5 Yr Treasury	0.32	1.22
USA 10 Yr T	0.76	1.66
USA 20 Yr T	1.30	2.06
Moody's Aaa	2.29	2.72
Moody's Baa	3.40	3.38
CAN 5 Yr T	0.35	1.34
CAN 10 Yr T	0.58	1.65

Money Market	2020	2021
USA Fed Funds	0.25	0.25
USA 3 Mo T-B	0.11	0.06
CAN tgt overnight rate	0.25	0.25
CAN 3 Mo T-B	0.09	0.12

Foreign Exchange	2020	2021
EUR/USD	1.17	1.16
GBP/USD	1.29	1.38
USD/CAD	1.32	1.24
USD/JPY	105.40	113.50

OCTOBER

M	T	W	T	F	S	S
						1
2	3	4	5	6	7	8
9	10	11	12	13	14	15
16	17	18	19	20	21	22
23	24	25	26	27	28	29
30	31					

NOVEMBER

M	T	W	T	F	S	S
	1	2	3	4	5	
6	7	8	9	10	11	12
13	14	15	16	17	18	19
20	21	22	23	24	25	26
27	28	29	30			

DECEMBER

M	T	W	T	F	S	S
				1	2	3
4	5	6	7	8	9	10
11	13	13	14	15	16	17
18	19	20	21	22	23	24
25	26	27	28	29	30	31

RETAIL
① Jan 21 to Apr 12   ② Oct 28 to Nov 29

The retail sector has two strong seasonal periods. The late January to mid-April seasonal period is the result of the retail sector's response to analysts putting forward positive economic expectations for the economy and consumer spending at the beginning of the year. Preceding the late January to mid-April period, the sector often performs poorly from late December to mid-January.

The second seasonal period for the retail sector occurs in the run-up period to Black Friday, from late October to late November. The retail sector tends to perform well in this period as the result of investors increasing their interest in the sector anticipating retail companies to benefit from increased sales during the holiday shopping season.

13% gain

The frequency of success in the late October to late November seasonal period is stronger than the spring seasonal period. On the other hand, the average percentage gain of the spring seasonal period is stronger. Overall, the spring seasonal period when considering both frequency and gain, is the best seasonal period.

2021/22 Performance Update.
In 2021, the retail sector underperformed the S&P 500 for most of the year. In the first half of the 2022, the retail sector continued its underperformance, including in its strong seasonal period. The retail sector has been adversely affected by slowing economic growth and high inflation translating into less discretionary spending.

(i) *Retail SP GIC Sector # 2550:*
An index of retail companies.
For more information on the retail
sector, see www.standardandpoors.com.

Retail* vs. S&P 500 - 1990 to 2021   Positive ▢

	Jan 21 to Apr 12		Oct 28 to Nov 29		Compound Growth	
Year	S&P 500	Retail	S&P 500	Retail	S&P 500	Retail
1990	1.5 %	9.6 %	3.8 %	9.9 %	5.4 %	20.5 %
1991	14.5	29.9	-2.3	2.7	11.8	33.4
1992	-2.9	-2.7	2.8	5.5	-0.2	2.7
1993	3.5	-0.6	-0.6	6.3	2.9	5.7
1994	-5.8	2.0	-2.3	0.4	-7.9	2.4
1995	9.1	7.4	4.8	9.5	14.4	17.6
1996	4.1	19.7	8.0	0.4	12.4	20.2
1997	-5.0	6.0	8.9	16.9	3.5	23.9
1998	13.5	20.1	11.9	20.4	27.0	44.5
1999	8.1	23.4	8.6	14.1	17.4	40.7
2000	1.5	5.8	-2.7	9.9	-1.3	16.2
2001	-11.8	-0.5	3.2	7.9	-9.0	7.4
2002	-1.5	6.7	4.3	-1.7	2.8	4.9
2003	-3.7	6.5	2.6	2.5	-1.2	9.2
2004	0.6	6.7	4.7	7.0	5.3	14.1
2005	1.1	-1.6	6.7	9.9	7.8	8.1
2006	2.1	3.4	1.6	0.2	3.8	3.6
2007	1.2	-0.7	-4.3	-7.5	-3.1	-8.1
2008	0.6	3.5	5.6	7.5	6.2	11.3
2009	6.4	25.1	2.6	3.6	9.2	29.6
2010	5.1	15.5	0.4	5.2	5.6	21.5
2011	2.6	4.4	-7.0	-4.5	-4.5	-0.3
2012	5.5	12.1	0.3	5.1	5.8	17.8
2013	6.9	10.1	2.6	5.0	9.7	15.5
2014	-1.3	-7.1	5.4	8.9	4.1	1.2
2015	3.9	15.5	1.2	3.9	5.2	19.9
2016	10.9	9.7	3.4	2.8	14.6	12.8
2017	3.2	4.6	1.7	4.4	5.0	9.2
2018	-5.2	1.6	3.0	0.9	-2.4	2.5
2019	8.9	10.7	3.9	0.4	13.1	11.1
2020	-16.2	-6.0	7.3	0.5	-10.1	-5.5
2021	7.2	7.8	2.3	5.3	9.6	13.5
Avg.	2.1 %	7.8 %	2.9 %	5.1 %	5.1 %	13.3 %
Fq>0	72 %	78 %	81 %	91 %	72 %	91 %

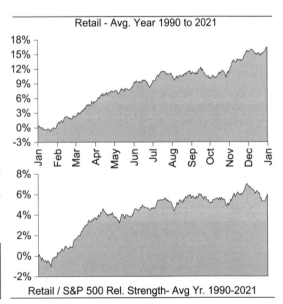

Retail - Avg. Year 1990 to 2021

Retail / S&P 500 Rel. Strength- Avg Yr. 1990-2021

Retail Performance

Retail Monthly % Gain (1990-2021)

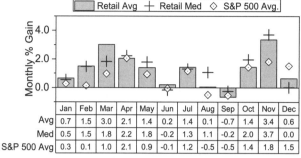

Legend: Retail Avg | + Retail Med | ◇ S&P 500 Avg.

	Jan	Feb	Mar	Apr	May	Jun	Jul	Aug	Sep	Oct	Nov	Dec
Avg	0.7	1.5	3.0	2.1	1.4	0.2	1.4	0.1	-0.7	1.4	3.4	0.6
Med	0.5	1.5	1.8	2.2	1.8	-0.2	1.3	1.1	-0.2	2.0	3.7	0.0
S&P 500 Avg	0.3	0.1	1.0	2.1	0.9	-0.1	1.2	-0.5	-0.5	1.4	1.8	1.5

Fq % Retail Gain > 0% (1990-2021)

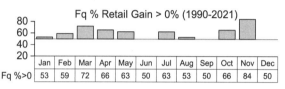

	Jan	Feb	Mar	Apr	May	Jun	Jul	Aug	Sep	Oct	Nov	Dec
Fq %>0	53	59	72	66	63	50	63	53	50	66	84	50

Fq % Retail Gain > S&P 500 % (1990-2021)

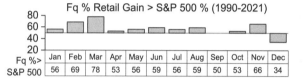

	Jan	Feb	Mar	Apr	May	Jun	Jul	Aug	Sep	Oct	Nov	Dec
Fq %> S&P 500	56	69	78	53	56	59	56	59	50	53	66	34

Retail % Gain 5 Year (2017-2021)

Legend: Retail Hi/Lo — Retail Avg. ■ Retail Med. ◇ S&P 500 Avg.

Retail Performance 2021-2022

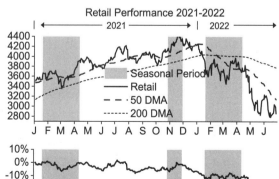

Legend: Seasonal Period — Retail — 50 DMA ···· 200 DMA

Relative Strength, % Gain vs. S&P 500

WEEK 43

Market Indices & Rates
Weekly Values**

Stock Markets	2020	2021
Dow	28,336	35,820
S&P500	3,465	4,605
Nasdaq	11,548	15,498
TSX	16,304	21,037
FTSE	5,860	7,238
DAX	12,646	15,689
Nikkei	23,517	28,893
Hang Seng	24,919	25,377

Commodities	2020	2021
Oil	39.67	83.57
Gold	1903.7	1769.2

Bond Yields	2020	2021
USA 5 Yr Treasury	0.37	1.18
USA 10 Yr T	0.85	1.55
USA 20 Yr T	1.41	1.98
Moody's Aaa	2.41	2.59
Moody's Baa	3.45	3.24
CAN 5 Yr T	0.39	1.51
CAN 10 Yr T	0.64	1.72

Money Market	2020	2021
USA Fed Funds	0.25	0.25
USA 3 Mo T-B	0.10	0.05
CAN tgt overnight rate	0.25	0.25
CAN 3 Mo T-B	0.09	0.14

Foreign Exchange	2020	2021
EUR/USD	1.19	1.16
GBP/USD	1.30	1.37
USD/CAD	1.31	1.24
USD/JPY	104.71	113.95

OCTOBER

M	T	W	T	F	S	S
						1
2	3	4	5	6	7	8
9	10	11	12	13	14	15
16	17	18	19	20	21	22
23	24	25	26	27	28	29
30	31					

NOVEMBER

M	T	W	T	F	S	S
	1	2	3	4	5	
6	7	8	9	10	11	12
13	14	15	16	17	18	19
20	21	22	23	24	25	26
27	28	29	30			

DECEMBER

M	T	W	T	F	S	S
			1	2	3	
4	5	6	7	8	9	10
11	13	13	14	15	16	17
18	19	20	21	22	23	24
25	26	27	28	29	30	31

INDUSTRIAL STRENGTH
① Oct 28 to Dec 31   ② Jan 23 to May 5

The industrial sector's seasonal trends are largely the same as the broad market, such as the S&P 500. Although the trends are similar, there still exists an opportunity to take advantage of the time period when the industrial sector tends to outperform.

> ### 11% gain & positive 85% of the time

Industrials tend to outperform in the favorable six month period for the stock market, but there is an opportunity to temporarily get out of the industrial sector in order to avoid a time period when the sector has on average, decreased before turning positive again.

The overall strategy is to be invested in the industrial sector from October 28 to December 31, sell at the end of the day on the 31, and re-enter the sector to be invested from January 23 to May 5.

It should be noted that longer term investors may decide to be invested during the whole time period from October 28 to May 5. Shorter term investors may decide to use technical analysis to determine, if and when, they should temporarily sell the industrials sector during its weak period from January 1 to January 22.

2021/22 Performance Update.
In 2021, the industrial sector started the year on a positive note outperforming the S&P 500, but economic growth concerns took their toll on the sector and it underperformed for the second half of 2021. In the first half of 2022, the industrial sector managed to outperform the S&P 500.

Industrials* vs. S&P 500 1989/90 to 2021/22 Positive ▢

Year	Oct 28 to Dec 31 S&P 500	Oct 28 to Dec 31 Ind.	Jan 23 to May 5 S&P 500	Jan 23 to May 5 Ind.	Compound Growth S&P 500	Compound Growth Ind.
1989/90	5.5 %	6.9 %	2.4 %	5.5 %	8.0 %	12.7 %
1990/91	8.4	10.7	16.0	15.2	25.7	27.5
1991/92	8.6	7.2	-0.3	-1.0	8.2	6.1
1992/93	4.1	6.3	1.9	5.4	6.1	12.0
1993/94	0.4	5.1	-4.9	-6.7	-4.5	-2.0
1994/95	-1.4	-0.5	11.9	12.4	10.3	11.8
1995/96	6.3	10.7	4.6	7.6	11.1	19.1
1996/97	5.7	4.5	5.6	5.2	11.6	9.9
1997/98	10.7	10.5	15.8	11.5	28.2	23.2
1998/99	15.4	10.5	10.0	19.5	26.9	32.1
1999/00	13.3	10.8	-0.6	4.5	12.6	15.8
2000/01	-4.3	1.8	-5.7	4.7	-9.7	6.6
2001/02	3.9	8.1	-4.1	-5.3	-0.3	2.4
2002/03	-2.0	-1.3	5.5	8.6	3.4	7.1
2003/04	7.8	11.6	-2.0	-3.3	5.7	7.9
2004/05	7.7	8.7	0.4	0.2	8.1	8.9
2005/06	5.9	7.6	5.1	14.3	11.3	23.0
2006/07	3.0	3.1	5.8	6.8	9.0	10.1
2007/08	-4.4	-3.4	7.4	9.7	2.7	6.0
2008/09	6.4	7.1	9.2	6.1	16.2	13.7
2009/10	4.9	6.4	6.8	13.4	12.0	20.6
2010/11	6.4	8.1	4.0	4.9	10.6	13.5
2011/12	-2.1	-1.0	4.1	0.3	1.9	-0.7
2012/13	1.0	4.1	8.2	4.9	9.3	9.2
2013/14	5.0	7.3	2.2	1.6	7.3	9.0
2014/15	5.0	5.2	1.3	-1.0	6.3	4.1
2015/16	-1.1	-1.2	7.5	12.8	6.4	11.4
2016/17	5.0	9.7	5.6	5.0	10.9	15.2
2017/18	3.6	4.2	-6.0	-9.5	-2.6	-5.7
2018/19	-5.7	-6.7	11.9	14.2	5.5	6.6
2019/20	6.9	3.8	-13.6	-25.5	-7.7	-22.7
2020/21	10.8	14.6	8.5	16.9	20.2	34.0
2021/22	4.7	2.6	-5.7	-5.0	-1.3	-2.5
Avg.	4.4 %	5.5 %	4.7 %	4.7 %	8.2 %	10.5 %
Fq > 0	79 %	82 %	76 %	76 %	82 %	85 %

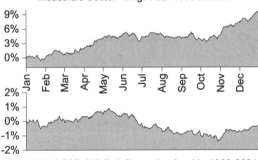

Industrials Sector - Avg. Year 1990 to 2021

Industrials / S&P 500 Rel. Strength - Avg Yr. 1990-2021

> Ⓨ *Alternate Strategy—*
> *Investors can bridge the gap between the two positive seasonal trends for the industrials sector by holding from October 28th to May 5th. Longer term investors may prefer this strategy, shorter term investors can use technical tools to determine the appropriate strategy.*

> ⓘ **The SP GICS Industrial Sector. For more information on the industrials sector, see www.standardandpoors.com*

Industrials Performance

Industrials Monthly % Gain (1990-2021)

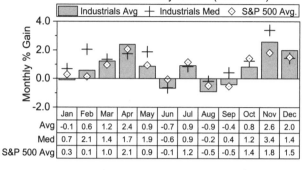

Legend: Industrials Avg · + Industrials Med · ◇ S&P 500 Avg.

Monthly % Gain

	Jan	Feb	Mar	Apr	May	Jun	Jul	Aug	Sep	Oct	Nov	Dec
Avg	-0.1	0.6	1.2	2.4	0.9	-0.7	0.9	-0.9	-0.4	0.8	2.6	2.0
Med	0.7	2.1	1.4	1.7	1.9	-0.6	0.9	-0.2	0.4	1.2	3.4	1.4
S&P 500 Avg	0.3	0.1	1.0	2.1	0.9	-0.1	1.2	-0.5	-0.5	1.4	1.8	1.5

Fq % Industrials Gain > 0% (1990-2021)

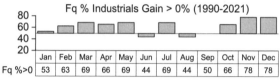

	Jan	Feb	Mar	Apr	May	Jun	Jul	Aug	Sep	Oct	Nov	Dec
Fq %>0	53	63	69	66	69	44	69	44	50	66	78	78

Fq % Industrials Gain > S&P 500 % (1990-2021)

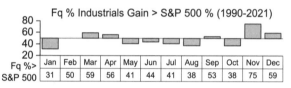

	Jan	Feb	Mar	Apr	May	Jun	Jul	Aug	Sep	Oct	Nov	Dec
Fq %> S&P 500	31	50	59	56	41	44	41	38	53	38	75	59

Industrials % Gain 5 Year (2017-2021)

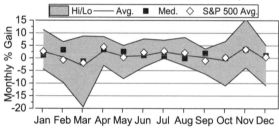

Legend: Hi/Lo — Avg. · ■ Med. · ◇ S&P 500 Avg.

Industrials Performance 2021-2022

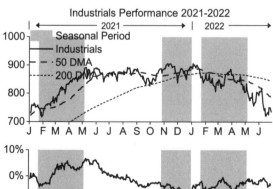

Seasonal Period · Industrials · 50 DMA · 200 DMA

Relative Strength, % Gain vs. S&P 500

Market Indices & Rates
Weekly Values**

Stock Markets	2020	2021
Dow	26,502	36,328
S&P500	3,270	4,698
Nasdaq	10,912	15,972
TSX	15,581	21,456
FTSE	5,577	7,304
DAX	11,556	16,054
Nikkei	22,977	29,612
Hang Seng	24,107	24,871

Commodities	2020	2021
Oil	35.79	81.27
Gold	1881.9	1801.9

Bond Yields	2020	2021
USA 5 Yr Treasury	0.38	1.04
USA 10 Yr T	0.88	1.45
USA 20 Yr T	1.43	1.88
Moody's Aaa	2.39	2.50
Moody's Baa	3.49	3.18
CAN 5 Yr T	0.40	1.36
CAN 10 Yr T	0.66	1.59

Money Market	2020	2021
USA Fed Funds	0.25	0.25
USA 3 Mo T-B	0.09	0.05
CAN tgt overnight rate	0.25	0.25
CAN 3 Mo T-B	0.09	0.14

Foreign Exchange	2020	2021
EUR/USD	1.16	1.16
GBP/USD	1.29	1.35
USD/CAD	1.33	1.25
USD/JPY	104.66	113.41

OCTOBER

M	T	W	T	F	S	S
						1
2	3	4	5	6	7	8
9	10	11	12	13	14	15
16	17	18	19	20	21	22
23	24	25	26	27	28	29
30	31					

NOVEMBER

M	T	W	T	F	S	S
	1	2	3	4	5	
6	7	8	9	10	11	12
13	14	15	16	17	18	19
20	21	22	23	24	25	26
27	28	29	30			

DECEMBER

M	T	W	T	F	S	S
				1	2	3
4	5	6	7	8	9	10
11	13	13	14	15	16	17
18	19	20	21	22	23	24
25	26	27	28	29	30	31

NOVEMBER

	MONDAY	TUESDAY	WEDNESDAY
WEEK 44	30	31	1 29
WEEK 45	6 24	7 23	8 22
WEEK 46	13 17	14 16	15 15
WEEK 47	20 10	21 9	22 8
WEEK 48	27 3	28 2	29 1

THURSDAY	FRIDAY
2 28	**3** 27
9 21	**10** 20
	USA Bond Market Closed-Veterans Day
	CAD Bond Market Closed-Remembrance Day
16 14	**17** 13
23 7	**24** 6
USA Market Closed-Thanksgiving Day	USA Early Market Close Thanksgiving
30	1

DECEMBER

M	T	W	T	F	S	S
				1	2	3
4	5	6	7	8	9	10
11	12	13	14	15	16	17
18	19	20	21	22	23	24
25	26	27	28	29	30	31

JANUARY

M	T	W	T	F	S	S
1	2	3	4	5	6	7
8	9	10	11	12	13	14
15	16	17	18	19	20	21
22	23	24	25	26	27	28
29	30	31				

FEBRUARY

M	T	W	T	F	S	S
			1	2	3	4
5	6	7	8	9	10	11
12	13	14	15	16	17	18
19	20	21	22	23	24	25
26	27	28				

MARCH

M	T	W	T	F	S	S
			1	2	3	4
5	6	7	8	9	10	11
12	13	14	15	16	17	18
19	20	21	22	23	24	25
26	27	28	29	30	31	

NOVEMBER
S U M M A R Y

S&P500 Cumulative Daily Gains for Avg Month 1950 to 2021

Prob. of Daily Gain

	Dow Jones	S&P 500	Nasdaq	TSX Comp
Month Rank	2	1	2	6
# Up	50	49	36	23
# Down	22	23	14	14
% Pos	69	68	72	62
% Avg. Gain	1.7	1.7	1.9	0.9

Dow & S&P 1950-2021, Nasdaq 1972-2021, TSX 1985-2021

♦ November, on average, is one of the better months of the year for the S&P 500. From 1950 to 2021, it has produced an average gain of 1.7% and has been positive 68% of the time. ♦ In November, the cyclical sectors tend to start increasing their relative performance compared to the S&P 500. The metals and mining sector starts its period of seasonal strength on November 19th. ♦ For investors looking for a short-term investment, the day before and the day after Thanksgiving are on average the two strongest days of the year for the S&P 500.

BEST / WORST NOVEMBER BROAD MKTS. 2012-2021

BEST NOVEMBER MARKETS
- ♦ Russell 2000 (2020) 18.3%
- ♦ Nikkei 225 (2020) 15.0%
- ♦ FTSE 100 (2020) 12.4%

WORST NOVEMBER MARKETS
- ♦ Russell 2000 (2021) -4.3%
- ♦ Dow (2021) -3.7%
- ♦ Nikkei 225 (2021) -3.7%

Index Values End of Month

	2012	2013	2014	2015	2016	2017	2018	2019	2020	2021
Dow	13,026	16,086	17,828	17,720	19,124	24,272	25,538	28,051	29,639	34,484
S&P 500	1,416	1,806	2,068	2,080	2,199	2,648	2,760	3,141	3,622	4,567
Nasdaq	3,010	4,060	4,792	5,109	5,324	6,874	7,331	8,665	12,199	15,538
TSX Comp.	12,239	13,395	14,745	13,470	15,083	16,067	15,198	17,040	17,190	20,660
Russell 1000	783	1,005	1,149	1,155	1,221	1,467	1,526	1,737	2,037	2,546
Russell 2000	822	1,143	1,173	1,198	1,322	1,544	1,533	1,625	1,820	2,199
FTSE 100	5,867	6,651	6,723	6,356	6,784	7,327	6,980	7,347	6,266	7,059
Nikkei 225	9,446	15,662	17,460	19,747	18,308	22,725	22,351	23,294	26,434	27,822

Percent Gain for November

	2012	2013	2014	2015	2016	2017	2018	2019	2020	2021
Dow	-0.5	3.5	2.5	0.3	5.4	3.8	1.7	3.7	11.8	-3.7
S&P 500	0.3	2.8	2.5	0.1	3.4	2.8	1.8	3.4	10.8	-0.8
Nasdaq	1.1	3.6	3.5	1.1	2.6	2.2	0.3	4.5	11.8	0.3
TSX Comp.	-1.5	0.3	0.9	-0.4	2.0	0.3	1.1	3.4	10.3	-1.8
Russell 1000	0.5	2.6	2.4	0.1	3.7	2.8	1.8	3.6	11.6	-1.5
Russell 2000	0.4	3.9	0.0	3.1	11.0	2.8	1.4	4.0	18.3	-4.3
FTSE 100	1.5	-1.2	2.7	-0.1	-2.5	-2.2	-2.1	1.4	12.4	-2.5
Nikkei 225	5.8	9.3	6.4	3.5	5.1	3.2	2.0	1.6	15.0	-3.7

November Market Avg. Performance 2012 to 2021[1]

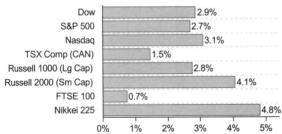

Dow		2.9%
S&P 500		2.7%
Nasdaq		3.1%
TSX Comp (CAN)		1.5%
Russell 1000 (Lg Cap)		2.8%
Russell 2000 (Sm Cap)		4.1%
FTSE 100		0.7%
Nikkei 225		4.8%

Interest Corner Nov[2]

	Fed Funds %[3]	3 Mo. T-Bill %[4]	10 Yr %[5]	20 Yr %[6]
2021	0.25	0.05	1.43	1.85
2020	0.25	0.08	0.84	1.37
2019	1.75	1.59	1.78	2.07
2018	2.25	2.37	3.01	3.19
2017	1.25	1.27	2.42	2.65

(1) Russell Data provided by Russell (2) Federal Reserve Bank of St. Louis- end of month values (3) Target rate set by FOMC (4)(5)(6) Constant yield maturities.

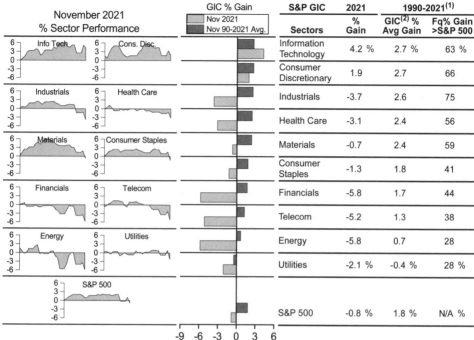

November 2021 % Sector Performance	GIC % Gain	S&P GIC	2021	1990-2021[1]	
	Nov 2021 / Nov 90-2021 Avg.	Sectors	% Gain	GIC[2] % Avg Gain	Fq% Gain >S&P 500
Info Tech		Information Technology	4.2 %	2.7 %	63 %
Cons. Disc.		Consumer Discretionary	1.9	2.7	66
Industrials		Industrials	-3.7	2.6	75
Health Care		Health Care	-3.1	2.4	56
Materials		Materials	-0.7	2.4	59
Consumer Staples		Consumer Staples	-1.3	1.8	41
Financials		Financials	-5.8	1.7	44
Telecom		Telecom	-5.2	1.3	38
Energy		Energy	-5.8	0.7	28
Utilities		Utilities	-2.1 %	-0.4 %	28 %
S&P 500		S&P 500	-0.8 %	1.8 %	N/A %

-9 -6 -3 0 3 6

Sector Commentary

♦ In November 2021, the S&P 500 produced a small loss of 0.8%. The rank of the sectors according to their seasonal trends, was generally followed with the information technology sector producing a gain of 4.2%. The weakest performing sectors were the financials sector and the energy sector, which both produced losses of 5.8%.

Sub-Sector Commentary

♦ Typically, the semiconductor sub-sector performs well in November. In 2021, the semiconductor sub-sector produced a strong gain of 11.1%. ♦ The homebuilders sub-sector typically performs well in November. In 2021, it followed its seasonal trend and produced a gain of 6.8%. ♦ Gold and silver typically perform poorly in November. In 2021, silver lost 4.8% and gold gained 2.0%.

SELECTED SUB-SECTORS[3]			
SOX (1995-2021)	11.1 %	4.2 %	63 %
Steel	-4.8	3.5	53
Home-builders	6.8	3.4	53
Retail	3.6	3.4	66
Biotech (1993-2021)	0.0	2.9	50
Transporta-tion	-4.7	2.8	53
Agriculture (1994-2021)	-3.2	2.5	36
Auto	3.1	2.3	53
Chemicals	-0.2	2.3	53
Pharma	-1.0	2.2	50
Railroads	-4.6	2.1	59
Banks	-6.3	1.9	50
Metals & Mining	-1.4	1.7	47
Gold	2.0	0.7	47
Silver	-4.8	0.4	43

(1) Sector data provided by Standard and Poors (2) GIC is short form for Global Industry Classification (3) Sub Sector data provided by Standard and Poors, except where marked by symbol.

MATERIAL STOCKS – MATERIAL GAINS
① Oct 28 to Jan 6   ② Jan 23 to May 5

Materials Composition – CAUTION

The U.S. materials sector is substantially different from the Canadian materials sector. The U.S. sector has over a 60% weight in chemical companies, versus the Canadian sector which has over a 60% weight in gold companies.

The materials sector (U.S.) generally performs well during the favorable six months of the year, from the end of October to the beginning of May. The sector is economically sensitive and is leveraged to economic forecasts.

Positive 14% of the time

The materials sector has two seasonal periods. The first period is from October 28 to January 6 and the second period is from January 23 to May 5.

The time period in between the two seasonal periods, from January 7 to January 22, has had an average loss of 2.2% and only been positive 42% of the time (1990 to 2022).

Investors may decide to bridge the gap between the two seasonal periods if the materials sector has strong momentum at the beginning of January. The complete materials strategy is to be invested from October 28 to January 6, out of the sector from January 7 to the 22, and back in from January 23 to May 5.

2021/22 Performance Update.
In 2021, the materials sector outperformed the S&P 500 in both of its strong seasonal periods. Overall, the sector slightly underperformed the S&P 500 for the year.

In the first half of the year, the materials sector started on a positive note, outperforming the S&P 500 into early June, but then corrected sharply relative to the S&P 500 as investors shifted to the defensive sectors of the stock market.

Materials* vs S&P 500 1989/90 to 2021/22 Positive

Year	Oct 28 to Jan 6 S&P 500	Oct 28 to Jan 6 Mat.	Jan 23 to May 5 S&P 500	Jan 23 to May 5 Mat.	Compound Growth S&P 500	Compound Growth Mat.
1989/90	5.1 %	9.1 %	2.4 %	-3.1 %	7.7 %	5.7 %
1990/91	5.4	9.2	16.0	15.3	22.2	26.0
1991/92	8.8	1.5	-0.3	5.5	8.5	7.1
1992/93	3.8	5.6	1.9	4.3	5.8	10.2
1993/94	0.5	9.4	-4.9	-5.3	-4.4	3.6
1994/95	-1.1	-3.5	11.9	6.1	10.7	2.4
1995/96	6.4	7.6	4.6	11.1	11.3	19.5
1996/97	6.7	2.3	5.6	2.3	12.6	4.6
1997/98	10.2	1.4	15.8	20.9	27.7	22.6
1998/99	19.4	6.1	10.0	31.5	31.3	39.6
1999/00	8.2	15.7	-0.6	-7.1	7.6	7.5
2000/01	-5.9	19.2	-5.7	15.1	-11.2	37.2
2001/02	6.2	8.5	-4.1	14.9	1.8	24.7
2002/03	3.5	9.2	5.5	2.7	9.2	12.1
2003/04	9.0	16.6	-2.0	-3.0	6.8	13.1
2004/05	5.6	5.4	0.4	0.3	6.0	5.8
2005/06	9.0	16.3	5.1	14.7	14.6	33.5
2006/07	2.4	3.2	5.8	10.7	8.3	14.2
2007/08	-8.1	-5.1	7.4	16.7	-1.2	10.8
2008/09	10.1	12.0	9.2	23.3	20.3	38.1
2009/10	6.9	13.8	6.8	3.0	14.2	17.2
2010/11	7.7	11.7	4.0	4.2	12.1	16.4
2011/12	-0.5	-2.3	4.1	-2.7	3.5	-4.9
2012/13	3.9	7.2	8.2	0.0	12.3	7.2
2013/14	3.8	3.1	2.2	4.3	6.1	7.5
2014/15	2.1	-0.7	1.3	2.9	3.4	2.2
2015/16	-3.7	-6.2	7.5	18.3	3.6	11.0
2016/17	6.8	8.6	5.6	4.5	12.8	13.5
2017/18	6.3	6.4	-6.0	-8.6	-0.1	-2,8
2018/19	-4.8	1.0	11.9	7.4	6.5	8.5
2019/20	7.4	2.2	-13.6	-15.0	-7.3	-13.2
2020/21	10.5	19.9	8.5	15.6	19.9	38.6
2021/22	3.2	5.6	-5.7	2.0	-2.7	7.7
Avg.	4.7 %	6.7 %	3.6 %	6.4 %	8.5 %	13.5 %
Fq > 0	82 %	85 %	73 %	76 %	82 %	91 %

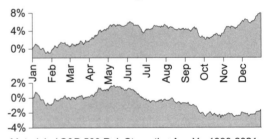

Materials Sector - Avg. Year 1990 to 2021

Materials / S&P 500 Rel. Strength - Avg Yr. 1990-2021

Ⓨ *Alternate Strategy—*
Investors can bridge the gap between the two positive seasonal trends for the materials sector by holding from October 28 to May 5. Longer term investors may prefer this strategy. Shorter term investors can use technical tools to determine the appropriate strategy.

ⓘ **The SP GICS Materials Sector encompasses a wide range of materials based companies.*
For more information on the materials sector, see www.standardandpoors.com

Materials Performance

Materials Monthly % Gain (1990-2021)

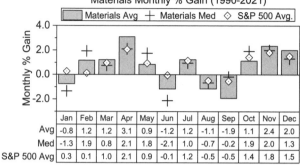

	Jan	Feb	Mar	Apr	May	Jun	Jul	Aug	Sep	Oct	Nov	Dec
Avg	-0.8	1.2	1.2	3.1	0.9	-1.2	1.2	-1.1	-1.9	1.1	2.4	2.0
Med	-1.3	1.9	0.8	2.1	1.8	-2.1	1.0	-0.7	-0.2	1.9	2.0	1.3
S&P 500 Avg	0.3	0.1	1.0	2.1	0.9	-0.1	1.2	-0.5	-0.5	1.4	1.8	1.5

Fq % Materials Gain > 0% (1990-2021)

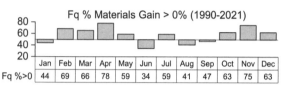

	Jan	Feb	Mar	Apr	May	Jun	Jul	Aug	Sep	Oct	Nov	Dec
Fq %>0	44	69	66	78	59	34	59	41	47	63	75	63

Fq % Materials Gain > S&P 500 % (1990-2021)

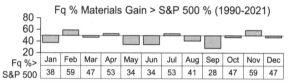

	Jan	Feb	Mar	Apr	May	Jun	Jul	Aug	Sep	Oct	Nov	Dec
Fq %> S&P 500	38	59	47	53	34	34	53	41	28	47	59	47

Materials % Gain 5 Year (2017-2021)

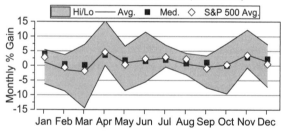

Materials Performance 2021-2022

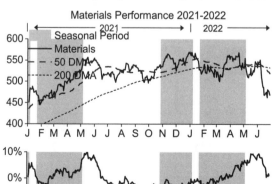

Relative Strength, % Gain vs. S&P 500

Market Indices & Rates
Weekly Values**

Stock Markets	2020	2021
Dow	28,323	36,100
S&P500	3,509	4,683
Nasdaq	11,895	15,861
TSX	16,283	21,769
FTSE	5,910	7,348
DAX	12,480	16,094
Nikkei	24,325	29,610
Hang Seng	25,713	25,328

Commodities	2020	2021
Oil	37.14	80.79
Gold	1940.8	1860.6

Bond Yields	2020	2021
USA 5 Yr Treasury	0.36	1.24
USA 10 Yr T	0.83	1.58
USA 20 Yr T	1.37	1.99
Moody's Aaa	2.31	2.61
Moody's Baa	3.34	3.27
CAN 5 Yr T	0.40	1.45
CAN 10 Yr T	0.65	1.67

Money Market	2020	2021
USA Fed Funds	0.25	0.25
USA 3 Mo T-B	0.10	0.05
CAN tgt overnight rate	0.25	0.25
CAN 3 Mo T-B	0.09	0.12

Foreign Exchange	2020	2021
EUR/USD	1.19	1.14
GBP/USD	1.32	1.34
USD/CAD	1.31	1.26
USD/JPY	103.35	113.89

NOVEMBER

M	T	W	T	F	S	S
		1	2	3	4	5
6	7	8	9	10	11	12
13	14	15	16	17	18	19
20	21	22	23	24	25	26
27	28	29	30			

DECEMBER

M	T	W	T	F	S	S
				1	2	3
4	5	6	7	8	9	10
11	12	13	14	15	16	17
18	19	20	21	22	23	24
25	26	27	28	29	30	31

JANUARY

M	T	W	T	F	S	S
1	2	3	4	5	6	7
8	9	10	11	12	13	14
15	16	17	18	19	20	21
22	23	24	25	26	27	28
29	30	31				

HOME DEPOT – BUILDING GAINS
① Oct 28 to Dec 31   ② Jan 9 to Apr 15

Home Depot is part of the consumer discretionary sector, and as such, has a similar seasonal period. Both Home Depot and the consumer discretionary sector start their seasonal periods on October 28. In the seasonal period from October 28 to December 31 (1989 to 2021), Home Depot has produced an average gain of 10.6% and has been positive 79% of the time

18% gain & positive 82% of the time

Home Depot has a second seasonal period from January 9 to April 15. In this period, Home Depot's strong seasonal period occurs at a similar time to the consumer discretionary and retail sectors' strong seasonal period.

Comparing the two seasonal periods, Home Depot has better performance in its October 28 to December 31 period compared to the January 9 to April 15 period.

Home Depot has a short period (January 1 to January 8) at the beginning of January where it tends to underperform the S&P 500. In this time period, during the years 1990 to 2022, on average Home Depot has lost 1.5% and has only outperformed the S&P 500, 36% of the time.

2021/22 Performance Update.
In 2021, Home Depot strongly outperformed the S&P 500 as the COVID home renovation phase continued. In December, Home Depot topped out and started to underperform the S&P 500. Home Depot managed to outperform the S&P 500 in its strong seasonal period from late October to late December in 2021. In 2022, Home Depot underperformed the S&P 500 in its strong seasonal period from late January to mid-April. Higher inflation reduced the demand for home renovation.

HD* vs. S&P 500 1989/90 to 2021/22 Positive ▢

Year	Oct 28 to Dec 31 S&P 500	Oct 28 to Dec 31 HD	Jan 9 to Apr 15 S&P 500	Jan 9 to Apr 15 HD	Compound Growth S&P 500	Compound Growth HD
1989/90	5.5%	9.3%	-2.7%	26.2%	2.7%	37.9%
1990/91	8.4	28.8	21.1	64.2	31.2	111.4
1991/92	8.6	23.3	-0.4	-0.2	8.1	23.1
1992/93	4.1	18.4	4.5	-9.6	8.8	7.0
1993/94	0.4	1.6	-5.1	8.1	-4.7	9.8
1994/95	-1.4	3.1	10.5	-3.4	9.0	-0.4
1995/96	6.3	29.5	3.9	4.3	10.4	35.0
1996/97	5.7	-9.3	0.8	10.7	6.6	0.5
1997/98	10.7	15.4	17.1	23.6	29.5	42.7
1998/99	15.4	49.7	3.8	8.4	19.7	62.2
1999/00	13.3	48.0	-5.9	-5.1	6.6	40.4
2000/01	-4.3	16.0	-8.7	-12.7	-12.6	1.3
2001/02	3.9	26.6	-5.0	-3.7	-1.3	21.9
2002/03	-2.0	-21.5	-2.1	28.4	-4.0	0.8
2003/04	7.8	-1.4	-0.3	0.7	7.5	-0.7
2004/05	7.7	4.8	-3.7	-12.8	3.7	-8.7
2005/06	5.9	2.8	0.3	1.8	6.2	4.7
2006/07	3.0	8.3	2.8	-4.1	5.9	4.0
2007/08	-4.4	-14.1	-4.0	12.9	-8.2	-3.0
2008/09	6.4	21.7	-6.3	5.3	-0.3	28.1
2009/10	4.9	11.3	5.8	21.3	11.0	34.9
2010/11	6.4	13.5	3.8	11.0	10.4	26.0
2011/12	-2.1	13.0	7.2	18.0	5.0	33.2
2012/13	1.0	3.0	6.5	14.3	7.6	17.7
2013/14	5.0	8.0	0.3	-7.4	5.3	0.0
2014/15	5.0	10.0	2.2	6.3	7.2	16.9
2015/16	-1.1	6.3	8.3	9.0	7.1	15.8
2016/17	5.0	9.7	2.3	9.3	7.4	19.8
2017/18	3.6	13.3	-3.3	-10.0	0.1	1.9
2018/19	-5.7	-0.2	12.9	15.2	6.4	14.9
2019/20	6.9	-6.8	-14.4	-10.5	-8.5	-16.6
2020/21	10.8	-4.1	9.0	19.9	20.8	15.1
2021/22	4.7	11.5	-6.1	-22.6	-1.7	-13.8
Avg.	4.4%	10.6%	1.7%	6.6%	6.1%	17.7%
Fq > 0	79%	79%	58%	63%	76%	82%

Home Depot- Avg. Year 1990 to 2021

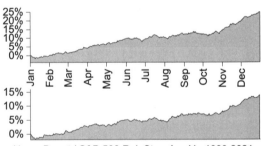

Home Depot / S&P 500 Rel. Str. - Avg Yr. 1990-2021

> **Alternate Strategy—**
> *Investors can bridge the gap between the two positive seasonal trends for Home Depot by holding from October 28th to April 15th. Longer term investors may prefer this strategy, shorter term investors can use technical tools to determine the appropriate strategy.*

> ⓘ ** Home Depot trades on the NYSE, adjusted for splits.*

Home Depot Performance

HD Monthly % Gain (1990-2021)

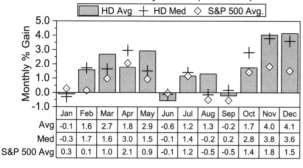

	Jan	Feb	Mar	Apr	May	Jun	Jul	Aug	Sep	Oct	Nov	Dec
Avg	-0.1	1.6	2.7	1.8	2.9	-0.6	1.2	1.3	-0.2	1.7	4.0	4.1
Med	-0.3	1.7	1.6	3.0	1.5	-0.1	1.4	-0.2	0.2	2.8	3.8	3.6
S&P 500 Avg	0.3	0.1	1.0	2.1	0.9	-0.1	1.2	-0.5	-0.5	1.4	1.8	1.5

Fq % HD Gain > 0% (1990-2021)

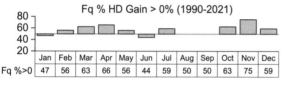

	Jan	Feb	Mar	Apr	May	Jun	Jul	Aug	Sep	Oct	Nov	Dec
Fq %>0	47	56	63	66	56	44	59	50	50	63	75	59

Fq % HD Gain > S&P 500 % (1990-2021)

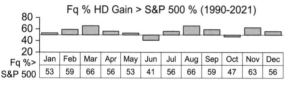

	Jan	Feb	Mar	Apr	May	Jun	Jul	Aug	Sep	Oct	Nov	Dec
Fq %> S&P 500	53	59	66	56	53	41	56	66	59	47	63	56

HD % Gain 5 Year (2017-2021)

HD Performance 2021-2022

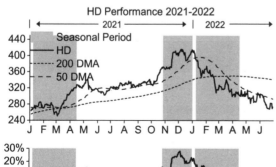

Relative Strength, % Gain vs. S&P 500

Market Indices & Rates
Weekly Values**

Stock Markets	2020	2021
Dow	29,480	35,602
S&P500	3,585	4,698
Nasdaq	11,829	16,057
TSX	16,676	21,555
FTSE	6,316	7,224
DAX	13,077	16,160
Nikkei	25,386	29,746
Hang Seng	26,157	25,050

Commodities	2020	2021
Oil	40.13	76.10
Gold	1890.9	1861.1

Bond Yields	2020	2021
USA 5 Yr Treasury	0.41	1.22
USA 10 Yr T	0.89	1.54
USA 20 Yr T	1.43	1.95
Moody's Aaa	2.35	2.63
Moody's Baa	3.33	3.27
CAN 5 Yr T	0.46	1.45
CAN 10 Yr T	0.73	1.66

Money Market	2020	2021
USA Fed Funds	0.25	0.25
USA 3 Mo T-B	0.09	0.05
CAN tgt overnight rate	0.25	0.25
CAN 3 Mo T-B	0.11	0.11

Foreign Exchange	2020	2021
EUR/USD	1.18	1.13
GBP/USD	1.32	1.35
USD/CAD	1.31	1.26
USD/JPY	104.63	113.99

NOVEMBER

M	T	W	T	F	S	S
		1	2	3	4	5
6	7	8	9	10	11	12
13	14	15	16	17	18	19
20	21	22	23	24	25	26
27	28	29	30			

DECEMBER

M	T	W	T	F	S	S
				1	2	3
4	5	6	7	8	9	10
11	12	13	14	15	16	17
18	19	20	21	22	23	24
25	26	27	28	29	30	31

JANUARY

M	T	W	T	F	S	S
1	2	3	4	5	6	7
8	9	10	11	12	13	14
15	16	17	18	19	20	21
22	23	24	25	26	27	28
29	30	31				

At the macro level, the metals and mining (M&M) sector is driven by future economic growth expectations. When worldwide growth expectations are increasing, there is a greater need for raw materials, and vice versa.

Within the macro trend, the M&M sector has traditionally followed the overall market cycle of performing well from autumn until spring. This is the time of year that investors have a positive outlook on the economy and as a result, the cyclical sectors tend to outperform, including the metals and mining sector.

14% gain

The metals and mining sector has two seasonal "sweet spots" – the first from November 19 to January 5 and the second from January 23 to May 5.

Investors have the option to hold and "bridge the gap" across the two sweet spots, but over the long-term, nimble traders have been able to capture extra value by being out of the sector from January 6 to the 22.

From a portfolio perspective, it is important to consider reducing exposure at the beginning of May. The danger of holding on too long is that the sector tends not to perform well in the late summer, particularly in September.

2021/22 Performance Update.
In 2021, the metals and mining sector slightly outperformed the S&P 500. In early 2022, the metals and mining sector performed very well and outperformed in its strong seasonal period.

For more information on the metals and mining sector, see www.standardandpoors.com

Metals & Mining* vs. S&P 500
1989/90 to 2021/22 — Positive

Year	Nov 19 to Jan 5 S&P 500	Nov 19 to Jan 5 M&M	Jan 23 to May 5 S&P 500	Jan 23 to May 5 M&M	Compound Growth S&P 500	Compound Growth M&M
1989/90	3.1 %	6.3 %	2.4 %	-4.6 %	5.6 %	1.4 %
1990/91	1.2	6.4	16.0	7.1	17.4	13.9
1991/92	8.9	1.0	-0.3	-1.7	8.5	-0.7
1992/93	2.7	12.5	1.9	3.2	4.7	16.1
1993/94	0.9	9.0	-4.9	-11.1	-4.1	-3.1
1994/95	-0.2	-1.2	11.9	-3.0	11.6	-4.1
1995/96	2.8	8.3	4.6	5.8	7.5	14.6
1996/97	1.5	-1.9	5.6	-1.2	7.2	-3.0
1997/98	4.1	-4.5	15.8	19.3	20.6	13.9
1998/99	8.8	-7.9	10.0	31.0	19.6	20.6
1999/00	-1.6	21.7	-0.6	-10.4	-2.2	9.1
2000/01	-5.1	17.0	-5.7	19.6	-10.5	40.0
2001/02	3.0	5.5	-4.1	12.8	-1.3	19.0
2002/03	0.9	9.3	5.5	3.2	6.4	12.8
2003/04	8.5	18.2	-2.0	-12.1	6.4	3.9
2004/05	0.0	-8.4	0.4	-4.0	0.4	-12.0
2005/06	2.0	17.3	5.1	27.3	7.2	49.4
2006/07	0.6	3.0	5.8	17.2	6.5	20.8
2007/08	-3.2	0.9	7.4	27.4	3.9	28.5
2008/09	8.0	43.8	9.2	30.6	17.9	87.8
2009/10	2.4	6.3	6.8	4.8	9.4	11.3
2010/11	6.7	15.0	4.0	-1.6	11.0	13.1
2011/12	5.4	1.2	4.1	-16.0	9.7	-15.0
2012/13	7.8	3.9	8.2	-16.8	16.6	-13.6
2013/14	2.2	1.2	2.2	2.6	4.4	3.8
2014/15	-1.5	-14.2	1.3	5.3	-0.3	-9.7
2015/16	-3.2	-3.4	7.5	76.3	4.1	70.2
2016/17	4.0	7.2	5.6	-10.8	9.8	-4.4
2017/18	6.4	24.3	-6.0	-11.5	0.0	9.9
2018/19	-7.5	-7.4	11.9	-2.6	3.5	-9.8
2019/20	3.6	9.7	-13.6	12.7	-10.5	23.6
2020/21	4.5	13.6	8.5	27.2	13.3	44.4
2021/22	-0.1	7.4	-5.7	13.7	-5.8	22.2
Avg.	2.3 %	6.7 %	3.6 %	7.3 %	6.0 %	14.4 %
Fq > 0	76 %	76 %	73 %	58 %	79 %	70 %

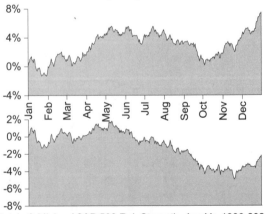

Metals & Mining - Avg. Year 1990 to 2021

Metals & Mining / S&P 500 Rel. Strength- Avg Yr. 1990-2021

Metals & Mining Performance

Metals & Mining Monthly % Gain (1990-2021)

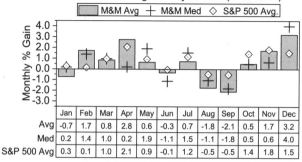

	Jan	Feb	Mar	Apr	May	Jun	Jul	Aug	Sep	Oct	Nov	Dec
Avg	-0.7	1.7	0.8	2.8	0.6	-0.3	0.7	-1.8	-2.1	0.5	1.7	3.2
Med	0.2	1.4	1.0	0.2	1.9	-1.1	1.5	-1.1	-1.8	0.5	0.6	4.0
S&P 500 Avg	0.3	0.1	1.0	2.1	0.9	-0.1	1.2	-0.5	-0.5	1.4	1.8	1.5

Fq % Metals & Mining Gain > 0% (1990-2021)

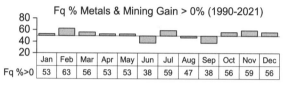

	Jan	Feb	Mar	Apr	May	Jun	Jul	Aug	Sep	Oct	Nov	Dec
Fq %>0	53	63	56	53	53	38	59	47	38	56	59	56

Fq % Metals & Mining Gain > S&P 500 % (1990-2021)

	Jan	Feb	Mar	Apr	May	Jun	Jul	Aug	Sep	Oct	Nov	Dec
Fq %> S&P 500	44	56	44	44	44	53	50	41	41	41	47	59

Metals & Mining % Gain 5 Year (2017-2021)

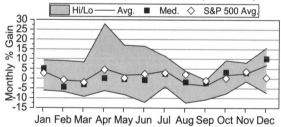

Metals & Mining Performance 2021-2022

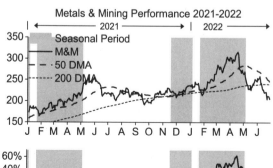

Relative Strength, % Gain vs. S&P 500

Market Indices & Rates — Weekly Values**

Stock Markets	2020	2021
Dow	29,263	34,899
S&P500	3,558	4,595
Nasdaq	11,855	15,492
TSX	17,019	21,126
FTSE	6,351	7,044
DAX	13,137	15,257
Nikkei	25,527	28,752
Hang Seng	26,452	24,081

Commodities	2020	2021
Oil	42.15	78.39
Gold	1875.7	1800.8

Bond Yields	2020	2021
USA 5 Yr Treasury	0.38	1.16
USA 10 Yr T	0.83	1.48
USA 20 Yr T	1.33	1.89
Moody's Aaa	2.24	2.61
Moody's Baa	3.18	3.30
CAN 5 Yr T	0.42	1.40
CAN 10 Yr T	0.65	1.61

Money Market	2020	2021
USA Fed Funds	0.25	0.25
USA 3 Mo T-B	0.07	0.06
CAN tgt overnight rate	0.25	0.25
CAN 3 Mo T-B	0.11	0.08

Foreign Exchange	2020	2021
EUR/USD	1.19	1.13
GBP/USD	1.33	1.33
USD/CAD	1.31	1.28
USD/JPY	103.86	113.38

NOVEMBER

M	T	W	T	F	S	S
		1	2	3	4	5
6	7	8	9	10	11	12
13	14	15	16	17	18	19
20	21	22	23	24	25	26
27	28	29	30			

DECEMBER

M	T	W	T	F	S	S
				1	2	3
4	5	6	7	8	9	10
11	12	13	14	15	16	17
18	19	20	21	22	23	24
25	26	27	28	29	30	31

JANUARY

M	T	W	T	F	S	S
1	2	3	4	5	6	7
8	9	10	11	12	13	14
15	16	17	18	19	20	21
22	23	24	25	26	27	28
29	30	31				

UPS – DELIVERING RETURNS

UPS
①LONG (Oct10-Dec8)
②SELL SHORT (Dec9-Mar1)

In recent years, Amazon has shown an increasing interest in delivering its own packages, rather than using package delivery companies. Although this trend is expected to continue, consideration should still be given to investing in UPS in its seasonal period before Christmas, as this is when UPS would still be expected to outperform the S&P 500.

Investors look for an activity that could drive a stock price higher. In UPS' case investors typically become more interested in the stock just before the holiday season. The logic is that a busy time of year will help increase earnings, which should raise the stock price.

12% growth & positive 86% of the time

The best time to get into UPS is before most investors become excited about the stock. When maximum investor interest for the stock occurs, it has been best to exit.

"Get in before everyone else and exit once everyone is in." In other words, the seasonal trend takes advantage of human behavioral tendencies.

Investors typically do not want to invest in UPS at the times of the year when its stock price lacks a near-term catalyst. January and February are low activity months for UPS. As a result, investors tend to reduce their buying of package delivery companies at the end of the year and into the beginning of March.

2021/22 Performance Update.
In 2021, UPS was volatile but managed to slightly outperform the S&P

ⓘ *UPS trades on the NYSE, adjusted for splits.*

UPS* vs. S&P 500 2000/01 to 2020/21

Positive Long ▨   Negative Short ☐

Year	Oct 10 to Dec 8 S&P 500	UPS	Dec 9 to Mar 1 S&P 500	UPS	Compound Growth S&P 500	UPS
2000/01	-2.3 %	12.0 %	-9.4 %	-12.1 %	-11.5 %	25.5 %
2001/02	9.6	12.1	-2.3	3.3	7.1	8.5
2002/03	17.4	6.5	-7.8	-10.2	8.3	17.4
2003/04	2.9	11.1	8.1	-4.9	11.3	16.5
2004/05	5.4	14.5	2.3	-11.0	7.9	27.1
2005/06	5.0	9.6	2.8	0.4	8.0	9.2
2006/07	4.4	5.6	-0.5	-10.2	3.9	16.3
2007/08	-3.9	-3.5	-11.6	-5.3	-15.0	1.6
2008/09	0.0	10.6	-19.2	-29.8	-19.2	43.5
2009/10	1.9	3.2	2.2	1.9	4.1	1.2
2010/11	5.4	6.6	6.4	0.5	12.1	6.1
2011/12	6.8	8.7	11.3	6.8	18.9	1.3
2012/13	-1.6	0.2	7.1	13.3	5.3	-13.1
2013/14	9.0	15.5	3.0	-6.5	12.3	23.0
2014/15	6.9	14.2	2.1	-7.7	9.1	22.9
2015/16	2.4	-2.4	-4.1	-2.8	-1.8	0.3
2016/17	4.3	9.4	6.7	-10.2	11.2	20.5
2017/18	4.2	2.1	1.0	-11.0	5.2	13.3
2018/19	-8.6	-10.7	6.5	6.5	-2.7	-16.5
2019/20	7.8	3.2	-6.1	-23.0	1.2	27.0
2020/21	6.5	-4.8	5.4	-3.0	12.2	-1.9
2021/22	7.1	11.6	-8.4	0.4	-1.9	11.1
Avg.	4.1 %	6.1 %	-0.2 %	-5.4 %	3.9 %	11.9 %
Fq>0	77 %	82 %	59 %	36 %	73 %	86 %

500. UPS managed to outperform the S&P 500 in its strong seasonal period from mid-October to mid-December. UPS performed well from mid-December to early March when it typically performs poorly. UPS' performance continued to volatile in the first half of 2022.

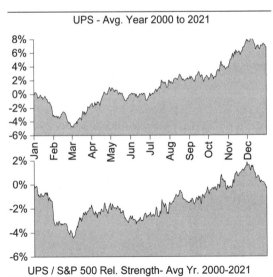

UPS - Avg. Year 2000 to 2021

UPS / S&P 500 Rel. Strength- Avg. Yr. 2000-2021

UPS Performance

UPS Monthly % Gain (2000-2021)

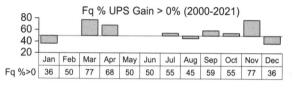

	Jan	Feb	Mar	Apr	May	Jun	Jul	Aug	Sep	Oct	Nov	Dec
Avg	-3.2	-1.7	3.6	2.5	-0.8	-0.1	2.6	0.1	0.1	1.7	3.9	-1.3
Med	-3.4	0.2	2.4	0.9	-0.3	-0.0	0.4	-0.5	1.0	1.7	4.2	-1.3
S&P 500 Avg	-0.1	-0.3	1.3	1.8	1.3	-0.7	0.6	-1.1	-0.6	1.5	1.4	2.0

Fq % UPS Gain > 0% (2000-2021)

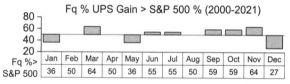

	Jan	Feb	Mar	Apr	May	Jun	Jul	Aug	Sep	Oct	Nov	Dec
Fq %>0	36	50	77	68	50	50	55	45	59	55	77	36

Fq % UPS Gain > S&P 500 % (2000-2021)

	Jan	Feb	Mar	Apr	May	Jun	Jul	Aug	Sep	Oct	Nov	Dec
Fq %> S&P 500	36	50	64	50	36	55	55	50	59	59	64	27

UPS % Gain 5 Year (2017-2021)

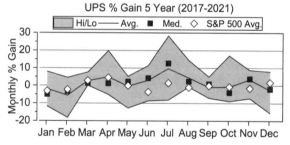

UPS Performance 2021-2022

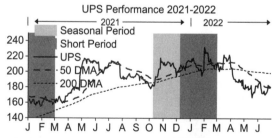

Relative Strength, % Gain vs. S&P 500

Market Indices & Rates
Weekly Values**

Stock Markets	2020	2021
Dow	29,910	34,580
S&P500	3,638	4,538
Nasdaq	12,206	15,085
TSX	17,397	20,633
FTSE	6,368	7,122
DAX	13,336	15,170
Nikkei	26,645	28,030
Hang Seng	26,895	23,767

Commodities	2020	2021
Oil	45.51	66.26
Gold	1779.3	1767.6

Bond Yields	2020	2021
USA 5 Yr Treasury	0.37	1.13
USA 10 Yr T	0.84	1.35
USA 20 Yr T	1.36	1.77
Moody's Aaa	2.20	2.49
Moody's Baa	3.16	3.16
CAN 5 Yr T	0.43	1.33
CAN 10 Yr T	0.68	1.44

Money Market	2020	2021
USA Fed Funds	0.25	0.25
USA 3 Mo T-B	0.09	0.06
CAN tgt overnight rate	0.25	0.25
CAN 3 Mo T-B	0.12	0.03

Foreign Exchange	2020	2021
EUR/USD	1.20	1.13
GBP/USD	1.33	1.32
USD/CAD	1.30	1.28
USD/JPY	104.09	112.80

NOVEMBER

M	T	W	T	F	S	S
		1	2	3	4	5
6	7	8	9	10	11	12
13	14	15	16	17	18	19
20	21	22	23	24	25	26
27	28	29	30			

DECEMBER

M	T	W	T	F	S	S
				1	2	3
4	5	6	7	8	9	10
11	12	13	14	15	16	17
18	19	20	21	22	23	24
25	26	27	28	29	30	31

JANUARY

M	T	W	T	F	S	S
1	2	3	4	5	6	7
8	9	10	11	12	13	14
15	16	17	18	19	20	21
22	23	24	25	26	27	28
29	30	31				

DECEMBER

	MONDAY	TUESDAY	WEDNESDAY
WEEK 48	27	28	29
WEEK 49	**4** 27	**5** 26	**6** 25
WEEK 50	**11** 20	**12** 19	**13** 18
WEEK 51	**18** 13	**19** 12	**20** 11
WEEK 52	**25** 6 CAN Market Closed- Christmas Day USA Market Closed- Christmas Day	**26** 5 CAN Market Closed- Boxing Day	**27** 4

THURSDAY		FRIDAY	
30	30	**1**	30
7	24	**8**	23
14	17	**15**	16
21	10	**22**	9
28	3	**29**	2

JANUARY

M	T	W	T	F	S	S
1	2	3	4	5	6	7
8	9	10	11	12	13	14
15	16	17	18	19	20	21
22	23	24	25	26	27	28
29	30	31				

FEBRUARY

M	T	W	T	F	S	S
			1	2	3	4
5	6	7	8	9	10	11
12	13	14	15	16	17	18
19	20	21	22	23	24	25
26	27	28				

MARCH

M	T	W	T	F	S	S
			1	2	3	4
5	6	7	8	9	10	11
12	13	14	15	16	17	18
19	20	21	22	23	24	25
26	27	28	29	30	31	

APRIL

M	T	W	T	F	S	S
					1	2
3	4	5	6	7	8	9
10	11	12	13	14	15	16
17	18	19	20	21	22	23
24	25	26	27	28	29	30

DECEMBER
S U M M A R Y

	Dow Jones	S&P 500	Nasdaq	TSX Comp
Month Rank	3	3	4	1
# Up	51	54	30	31
# Down	21	18	20	6
% Pos	71	75	60	84
% Avg. Gain	1.6	1.5	1.5	1.7

Dow & S&P 1950-2021, Nasdaq 1972-2021, TSX 1985-2021

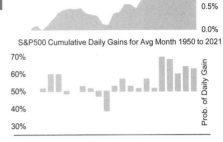

S&P500 Cumulative Daily Gains for Avg Month 1950 to 2021

Prob. of Daily Gain

♦ December is typically one of the strongest months of the year for the S&P 500. From 1950 to 2021, the S&P 500 produced an average gain of 1.5% and was positive 75% of the time. ♦ Most of the gains for the S&P 500 tend to occur in the second half of the month. ♦ The Nasdaq tends to outperform the S&P 500 starting mid-December. ♦ The small cap sector typically starts to outperform the S&P 500 mid-month.

BEST / WORST DECEMBER BROAD MKTS. 2012-2021

BEST DECEMBER MARKETS
- ♦ Nikkei 225 (2012) 10.0%
- ♦ Russell 2000 (2020) 8.5%
- ♦ Nasdaq (2020) 5.7%

WORST DECEMBER MARKETS
- ♦ Russell 2000 (2018) -12.0%
- ♦ Nikkei 225 (2018) -10.5%
- ♦ Nasdaq (2018) -9.5%

Index Values End of Month

	2012	2013	2014	2015	2016	2017	2018	2019	2020	2021
Dow	13,104	16,577	17,823	17,425	19,763	24,719	23,327	28,538	30,606	36,338
S&P 500	1,426	1,848	2,059	2,044	2,239	2,674	2,507	3,231	3,756	4,766
Nasdaq	3,020	4,177	4,736	5,007	5,383	6,903	6,635	8,973	12,888	15,645
TSX Comp.	12,434	13,622	14,632	13,010	15,288	16,209	14,323	17,063	17,433	21,223
Russell 1000	790	1,030	1,144	1,132	1,242	1,482	1,384	1,784	2,121	2,646
Russell 2000	849	1,164	1,205	1,136	1,357	1,536	1,349	1,668	1,975	2,245
FTSE 100	5,898	6,749	6,566	6,242	7,143	7,688	6,728	7,542	6,461	7,385
Nikkei 225	10,395	16,291	17,451	19,034	19,114	22,765	20,015	23,657	27,444	28,792

Percent Gain for December

	2012	2013	2014	2015	2016	2017	2018	2019	2020	2021
Dow	0.6	3.0	0.0	-1.7	3.3	1.8	-8.7	1.7	3.3	5.4
S&P 500	0.7	2.4	-0.4	-1.8	1.8	1.0	-9.2	2.9	3.7	4.4
Nasdaq	0.3	2.9	-1.2	-2.0	1.1	0.4	-9.5	3.5	5.7	0.7
TSX Comp.	1.6	1.7	-0.8	-3.4	1.4	0.9	-5.8	0.1	1.4	2.7
Russell 1000	0.8	2.5	-0.4	-2.0	1.7	1.0	-9.3	2.7	4.1	3.9
Russell 2000	3.3	1.8	2.7	-5.2	2.6	-0.6	-12.0	2.7	8.5	2.1
FTSE 100	0.5	1.5	-2.3	-1.8	5.3	4.9	-3.6	2.7	3.1	4.6
Nikkei 225	10.0	4.0	-0.1	-3.6	4.4	0.2	-10.5	1.6	3.8	3.5

December Market Avg. Performance 2012 to 2021[1]

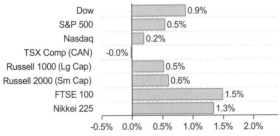

Dow	0.9%
S&P 500	0.5%
Nasdaq	0.2%
TSX Comp (CAN)	-0.0%
Russell 1000 (Lg Cap)	0.5%
Russell 2000 (Sm Cap)	0.6%
FTSE 100	1.5%
Nikkei 225	1.3%

Interest Corner Dec[2]

	Fed Funds % [3]	3 Mo. T-Bill % [4]	10 Yr % [5]	20 Yr % [6]
2021	0.25	0.06	1.52	1.94
2020	0.25	0.09	0.93	1.45
2019	1.75	1.55	1.92	2.25
2018	2.50	2.45	2.69	2.87
2017	1.50	1.39	2.40	2.58

(1) Russell Data provided by Russell (2) Federal Reserve Bank of St. Louis- end of month values (3) Target rate set by FOMC (4)(5)(6) Constant yield maturities.

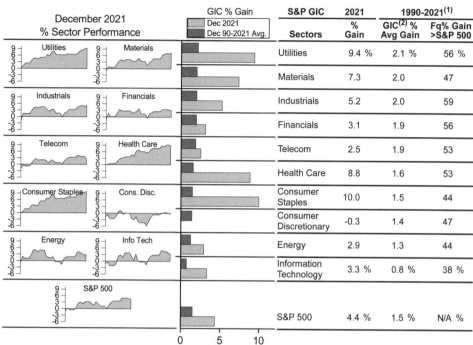

S&P GIC Sectors	2021 % Gain	1990-2021[1] GIC[2] % Avg Gain	Fq% Gain >S&P 500
Utilities	9.4 %	2.1 %	56 %
Materials	7.3	2.0	47
Industrials	5.2	2.0	59
Financials	3.1	1.9	56
Telecom	2.5	1.9	53
Health Care	8.8	1.6	53
Consumer Staples	10.0	1.5	44
Consumer Discretionary	-0.3	1.4	47
Energy	2.9	1.3	44
Information Technology	3.3 %	0.8 %	38 %
S&P 500	4.4 %	1.5 %	N/A %

Sector Commentary

♦ In December 2021, the S&P 500 produced a strong gain of 4.4%. ♦ All of the major sectors were positive except for the consumer discretionary sector which lost 0.3%. ♦ In December, interest rates were rising and yet the consumer staples sector managed to produce a gain of 10%. ♦ The other defensive sectors also outperformed the S&P 500. The health care sector produced a gain of 8.8% and the utilities sector managed to produce a gain of 9.4%. ♦ The defensive sectors outperforming the S&P 500, strongly when interest rates were moving higher and the overall market performing well was a sign that investors were becoming more cautious and the stock market was becoming more susceptible to a correction.

Sub-Sector Commentary

♦ In December 2021, the homebuilders sub-sector followed its seasonal trend of strong performance with a gain of 11.7%. ♦ December is the first full month of the metals & mining strong seasonal period. In December, the metals & mining sub-sector produced a gain of 11.5%

SELECTED SUB-SECTORS[3]			
Homebuilders	11.7 %	6.1 %	75 %
Steel	7.4	3.9	59
Metals & Mining	11.5	3.2	59
Biotech (1993-2021)	4.3	2.9	43
Agriculture (1994-2021)	8.6	2.1	54
Silver	1.0	1.9	57
Banks	-0.2	1.8	59
Chemicals	6.9	1.7	53
Pharma	9.4	1.4	50
Railroads	8.2	1.3	47
SOX (1995-2021)	2.9	1.2	48
Transportation	7.6	0.7	38
Retail	-1.3	0.6	34
Auto	-5.5	0.4	31
Gold	0.1	0.4	38

BRINK'S
(NEW) BCO
December 1 to December 31

Brink's provides secure transportation, cash management and other security related services.

If there were one month of the year to invest in Brink's it would have to be December on a seasonal basis. Brink's has a strong track record of performing well in the last month of the year.

73% of the time
better than the S&P 500

From 1996 to 2021, in the month of December, Brink's has produced a average gain of 5.8% and has been positive 77% of the time. In the same time period, Brink's has outperformed the S&P 500, 73% of the time.

Brink's tends to perform well in the month of November, but its performance is not as strong as in December. In addition, it is typically the second half of November that provides the biggest benefit. Investors should be on the watch for Brink's starting to outperform the S&P 500 in late November.

Over the last five years, Brink's has on average been slightly positive in December. November has been one of the strongest months of the year in the same time period.

BCO vs. S&P 500 1996 to 2021

Nov 15 to Dec 31	S&P 500	Positive BCO	Diff
1996	-2.2 %	5.9 %	8.0 %
1997	1.6	9.9	8.3
1998	5.6	6.3	0.6
1999	5.8	15.8	10.0
2000	0.4	31.4	31.0
2001	0.8	7.2	6.5
2002	-6.0	-2.0	4.0
2003	5.1	1.8	-3.2
2004	3.2	2.4	-0.9
2005	-0.1	3.8	3.9
2006	1.3	13.9	12.6
2007	-0.9	-6.6	-5.8
2008	0.8	23.5	22.7
2009	1.8	8.3	6.5
2010	6.5	9.5	3.0
2011	0.9	9.2	8.3
2012	0.7	3.9	3.2
2013	2.4	1.8	-0.5
2014	-0.4	12.5	12.9
2015	-1.8	-10.3	-8.6
2016	1.8	2.1	0.3
2017	1.0	-2.7	-3.6
2018	-9.2	-8.7	0.5
2019	2.9	-2.5	-5.4
2020	3.7	7.3	3.6
2021	4.4	7.2	2.8
Avg.	1.2 %	5.8 %	4.6 %
Fq > 0	73 %	77 %	73 %

Investors should also note that Brink's tends to underperform the S&P 500 in the months early in the new year: January and February. Investors should be nimble in exiting Brink's towards the end of December if Brink's starts to underperform.

2021/22 Performance Update.
In 2021, Brink's underperformed the S&P 500 for the whole year, but managed to outperform the S&P 500 in its seasonal period.

In 2022, In the first six months of the year, Brink's lost ground, but managed to outperform the S&P 500.

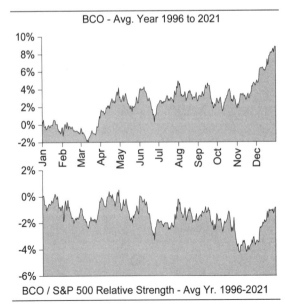

BCO - Avg. Year 1996 to 2021

BCO / S&P 500 Relative Strength - Avg Yr. 1996-2021

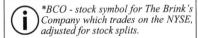

BCO - stock symbol for The Brink's Company which trades on the NYSE, adjusted for stock splits.

Brink's Performance

BCO Monthly % Gain (1996-2021)

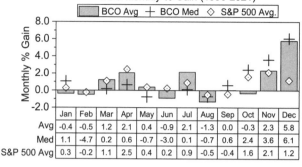

	Jan	Feb	Mar	Apr	May	Jun	Jul	Aug	Sep	Oct	Nov	Dec
Avg	-0.4	-0.5	1.2	2.1	0.4	-0.9	2.1	-1.3	0.0	-0.3	2.3	5.8
Med	1.1	-4.7	0.2	0.6	-0.7	-3.0	0.1	-0.7	0.6	2.4	3.6	6.1
S&P 500 Avg	0.3	-0.2	1.1	2.5	0.4	0.2	0.9	-0.5	-0.4	1.6	2.1	1.2

Fq % BCO Gain > 0% (1996-2021)

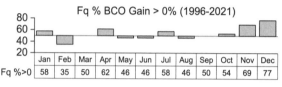

	Jan	Feb	Mar	Apr	May	Jun	Jul	Aug	Sep	Oct	Nov	Dec
Fq %>0	58	35	50	62	46	46	58	46	50	54	69	77

Fq % BCO Gain > S&P 500 % (1996-2021)

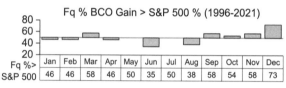

	Jan	Feb	Mar	Apr	May	Jun	Jul	Aug	Sep	Oct	Nov	Dec
Fq %> S&P 500	46	46	58	46	50	35	50	38	58	54	58	73

BCO % Gain 5 Year (2017-2021)

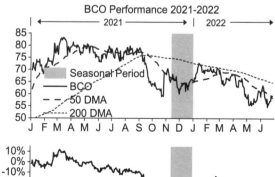

BCO Performance 2021-2022

Relative Strength, % Gain vs. S&P 500

WEEK 49

Market Indices & Rates
Weekly Values**

Stock Markets	2020	2021
Dow	30,218	35,971
S&P500	3,699	4,712
Nasdaq	12,464	15,631
TSX	17,521	20,891
FTSE	6,550	7,292
DAX	13,299	15,623
Nikkei	26,751	28,438
Hang Seng	26,836	23,996

Commodities	2020	2021
Oil	46.26	71.67
Gold	1843.0	1779.8

Bond Yields	2020	2021
USA 5 Yr Treasury	0.42	1.25
USA 10 Yr T	0.97	1.48
USA 20 Yr T	1.53	1.91
Moody's Aaa	2.26	2.67
Moody's Baa	3.20	3.31
CAN 5 Yr T	0.50	1.32
CAN 10 Yr T	0.80	1.47

Money Market	2020	2021
USA Fed Funds	0.25	0.25
USA 3 Mo T-B	0.09	0.06
CAN tgt overnight rate	0.25	0.25
CAN 3 Mo T-B	0.12	0.00

Foreign Exchange	2020	2021
EUR/USD	1.21	1.13
GBP/USD	1.34	1.33
USD/CAD	1.28	1.27
USD/JPY	104.17	113.44

DECEMBER

M	T	W	T	F	S	S
				1	2	3
4	5	6	7	8	9	10
11	12	13	14	15	16	17
18	19	20	21	22	23	24
25	26	27	28	29	30	31

JANUARY

M	T	W	T	F	S	S
1	2	3	4	5	6	7
8	9	10	11	12	13	14
15	16	17	18	19	20	21
22	23	24	25	26	27	28
29	30	31				

FEBRUARY

M	T	W	T	F	S	
			1	2	3	4
5	6	7	8	9	10	11
12	13	14	15	16	17	18
19	20	21	22	23	24	25
26	27	28	29			

10-YR Inflation Break-Even (B/E) rate

The 10YR inflation break-even rate is representative of investors' expectations for inflation over the next ten years. It is approximately calculated by subtracting the yield on the 10 Year Treasury Inflation Protected bonds (TIPS) from the yield on 10 Year US Treasury 10 year bonds.

The Federal Reserve went from declaring that inflation was not a problem before the COVID-19 pandemic, to it is transitory during the pandemic to we have to get it under control.

58% increase & positive 89% of the time

Investors have on average adjusted their expectations upwards for inflation towards the end of the year and into early March of the following year. The most probable cause of this phenomenon is investors adjusting their expectations based upon overly optimistic full year analyst forecasts that generally get published at the end of the year and the beginning of the next year.

10 YR Inflation Break-Even*
2003/04 to 2021/22

Positive	
Dec 20 to Mar 7	B/E
2003/04	8.6 %
2004/05	4.3
2005/06	10.3
2006/07	2.2
2007/08	9.4
2008/09	440.0*
2009/10	-1.3
2010/11	10.1
2011/12	13.4
2012/13	3.2
2013/14	3.7
2014/15	8.9
2015/16	1.4
2016/17	9.1
2017/18	11.5
2018/19	5.6
2019/20	-26.0
2020/21	13.8
2021/22	16.4
Avg	58 %
Fq > 0	89 %

*2008/09 data has been excluded from average and frequency % positive data.

10-YR B/E Inflation - Avg. Year 2003 to 2021

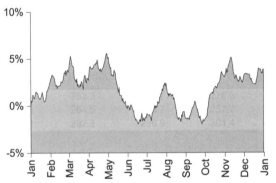

*Excludes 2008-2009 due to extreme volatility

At the retail level, one of the better methods of taking advantage of the 10YR-B/E strategy is to invest in an ETF that invests in Treasury Inflation Protected TIPS bonds and to short sell an ETF that represents the US 10YR Government bonds of the same maturity. It is important to consider the full risk of the trade, including all of the costs that go along with short selling.

Although most investors will probably not invest directly in a B/E spread trade, investors can still benefit from understanding the impact of investing in other sectors of the stock and bond markets that are affected by changing inflation expectations.

2021/22 Performance Update.

In 2021, the B/E 10YR inflation rate moved up higher for most of the year, including in its strong seasonal period. The CPI inflation rate was moving higher in 2021 and investors continued to extrapolate expected inflation higher in the future.

In 2022, early in the year, inflation expectations moved sharply higher. The stock market, responded with a move lower. Inflation expectations were positive in their strong seasonal period in 2022.

> *For more information on 10yr break-even inflation rates, see www.https://fred.stlouisfed.org/series/T10YIE*

10YR Inflation Break-Even Performance

*2008 & 2009 removed due to extreme volatility

10-YR Inflation Break-Even (B/E) Rate Monthly % Gain (2003-2021)*

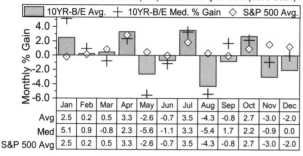

	Jan	Feb	Mar	Apr	May	Jun	Jul	Aug	Sep	Oct	Nov	Dec
Avg	2.5	0.2	0.5	3.3	-2.6	-0.7	3.5	-4.3	-0.8	2.7	-3.0	-2.0
Med	5.1	0.9	-0.8	2.3	-5.6	-1.1	3.3	-5.4	1.7	2.2	-0.9	0.0
S&P 500 Avg	2.5	0.2	0.5	3.3	-2.6	-0.7	3.5	-4.3	-0.8	2.7	-3.0	-2.0

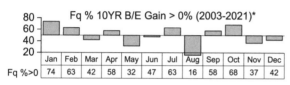

Fq % 10YR B/E Gain > 0% (2003-2021)*

	Jan	Feb	Mar	Apr	May	Jun	Jul	Aug	Sep	Oct	Nov	Dec
Fq %>0	74	63	42	58	32	47	63	16	58	68	37	42

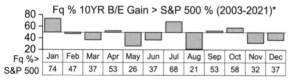

Fq % 10YR B/E Gain > S&P 500 % (2003-2021)*

	Jan	Feb	Mar	Apr	May	Jun	Jul	Aug	Sep	Oct	Nov	Dec
Fq %> S&P 500	74	47	37	53	26	37	68	21	53	58	32	37

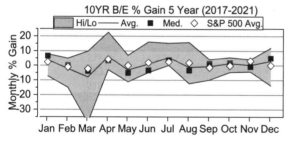

10YR B/E % Gain 5 Year (2017-2021)

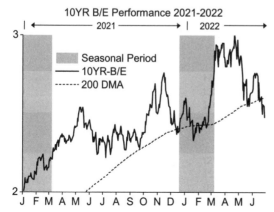

10YR B/E Performance 2021-2022

Market Indices & Rates Weekly Values**

Stock Markets	2020	2021
Dow	30,046	35,365
S&P500	3,663	4,621
Nasdaq	12,378	15,170
TSX	17,549	20,739
FTSE	6,547	7,270
DAX	13,114	15,532
Nikkei	26,653	28,546
Hang Seng	26,506	23,193

Commodities	2020	2021
Oil	46.57	70.86
Gold	1842.0	1807.7

Bond Yields	2020	2021
USA 5 Yr Treasury	0.37	1.18
USA 10 Yr T	0.90	1.41
USA 20 Yr T	1.42	1.87
Moody's Aaa	2.27	2.63
Moody's Baa	3.13	3.28
CAN 5 Yr T	0.44	1.18
CAN 10 Yr T	0.71	1.32

Money Market	2020	2021
USA Fed Funds	0.25	0.25
USA 3 Mo T-B	0.08	0.05
CAN tgt overnight rate	0.25	0.25
CAN 3 Mo T-B	0.13	0.05

Foreign Exchange	2020	2021
EUR/USD	1.21	1.12
GBP/USD	1.32	1.32
USD/CAD	1.28	1.29
USD/JPY	104.04	113.63

DECEMBER

M	T	W	T	F	S	S
				1	2	3
4	5	6	7	8	9	10
11	12	13	14	15	16	17
18	19	20	21	22	23	24
25	26	27	28	29	30	31

JANUARY

M	T	W	T	F	S	S
1	2	3	4	5	6	7
8	9	10	11	12	13	14
15	16	17	18	19	20	21
22	23	24	25	26	27	28
29	30	31				

FEBRUARY

M	T	W	T	F	S	S
		1	2	3	4	
5	6	7	8	9	10	11
12	13	14	15	16	17	18
19	20	21	22	23	24	25
26	27	28	29			

DO THE "NAZ" WITH SANTA
Nasdaq Gives More at Christmas – Dec 15 to Jan 23

One of the best times to invest in the major stock markets is the period around Christmas. The markets are generally positive at this time of the year as investors reposition their portfolios for the start of the new year. A lot of investors are familiar with the *Small Cap Effect* opportunity that starts approximately at this time of the year, where small caps tend to outperform from mid-December until the beginning of March (*see Small Cap Effect*), but few investors know that the last half of December and the first half of January is also a seasonally strong period for the Nasdaq.

80% of time better than S&P 500

The Nasdaq tends to perform well in the last two weeks of December, as investors typically increase their investment allocation to higher beta investments, including the Nasdaq, to finish the year.

In addition, the major sector drivers of the Nasdaq (biotech and technology), tend to perform well in the second half of December and the first half of January. Biotech tends to perform well in the last half of December, and technology tends to perform well in the first half of January. The end result is a Nasdaq Christmas trade that lasts from December 15 to January 23. In this time period, for the years 1971/72 to 2021/22, the Nasdaq has outperformed the S&P 500 by an average 1.9% per year. This rate of return is considered to be very high given that the length of the favorable period is just over one month. Even more impressive is the 80% frequency that the Nasdaq has outperformed the S&P 500.

Nasdaq vs. S&P 500 Dec 15th to Jan 23rd 1971/72 To 2021/22		
Dec 15 to Jan 23 S&P 500	Positive Nasdaq	Diff
1971/72 6.1 %	7.5 %	1.3 %
1972/73 0.0	-0.7	-0.7
1973/74 4.1	6.8	2.8
1974/75 7.5	8.9	1.4
1975/76 13.0	13.8	0.9
1976/77 -1.7	2.8	4.5
1977/78 -5.1	-3.5	1.6
1978/79 4.7	6.2	1.4
1979/80 4.1	5.6	1.5
1980/81 0.8	3.3	2.5
1981/82 -6.0	-5.0	1.0
1982/83 4.7	5.5	0.8
1983/84 0.9	1.4	0.4
1984/85 9.0	13.3	4.3
1985/86 -2.7	0.8	3.5
1986/87 9.2	10.2	1.0
1987/88 1.8	9.1	7.3
1988/89 3.3	4.6	1.3
1989/90 -5.5	-3.8	1.7
1990/91 1.0	4.1	3.1
1991/92 7.9	15.2	7.2
1992/93 0.8	7.2	6.4
1993/94 2.5	5.7	3.2
1994/95 2.4	4.7	2.3
1995/96 -0.7	-1.0	-0.3
1996/97 6.7	7.3	0.6
1997/98 0.4	2.6	2.1
1998/99 7.4	18.9	11.6
1999/00 2.7	18.6	15.9
2000/01 1.5	4.1	2.6
2001/02 0.5	-1.6	-2.0
2002/03 -0.2	1.9	2.1
2003/04 6.3	9.0	2.7
2004/05 -3.0	-5.8	-2.9
2005/06 -0.7	-0.6	0.1
2006/07 0.2	-0.9	-1.1
2007/08 -8.8	-12.1	-3.3
2008/09 -5.4	-4.1	1.3
2009/10 -2.0	-0.3	1.7
2010/11 3.4	2.4	-1.0
2011/12 8.6	9.6	1.1
2012/13 5.8	6.1	0.4
2013/14 3.0	5.5	2.5
2014/15 2.5	2.2	-0.2
2015/16 -5.7	-7.3	-1.6
2016/17 0.5	2.1	1.6
2017/18 7.1	8.8	1.8
2018/19 1.5	1.7	0.2
2019/20 4.9	7.6	2.7
2020/21 5.3	8.9	3.5
2021/22 -5.1	-9.6	-4.5
Avg 1.9 %	3.9 %	1.9 %
Fq > 0 71 %	73 %	80 %

Nasdaq - Avg. Year 1972 to 2021

Nasdaq / SP 500 Relative Strength - Avg Yr. 1972-2021

Ⓨ *Alternate Strategy — For those investors who favor the Nasdaq, an alternative strategy is to invest in the Nasdaq at an earlier date: October 28th. Historically, on average the Nasdaq has started its outperformance at this time. The "Do the Naz with Santa" strategy focuses on the sweet spot of the Nasdaq's outperformance.*

Nasdaq Performance

Nasdaq Monthly % Gain (1972-2021)

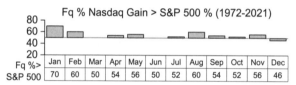

	Jan	Feb	Mar	Apr	May	Jun	Jul	Aug	Sep	Oct	Nov	Dec
Avg	2.9	0.1	0.5	1.4	1.3	1.0	-0.1	0.3	-0.9	0.3	1.7	1.8
Med	3.1	-0.5	0.8	1.7	2.8	1.5	-0.5	1.8	0.2	1.1	2.6	0.8
S&P 500 Avg	1.2	0.1	0.9	1.8	0.7	0.5	0.7	0.1	-0.8	1.0	1.5	1.3

Fq % Nasdaq Gain > 0% (1972-2021)

	Jan	Feb	Mar	Apr	May	Jun	Jul	Aug	Sep	Oct	Nov	Dec
Fq %>0	66	54	62	66	62	58	58	56	52	56	72	60

Fq % Nasdaq Gain > S&P 500 % (1972-2021)

	Jan	Feb	Mar	Apr	May	Jun	Jul	Aug	Sep	Oct	Nov	Dec
Fq %> S&P 500	70	60	50	54	56	50	52	60	54	52	56	46

Nasdaq % Gain 5 Year (2017-2021)

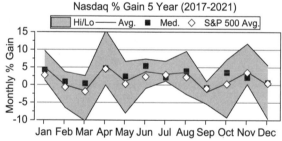

Nasdaq Performance 2021-2022

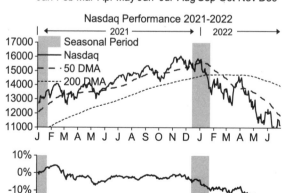

Relative Strength, % Gain vs. S&P 500

Market Indices & Rates
Weekly Values**

Stock Markets	2020	2021
Dow	30,179	35,951
S&P500	3,709	4,726
Nasdaq	12,756	15,653
TSX	17,535	21,230
FTSE	6,529	7,372
DAX	13,631	15,756
Nikkei	26,763	28,783
Hang Seng	26,499	23,224

Commodities	2020	2021
Oil	49.10	73.74
Gold	1879.8	1805.2

Bond Yields	2020	2021
USA 5 Yr Treasury	0.39	1.25
USA 10 Yr T	0.95	1.50
USA 20 Yr T	1.49	1.94
Moody's Aaa	2.32	2.74
Moody's Baa	3.19	3.36
CAN 5 Yr T	0.45	1.29
CAN 10 Yr T	0.75	1.46

Money Market	2020	2021
USA Fed Funds	0.25	0.25
USA 3 Mo T-B	0.08	0.07
CAN tgt overnight rate	0.25	0.25
CAN 3 Mo T-B	0.10	0.16

Foreign Exchange	2020	2021
EUR/USD	1.23	1.13
GBP/USD	1.35	1.34
USD/CAD	1.28	1.28
USD/JPY	103.30	114.38

DECEMBER

M	T	W	T	F	S	S
				1	2	3
4	5	6	7	8	9	10
11	12	13	14	15	16	17
18	19	20	21	22	23	24
25	26	27	28	29	30	31

JANUARY

M	T	W	T	F	S	S
1	2	3	4	5	6	7
8	9	10	11	12	13	14
15	16	17	18	19	20	21
22	23	24	25	26	27	28
29	30	31				

FEBRUARY

M	T	W	T	F	S	
			1	2	3	4
5	6	7	8	9	10	11
12	13	14	15	16	17	18
19	20	21	22	23	24	25
26	27	28	29			

SMALL CAP (SMALL COMPANY) EFFECT
Small Companies Outperform - Dec 19 to Mar 7

At different stages of the business cycle, small capitalization companies (small caps represented by Russell 2000), perform better than large capitalization companies (large caps represented by Russell 1000).

Evidence shows that the small caps relative outperformance also has a seasonal component as they typically outperform large caps from December 19 to March 7.

> **5% gain and**
> **positive 74% of the time**

Russell 2000 - Avg. Year 1979 to 2021

Russell 2000 / Russell 1000 - Avg Yr. 1979-2021

In recent times, the *January Effect* start date has shifted to mid-December and is more pronounced for small caps as their prices are more volatile than large caps.

At the beginning of the year, small cap stocks benefit from a phenomenon that I have coined, "beta out of the gate, and coast." If small cap stocks are outperforming at the beginning of the year, money managers will gravitate to the sector in order to produce returns that are above their index benchmark.

Once above average returns have been "locked in," the managers then rotate from their small cap overweight positions back to index large cap positions and coast for the rest of the year with above average returns. The overall process boosts small cap stocks at the beginning of the year.

Russell 2000 vs. Russell 1000* % Gains
Dec 19th to Mar 7th 1979/80 to 2021/22
Positive

Dec 19 - Mar 7	Russell 1000	Russell 2000	Diff
1979/80	-1.3 %	-0.4 %	0.9 %
1980/81	-2.8	4.0	6.8
1981/82	-12.4	-12.1	0.3
1982/83	11.8	19.8	8.0
1983/84	-6.4	-7.5	-1.1
1984/85	7.7	17.1	9.4
1985/86	8.2	11.7	3.5
1986/87	17.2	21.3	4.1
1987/88	8.3	16.4	8.0
1988/89	6.9	9.1	2.5
1989/90	-2.0	-1.9	0.2
1990/91	14.6	29.0	14.4
1991/92	6.0	16.8	10.8
1992/93	1.4	5.0	3.5
1993/94	0.5	5.7	5.3
1994/95	5.3	5.5	0.2
1995/96	8.3	7.8	-0.5
1996/97	9.5	3.5	-6.0
1997/98	10.2	10.3	0.1
1998/99	7.3	0.2	-7.2
1999/00	-1.7	27.7	29.4
2000/01	-5.2	4.7	9.8
2001/02	1.6	1.9	0.4
2002/03	-6.7	-7.8	-1.0
2003/04	6.4	9.6	3.3
2004/05	2.8	0.3	-2.5
2005/06	0.8	5.6	4.7
2006/07	-1.6	-0.8	0.9
2007/08	-10.9	-12.5	-1.5
2008/09	-22.2	-26.7	-4.5
2009/10	3.6	9.1	5.5
2010/11	5.5	4.2	-1.3
2011/12	11.3	10.2	-1.1
2012/13	7.1	10.3	3.1
2013/14	4.2	6.1	2.0
2014/15	1.0	2.1	1.1
2015/16	-0.3	-2.4	-2.1
2016/17	4.8	0.8	-4.1
2017/18	1.5	1.7	0.2
2018/19	8.4	10.6	2.2
2019/20	-6.8	-12.8	-5.9
2020/21	3.2	11.3	8.0
2021/22	-9.8	-10.2	-0.5
Avg.	2.2 %	4.8 %	2.5 %
Fq > 0	67 %	74 %	65 %

2021/22 Performance Update.
In 2021, after the end of its seasonal period in March, the small cap sector started to underperform the S&P 500 and continued for most of the rest of the year. In the first half of 2022, the small cap sector performed poorly.

(i) *Russell 2000 (small cap index): The 2000 smallest companies in the Russell 3000 stock index (a broad market index). Russell 1000 (large cap index): The 1000 largest companies in the Russell 3000 stock index.*

Small Caps Performance

Russell 2000 Monthly % Gain (1979-2021)

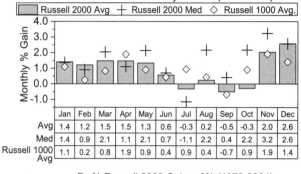

Russell 2000 Avg + Russell 2000 Med ◇ Russell 1000 Avg.

	Jan	Feb	Mar	Apr	May	Jun	Jul	Aug	Sep	Oct	Nov	Dec
Avg	1.4	1.2	1.5	1.5	1.3	0.6	-0.3	0.2	-0.5	-0.3	2.0	2.6
Med	1.4	0.9	2.1	1.1	2.1	0.7	-1.1	2.2	0.4	2.2	3.2	2.6
Russell 1000 Avg	1.1	0.2	0.8	1.9	0.9	0.4	0.9	0.4	-0.7	0.9	1.9	1.4

Fq % Russell 2000 Gain > 0% (1979-2021)

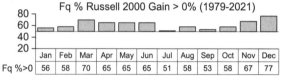

	Jan	Feb	Mar	Apr	May	Jun	Jul	Aug	Sep	Oct	Nov	Dec
Fq %>0	56	58	70	65	65	65	51	58	53	58	67	77

Fq % Russell 2000 Gain > Russell 1000 % (1979-2021)

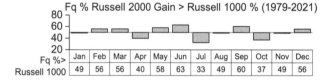

	Jan	Feb	Mar	Apr	May	Jun	Jul	Aug	Sep	Oct	Nov	Dec
Fq %> Russell 1000	49	56	56	40	58	63	33	49	60	37	49	56

Russell 2000 % Gain 5 Year (2017-2021)

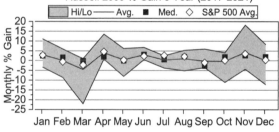

Hi/Lo —— Avg. ■ Med. ◇ S&P 500 Avg.

Russell 2000 Performance 2021-2022

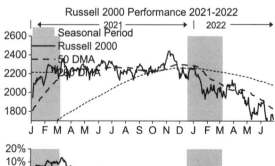

Relative Strength, % Gain vs. Russell 1000

Market Indices & Rates
Weekly Values**

Stock Markets	2020	2021
Dow	30,200	36,338
S&P500	3,703	4,766
Nasdaq	12,805	15,645
TSX	17,624	21,223
FTSE	6,502	7,385
DAX	13,587	15,885
Nikkei	26,657	28,792
Hang Seng	26,387	23,398

Commodities	2020	2021
Oil	48.08	76.99
Gold	1875.0	1805.9

Bond Yields	2020	2021
USA 5 Yr Treasury	0.37	1.26
USA 10 Yr T	0.94	1.52
USA 20 Yr T	1.46	1.94
Moody's Aaa	2.26	2.66
Moody's Baa	3.17	3.34
CAN 5 Yr T	0.43	1.26
CAN 10 Yr T	0.72	1.43

Money Market	2020	2021
USA Fed Funds	0.25	0.25
USA 3 Mo T-B	0.09	0.06
CAN tgt overnight rate	0.25	0.25
CAN 3 Mo T-B	0.09	0.16

Foreign Exchange	2020	2021
EUR/USD	1.22	1.14
GBP/USD	1.36	1.35
USD/CAD	1.29	1.26
USD/JPY	103.43	115.08

DECEMBER

M	T	W	T	F	S	S
				1	2	3
4	5	6	7	8	9	10
11	12	13	14	15	16	17
18	19	20	21	22	23	24
25	26	27	28	29	30	31

JANUARY

M	T	W	T	F	S	S
1	2	3	4	5	6	7
8	9	10	11	12	13	14
15	16	17	18	19	20	21
22	23	24	25	26	27	28
29	30	31				

FEBRUARY

M	T	W	T	F	S	S
				1	2	3	4
5	6	7	8	9	10	11
12	13	14	15	16	17	18
19	20	21	22	23	24	25
26	27	28	29			

FINANCIALS (U.S.) YEAR END CLEAN UP
December 15 to April 13

The main driver for the strong seasonal performance of the financial sector has been the year-end earnings of the banks that start to report in mid-January. A strong performance from mid-December has been the result of investors getting into the market early to take advantage of positive year-end earnings.

5% gain

In recent years, the financial sector has become more sensitive to interest rate movements. When interest rates have been rising and the yield curve steepening, banks have benefited from an increase in net interest margins and vice versa.

The strongest month of the year on an average basis for the banking sector has been April over the long-term. This trend has also occurred over the last five years.

Dec 15 to Apr 13	S&P 500	Positive Financials	Diff
1989/90	-1.9 %	-9.9 %	-8.0 %
1990/91	16.4	29.2	12.8
1991/92	5.6	9.2	3.5
1992/93	3.8	17.9	14.1
1993/94	-3.6	-0.4	3.2
1994/95	11.9	14.0	2.1
1995/96	3.2	5.5	2.3
1996/97	1.2	4.7	3.4
19/9798	16.4	19.7	3.3
1998/99	18.3	24.9	6.6
1999/00	2.7	4.0	1.3
2000/01	-11.7	-4.8	6.9
2001/02	-1.1	6.5	7.6
2002/03	-2.4	-1.8	0.6
2003/04	5.2	6.7	1.5
2004/05	-2.5	-6.2	-3.7
2005/06	1.3	1.1	-0.2
2006/07	1.9	-2.2	-4.1
2007/08	-9.2	-14.1	-4.9
2008/09	-2.4	-7.0	-4.6
2009/10	7.5	15.2	7.8
2010/11	5.9	4.6	-1.3
2011/12	13.1	20.7	7.7
2012/13	12.4	16.0	3.6
2013/14	2.3	1.0	-1.3
2014/15	4.5	1.1	-3.4
2015/16	3.0	-2.0	-5.0
2016/17	3.4	-2.0	-5.4
2017/18	0.2	-0.6	-0.7
2018/19	11.8	12.5	0.6
2019/20	-12.8	-26.2	-13.4
2020/21	13.5	24.7	11.2
2021/22	-4.0	-3.8	0.2
Avg.	3.4 %	4.8 %	1.3 %
Fq > 0	70 %	61 %	61 %

Financials* vs. S&P 500 1989/90 to 2021/22

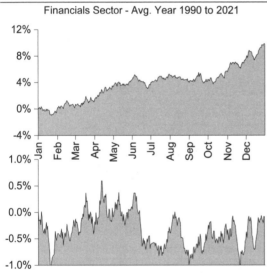

Financials Sector - Avg. Year 1990 to 2021

Financials / S&P 500 Relative Strength - Avg. Yr. 1990-2021

The seasonal trend for the banking sector has not been as strong in recent years compared to the 1990's, particularly when the banking sector has struggled. Nevertheless, seasonal investors would be wise to consider concentrating their financial investments during the sector's strong seasonal period that lasts from mid-December to mid-April.

It should be noted that Canadian banks have different year-ends and different seasonal periods compared to the US banks.

2021/22 Performance Update.
In 2021, the financial sector outperformed the S&P 500 as rising interesting rates boosted bank net interest margins.

At the end of 2021, the financial sector performed particularly well, but gave back some of its gains late in its seasonal period. Nevertheless, the financial sector managed to outperform the S&P 500 in its strong seasonal period from mid-December to mid-April.

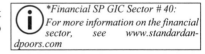

*Financial SP GIC Sector # 40:
For more information on the financial sector, see www.standardandpoors.com

Financials Performance

Financials Monthly % Gain (1990-2021)

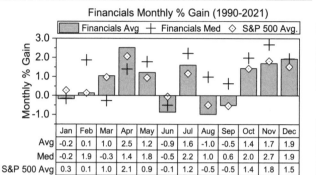

Legend: Financials Avg | Financials Med | S&P 500 Avg.

	Jan	Feb	Mar	Apr	May	Jun	Jul	Aug	Sep	Oct	Nov	Dec
Avg	-0.2	0.1	1.0	2.5	1.2	-0.9	1.6	-1.0	-0.5	1.4	1.7	1.9
Med	-0.2	1.9	-0.3	1.4	1.8	-0.5	2.2	1.0	0.6	2.0	2.7	1.9
S&P 500 Avg	0.3	0.1	1.0	2.1	0.9	-0.1	1.2	-0.5	-0.5	1.4	1.8	1.5

Fq % Financials Gain > 0% (1990-2021)

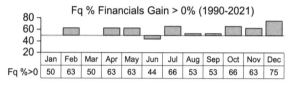

	Jan	Feb	Mar	Apr	May	Jun	Jul	Aug	Sep	Oct	Nov	Dec
Fq %>0	50	63	50	63	63	44	66	53	53	66	63	75

Fq % Financials Gain > S&P 500 % (1990-2021)

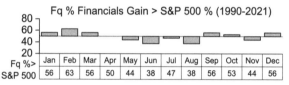

	Jan	Feb	Mar	Apr	May	Jun	Jul	Aug	Sep	Oct	Nov	Dec
Fq %> S&P 500	56	63	56	50	44	38	47	38	56	53	44	56

Financials % Gain 5 Year (2017-2021)

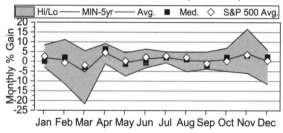

Legend: Hi/Lo | MIN-5yr | Avg. | Med. | S&P 500 Avg.

Financials Performance 2021-2022

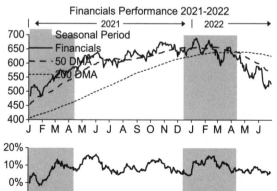

Relative Strength, % Gain vs. S&P 500

JANUARY

M	T	W	T	F	S	S
1	2	3	4	5	6	7
8	9	10	11	12	13	14
15	16	17	18	19	20	21
22	23	24	25	26	27	28
29	30	31				

FEBRUARY

M	T	W	T	F	S	S
			1	2	3	4
5	6	7	8	9	10	11
12	13	14	15	16	17	18
19	20	21	22	23	24	25
26	27	28	29			

MARCH

M	T	W	T	F	S	S
				1	2	3
4	5	6	7	8	9	10
11	12	13	14	15	16	17
18	19	20	21	22	23	24
25	26	27	28	29	30	31

APRIL

M	T	W	T	F	S	S
1	2	3	4	5	6	7
8	9	10	11	12	13	14
15	16	17	18	19	20	21
22	23	24	25	26	27	28
29	30					

MAY

M	T	W	T	F	S	S
	1	2	3	4	5
6	7	8	9	10	11	12
13	14	15	16	17	18	19
20	21	22	23	24	25	26
27	28	29	30	31		

JUNE

M	T	W	T	F	S	S
						1
2	3	4	5	6	7	8
9	10	11	12	13	14	15
16	17	18	19	20	21	22
23	24	25	26	27	28	29
30						

APPENDIX

STOCK MARKET RETURNS

STOCK MKT — S&P 500 PERCENT CHANGES

	JAN	FEB	MAR	APR	MAY	JUN
1950	1.5 %	1.0 %	0.4 %	4.5 %	3.9 %	— 5.8 %
1951	6.1	0.6	— 1.8	4.8	— 4.1	— 2.6
1952	1.6	— 3.6	4.8	— 4.3	2.3	4.6
1953	— 0.7	— 1.8	— 2.4	— 2.6	— 0.3	— 1.6
1954	5.1	0.3	3.0	4.9	3.3	0.1
1955	1.8	0.4	— 0.5	3.8	— 0.1	8.2
1956	— 3.6	3.5	6.9	— 0.2	— 6.6	3.9
1957	— 4.2	— 3.3	2.0	3.7	3.7	— 0.1
1958	4.3	2.1	3.1	3.2	1.5	2.6
1959	0.4	— 0.1	0.1	3.9	1.9	— 0.4
1960	— 7.1	0.9	— 1.4	— 1.8	2.7	2.0
1961	6.3	2.7	2.6	0.4	1.9	— 2.9
1962	— 3.8	1.6	— 0.6	— 6.2	— 8.6	— 8.2
1963	4.9	— 2.9	3.5	4.9	1.4	— 2.0
1964	2.7	1.0	1.5	0.6	1.1	1.6
1965	3.3	— 0.1	— 1.5	3.4	— 0.8	— 4.9
1966	0.5	— 1.8	— 2.2	2.1	— 5.4	— 1.6
1967	7.8	0.2	3.9	4.2	— 5.2	1.8
1968	— 4.4	— 3.1	0.9	8.0	1.3	0.9
1969	— 0.8	— 4.7	3.4	2.1	— 0.2	— 5.6
1970	— 7.6	5.3	0.1	— 9.0	— 6.1	— 5.0
1971	4.0	0.9	3.7	3.6	— 4.2	— 0.9
1972	1.8	2.5	0.6	0.4	1.7	— 2.2
1973	— 1.7	— 3.7	— 0.1	— 4.1	— 1.9	— 0.7
1974	— 1.0	— 0.4	— 2.3	— 3.9	— 3.4	— 1.5
1975	12.3	6.0	2.2	4.7	4.4	4.4
1976	11.8	— 1.1	3.1	— 1.1	— 1.4	4.1
1977	— 5.1	— 2.2	— 1.4	0.0	— 2.4	4.5
1978	— 6.2	— 2.5	2.5	8.5	0.4	— 1.8
1979	4.0	— 3.7	5.5	0.2	— 2.6	3.9
1980	5.8	— 0.4	— 10.2	4.1	4.7	2.7
1981	— 4.6	1.3	3.6	— 2.3	— 0.2	— 1.0
1982	— 1.8	— 6.1	— 1.0	4.0	— 3.9	— 2.0
1983	3.3	1.9	3.3	7.5	— 1.2	3.2
1984	— 0.9	— 3.9	1.3	0.5	— 5.9	1.7
1985	7.4	0.9	— 0.3	— 0.5	5.4	1.2
1986	0.2	7.1	5.3	— 1.4	5.0	1.4
1987	13.2	3.7	2.6	— 1.1	0.6	4.8
1988	4.0	4.2	— 3.3	0.9	0.3	4.3
1989	7.1	— 2.9	2.1	5.0	3.5	— 0.8
1990	— 6.9	0.9	2.4	— 2.7	9.2	— 0.9
1991	4.2	6.7	2.2	0.0	3.9	— 4.8
1992	— 2.0	1.0	— 2.2	2.8	0.1	— 1.7
1993	0.7	1.0	1.9	— 2.5	2.3	0.1
1994	3.3	— 3.0	— 4.6	1.2	1.2	— 2.7
1995	2.4	3.6	2.7	2.8	3.6	2.1
1996	3.3	0.7	0.8	1.3	2.3	0.2
1997	6.1	0.6	— 4.3	5.8	5.9	4.3
1998	1.0	7.0	5.0	0.9	— 1.9	3.9
1999	4.1	— 3.2	3.9	3.8	— 2.5	5.4
2000	— 5.1	— 2.0	9.7	— 3.1	— 2.2	2.4
2001	3.5	— 9.2	— 6.4	7.7	0.5	— 2.5
2002	— 1.6	— 2.1	3.7	— 6.1	— 0.9	— 7.2
2003	— 2.7	— 1.7	0.8	8.1	5.1	1.1
2004	1.7	1.2	— 1.6	— 1.7	1.2	1.8
2005	— 2.5	1.9	— 1.9	— 2.0	3.0	0.0
2006	2.5	0.0	1.1	1.2	— 3.1	0.0
2007	1.4	— 2.2	1.0	4.3	3.3	— 1.8
2008	— 6.1	— 3.5	— 0.6	4.8	1.1	— 8.6
2009	— 8.6	— 11.0	8.5	9.4	5.3	0.0
2010	— 3.7	2.9	5.9	1.5	— 8.2	— 5.4
2011	2.3	3.2	— 0.1	2.8	— 1.4	— 1.8
2012	4.4	4.1	3.1	— 0.7	— 6.3	4.0
2013	5.0	1.1	3.6	1.8	2.1	— 1.5
2014	— 3.6	4.3	0.7	0.6	2.1	1.9
2015	— 3.1	5.5	— 1.7	0.9	1.0	— 2.1
2016	— 5.1	— 0.4	6.6	0.3	1.5	0.1
2017	1.8	3.7	0.0	0.9	1.2	0.5
2018	5.6	— 3.9	— 2.7	0.3	2.2	0.5
2019	7.9	3.0	1.8	3.9	— 6.6	6.9
2020	— 0.2	8.4	— 12.5	12.7	4.5	1.8
2021	— 1.1	2.6	4.2	5.2	0.5	2.2
FQ POS*	43/72	40/72	46/72	51/72	43/72	40/72
% FQ POS*	60 %	56 %	64 %	71 %	60 %	56 %
AVG GAIN*	1.1 %	0.0 %	1.0 %	1.7 %	0.2 %	0.1 %
RANK GAIN*	5	11	6	2	8	9

S&P 500
PERCENT CHANGES 🇺🇸 STOCK MKT

JUL	AUG	SEP	OCT	NOV	DEC		YEAR
0.8 %	3.3 %	5.6 %	0.4 %	− 0.1 %	4.6 %	**1950**	21.7 %
6.9	3.9	− 0.1	− 1.4	− 0.3	3.9	**1951**	16.5
1.8	− 1.5	− 2.0	− 0.1	4.6	3.5	**1952**	11.8
2.5	− 5.8	0.1	5.1	0.9	0.2	**1953**	− 6.6
5.7	− 3.4	8.3	− 1.9	8.1	5.1	**1954**	45.0
6.1	− 0.8	1.1	− 3.0	7.5	− 0.1	**1955**	26.4
5.2	− 3.8	− 4.5	0.5	− 1.1	3.5	**1956**	2.6
1.1	− 5.6	− 6.2	− 3.2	1.6	− 4.1	**1957**	− 14.3
4.3	1.2	4.8	2.5	2.2	5.2	**1958**	38.1
3.5	− 1.5	− 4.6	1.1	1.3	2.8	**1959**	8.5
− 2.5	2.6	− 6.0	− 0.2	4.0	4.6	**1960**	− 3.0
3.3	2.0	− 2.0	2.8	3.9	0.3	**1961**	23.1
6.4	1.5	− 4.8	0.4	10.2	1.3	**1962**	− 11.8
− 0.3	4.9	− 1.1	3.2	− 1.1	2.4	**1963**	18.9
1.8	− 1.6	2.9	0.8	− 0.5	0.4	**1964**	13.0
1.3	2.3	3.2	2.7	− 0.9	0.9	**1965**	9.1
− 1.3	− 7.8	− 0.7	4.8	0.3	− 0.1	**1966**	− 13.1
4.5	− 1.2	3.3	− 3.5	0.8	2.6	**1967**	20.1
− 1.8	1.1	3.9	0.7	4.8	− 4.2	**1968**	7.7
− 6.0	4.0	− 2.5	4.3	− 3.4	− 1.9	**1969**	− 11.4
7.3	4.4	3.4	− 1.2	4.7	5.7	**1970**	0.1
− 3.2	3.6	− 0.7	− 4.2	− 0.3	8.6	**1971**	10.8
0.2	3.4	− 0.5	0.9	4.6	1.2	**1972**	15.6
3.8	− 3.7	4.0	− 0.1	− 11.4	1.7	**1973**	− 17.4
− 7.8	− 9.0	− 11.9	16.3	− 5.3	− 2.0	**1974**	− 29.7
− 6.8	− 2.1	− 3.5	6.2	2.5	− 1.2	**1975**	31.5
− 0.8	− 0.5	2.3	− 2.2	− 0.8	5.2	**1976**	19.1
− 1.6	− 2.1	− 0.2	− 4.3	2.7	0.3	**1977**	− 11.5
5.4	2.6	− 0.7	− 9.2	1.7	1.5	**1978**	1.1
0.9	5.3	0.0	− 6.9	4.3	1.7	**1979**	12.3
6.5	0.6	2.5	1.6	10.2	− 3.4	**1980**	25.8
− 0.2	− 6.2	− 5.4	4.9	3.7	− 3.0	**1981**	9.7
− 2.3	11.6	0.8	11.0	3.6	1.5	**1982**	14.8
3.0	1.1	1.0	− 1.5	1.7	− 0.9	**1983**	17.3
− 1.6	10.6	− 0.3	0.0	− 1.5	2.2	**1984**	1.4
− 0.5	− 1.2	− 3.5	4.3	6.5	4.5	**1985**	26.3
− 5.9	7.1	− 8.5	5.5	2.1	− 2.8	**1986**	14.6
4.8	3.5	− 2.4	− 21.8	− 8.5	7.3	**1987**	2.0
− 0.5	− 3.9	4.0	2.6	− 1.9	1.5	**1988**	12.4
8.8	1.6	− 0.7	− 2.5	1.7	2.1	**1989**	27.3
− 0.5	− 9.4	− 5.1	− 0.7	6.0	2.5	**1990**	− 6.6
4.5	2.0	− 1.9	1.2	− 4.4	11.2	**1991**	26.3
3.9	− 2.4	0.9	0.2	3.0	1.0	**1992**	4.5
− 0.5	3.4	− 1.0	1.9	− 1.3	1.0	**1993**	7.1
3.1	3.8	− 2.7	2.1	− 4.0	1.2	**1994**	− 1.5
3.2	0.0	4.0	− 0.5	4.1	1.7	**1995**	34.1
− 4.6	1.9	5.4	2.6	7.3	− 2.2	**1996**	20.3
7.8	− 5.7	5.3	− 3.4	4.5	1.6	**1997**	31.0
− 1.2	− 14.6	6.2	8.0	5.9	5.6	**1998**	26.7
− 3.2	− 0.6	2.9	6.3	1.9	5.8	**1999**	19.5
− 1.6	6.1	− 5.3	− 0.5	− 8.0	0.4	**2000**	− 10.1
− 1.1	− 6.4	− 8.2	1.8	7.5	0.8	**2001**	− 13.0
− 7.9	0.5	− 11.0	8.6	5.7	− 6.0	**2002**	− 23.4
1.6	1.8	− 1.2	5.5	0.7	5.1	**2003**	26.4
-3.4	0.2	0.9	1.4	3.9	3.2	**2004**	9.0
3.6	1.1	0.7	− 1.8	3.5	− 0.1	**2005**	3.0
0.5	2.1	2.5	3.2	1.6	1.3	**2006**	13.6
3.2	1.3	3.6	1.5	− 4.4	− 0.9	**2007**	3.5
− 1.0	1.2	− 9.1	− 16.9	− 7.5	0.8	**2008**	-38.5
7.4	3.4	3.6	− 2.0	5.7	1.8	**2009**	23.5
6.9	− 4.7	8.8	3.7	− 0.2	6.5	**2010**	12.8
2.1	− 5.7	− 7.2	10.8	− 0.5	0.9	**2011**	0.0
1.3	2.0	2.4	− 2.0	0.3	0.7	**2012**	13.4
4.9	− 3.1	3.0	4.5	2.8	2.4	**2013**	29.6
− 1.5	3.8	− 1.6	2.3	2.5	− 0.4	**2014**	11.4
2.0	− 6.3	− 2.6	8.3	0.1	− 1.8	**2015**	− 0.7
3.6	− 0.1	− 0.1	− 1.9	3.4	1.8	**2016**	9.5
1.9	0.1	1.9	2.2	2.8	1.0	**2017**	19.4
3.6	3.0	0.4	− 6.9	1.8	− 9.2	**2018**	− 6.2
1.3	− 1.8	1.7	2.0	3.4	2.9	**2019**	28.9
5.5	7.0	− 3.9	− 2.8	10.8	3.7	**2020**	16.3
2.3	2.9	− 4,8	6.9	− 0.8	4.4	**2021**	26.9
42/72	40/72	32/72	43/72	49/72	54/72		53/72
58 %	56 %	44 %	60 %	68 %	75 %		74 %
1.1 %	0.1 %	− 0.5 %	0.9 %	1.7 %	1.5 %		9.5 %
4	10	12	7	1	3		

S&P 500 MONTH CLOSING VALUES

	JAN	FEB	MAR	APR	MAY	JUN
1950	17	17	17	18	19	18
1951	22	22	21	22	22	21
1952	24	23	24	23	24	25
1953	26	26	25	25	25	24
1954	26	26	27	28	29	29
1955	37	37	37	38	38	41
1956	44	45	48	48	45	47
1957	45	43	44	46	47	47
1958	42	41	42	43	44	45
1959	55	55	55	58	59	58
1960	56	56	55	54	56	57
1961	62	63	65	65	67	65
1962	69	70	70	65	60	55
1963	66	64	67	70	71	69
1964	77	78	79	79	80	82
1965	88	87	86	89	88	84
1966	93	91	89	91	86	85
1967	87	87	90	94	89	91
1968	92	89	90	97	99	100
1969	103	98	102	104	103	98
1970	85	90	90	82	77	73
1971	96	97	100	104	100	99
1972	104	107	107	108	110	107
1973	116	112	112	107	105	104
1974	97	96	94	90	87	86
1975	77	82	83	87	91	95
1976	101	100	103	102	100	104
1977	102	100	98	98	96	100
1978	89	87	89	97	97	96
1979	100	96	102	102	99	103
1980	114	114	102	106	111	114
1981	130	131	136	133	133	131
1982	120	113	112	116	112	110
1983	145	148	153	164	162	168
1984	163	157	159	160	151	153
1985	180	181	181	180	190	192
1986	212	227	239	236	247	251
1987	274	284	292	288	290	304
1988	257	268	259	261	262	274
1989	297	289	295	310	321	318
1990	329	332	340	331	361	358
1991	344	367	375	375	390	371
1992	409	413	404	415	415	408
1993	439	443	452	440	450	451
1994	482	467	446	451	457	444
1995	470	487	501	515	533	545
1996	636	640	646	654	669	671
1997	786	791	757	801	848	885
1998	980	1049	1102	1112	1091	1134
1999	1280	1238	1286	1335	1302	1373
2000	1394	1366	1499	1452	1421	1455
2001	1366	1240	1160	1249	1256	1224
2002	1130	1107	1147	1077	1067	990
2003	856	841	848	917	964	975
2004	1131	1145	1126	1107	1121	1141
2005	1181	1204	1181	1157	1192	1191
2006	1280	1281	1295	1311	1270	1270
2007	1438	1407	1421	1482	1531	1503
2008	1379	1331	1323	1386	1400	1280
2009	826	735	798	873	919	919
2010	1074	1104	1169	1187	1089	1031
2011	1286	1327	1326	1364	1345	1321
2012	1312	1366	1408	1398	1310	1362
2013	1498	1515	1569	1598	1631	1606
2014	1783	1869	1872	1884	1924	1960
2015	1995	2105	2068	2086	2107	2063
2016	1940	1932	2060	2065	2097	2099
2017	2279	2364	2363	2384	2412	2423
2018	2824	2714	2641	2648	2705	2718
2019	2704	2784	2834	2946	2752	2942
2020	3226	2954	2585	2912	3044	3100
2021	3714	3811	3973	4181	4204	4298

S&P 500 MONTH CLOSING VALUES

STOCK MKT

JUL	AUG	SEP	OCT	NOV	DEC	
18	18	19	20	20	20	**1950**
22	23	23	23	23	24	**1951**
25	25	25	25	26	27	**1952**
25	23	23	25	25	25	**1953**
31	30	32	32	34	36	**1954**
44	43	44	42	46	45	**1955**
49	48	45	46	45	47	**1956**
48	45	42	41	42	40	**1957**
47	48	50	51	52	55	**1958**
61	60	57	58	58	60	**1959**
56	57	54	53	56	58	**1960**
67	68	67	69	71	72	**1961**
58	59	56	57	62	63	**1962**
69	73	72	74	73	75	**1963**
83	82	84	85	84	85	**1964**
85	87	90	92	92	92	**1965**
84	77	77	80	80	80	**1966**
95	94	97	93	94	96	**1967**
98	99	103	103	108	104	**1968**
92	96	93	97	94	92	**1969**
78	82	84	83	87	92	**1970**
96	99	98	94	94	102	**1971**
107	111	111	112	117	118	**1972**
108	104	108	108	96	98	**1973**
79	72	64	74	70	69	**1974**
89	87	84	89	91	90	**1975**
103	103	105	103	102	107	**1976**
99	97	97	92	95	95	**1977**
101	103	103	93	95	96	**1978**
104	109	109	102	106	108	**1979**
122	122	125	127	141	136	**1980**
131	123	116	122	126	123	**1981**
107	120	120	134	139	141	**1982**
163	164	166	164	166	165	**1983**
151	167	166	166	164	167	**1984**
191	189	182	190	202	211	**1985**
236	253	231	244	249	242	**1986**
319	330	322	252	230	247	**1987**
272	262	272	279	274	278	**1988**
346	351	349	340	346	353	**1989**
356	323	306	304	322	330	**1990**
388	395	388	392	375	417	**1991**
424	414	418	419	431	436	**1992**
448	464	459	468	462	466	**1993**
458	475	463	472	454	459	**1994**
562	562	584	582	605	616	**1995**
640	652	687	705	757	741	**1996**
954	899	947	915	955	970	**1997**
1121	957	1017	1099	1164	1229	**1998**
1329	1320	1283	1363	1389	1469	**1999**
1431	1518	1437	1429	1315	1320	**2000**
1211	1134	1041	1060	1139	1148	**2001**
912	916	815	886	936	880	**2002**
990	1008	996	1051	1058	1112	**2003**
1102	1104	1115	1130	1174	1212	**2004**
1234	1220	1229	1207	1249	1248	**2005**
1277	1304	1336	1378	1401	1418	**2006**
1455	1474	1527	1549	1481	1468	**2007**
1267	1283	1165	969	896	903	**2008**
987	1021	1057	1036	1096	1115	**2009**
1102	1049	1141	1183	1181	1258	**2010**
1292	1219	1131	1253	1247	1258	**2011**
1379	1407	1441	1412	1416	1426	**2012**
1686	1633	1682	1757	1806	1848	**2013**
1931	2003	1972	2018	2068	2059	**2014**
2104	1972	1920	2079	2080	2044	**2015**
2174	2171	2168	2126	2199	2239	**2016**
2470	2472	2519	2575	2648	2674	**2017**
2816	2902	2914	2712	2760	2507	**2018**
2980	2926	2977	3038	3141	3231	**2019**
3271	3500	3363	3270	3622	3756	**2020**
4395	4523	4308	4605	4567	4766	**2021**

DOW JONES PERCENT MONTH CHANGES

	JAN	FEB	MAR	APR	MAY	JUN
1950	0.8 %	0.8 %	1.3 %	4.0 %	4.2 %	− 6.4 %
1951	5.7	1.3	− 1.7	4.5	− 3.6	− 2.8
1952	0.6	− 3.9	3.6	− 4.4	2.1	4.3
1953	− 0.7	− 2.0	− 1.5	− 1.8	− 0.9	− 1.5
1954	4.1	0.7	3.1	5.2	2.6	1.8
1955	1.1	0.8	− 0.5	3.9	− 0.2	6.2
1956	− 3.6	2.8	5.8	0.8	− 7.4	3.1
1957	− 4.1	− 3.0	2.2	4.1	2.1	− 0.3
1958	3.3	− 2.2	1.6	2.0	1.5	3.3
1959	1.8	1.6	− 0.3	3.7	3.2	0.0
1960	− 8.4	1.2	− 2.1	− 2.4	4.0	2.4
1961	5.2	2.1	2.2	0.3	2.7	− 1.8
1962	− 4.3	1.2	− 0.2	− 5.9	− 7.8	− 8.5
1963	4.7	− 2.9	3.0	5.2	1.3	− 2.8
1964	2.9	1.9	1.6	− 0.3	1.2	1.3
1965	3.3	0.1	− 1.6	3.7	− 0.5	− 5.4
1966	1.5	− 3.2	− 2.8	1.0	− 5.3	− 1.6
1967	8.2	− 1.2	3.2	3.6	− 5.0	0.9
1968	− 5.5	− 1.8	0.0	8.5	− 1.4	− 0.1
1969	0.2	− 4.3	3.3	1.6	− 1.3	− 6.9
1970	− 7.0	4.5	1.0	− 6.3	− 4.8	− 2.4
1971	3.5	1.2	2.9	4.1	− 3.6	− 1.8
1972	1.3	2.9	1.4	1.4	0.7	− 3.3
1973	− 2.1	− 4.4	− 0.4	− 3.1	− 2.2	− 1.1
1974	0.6	0.6	− 1.6	− 1.2	− 4.1	0.0
1975	14.2	5.0	3.9	6.9	1.3	5.6
1976	14.4	− 0.3	2.8	− 0.3	− 2.2	2.8
1977	− 5.0	− 1.9	− 1.8	0.8	− 3.0	2.0
1978	− 7.4	− 3.6	2.1	10.5	0.4	− 2.6
1979	4.2	− 3.6	6.6	− 0.8	− 3.8	2.4
1980	4.4	− 1.5	− 9.0	4.0	4.1	2.0
1981	− 1.7	2.9	3.0	− 0.6	− 0.6	− 1.5
1982	− 0.4	− 5.4	− 0.2	3.1	− 3.4	− 0.9
1983	2.8	3.4	1.6	8.5	− 2.1	1.8
1984	− 3.0	− 5.4	0.9	0.5	− 5.6	2.5
1985	6.2	− 0.2	− 1.3	− 0.7	4.6	1.5
1986	1.6	8.8	6.4	− 1.9	5.2	0.9
1987	13.8	3.1	3.6	− 0.8	0.2	5.5
1988	1.0	5.8	− 4.0	2.2	− 0.1	5.4
1989	8.0	− 3.6	1.6	5.5	2.5	− 1.6
1990	− 5.9	1.4	3.0	− 1.9	8.3	0.1
1991	3.9	5.3	1.1	− 0.9	4.8	− 4.0
1992	1.7	1.4	− 1.0	3.8	1.1	− 2.3
1993	0.3	1.8	1.9	− 0.2	2.9	− 0.3
1994	6.0	− 3.7	− 5.1	1.3	2.1	− 3.5
1995	0.2	4.3	3.7	3.9	3.3	2.0
1996	5.4	1.7	1.9	− 0.3	1.3	0.2
1997	5.7	0.9	− 4.3	6.5	4.6	4.7
1998	0.0	8.1	3.0	3.0	− 1.8	0.6
1999	1.9	− 0.6	5.2	10.2	− 2.1	3.9
2000	− 4.5	− 7.4	7.8	− 1.7	− 2.0	− 0.7
2001	0.9	− 3.6	− 5.9	8.7	1.6	− 3.8
2002	1.0	1.9	2.9	− 4.4	− 0.2	− 6.9
2003	− 3.5	− 2.0	1.3	6.1	4.4	1.5
2004	0.3	0.9	− 2.1	− 1.3	− 0.4	2.4
2005	− 2.7	2.6	− 2.4	− 3.0	2.7	− 1.8
2006	1.4	1.2	1.1	2.3	− 1.7	− 0.2
2007	1.3	− 2.8	0.7	5.7	4.3	− 1.6
2008	− 4.6	− 3.0	0.0	4.5	− 1.4	− 10.2
2009	− 8.8	− 11.7	7.7	7.3	4.1	− 0.6
2010	− 3.5	2.6	5.1	1.4	− 7.9	− 3.6
2011	2.7	2.8	0.8	4.0	− 1.9	− 1.2
2012	3.4	3.8	2.0	0.0	− 6.2	3.9
2013	5.8	4.8	3.7	1.8	1.9	− 1.4
2014	− 5.3	5.8	0.8	0.7	0.8	0.7
2015	− 3.7	6.8	− 2.0	0.4	1.0	− 2.2
2016	− 5.5	0.3	7.1	0.5	0.1	0.8
2017	0.5	4.8	− 0.7	1.3	0.3	1.6
2018	5.8	− 4.3	− 3.7	0.2	1.0	0.6
2019	7.2	3.7	0.0	2.6	− 6.7	7.2
2020	− 0.2	− 8.4	− 12.5	12.7	4.5	1.8
2021	− 2.0	3.2	6.6	2.7	1.9	− 0.1
FQ POS	45/72	42/72	46/72	50/72	39/72	34/72
% FQ POS	63 %	58 %	64 %	69 %	54 %	47 %
AVG GAIN	1.0 %	0.3 %	0.9 %	2.1 %	0.0 %	− 0.1 %
RANK GAIN	5	8	6	1	9	11

DOW JONES PERCENT MONTH CHANGES — STOCK MKT

JUL	AUG	SEP	OCT	NOV	DEC		YEAR
0.1 %	3.6 %	4.4 %	− 0.6 %	1.2 %	3.4 %	1950	17.6 %
6.3	4.8	0.3	− 3.2	− 0.4	3.0	1951	14.4
1.9	− 1.6	− 1.6	− 0.5	5.4	2.9	1952	8.4
2.6	− 5.2	1.1	4.5	2.0	− 0.2	1953	− 3.8
4.3	− 3.5	7.4	− 2.3	9.9	4.6	1954	44.0
3.2	0.5	− 0.3	− 2.5	6.2	1.1	1955	20.8
5.1	− 3.1	− 5.3	1.0	− 1.5	5.6	1956	2.3
1.0	− 4.7	− 5.8	− 3.4	2.0	− 3.2	1957	− 12.8
5.2	1.1	4.6	2.1	2.6	4.7	1958	34.0
4.9	− 1.6	− 4.9	2.4	1.9	3.1	1959	16.4
− 3.7	1.5	− 7.3	0.1	2.9	3.1	1960	− 9.3
3.1	2.1	− 2.6	0.4	2.5	1.3	1961	18.7
6.5	1.9	− 5.0	1.9	10.1	0.4	1962	− 10.8
− 1.6	4.9	0.5	3.1	− 0.6	1.7	1963	17.0
1.2	− 0.3	4.4	− 0.3	0.3	− 0.1	1964	14.6
1.6	1.3	4.2	3.2	− 1.5	2.4	1965	10.9
− 2.6	− 7.0	− 1.8	4.2	− 1.9	− 0.7	1966	− 18.9
5.1	− 0.3	2.8	− 5.1	− 0.4	3.3	1967	15.2
1.6	1.5	4.4	1.8	3.4	− 4.2	1968	4.3
− 6.6	2.6	− 2.8	5.3	− 5.1	− 1.5	1969	− 15.2
7.4	4.2	− 0.5	− 0.7	5.1	5.6	1970	4.8
− 3.7	4.6	− 1.2	− 5.4	− 0.9	7.1	1971	6.1
− 0.5	4.2	− 1.1	0.2	6.6	0.2	1972	14.6
3.9	− 4.2	6.7	1.0	− 14.0	3.5	1973	− 16.6
− 5.6	− 10.4	− 10.4	9.5	− 7.0	− 0.4	1974	− 27.6
− 5.4	0.5	− 5.0	5.3	3.0	− 1.0	1975	38.3
− 1.8	− 1.1	1.7	− 2.6	− 1.8	6.1	1976	17.9
− 2.9	− 3.2	− 1.7	− 3.4	1.4	0.2	1977	− 17.3
5.3	1.7	− 1.3	− 8.5	0.8	0.8	1978	3.2
0.5	4.9	− 1.0	− 7.2	0.8	2.0	1979	4.2
7.8	− 0.3	0.0	− 0.8	7.4	− 2.9	1980	14.9
− 2.5	− 7.4	− 3.6	0.3	4.3	− 1.6	1981	9.2
− 0.4	11.5	− 0.6	10.6	4.8	0.7	1982	19.6
− 1.9	1.4	1.4	− 0.6	4.1	− 1.4	1983	20.3
− 1.5	9.8	− 1.4	0.1	− 1.5	1.9	1984	3.7
0.9	− 1.0	− 0.4	3.4	7.1	5.1	1985	27.7
− 6.2	6.9	− 6.9	6.2	1.9	− 1.0	1986	22.6
6.4	3.5	− 2.5	− 23.2	− 8.0	5.7	1987	2.3
− 0.6	− 4.6	4.0	1.7	− 1.6	2.6	1988	11.9
9.0	2.9	− 1.6	− 1.8	2.3	1.7	1989	27.0
0.9	− 10.0	− 6.2	− 0.4	4.8	2.9	1990	− 4.3
4.1	0.6	− 0.9	1.7	− 5.7	9.5	1991	20.3
2.3	− 4.0	0.4	− 1.4	2.4	− 0.1	1992	4.2
0.7	3.2	− 2.6	3.5	0.1	1.9	1993	13.7
3.8	4.0	− 1.8	1.7	− 4.3	2.5	1994	2.1
3.3	− 2.1	3.9	− 0.7	6.7	0.8	1995	33.5
− 2.2	1.6	4.7	2.5	8.2	− 1.1	1996	26.0
7.2	− 7.3	4.2	− 6.3	5.1	1.1	1997	22.6
− 0.8	− 15.1	4.0	9.6	6.1	0.7	1998	16.1
− 2.9	1.6	− 4.5	3.8	1.4	5.3	1999	24.7
0.7	6.6	− 5.0	3.0	− 5.1	3.6	2000	− 5.8
0.2	− 5.4	− 11.1	2.6	8.6	1.7	2001	− 7.1
− 5.5	− 0.8	− 12.4	10.6	5.9	− 6.2	2002	− 16.8
2.8	2.0	− 1.5	5.7	− 0.2	6.9	2003	25.3
− 2.8	0.3	− 0.9	− 0.5	4.0	3.4	2004	3.1
3.6	− 1.5	0.8	− 1.2	3.5	− 0.8	2005	− 0.6
0.3	1.7	2.6	3.4	1.2	2.0	2006	16.3
− 1.5	1.1	4.0	0.2	− 4.0	− 0.8	2007	6.4
0.2	1.5	− 6.0	− 14.1	− 5.3	− 0.6	2008	− 33.8
8.6	3.5	2.3	0.0	6.5	0.8	2009	18.8
7.1	− 4.3	7.7	3.1	− 1.0	5.2	2010	11.0
− 2.2	− 4.4	− 6.0	9.5	0.8	1.4	2011	5.5
1.0	0.6	2.6	− 2.5	− 0.5	0.6	2012	7.3
4.0	− 4.4	2.2	2.8	3.5	3.0	2013	26.5
− 1.6	3.2	− 0.3	2.0	2.5	0.0	2014	7.5
0.4	− 6.6	− 1.5	8.5	0.3	− 2.2	2015	− 2.2
2.8	− 0.2	− 0.5	− 0.9	5.4	3.3	2016	13.4
2.5	0.3	2.1	4.3	3.8	1.8	2017	25.1
4.7	2.2	1.9	− 5.1	1.7	− 8.7	2018	− 5.6
1.0	− 1.7	1.9	0.5	3.7	1.7	2019	22.3
5.5	7.0	− 3.9	− 2.8	10.8	3.7	2020	16.3
1.3	1.2	− 4.3	5.8	− 3.7	5.4	2021	18.7
46/72	40/72	29/72	42/72	50/72	50/72		52/72
65 %	56 %	41 %	59 %	69 %	70 %		72 %
1.3 %	− 0.1 %	− 0.7 %	0.5 %	1.7 %	1.5 %		8.3 %
4	10	12	7	2	3		

DOW JONES
MONTH CLOSING VALUES

	JAN	FEB	MAR	APR	MAY	JUN
1950	202	203	206	214	223	209
1951	249	252	248	259	250	243
1952	271	260	270	258	263	274
1953	290	284	280	275	272	268
1954	292	295	304	319	328	334
1955	409	412	410	426	425	451
1956	471	484	512	516	478	493
1957	479	465	475	494	505	503
1958	450	440	447	456	463	478
1959	594	604	602	624	644	644
1960	623	630	617	602	626	641
1961	648	662	677	679	697	684
1962	700	708	707	665	613	561
1963	683	663	683	718	727	707
1964	785	800	813	811	821	832
1965	903	904	889	922	918	868
1966	984	952	925	934	884	870
1967	850	839	866	897	853	860
1968	856	841	841	912	899	898
1969	946	905	936	950	938	873
1970	744	778	786	736	700	684
1971	869	879	904	942	908	891
1972	902	928	941	954	961	929
1973	999	955	951	921	901	892
1974	856	861	847	837	802	802
1975	704	739	768	821	832	879
1976	975	973	1000	997	975	1003
1977	954	936	919	927	899	916
1978	770	742	757	837	841	819
1979	839	809	862	855	822	842
1980	876	863	786	817	851	868
1981	947	975	1004	998	992	977
1982	871	824	823	848	820	812
1983	1076	1113	1130	1226	1200	1222
1984	1221	1155	1165	1171	1105	1132
1985	1287	1284	1267	1258	1315	1336
1986	1571	1709	1819	1784	1877	1893
1987	2158	2224	2305	2286	2292	2419
1988	1958	2072	1988	2032	2031	2142
1989	2342	2258	2294	2419	2480	2440
1990	2591	2627	2707	2657	2877	2881
1991	2736	2882	2914	2888	3028	2907
1992	3223	3268	3236	3359	3397	3319
1993	3310	3371	3435	3428	3527	3516
1994	3978	3832	3636	3682	3758	3625
1995	3844	4011	4158	4321	4465	4556
1996	5395	5486	5587	5569	5643	5655
1997	6813	6878	6584	7009	7331	7673
1998	7907	8546	8800	9063	8900	8952
1999	9359	9307	9786	10789	10560	10971
2000	10941	10128	10922	10734	10522	10448
2001	10887	10495	9879	10735	10912	10502
2002	9920	10106	10404	9946	9925	9243
2003	8054	7891	7992	8480	8850	8985
2004	10488	10584	10358	10226	10188	10435
2005	10490	10766	10504	10193	10467	10275
2006	10865	10993	11109	11367	11168	11150
2007	12622	12269	12354	13063	13628	13409
2008	12650	12266	12263	12820	12638	11350
2009	8001	7063	7609	8168	8500	8447
2010	10067	10325	10857	11009	10137	9774
2011	11892	12226	12320	12811	12570	12414
2012	12633	12952	13212	13214	12393	12880
2013	13861	14054	14579	14840	15116	14910
2014	15699	16322	16458	16581	16717	16827
2015	17165	18133	17776	17841	18011	17620
2016	16466	16517	17685	17774	17787	17930
2017	19864	20812	20663	20941	21009	21350
2018	26149	25029	24103	24163	24416	24271
2019	25000	25916	25929	26593	24815	26600
2020	28256	25409	21917	24346	25383	25813
2021	29983	30932	32982	33875	34529	34503

DOW JONES
MONTH CLOSING VALUES

STOCK MKT

JUL	AUG	SEP	OCT	NOV	DEC	
209	217	226	225	228	235	**1950**
258	270	271	262	261	269	**1951**
280	275	271	269	284	292	**1952**
275	261	264	276	281	281	**1953**
348	336	361	352	387	404	**1954**
466	468	467	455	483	488	**1955**
518	502	475	480	473	500	**1956**
509	484	456	441	450	436	**1957**
503	509	532	543	558	584	**1958**
675	664	632	647	659	679	**1959**
617	626	580	580	597	616	**1960**
705	720	701	704	722	731	**1961**
598	609	579	590	649	652	**1962**
695	729	733	755	751	763	**1963**
841	839	875	873	875	874	**1964**
882	893	931	961	947	969	**1965**
847	788	774	807	792	786	**1966**
904	901	927	880	876	905	**1967**
883	896	936	952	985	944	**1968**
816	837	813	856	812	800	**1969**
734	765	761	756	794	839	**1970**
858	898	887	839	831	890	**1971**
925	964	953	956	1018	1020	**1972**
926	888	947	957	822	851	**1973**
757	679	608	666	619	616	**1974**
832	835	794	836	861	852	**1975**
985	974	990	965	947	1005	**1976**
890	862	847	818	830	831	**1977**
862	877	866	793	799	805	**1978**
846	888	879	816	822	839	**1979**
935	933	932	925	993	964	**1980**
952	882	850	853	889	875	**1981**
809	901	896	992	1039	1047	**1982**
1199	1216	1233	1225	1276	1259	**1983**
1115	1224	1207	1207	1189	1212	**1984**
1348	1334	1329	1374	1472	1547	**1985**
1775	1898	1768	1878	1914	1896	**1986**
2572	2663	2596	1994	1834	1939	**1987**
2129	2032	2113	2149	2115	2169	**1988**
2661	2737	2693	2645	2706	2753	**1989**
2905	2614	2453	2442	2560	2634	**1990**
3025	3044	3017	3069	2895	3169	**1991**
3394	3257	3272	3226	3305	3301	**1992**
3540	3651	3555	3681	3684	3754	**1993**
3765	3913	3843	3908	3739	3834	**1994**
4709	4611	4789	4756	5075	5117	**1995**
5529	5616	5882	6029	6522	6448	**1996**
8223	7622	7945	7442	7823	7908	**1997**
8883	7539	7843	8592	9117	9181	**1998**
10655	10829	10337	10730	10878	11453	**1999**
10522	11215	10651	10971	10415	10788	**2000**
10523	9950	8848	9075	9852	10022	**2001**
8737	8664	7592	8397	8896	8342	**2002**
9234	9416	9275	9801	9782	10454	**2003**
10140	10174	10080	10027	10428	10783	**2004**
10641	10482	10569	10440	10806	10718	**2005**
11186	11381	11679	12801	12222	12463	**2006**
13212	13358	13896	13930	13372	13265	**2007**
11378	11544	10851	9325	8829	8776	**2008**
9172	9496	9712	9713	10345	10428	**2009**
10466	10015	10788	11118	11006	11578	**2010**
12143	11614	10913	11955	12046	12218	**2011**
13009	13091	13437	13096	13026	13104	**2012**
15500	14810	15130	15546	16086	16577	**2013**
16563	17098	17043	17391	17828	17823	**2014**
17690	16528	16285	17664	17720	17425	**2015**
18432	18401	18308	18142	19124	19763	**2016**
21891	21948	22405	23377	24272	24719	**2017**
25415	25965	26458	25166	25538	23327	**2018**
26864	26403	26917	27046	28051	28538	**2019**
26428	28430	27782	26502	29639	30606	**2020**
34935	35361	33844	35820	34484	36338	**2021**

NASDAQ PERCENT MONTH CHANGES

	JAN	FEB	MAR	APR	MAY	JUN
1972	4.2	5.5	2.2	2.5	0.9	— 1.8
1973	— 4.0	— 6.2	— 2.4	— 8.2	— 4.8	— 1.6
1974	3.0	— 0.6	— 2.2	— 5.9	— 7.7	— 5.3
1975	16.6	4.6	3.6	3.8	5.8	4.7
1976	12.1	3.7	0.4	— 0.6	— 2.3	2.6
1977	— 2.4	— 1.0	— 0.5	1.4	0.1	4.3
1978	— 4.0	0.6	4.7	8.5	4.4	0.0
1979	6.6	— 2.6	7.5	1.6	— 1.8	5.1
1980	7.0	— 2.3	— 17.1	6.9	7.5	4.9
1981	— 2.2	0.1	6.1	3.1	3.1	— 3.5
1982	— 3.8	— 4.8	— 2.1	5.2	— 3.3	— 4.1
1983	6.9	5.0	3.9	8.2	5.3	3.2
1984	— 3.7	— 5.9	— 0.7	— 1.3	— 5.9	2.9
1985	12.8	2.0	— 1.8	0.5	3.6	1.9
1986	3.4	7.1	4.2	2.3	4.4	1.3
1987	12.4	8.4	1.2	— 2.9	— 0.3	2.0
1988	4.3	6.5	2.1	1.2	— 2.3	6.6
1989	5.2	— 0.4	1.8	5.1	4.3	— 2.4
1990	— 8.6	2.4	2.3	— 3.5	9.3	0.7
1991	10.8	9.4	6.4	0.5	4.4	— 6.0
1992	5.8	2.1	— 4.7	— 4.2	1.1	— 3.7
1993	2.9	— 3.7	2.9	— 4.2	5.9	0.5
1994	3.0	— 1.0	— 6.2	— 1.3	0.2	— 4.0
1995	0.4	5.1	3.0	3.3	2.4	8.0
1996	0.7	3.8	0.1	8.1	4.4	— 4.7
1997	6.9	— 5.1	— 6.7	3.2	11.1	3.0
1998	3.1	9.3	3.7	1.8	— 4.8	6.5
1999	14.3	— 8.7	7.6	3.3	— 2.8	8.7
2000	— 3.2	19.2	— 2.6	— 15.6	— 11.9	16.6
2001	12.2	— 22.4	— 14.5	15.0	— 0.3	2.4
2002	— 0.8	— 10.5	6.6	— 8.5	— 4.3	— 9.4
2003	— 1.1	1.3	0.3	9.2	9.0	1.7
2004	3.1	— 1.8	— 1.8	— 3.7	3.5	3.1
2005	— 5.2	— 0.5	— 2.6	— 3.9	7.6	— 0.5
2006	4.6	— 1.1	2.6	— 0.7	— 6.2	— 0.3
2007	2.0	— 1.9	0.2	4.3	3.1	0.0
2008	— 9.9	— 5.0	0.3	5.9	4.6	— 9.1
2009	— 6.4	— 6.7	10.9	12.3	3.3	3.4
2010	— 5.4	4.2	7.1	2.6	— 8.3	— 6.5
2011	1.8	3.0	0.0	3.3	— 1.3	— 2.2
2012	8.0	5.4	4.2	— 1.5	— 7.2	3.8
2013	4.1	0.6	3.4	1.9	3.8	— 1.5
2014	— 1.7	5.0	— 2.5	— 2.0	3.1	3.9
2015	— 2.1	7.1	— 1.3	0.8	2.6	— 1.6
2016	— 7.9	— 1.2	6.8	— 1.9	3.6	— 2.1
2017	4.3	3.8	1.5	2.3	2.5	— 0.9
2018	7.4	— 1.9	— 2.9	0.0	5.3	0.9
2019	9.7	3.4	2.6	4.7	— 7.9	7.4
2020	2.0	— 6.4	— 10.1	15.4	6.8	6.0
2021	1.4	0.9	0.4	5.4	— 1.5	5.5
FQ POS	33/50	27/50	31/50	33/50	31/50	29/50
% FQ POS	66 %	54 %	62 %	66 %	62 %	58 %
AVG GAIN	2.6 %	0.6 %	0.6 %	1.7 %	1.0 %	1.0 %
RANK GAIN	1	10	9	3	5	6

NASDAQ PERCENT MONTH CHANGES

STOCK MKT

JUL	AUG	SEP	OCT	NOV	DEC		YEAR
— 1.8	1.7	— 0.3	0.5	2.1	0.6	**1972**	17.2
7.6	— 3.5	6.0	— 0.9	— 15.1	— 1.4	**1973**	— 31.1
— 7.9	— 10.9	— 10.7	17.2	— 3.5	— 5.0	**1974**	— 35.1
— 4.4	— 5.0	— 5.9	3.6	2.4	— 1.5	**1975**	29.8
1.1	— 1.7	1.7	— 1.0	0.9	7.4	**1976**	26.1
0.9	— 0.5	0.7	— 3.3	5.8	1.8	**1977**	7.3
5.0	6.9	— 1.6	— 16.4	3.2	2.9	**1978**	12.3
2.3	6.4	— 0.3	— 9.6	6.4	4.8	**1979**	28.1
8.9	5.7	3.4	2.7	8.0	— 2.8	**1980**	33.9
— 1.9	— 7.5	— 8.0	8.4	3.1	— 2.7	**1981**	— 3.2
— 2.3	6.2	5.6	13.3	9.3	0.0	**1982**	18.7
— 4.6	— 3.8	1.4	— 7.4	4.1	— 2.5	**1983**	19.9
— 4.2	10.9	— 1.8	— 1.2	— 1.9	1.9	**1984**	— 11.3
1.7	— 1.2	— 5.8	4.4	7.4	3.5	**1985**	31.5
— 8.4	3.1	— 8.4	2.9	— 0.3	— 3.0	**1986**	7.4
2.4	4.6	— 2.4	— 27.2	— 5.6	8.3	**1987**	— 5.2
— 1.9	— 2.8	2.9	— 1.3	— 2.9	2.7	**1988**	15.4
4.2	3.4	0.8	— 3.7	0.1	— 0.3	**1989**	19.2
— 5.2	— 13.0	— 9.6	— 4.3	8.9	4.1	**1990**	— 17.8
5.5	4.7	0.2	3.1	— 3.5	11.9	**1991**	56.9
3.1	— 3.0	3.6	3.8	7.9	3.7	**1992**	15.5
0.1	5.4	2.7	2.2	— 3.2	3.0	**1993**	14.7
2.3	6.0	— 0.2	1.7	— 3.5	0.2	**1994**	— 3.2
7.3	1.9	2.3	— 0.7	2.2	— 0.7	**1995**	39.9
— 8.8	5.6	7.5	— 0.4	5.8	— 0.1	**1996**	22.7
10.5	— 0.4	6.2	-5.5	0.4	— 1.9	**1997**	21.6
— 1.2	— 19.9	13.0	4.6	10.1	12.5	**1998**	39.6
— 1.8	3.8	0.2	8.0	12.5	22.0	**1999**	85.6
— 5.0	11.7	— 12.7	— 8.3	— 22.9	— 4.9	**2000**	— 39.3
— 6.2	— 10.9	— 17.0	12.8	14.2	1.0	**2001**	— 21.1
— 9.2	— 1.0	— 10.9	13.5	11.2	— 9.7	**2002**	— 31.5
6.9	4.3	— 1.3	8.1	1.5	2.2	**2003**	50.0
— 7.8	— 2.6	3.2	4.1	6.2	3.7	**2004**	8.6
6.2	— 1.5	0.0	— 1.5	5.3	— 1.2	**2005**	1.4
— 3.7	4.4	3.4	4.8	2.7	— 0.7	**2006**	9.5
— 2.2	2.0	4.0	5.8	— 6.9	— 0.3	**2007**	9.8
1.4	1.8	— 11.6	— 17.7	— 10.8	2.7	**2008**	— 40.5
7.8	1.5	5.6	— 3.6	4.9	5.8	**2009**	43.9
6.9	— 6.2	12.0	5.9	— 0.4	6.2	**2010**	16.9
— 0.6	— 6.4	— 6.4	11.1	— 2.4	— 0.6	**2011**	— 1.8
0.2	4.3	1.6	— 4.5	1.1	0.3	**2012**	15.9
6.6	— 1.0	5.1	3.9	3.6	2.9	**2013**	38.3
— 0.9	4.8	— 1.9	3.1	3.5	— 1.2	**2014**	13.4
2.8	— 6.9	— 3.3	9.4	1.1	— 2.0	**2015**	5.7
6.6	1.0	1.9	— 2.3	2.6	1.1	**2016**	7.5
3.4	1.3	1.0	3.6	2.2	0.4	**2017**	28.2
2.2	5.7	— 0.8	— 9.2	0.3	— 9.5	**2018**	— 3.9
2.1	— 2.6	0.5	3.7	4.5	3.5	**2019**	35.2
6.8	9.6	— 5.2	— 2.3	11.8	5.7	**2020**	43.6
1.2	4.0	— 5.3	7.3	0.3	0.7	**2021**	21.4
29/50	28/50	26/50	28/50	36/50	30/50		37/50
58 %	56 %	52 %	56 %	72 %	60 %		74 %
0.7 %	0.4 %	— 0.7 %	0.8 %	1.9 %	1.5 %		13.4 %
8	11	12	7	2	4		

NASDAQ MONTH
CLOSING VALUES

	JAN	FEB	MAR	APR	MAY	JUN
1972	119	125	128	131	133	130
1973	128	120	117	108	103	101
1974	95	94	92	87	80	76
1975	70	73	76	79	83	87
1976	87	90	91	90	88	90
1977	96	95	94	95	96	100
1978	101	101	106	115	120	120
1979	126	123	132	134	131	138
1980	162	158	131	140	150	158
1981	198	198	210	217	223	216
1982	188	179	176	185	179	171
1983	248	261	271	293	309	319
1984	268	253	251	247	233	240
1985	279	284	279	281	291	296
1986	336	360	375	383	400	406
1987	392	425	430	418	417	425
1988	345	367	375	379	370	395
1989	401	400	407	428	446	435
1990	416	426	436	420	459	462
1991	414	453	482	485	506	476
1992	620	633	604	579	585	564
1993	696	671	690	661	701	704
1994	800	793	743	734	735	706
1995	755	794	817	844	865	933
1996	1060	1100	1101	1191	1243	1185
1997	1380	1309	1222	1261	1400	1442
1998	1619	1771	1836	1868	1779	1895
1999	2506	2288	2461	2543	2471	2686
2000	3940	4697	4573	3861	3401	3966
2001	2773	2152	1840	2116	2110	2161
2002	1934	1731	1845	1688	1616	1463
2003	1321	1338	1341	1464	1596	1623
2004	2066	2030	1994	1920	1987	2048
2005	2062	2052	1999	1922	2068	2057
2006	2306	2281	2340	2323	2179	2172
2007	2464	2416	2422	2525	2605	2603
2008	2390	2271	2279	2413	2523	2293
2009	1476	1378	1529	1717	1774	1835
2010	2147	2238	2398	2461	2257	2109
2011	2700	2782	2781	2874	2835	2774
2012	2814	2967	3092	3046	2827	2935
2013	3142	3160	3268	3329	3456	3403
2014	4104	4308	4199	4115	4243	4408
2015	4635	4964	4901	4941	5070	4987
2016	4614	4558	4870	4775	4948	4843
2017	5615	5825	5912	6048	6199	6140
2018	7411	7273	7063	7066	7442	7510
2019	7282	7533	7729	8095	7453	8006
2020	9151	8567	7700	8890	9490	10059
2021	13071	13192	13247	13963	13749	14504

NASDAQ MONTH CLOSING VALUES

STOCK MKT

JUL	AUG	SEP	OCT	NOV	DEC	
128	130	130	130	133	134	**1972**
109	105	111	110	94	92	**1973**
70	62	56	65	63	60	**1974**
83	79	74	77	79	78	**1975**
91	90	91	90	91	98	**1976**
101	100	101	98	103	105	**1977**
126	135	133	111	115	118	**1978**
141	150	150	136	144	151	**1979**
172	182	188	193	208	202	**1980**
212	196	180	195	201	196	**1981**
167	178	188	213	232	232	**1982**
304	292	297	275	286	279	**1983**
230	255	250	247	242	247	**1984**
301	298	280	293	314	325	**1985**
371	383	351	361	360	349	**1986**
435	455	444	323	305	331	**1987**
387	377	388	383	372	381	**1988**
454	469	473	456	456	455	**1989**
438	381	345	330	359	374	**1990**
502	526	527	543	524	586	**1991**
581	563	583	605	653	677	**1992**
705	743	763	779	754	777	**1993**
722	766	764	777	750	752	**1994**
1001	1020	1044	1036	1059	1052	**1995**
1081	1142	1227	1222	1293	1291	**1996**
1594	1587	1686	1594	1601	1570	**1997**
1872	1499	1694	1771	1950	2193	**1998**
2638	2739	2746	2966	3336	4069	**1999**
3767	4206	3673	3370	2598	2471	**2000**
2027	1805	1499	1690	1931	1950	**2001**
1328	1315	1172	1330	1479	1336	**2002**
1735	1810	1787	1932	1960	2003	**2003**
1887	1838	1897	1975	2097	2175	**2004**
2185	2152	2152	2120	2233	2205	**2005**
2091	2184	2258	2367	2432	2415	**2006**
2546	2596	2702	2859	2661	2652	**2007**
2326	2368	2092	1721	1536	1577	**2008**
1979	2009	2122	2045	2145	2269	**2009**
2255	2114	2369	2507	2498	2653	**2010**
2756	2579	2415	2684	2620	2605	**2011**
2940	3067	3116	2977	3010	3020	**2012**
3626	3590	3771	3920	4060	4177	**2013**
4370	4580	4493	4631	4792	4736	**2014**
5128	4777	4620	5054	5109	5007	**2015**
5162	5213	5312	5189	5324	5383	**2016**
6348	6429	6496	6728	6874	6903	**2017**
7672	8110	8046	7306	7331	6635	**2018**
8175	7963	7999	8292	8665	8973	**2019**
10745	11775	11168	10912	12199	12888	**2020**
14673	15259	14449	15498	15538	15645	**2021**

S&P/TSX MONTH PERCENT CHANGES

	JAN	FEB	MAR	APR	MAY	JUN
1985	8.1	0.0	0.7	0.8	3.8	— 0.8
1986	— 1.7	0.5	6.7	1.1	1.4	— 1.2
1987	9.2	4.5	6.9	— 0.6	— 0.9	1.5
1988	— 3.3	4.8	3.4	0.8	— 2.7	5.9
1989	6.7	— 1.2	0.2	1.4	2.2	1.5
1990	— 6.7	— 0.5	— 1.3	— 8.2	6.7	— 0.6
1991	0.5	5.8	1.0	-0.8	2.2	— 2.3
1992	2.4	— 0.4	— 4.7	— 1.7	1.0	0.0
1993	— 1.3	4.4	4.4	5.2	2.5	2.2
1994	5.4	— 2.9	— 2.1	— 1.4	1.4	— 7.0
1995	— 4.7	2.7	4.6	— 0.8	4.0	1.8
1996	5.4	— 0.7	0.8	3.5	1.9	— 3.9
1997	3.1	0.8	— 5.0	2.2	6.8	0.9
1998	0.0	5.9	6.6	1.4	— 1.0	— 2.9
1999	3.8	— 6.2	4.5	6.3	— 2.5	2.5
2000	0.8	7.6	3.7	— 1.2	— 1.0	10.2
2001	4.3	— 13.3	— 5.8	4.5	2.7	— 5.2
2002	— 0.5	— 0.1	2.8	— 2.4	— 0.1	— 6.7
2003	— 0.7	— 0.2	— 3.2	3.8	4.2	1.8
2004	3.7	3.1	— 2.3	— 4.0	2.1	1.5
2005	— 0.5	5.0	— 0.6	— 3.5	3.6	3.1
2006	6.0	— 2.2	3.6	0.8	— 3.8	— 1.1
2007	1.0	0.1	0.9	1.9	4.8	— 1.1
2008	— 4.9	3.3	— 1.7	4.4	5.6	— 1.7
2009	— 3.3	— 6.6	7.4	6.9	11.2	0.0
2010	— 5.5	4.8	3.5	1.4	— 3.7	— 4.0
2011	0.8	4.3	— 0.1	— 1.2	— 1.0	— 3.6
2012	4.2	1.5	— 2.0	— 0.8	— 6.3	0.7
2013	2.0	1.1	— 0.6	— 2.3	1.6	— 4.1
2014	0.5	3.8	0.9	2.2	— 0.3	3.7
2015	0.3	3.8	— 2.2	2.2	— 1.4	— 3.1
2016	— 1.4	0.3	4.9	3.4	0.8	0.0
2017	0.6	0.1	1.0	0.2	— 1.5	— 1.1
2018	— 1.6	— 3.2	— 0.5	1.6	2.9	1.3
2019	8.5	2.9	0.6	3.0	— 3.3	2.1
2020	1.5	— 6.1	— 17.7	10.5	2.8	2.1
2021	— 0.6	4.2	3.5	2.2	3.3	2.2
FQ POS	23/37	23/37	22/37	24/37	23/37	18/37
% FQ POS	62 %	62 %	59 %	65 %	62 %	49 %
AVG GAIN	1.1 %	0.9 %	0.6 %	1.2 %	1.3 %	-0.2 %
RANK GAIN	4	7	8	3	2	11

S&P/TSX MONTH PERCENT CHANGES 🍁 STOCK MKT

JUL	AUG	SEP	OCT	NOV	DEC	YEAR	
2.4	1.5	— 6.7	1.6	6.8	1.3	**1985**	20.5
— 4.9	3.2	— 1.6	1.6	0.7	0.6	**1986**	6.0
7.8	— 0.9	— 2.3	— 22.6	— 1.4	6.1	**1987**	3.1
— 1.9	— 2.7	— 0.1	3.4	— 3.0	2.9	**1988**	7.3
5.6	1.0	— 1.7	— 0.6	0.6	0.7	**1989**	17.1
0.5	— 6.0	— 5.6	— 2.5	2.3	3.4	**1990**	— 18.0
2.1	— 0.6	— 3.7	3.8	— 1.9	1.9	**1991**	7.8
1.6	— 1.2	— 3.1	1.2	— 1.6	2.1	**1992**	— 4.6
0.0	4.3	— 3.6	6.6	— 1.8	3.4	**1993**	29.0
3.8	4.1	0.1	— 1.4	— 4.6	2.9	**1994**	— 2.5
1.9	— 2.1	0.3	— 1.6	4.5	1.1	**1995**	11.9
— 2.3	4.3	2.9	5.8	7.5	— 1.5	**1996**	25.7
6.8	— 3.9	6.5	— 2.8	— 4.8	2.9	**1997**	13.0
— 5.9	— 20.2	1.5	10.6	2.2	2.2	**1998**	— 3.2
1.0	— 1.6	— 0.2	4.3	3.6	11.9	**1999**	29.7
2.1	8.1	— 7.7	— 7.1	— 8.5	1.3	**2000**	6.2
— 0.6	— 3.8	— 7.6	0.7	7.8	3.5	**2001**	— 13.9
— 7.6	0.1	— 6.5	1.1	5.1	0.7	**2002**	— 14.0
3.9	3.6	— 1.3	4.7	1.1	4.6	**2003**	24.3
— 1.0	— 1.0	3.5	2.3	1.8	2.4	**2004**	12.5
5.3	2.4	3.2	— 5.7	4.2	4.1	**2005**	21.9
1.9	2.1	— 2.6	5.0	3.3	1.2	**2006**	14.5
— 0.3	— 1.5	3.2	3.7	— 6.4	1.1	**2007**	7.2
— 6.0	1.3	— 14.7	— 16.9	— 5.0	— 3.1	**2008**	— 35.0
4.0	0.8	4.8	— 4.2	4.9	2.6	**2009**	30.7
3.7	1.7	3.8	2.5	2.2	3.8	**2010**	14.4
— 2.7	— 1.4	— 9.0	5.4	— 0.4	— 2.0	**2011**	— 11.1
0.6	2.4	3.1	0.9	— 1.5	1.6	**2012**	4.0
2.9	1.3	1.1	4.5	0.3	1.7	**2013**	9.6
1.2	1.9	— 4.3	— 2.3	0.9	— 0.8	**2014**	7.4
— 0.6	— 4.2	— 4.0	1.7	— 0.4	— 3.4	**2015**	— 11.1
3.7	0.1	0.9	0.4	2.0	1.4	**2016**	17.5
— 0.3	0.4	2.8	2.5	0.3	0.9	**2017**	6.0
1.0	— 1.0	— 1.2	— 6.5	1.1	— 5.8	**2018**	— 11.8
0.1	0.2	1.3	— 1.1	3.4	0.1	**2019**	19.1
4.2	2.1	— 2.4	— 3.4	10.3	1.4	**2020**	2.2
0.6	1.5	— 2.5	4.8	— 1.8	2.7	**2021**	21.7
25/37	22/37	15/37	23/37	23/37	31/37		27/37
68 %	59 %	41 %	62 %	62 %	84 %		73 %
0.9 %	— 0.1 %	— 1.4 %	0.0 %	0.9 %	1.7 %		7.2 %
5	11	12	9	6	1		

S&P/TSX MONTH CLOSING VALUES

	JAN	FEB	MAR	APR	MAY	JUN
1985	2595	2595	2613	2635	2736	2713
1986	2843	2856	3047	3079	3122	3086
1987	3349	3499	3739	3717	3685	3740
1988	3057	3205	3314	3340	3249	3441
1989	3617	3572	3578	3628	3707	3761
1990	3704	3687	3640	3341	3565	3544
1991	3273	3462	3496	3469	3546	3466
1992	3596	3582	3412	3356	3388	3388
1993	3305	3452	3602	3789	3883	3966
1994	4555	4424	4330	4267	4327	4025
1995	4018	4125	4314	4280	4449	4527
1996	4968	4934	4971	5147	5246	5044
1997	6110	6158	5850	5977	6382	6438
1998	6700	7093	7559	7665	7590	7367
1999	6730	6313	6598	7015	6842	7010
2000	8481	9129	9462	9348	9252	10196
2001	9322	8079	7608	7947	8162	7736
2002	7649	7638	7852	7663	7656	7146
2003	6570	6555	6343	6586	6860	6983
2004	8521	8789	8586	8244	8417	8546
2005	9204	9668	9612	9275	9607	9903
2006	11946	11688	12111	12204	11745	11613
2007	13034	13045	13166	13417	14057	13907
2008	13155	13583	13350	13937	14715	14467
2009	8695	8123	8720	9325	10370	10375
2010	11094	11630	12038	12211	11763	11294
2011	13552	14137	14116	13945	13803	13301
2012	12452	12644	12392	12293	11513	11597
2013	12685	12822	12750	12457	12650	12129
2014	13695	14210	14335	14652	14604	15146
2015	14674	15234	14902	15225	15014	14553
2016	12822	12860	13494	13951	14066	14065
2017	15386	15399	15548	15586	15350	15182
2018	15952	15443	15367	15608	16062	16278
2019	15541	15999	16102	16581	16037	16382
2020	17318	16263	13379	14781	15193	15515
2021	17337	18060	18701	19108	19731	20166

S&P/TSX PERCENT CLOSING VALUES

JUL	AUG	SEP	OCT	NOV	DEC	
2779	2820	2632	2675	2857	2893	**1985**
2935	3028	2979	3027	3047	3066	**1986**
4030	3994	3902	3019	2978	3160	**1987**
3377	3286	3284	3396	3295	3390	**1988**
3971	4010	3943	3919	3943	3970	**1989**
3561	3346	3159	3081	3151	3257	**1990**
3540	3518	3388	3516	3449	3512	**1991**
3443	3403	3298	3336	3283	3350	**1992**
3967	4138	3991	4256	4180	4321	**1993**
4179	4350	4354	4292	4093	4214	**1994**
4615	4517	4530	4459	4661	4714	**1995**
4929	5143	5291	5599	6017	5927	**1996**
6878	6612	7040	6842	6513	6699	**1997**
6931	5531	5614	6208	6344	6486	**1998**
7081	6971	6958	7256	7520	8414	**1999**
10406	11248	10378	9640	8820	8934	**2000**
7690	7399	6839	6886	7426	7688	**2001**
6605	6612	6180	6249	6570	6615	**2002**
7258	7517	7421	7773	7859	8221	**2003**
8458	8377	8668	8871	9030	9247	**2004**
10423	10669	11012	10383	10824	11272	**2005**
11831	12074	11761	12345	12752	12908	**2006**
13869	13660	14099	14625	13689	13833	**2007**
13593	13771	11753	9763	9271	8988	**2008**
10787	10868	11935	10911	11447	11746	**2009**
11713	11914	12369	12676	12953	13443	**2010**
12946	12769	11624	12252	12204	11955	**2011**
11665	11949	12317	12423	12239	12434	**2012**
12487	12654	12787	13361	13395	13622	**2013**
15331	15626	14961	14613	14745	14632	**2014**
14468	13859	13307	13529	13470	13010	**2015**
14583	14598	14726	14787	15083	15288	**2016**
15144	15212	15635	16026	16067	16209	**2017**
16434	16263	16073	15027	15198	14323	**2018**
16407	16442	16659	16483	17040	17063	**2019**
16169	16514	16121	15581	17190	17433	**2020**
20288	20583	20070	21037	20660	21223	**2021**

10 BEST   ## 10 WORST

YEARS

	Close	Change	Change
1954	36	11 pt	45.0 %
1958	55	15	38.1
1995	616	157	34.1
1975	90	22	31.5
1997	970	230	31.0
2013	1848	422	29.6
2019	3231	724	28.9
1989	353	76	27.3
2021	4,766	1010	26.9
1998	1229	259	26.7

YEARS

	Close	Change	Change
2008	903	− 566 pt	− 38.5 %
1974	69	− 29	− 29.7
2002	880	− 268	− 23.4
1973	98	− 21	− 17.4
1957	40	− 7	− 14.3
1966	80	− 12	− 13.1
2001	1148	− 172	− 13.0
1962	63	− 8	− 11.8
1977	95	− 12	− 11.5
1969	92	− 12	− 11.4

MONTHS

	Close	Change	Change
Oct 1974	74	10 pt	16.3 %
Apr 2020	2912	328	12.7
Aug 1982	120	12	11.6
Dec 1991	417	42	11.2
Oct 1982	134	13	11.0
Oct 2011	1253	122	10.8
Nov 2020	3622	352	10.8
Aug 1984	167	16	10.6
Nov 1980	141	13	10.2
Nov 1962	62	6	10.2

MONTHS

	Close	Change	Change
Oct 1987	252	− 70 pt	− 21.8 %
Oct 2008	969	− 196	− 16.8
Aug 1998	957	− 163	− 14.6
Mar 2020	2584	− 370	− 12.5
Sep 1974	64	− 9	− 11.9
Nov 1973	96	− 12	− 11.4
Sep 2002	815	− 101	− 11.0
Feb 2009	735	− 91	− 11.0
Mar 1980	102	− 12	− 10.2
Aug 1990	323	− 34	− 9.4

DAYS

		Close	Change	Change
Mon	2008 Oct 13	1003	104 pt	11.6 %
Tue	2008 Oct 28	941	92	10.8
Tue	2020 Mar 24	2447	210	9.4
Fri	2020 Mar 13	2711	230	9.3
Wed	1987 Oct 21	258	22	9.1
Mon	2009 Mar 23	883	54	7.1
Mon	2020 Apr 6	2667	175	7.0
Thu	2008 Nov 13	911	59	6.9
Mon	2008 Nov 24	852	52	6.5
Tues	2009 Mar 10	720	43	6.4

DAYS

		Close	Change	Change
Mon	1987 Oct 19	225	− 58 pt	− 20.5 %
Mon	2020 Mar 16	2386	− 325	− 12.0
Thu	2020 Mar 12	2481	− 261	− 9.5
Wed	2008 Oct 15	908	− 90	− 9.0
Mon	2008 Dec 01	816	− 80	− 8.9
Mon	2008 Sep 29	1106	− 107	− 8.8
Mon	1987 Oct 26	228	− 21	− 8.3
Thu	2008 Oct 09	910	− 75	− 7.6
Mon	2020 Mar 9	2747	− 226	− 7.6
Mon	1997 Oct 27	877	− 65	− 6.9

10 BEST

10 WORST

YEARS

	Close	Change	Change
1954	404	124 pt	44.0 %
1975	852	236	38.3
1958	584	148	34.0
1995	5117	1283	33.5
1985	1547	335	27.7
1989	2753	585	27.0
2013	16577	3473	26.5
1996	6448	1331	26.0
2003	10454	2112	25.3
1999	11453	2272	25.2

YEARS

	Close	Change	Change
2008	8776	− 4488 pt	− 33.8 %
1974	616	− 235	− 27.6
1966	786	− 184	− 18.9
1977	831	− 174	− 17.3
2002	8342	− 1680	− 16.8
1973	851	− 169	− 16.6
1969	800	− 143	− 15.2
1957	436	− 64	− 12.8
1962	652	− 79	− 10.8
1960	616	− 64	− 9.3

MONTHS

	Close	Change	Change
Nov 2020	29639	3137 pt	11.8 %
Aug 1982	901	93	11.5
Oct 1982	992	95	10.6
Apr 2020	24246	2429	11.1
Oct 2002	8397	805	10.6
Apr 1978	837	80	10.5
Apr 1999	10789	1003	10.2
Nov 1962	649	60	10.1
Nov 1954	387	35	9.9
Aug 1984	1224	109	9.8

MONTHS

	Close	Change	Change
Oct 1987	1994	− 603 pt	− 23.2 %
Aug 1998	7539	− 1344	− 15.1
Oct 2008	9325	− 1526	− 14.1
Nov 1973	822	− 134	− 14.0
Mar 2020	21917	3492	13.7
Sep 2002	7592	− 1072	− 12.4
Feb 2009	7063	− 938	− 11.7
Sep 2001	8848	− 1102	− 11.1
Sep 1974	608	− 71	− 10.4
Aug 1974	679	− 79	− 10.4

DAYS

		Close	Change	Change
Tue	2020 Mar 24	20705	2113 pt	11.4 %
Mon	2008 Oct 13	9388	936	11.1
Tue	2008 Oct 28	9065	889	10.9
Wed	1987 Oct 21	2028	187	10.2
Fri	2020 Mar 13	23186	1985	9.4
Mon	2020 Apr 6	22680	1627	7.7
Mon	2009 Mar 23	7776	497	6.8
Thu	2008 Nov 13	8835	553	6.7
Fri	2008 Nov 21	8046	494	6.5
Thu	2020 Mar 26	22552	1352	6.4

DAYS

		Close	Change	Change
Mon	1987 Oct 19	1739	− 508 pt	− 22.6 %
Mon	2020 Mar 16	20189	− 2997	− 12.9
Thu	2020 Mar 12	20201	− 2353	− 10.0
Mon	1987 Oct 26	1794	− 157	− 8.0
Wed	2008 Oct 15	8578	− 733	− 7.9
Mon	2020 Mar 9	23851	2014	− 7.8
Mon	2008 Dec 01	8149	− 680	− 7.7
Thu	2008 Oct 09	8579	− 679	− 7.3
Mon	1997 Oct 27	8366	− 554	− 7.2
Mon	2001 Sep 17	8921	− 685	− 7.1

10 BEST

10 WORST

YEARS

	Close	Change	Change
1999	4069	1877 pt	85.6 %
1991	586	213	56.9
2003	2003	668	50.0
2009	2269	692	43.9
1995	1052	300	39.9
1998	2193	622	39.6
2013	4161	1157	38.3
2019	8973	2337	35.2
1980	202	51	33.9
1985	325	78	31.5

YEARS

	Close	Change	Change
2008	1577	– 1075 pt	– 40.5 %
2000	2471	– 1599	– 39.3
1974	60	– 32	– 35.1
2002	1336	– 615	– 31.5
1973	92	– 42	– 31.1
2001	1950	– 520	– 21.1
1990	374	– 81	– 17.8
1984	247	– 32	– 11.3
1987	331	– 18	– 5.2
2018	6635	– 268	– 3.9

MONTHS

	Close	Change	Change
Dec 1999	4069	733 pt	22.0 %
Feb 2000	4697	756	19.2
Oct 1974	65	10	17.2
Jun 2000	3966	565	16.6
Apr 2020	8890	1189	15.4
Apr 2001	2116	276	15.0
Nov 2001	1931	240	14.2
Oct 2002	1330	158	13.5
Oct 1982	1771	25	13.3
Sep 1998	1694	195	13.0

MONTHS

	Close	Change	Change
Oct 1987	323	– 121 pt	– 27.2 %
Nov 2000	2598	– 772	– 22.9
Feb 2001	2152	– 621	– 22.4
Aug 1998	1499	– 373	– 19.9
Oct 2008	1721	– 371	– 17.7
Mar 1980	131	– 27	– 17.1
Sep 2001	1499	– 307	– 17.0
Oct 1978	111	– 22	– 16.4
Apr 2000	3861	– 712	– 15.6
Nov 1973	94	– 17	– 15.1

DAYS

		Close	Change	Change
Wed	2001 Jan 3	2617	325 pt	14.2 %
Mon	2008 Oct 13	1844	195	11.8
Tue	2000 Dec 5	2890	274	10.5
Tue	2008 Oct 28	1649	144	9.5
Fri	2020 Mar 13	7875	673	9.3
Thu	2001 Apr 5	1785	146	8.9
Wed	2001 Apr 18	2079	156	8.1
	2020 Mar 24		557	8.1
Tue	2000 May 30	3459	254	7.9
Fri	2000 Oct 13	3317	242	7.9

DAYS

		Close	Change	Change
Mon	2020 Mar 16	6905	– 970 pt	– 12.3 %
Mon	1987 Oct 19	360	– 46	– 11.3
Fri	2000 Apr 14	3321	– 355	– 9.7
Thu	2020 Mar 12	7202	– 750	– 9.4
Mon	2008 Sep 29	1984	– 200	– 9.1
Mon	1987 Oct 26	299	– 30	– 9.0
Tue	1987 Oct 20	328	– 32	– 9.0
Mon	2008 Dec 01	1398	– 138	– 9.0
Mon	1998 Aug 31	1499	– 140	– 8.6
Wed	2008 Oct 15	1628	– 151	– 8.5

10 BEST

10 WORST

YEARS

	Close	Change	Change
2009	8414	2758 pt	30.7 %
1999	4321	1928	29.7
1993	5927	971	29.0
1996	8221	1213	25.7
2003	11272	1606	24.3
2005	2893	2026	21.9
2021	21223	3789	21.7
1985	3970	500	20.8
2019	17063	1842	27.4
1989	12908	580	17.1

YEARS

	Close	Change	Change
2008	8988	– 4845 pt	– 35.0 %
1990	3257	– 713	– 18.0
2002	6615	– 1074	– 14.0
2001	7688	– 1245	– 13.9
2018	14323	– 1886	– 11.6
2015	13010	– 1622	– 11.1
2011	11955	– 1488	– 11.1
1992	3350	– 162	– 4.6
1998	6486	– 214	– 3.2
1994	4214	– 108	– 2.5

MONTHS

	Close	Change	Change
Dec 1999	8414	891 pt	11.8 %
May 2009	8500	1045	11.2
Oct 1998	6208	594	10.6
Apr 2020	14781	1402	10.5
Nov 2020	17190	1610	10.3
Jun 2000	10196	943	10.2
Jan 1985	2595	195	8.1
Aug 2000	11248	842	8.1
Nov 2001	7426	540	7.8
Jul 1987	4030	290	7.8

MONTHS

	Close	Change	Change
Oct 1987	3019	– 883 pt	– 22.6 %
Aug 1998	5531	– 1401	– 20.2
Mar 2020	13379	– 2884	– 17.7
Oct 2008	9763	– 1990	– 16.9
Sep 2008	11753	– 2018	– 14.7
Feb 2001	8079	– 1243	– 13.3
Sep 2011	11624	– 1145	– 9.0
Nov 2000	8820	– 820	– 8.5
Apr 1990	3341	– 299	– 8.2
Sep 2000	10378	– 870	– 7.7

DAYS

		Close	Change	Change
Tue	2020 Mar 24	12571	1342 pt	12.0 %
Tue	2008 Oct 14	9956	891	9.8
Mon	2020 Mar 13	13716	1208	9.7
Wed	1987 Oct 21	3246	269	9.0
Mon	2008 Oct 20	10251	689	7.2
Tue	2008 Oct 28	9152	614	7.2
Fri	2008 Sep 19	12913	848	7.0
Fri	2008 Nov 28	9271	517	5.9
Fri	2008 Nov 21	8155	431	5.6
Mon	2008 Dec 08	8567	450	5.5

DAYS

		Close	Change	Change
Wed	2020 Mar 12	12508	– 1762 pt	– 12.3 %
Mon	1987 Oct 19	3192	– 407	– 11.3
Mon	2020 Mar 9	14514	– 1661	– 10.3
Mon	2020 Mar 16	12360	– 1356	– 9.9
Mon	2008 Dec 01	8406	– 864	– 9.3
Thu	2008 Nov 20	7725	– 766	– 9.0
Mon	2008 Oct 27	8537	– 757	– 8.1
Wed	2000 Oct 25	9512	– 840	– 8.1
Wed	2020 Mar 18	11721	– 964	– 7.6
Mon	1987 Oct 26	2846	– 233	– 7.6

BOND YIELDS

	JAN	FEB	MAR	APR	MAY	JUN
1954	2.48	2.47	2.37	2.29	2.37	2.38
1955	2.61	2.65	2.68	2.75	2.76	2.78
1956	2.9	2.84	2.96	3.18	3.07	3
1957	3.46	3.34	3.41	3.48	3.6	3.8
1958	3.09	3.05	2.98	2.88	2.92	2.97
1959	4.02	3.96	3.99	4.12	4.31	4.34
1960	4.72	4.49	4.25	4.28	4.35	4.15
1961	3.84	3.78	3.74	3.78	3.71	3.88
1962	4.08	4.04	3.93	3.84	3.87	3.91
1963	3.83	3.92	3.93	3.97	3.93	3.99
1964	4.17	4.15	4.22	4.23	4.2	4.17
1965	4.19	4.21	4.21	4.2	4.21	4.21
1966	4.61	4.83	4.87	4.75	4.78	4.81
1967	4.58	4.63	4.54	4.59	4.85	5.02
1968	5.53	5.56	5.74	5.64	5.87	5.72
1969	6.04	6.19	6.3	6.17	6.32	6.57
1970	7.79	7.24	7.07	7.39	7.91	7.84
1971	6.24	6.11	5.7	5.83	6.39	6.52
1972	5.95	6.08	6.07	6.19	6.13	6.11
1973	6.46	6.64	6.71	6.67	6.85	6.9
1974	6.99	6.96	7.21	7.51	7.58	7.54
1975	7.5	7.39	7.73	8.23	8.06	7.86
1976	7.74	7.79	7.73	7.56	7.9	7.86
1977	7.21	7.39	7.46	7.37	7.46	7.28
1978	7.96	8.03	8.04	8.15	8.35	8.46
1979	9.1	9.1	9.12	9.18	9.25	8.91
1980	10.8	12.41	12.75	11.47	10.18	9.78
1981	12.57	13.19	13.12	13.68	14.1	13.47
1982	14.59	14.43	13.86	13.87	13.62	14.3
1983	10.46	10.72	10.51	10.4	10.38	10.85
1984	11.67	11.84	12.32	12.63	13.41	13.56
1985	11.38	11.51	11.86	11.43	10.85	10.16
1986	9.19	8.7	7.78	7.3	7.71	7.8
1987	7.08	7.25	7.25	8.02	8.61	8.4
1988	8.67	8.21	8.37	8.72	9.09	8.92
1989	9.09	9.17	9.36	9.18	8.86	8.28
1990	8.21	8.47	8.59	8.79	8.76	8.48
1991	8.09	7.85	8.11	8.04	8.07	8.28
1992	7.03	7.34	7.54	7.48	7.39	7.26
1993	6.6	6.26	5.98	5.97	6.04	5.96
1994	5.75	5.97	6.48	6.97	7.18	7.1
1995	7.78	7.47	7.2	7.06	6.63	6.17
1996	5.65	5.81	6.27	6.51	6.74	6.91
1997	6.58	6.42	6.69	6.89	6.71	6.49
1998	5.54	5.57	5.65	5.64	5.65	5.5
1999	4.72	5	5.23	5.18	5.54	5.9
2000	6.66	6.52	6.26	5.99	6.44	6.1
2001	5.16	5.1	4.89	5.14	5.39	5.28
2002	5.04	4.91	5.28	5.21	5.16	4.93
2003	4.05	3.9	3.81	3.96	3.57	3.33
2004	4.15	4.08	3.83	4.35	4.72	4.73
2005	4.22	4.17	4.5	4.34	4.14	4.00
2006	4.42	4.57	4.72	4.99	5.11	5.11
2007	4.76	4.72	4.56	4.69	4.75	5.10
2008	3.74	3.74	3.51	3.68	3.88	4.10
2009	2.52	2.87	2.82	2.93	3.29	3.72
2010	3.73	3.69	3.73	3.85	3.42	3.20
2011	3.39	3.58	3.41	3.46	3.17	3.00
2012	1.97	1.97	2.17	2.05	1.80	1.62
2013	1.91	1.98	1.96	1.76	1.93	2.30
2014	2.86	2.71	2.72	2.71	2.56	2.60
2015	1.88	1.98	2.04	1.94	2.20	2.36
2016	2.09	1.78	1.89	1.81	1.81	1.64
2017	2.43	2.42	2.48	2.30	2.30	2.19
2018	2.58	2.86	2.84	2.87	2.98	2.91
2019	2.71	2.68	2.57	2.53	2.40	2.07
2020	1.76	1.50	0.87	0.66	0.67	0.73
2021	1.08	1.26	1.61	1.64	1.62	1.52

* Source: Federal Reserve Bank of St. Louis, monthly data calculated as average of business days

10 YEAR TREASURY 🇺🇸 BOND YIELDS

JUL	AUG	SEP	OCT	NOV	DEC	
2.3	2.36	2.38	2.43	2.48	2.51	**1954**
2.9	2.97	2.97	2.88	2.89	2.96	**1955**
3.11	3.33	3.38	3.34	3.49	3.59	**1956**
3.93	3.93	3.92	3.97	3.72	3.21	**1957**
3.2	3.54	3.76	3.8	3.74	3.86	**1958**
4.4	4.43	4.68	4.53	4.53	4.69	**1959**
3.9	3.8	3.8	3.89	3.93	3.84	**1960**
3.92	4.04	3.98	3.92	3.94	4.06	**1961**
4.01	3.98	3.98	3.93	3.92	3.86	**1962**
4.02	4	4.08	4.11	4.12	4.13	**1963**
4.19	4.19	4.2	4.19	4.15	4.18	**1964**
4.2	4.25	4.29	4.35	4.45	4.62	**1965**
5.02	5.22	5.18	5.01	5.16	4.84	**1966**
5.16	5.28	5.3	5.48	5.75	5.7	**1967**
5.5	5.42	5.46	5.58	5.7	6.03	**1968**
6.72	6.69	7.16	7.1	7.14	7.65	**1969**
7.46	7.53	7.39	7.33	6.84	6.39	**1970**
6.73	6.58	6.14	5.93	5.81	5.93	**1971**
6.11	6.21	6.55	6.48	6.28	6.36	**1972**
7.13	7.4	7.09	6.79	6.73	6.74	**1973**
7.81	8.04	8.04	7.9	7.68	7.43	**1974**
8.06	8.4	8.43	8.14	8.05	8	**1975**
7.83	7.77	7.59	7.41	7.29	6.87	**1976**
7.33	7.4	7.34	7.52	7.58	7.69	**1977**
8.64	8.41	8.42	8.64	8.81	9.01	**1978**
8.95	9.03	9.33	10.3	10.65	10.39	**1979**
10.25	11.1	11.51	11.75	12.68	12.84	**1980**
14.28	14.94	15.32	15.15	13.39	13.72	**1981**
13.95	13.06	12.34	10.91	10.55	10.54	**1982**
11.38	11.85	11.65	11.54	11.69	11.83	**1983**
13.36	12.72	12.52	12.16	11.57	11.5	**1984**
10.31	10.33	10.37	10.24	9.78	9.26	**1985**
7.3	7.17	7.45	7.43	7.25	7.11	**1986**
8.45	8.76	9.42	9.52	8.86	8.99	**1987**
9.06	9.26	8.98	8.8	8.96	9.11	**1988**
8.02	8.11	8.19	8.01	7.87	7.84	**1989**
8.47	8.75	8.89	8.72	8.39	8.08	**1990**
8.27	7.9	7.65	7.53	7.42	7.09	**1991**
6.84	6.59	6.42	6.59	6.87	6.77	**1992**
5.81	5.68	5.36	5.33	5.72	5.77	**1993**
7.3	7.24	7.46	7.74	7.96	7.81	**1994**
6.28	6.49	6.2	6.04	5.93	5.71	**1995**
6.87	6.64	6.83	6.53	6.2	6.3	**1996**
6.22	6.3	6.21	6.03	5.88	5.81	**1997**
5.46	5.34	4.81	4.53	4.83	4.65	**1998**
5.79	5.94	5.92	6.11	6.03	6.28	**1999**
6.05	5.83	5.8	5.74	5.72	5.24	**2000**
5.24	4.97	4.73	4.57	4.65	5.09	**2001**
4.65	4.26	3.87	3.94	4.05	4.03	**2002**
3.98	4.45	4.27	4.29	4.3	4.27	**2003**
4.5	4.28	4.13	4.1	4.19	4.23	**2004**
4.18	4.26	4.20	4.46	4.54	4.47	**2005**
5.09	4.88	4.72	4.73	4.60	4.56	**2006**
5.00	4.67	4.52	4.53	4.15	4.10	**2007**
4.01	3.89	3.69	3.81	3.53	2.42	**2008**
3.56	3.59	3.40	3.39	3.40	3.59	**2009**
3.01	2.70	2.65	2.54	2.76	3.29	**2010**
3.00	2.30	1.98	2.15	2.01	1.98	**2011**
1.53	1.68	1.72	1.75	1.65	1.72	**2012**
2.58	2.74	2.81	2.62	2.72	2.90	**2013**
2.54	2.42	2.53	2.30	2.33	2.21	**2014**
2.32	2.17	2.17	2.07	2.26	2.24	**2015**
1.50	1.56	1.63	1.76	2.14	2.49	**2016**
2.32	2.21	2.20	2.36	2.35	2.40	**2017**
2.89	2.89	3.00	3.15	3.12	2.83	**2018**
2.06	1.63	1.70	1.71	1.81	1.86	**2019**
0.62	0.65	0.68	0.79	0.87	0.93	**2020**
1.32	1.28	1.37	1.58	1.56	1.47	**2021**

BOND YIELDS 5 YEAR TREASURY*

	JAN	FEB	MAR	APR	MAY	JUN
1954	2.17	2.04	1.93	1.87	1.92	1.92
1955	2.32	2.38	2.48	2.55	2.56	2.59
1956	2.84	2.74	2.93	3.20	3.08	2.97
1957	3.47	3.39	3.46	3.53	3.64	3.83
1958	2.88	2.78	2.64	2.46	2.41	2.46
1959	4.01	3.96	3.99	4.12	4.35	4.50
1960	4.92	4.69	4.31	4.29	4.49	4.12
1961	3.67	3.66	3.60	3.57	3.47	3.81
1962	3.94	3.89	3.68	3.60	3.66	3.64
1963	3.58	3.66	3.68	3.74	3.72	3.81
1964	4.07	4.03	4.14	4.15	4.05	4.02
1965	4.10	4.15	4.15	4.15	4.15	4.15
1966	4.86	4.98	4.92	4.83	4.89	4.97
1967	4.70	4.74	4.54	4.51	4.75	5.01
1968	5.54	5.59	5.76	5.69	6.04	5.85
1969	6.25	6.34	6.41	6.30	6.54	6.75
1970	8.17	7.82	7.21	7.50	7.97	7.85
1971	5.89	5.56	5.00	5.65	6.28	6.53
1972	5.59	5.69	5.87	6.17	5.85	5.91
1973	6.34	6.60	6.80	6.67	6.80	6.69
1974	6.95	6.82	7.31	7.92	8.18	8.10
1975	7.41	7.11	7.30	7.99	7.72	7.51
1976	7.46	7.45	7.49	7.25	7.59	7.61
1977	6.58	6.83	6.93	6.79	6.94	6.76
1978	7.77	7.83	7.86	7.98	8.18	8.36
1979	9.20	9.13	9.20	9.25	9.24	8.85
1980	10.74	12.60	13.47	11.84	9.95	9.21
1981	12.77	13.41	13.41	13.99	14.63	13.95
1982	14.65	14.54	13.98	14.00	13.75	14.43
1983	10.03	10.26	10.08	10.02	10.03	10.63
1984	11.37	11.54	12.02	12.37	13.17	13.48
1985	10.93	11.13	11.52	11.01	10.34	9.60
1986	8.68	8.34	7.46	7.05	7.52	7.64
1987	6.64	6.79	6.79	7.57	8.26	8.02
1988	8.18	7.71	7.83	8.19	8.58	8.49
1989	9.15	9.27	9.51	9.30	8.91	8.29
1990	8.12	8.42	8.60	8.77	8.74	8.43
1991	7.70	7.47	7.77	7.70	7.70	7.94
1992	6.24	6.58	6.95	6.78	6.69	6.48
1993	5.83	5.43	5.19	5.13	5.20	5.22
1994	5.09	5.40	5.94	6.52	6.78	6.70
1995	7.76	7.37	7.05	6.86	6.41	5.93
1996	5.36	5.38	5.97	6.30	6.48	6.69
1997	6.33	6.20	6.54	6.76	6.57	6.38
1998	5.42	5.49	5.61	5.61	5.63	5.52
1999	4.60	4.91	5.14	5.08	5.44	5.81
2000	6.58	6.68	6.50	6.26	6.69	6.30
2001	4.86	4.89	4.64	4.76	4.93	4.81
2002	4.34	4.30	4.74	4.65	4.49	4.19
2003	3.05	2.90	2.78	2.93	2.52	2.27
2004	3.12	3.07	2.79	3.39	3.85	3.93
2005	3.71	3.77	4.17	4.00	3.85	3.77
2006	4.35	4.57	4.72	4.90	5.00	5.07
2007	4.75	4.71	4.48	4.59	4.67	5.03
2008	2.98	2.78	2.48	2.84	3.15	3.49
2009	1.60	1.87	1.82	1.86	2.13	2.71
2010	2.48	2.36	2.43	2.58	2.18	2.00
2011	1.99	2.26	2.11	2.17	1.84	1.58
2012	0.84	0.83	1.02	0.89	0.76	0.71
2013	0.81	0.85	0.82	0.71	0.84	1.20
2014	1.65	1.52	1.64	1.70	1.59	1.68
2015	1.37	1.47	1.52	1.35	1.54	1.68
2016	1.52	1.22	1.38	1.26	1.30	1.17
2017	1.92	1.90	2.01	1.82	1.84	1.77
2018	2.38	2.60	2.63	2.70	2.82	2.78
2019	2.54	2.49	2.37	2.33	2.19	1.83
2020	1.56	1.32	0.59	0.39	0.34	0.34
2021	0.45	0.54	0.82	0.86	0.82	0.84

* Source: Federal Reserve Bank of St. Louis, monthly data calculated as average of business days

5 YEAR TREASURY 🇺🇸 BOND YIELDS

JUL	AUG	SEP	OCT	NOV	DEC	
1.85	1.90	1.96	2.02	2.09	2.16	**1954**
2.72	2.86	2.85	2.76	2.81	2.93	**1955**
3.12	3.41	3.47	3.40	3.56	3.70	**1956**
4.00	4.00	4.03	4.08	3.72	3.08	**1957**
2.77	3.29	3.69	3.78	3.70	3.82	**1958**
4.58	4.57	4.90	4.72	4.75	5.01	**1959**
3.79	3.62	3.61	3.76	3.81	3.67	**1960**
3.84	3.96	3.90	3.80	3.82	3.91	**1961**
3.80	3.71	3.70	3.64	3.60	3.56	**1962**
3.89	3.89	3.96	3.97	4.01	4.04	**1963**
4.03	4.05	4.08	4.07	4.04	4.09	**1964**
4.15	4.20	4.25	4.34	4.46	4.72	**1965**
5.17	5.50	5.50	5.27	5.36	5.00	**1966**
5.23	5.31	5.40	5.57	5.78	5.75	**1967**
5.60	5.50	5.48	5.55	5.66	6.12	**1968**
7.01	7.03	7.57	7.51	7.53	7.96	**1969**
7.59	7.57	7.29	7.12	6.47	5.95	**1970**
6.85	6.55	6.14	5.93	5.78	5.69	**1971**
5.97	6.02	6.25	6.18	6.12	6.16	**1972**
7.33	7.63	7.05	6.77	6.92	6.80	**1973**
8.38	8.63	8.37	7.97	7.68	7.31	**1974**
7.92	8.33	8.37	7.97	7.80	7.76	**1975**
7.49	7.31	7.13	6.75	6.52	6.10	**1976**
6.84	7.03	7.04	7.32	7.34	7.48	**1977**
8.54	8.33	8.43	8.61	8.84	9.08	**1978**
8.90	9.06	9.41	10.63	10.93	10.42	**1979**
9.53	10.84	11.62	11.86	12.83	13.25	**1980**
14.79	15.56	15.93	15.41	13.38	13.60	**1981**
14.07	13.00	12.25	10.80	10.38	10.22	**1982**
11.21	11.63	11.43	11.28	11.41	11.54	**1983**
13.27	12.68	12.53	12.06	11.33	11.07	**1984**
9.70	9.81	9.81	9.69	9.28	8.73	**1985**
7.06	6.80	6.92	6.83	6.76	6.67	**1986**
8.01	8.32	8.94	9.08	8.35	8.45	**1987**
8.66	8.94	8.69	8.51	8.79	9.09	**1988**
7.83	8.09	8.17	7.97	7.81	7.75	**1989**
8.33	8.44	8.51	8.33	8.02	7.73	**1990**
7.91	7.43	7.14	6.87	6.62	6.19	**1991**
5.84	5.60	5.38	5.60	6.04	6.08	**1992**
5.09	5.03	4.73	4.71	5.06	5.15	**1993**
6.91	6.88	7.08	7.40	7.72	7.78	**1994**
6.01	6.24	6.00	5.86	5.69	5.51	**1995**
6.64	6.39	6.60	6.27	5.97	6.07	**1996**
6.12	6.16	6.11	5.93	5.80	5.77	**1997**
5.46	5.27	4.62	4.18	4.54	4.45	**1998**
5.68	5.84	5.80	6.03	5.97	6.19	**1999**
6.18	6.06	5.93	5.78	5.70	5.17	**2000**
4.76	4.57	4.12	3.91	3.97	4.39	**2001**
3.81	3.29	2.94	2.95	3.05	3.03	**2002**
2.87	3.37	3.18	3.19	3.29	3.27	**2003**
3.69	3.47	3.36	3.35	3.53	3.60	**2004**
3.98	4.12	4.01	4.33	4.45	4.39	**2005**
5.04	4.82	4.67	4.69	4.58	4.53	**2006**
4.88	4.43	4.20	4.20	3.67	3.49	**2007**
3.30	3.14	2.88	2.73	2.29	1.52	**2008**
2.46	2.57	2.37	2.33	2.23	2.34	**2009**
1.76	1.47	1.41	1.18	1.35	1.93	**2010**
1.54	1.02	0.90	1.06	0.91	0.89	**2011**
0.62	0.71	0.67	0.71	0.67	0.70	**2012**
1.40	1.52	1.60	1.37	1.37	1.58	**2013**
1.70	1.63	1.77	1.55	1.62	1.64	**2014**
1.63	1.54	1.49	1.39	1.67	1.70	**2015**
1.07	1.13	1.18	1.27	1.60	1.96	**2016**
1.87	1.78	1.80	1.98	2.05	2.18	**2017**
2.78	2.77	2.89	3.00	2.95	2.68	**2018**
1.83	1.49	1.57	1.53	1.64	1.68	**2019**
0.28	0.27	0.27	0.34	0.39	0.39	**2020**
0.76	0.77	0.86	1.11	1.20	1.23	**2021**

BOND YIELDS 3 MONTH TREASURY

	JAN	FEB	MAR	APR	MAY	JUN
1982	12.92	14.28	13.31	13.34	12.71	13.08
1983	8.12	8.39	8.66	8.51	8.50	9.14
1984	9.26	9.46	9.89	10.07	10.22	10.26
1985	8.02	8.56	8.83	8.22	7.73	7.18
1986	7.30	7.29	6.76	6.24	6.33	6.40
1987	5.58	5.75	5.77	5.82	5.85	5.85
1988	6.00	5.84	5.87	6.08	6.45	6.66
1999	8.56	8.84	9.14	8.96	8.74	8.43
1990	7.90	8.00	8.17	8.04	8.01	7.99
1991	6.41	6.12	6.09	5.83	5.63	5.75
1992	3.91	3.95	4.14	3.84	3.72	3.75
1993	3.07	2.99	3.01	2.93	3.03	3.14
1994	3.04	3.33	3.59	3.78	4.27	4.25
1995	5.90	5.94	5.91	5.84	5.85	5.64
1996	5.15	4.96	5.10	5.09	5.15	5.23
1997	5.17	5.14	5.28	5.30	5.20	5.07
1998	5.18	5.23	5.16	5.08	5.14	5.12
1999	4.45	4.56	4.57	4.41	4.63	4.72
2000	5.50	5.73	5.86	5.82	5.99	5.86
2001	5.29	5.01	4.54	3.97	3.70	3.57
2002	1.68	1.76	1.83	1.75	1.76	1.73
2003	1.19	1.19	1.15	1.15	1.09	0.94
2004	0.90	0.94	0.95	0.96	1.04	1.29
2005	2.37	2.58	2.80	2.84	2.90	3.04
2006	4.34	4.54	4.63	4.72	4.84	4.92
2007	5.11	5.16	5.08	5.01	4.87	4.74
2008	2.82	2.17	1.28	1.31	1.76	1.89
2009	0.13	0.30	0.22	0.16	0.18	0.18
2010	0.06	0.11	0.15	0.16	0.16	0.12
2011	0.15	0.13	0.10	0.06	0.04	0.04
2012	0.03	0.09	0.08	0.08	0.09	0.09
2013	0.07	0.10	0.09	0.06	0.04	0.05
2014	0.04	0.05	0.05	0.03	0.03	0.04
2015	0.03	0.02	0.03	0.02	0.02	0.02
2016	0.26	0.31	0.30	0.23	0.28	0.27
2017	0.52	0.53	0.75	0.81	0.90	1.00
2018	1.43	1.59	1.73	1.79	1.90	1.94
2019	2.42	2.44	2.45	2.43	2.40	2.22
2020	1.55	1.54	0.30	0.14	0.13	0.16
2021	0.08	0.04	0.30	0.02	0.02	0.04

* Source: Federal Reserve Bank of St. Louis, monthly data calculated as average of business days

3 MONTH TREASURY  BOND YIELDS

JUL	AUG	SEP	OCT	NOV	DEC	
11.86	9.00	8.19	7.97	8.35	8.20	**1982**
9.45	9.74	9.36	8.99	9.11	9.36	**1983**
10.53	10.90	10.80	10.12	8.92	8.34	**1984**
7.32	7.37	7.33	7.40	7.48	7.33	**1985**
6.00	5.69	5.35	5.32	5.50	5.68	**1986**
5.88	6.23	6.62	6.35	5.89	5.96	**1987**
6.95	7.30	7.48	7.60	8.03	8.35	**1988**
8.15	8.17	8.01	7.90	7.94	7.88	**1999**
7.87	7.69	7.60	7.40	7.29	6.95	**1990**
5.75	5.50	5.37	5.14	4.69	4.18	**1991**
3.28	3.20	2.97	2.93	3.21	3.29	**1992**
3.11	3.09	3.01	3.09	3.18	3.13	**1993**
4.46	4.61	4.75	5.10	5.45	5.76	**1994**
5.59	5.57	5.43	5.44	5.52	5.29	**1995**
5.30	5.19	5.24	5.12	5.17	5.04	**1996**
5.19	5.28	5.08	5.11	5.28	5.30	**1997**
5.09	5.04	4.74	4.07	4.53	4.50	**1998**
4.69	4.87	4.82	5.02	5.23	5.36	**1999**
6.14	6.28	6.18	6.29	6.36	5.94	**2000**
3.59	3.44	2.69	2.20	1.91	1.72	**2001**
1.71	1.65	1.66	1.61	1.25	1.21	**2002**
0.92	0.97	0.96	0.94	0.95	0.91	**2003**
1.36	1.50	1.68	1.79	2.11	2.22	**2004**
3.29	3.52	3.49	3.79	3.97	3.97	**2005**
5.08	5.09	4.93	5.05	5.07	4.97	**2006**
4.96	4.32	3.99	4.00	3.35	3.07	**2007**
1.66	1.75	1.15	0.69	0.19	0.03	**2008**
0.18	0.17	0.12	0.07	0.05	0.05	**2009**
0.16	0.16	0.15	0.13	0.14	0.14	**2010**
0.04	0.02	0.01	0.02	0.01	0.01	**2011**
0.10	0.10	0.11	0.10	0.09	0.07	**2012**
0.04	0.04	0.02	0.05	0.07	0.07	**2013**
0.03	0.03	0.02	0.02	0.02	0.03	**2014**
0.03	0.07	0.02	0.02	0.13	0.23	**2015**
0.30	0.30	0.29	0.33	0.45	0.51	**2016**
1.09	1.03	1.05	1.09	1.25	1.34	**2017**
1.99	2.07	2.17	2.29	2.37	2.41	**2018**
2.15	1.99	1.93	1.68	1.57	1.57	**2019**
0.13	0.10	0.11	0.10	0.09	0.09	**2020**
0.05	0.05	0.04	0.05	0.05	0.06	**2021**

BOND YIELDS — MOODY'S SEASONED CORPORATE Aaa*

	JAN	FEB	MAR	APR	MAY	JUN
1950	2.57	2.58	2.58	2.60	2.61	2.62
1951	2.66	2.66	2.78	2.87	2.89	2.94
1952	2.98	2.93	2.96	2.93	2.93	2.94
1953	3.02	3.07	3.12	3.23	3.34	3.40
1954	3.06	2.95	2.86	2.85	2.88	2.90
1955	2.93	2.93	3.02	3.01	3.04	3.05
1956	3.11	3.08	3.10	3.24	3.28	3.26
1957	3.77	3.67	3.66	3.67	3.74	3.91
1958	3.60	3.59	3.63	3.60	3.57	3.57
1959	4.12	4.14	4.13	4.23	4.37	4.46
1960	4.61	4.56	4.49	4.45	4.46	4.45
1961	4.32	4.27	4.22	4.25	4.27	4.33
1962	4.42	4.42	4.39	4.33	4.28	4.28
1963	4.21	4.19	4.19	4.21	4.22	4.23
1964	4.39	4.36	4.38	4.40	4.41	4.41
1965	4.43	4.41	4.42	4.43	4.44	4.46
1966	4.74	4.78	4.92	4.96	4.98	5.07
1967	5.20	5.03	5.13	5.11	5.24	5.44
1968	6.17	6.10	6.11	6.21	6.27	6.28
1969	6.59	6.66	6.85	6.89	6.79	6.98
1970	7.91	7.93	7.84	7.83	8.11	8.48
1971	7.36	7.08	7.21	7.25	7.53	7.64
1972	7.19	7.27	7.24	7.30	7.30	7.23
1973	7.15	7.22	7.29	7.26	7.29	7.37
1974	7.83	7.85	8.01	8.25	8.37	8.47
1975	8.83	8.62	8.67	8.95	8.90	8.77
1976	8.60	8.55	8.52	8.40	8.58	8.62
1977	7.96	8.04	8.10	8.04	8.05	7.95
1978	8.41	8.47	8.47	8.56	8.69	8.76
1979	9.25	9.26	9.37	9.38	9.50	9.29
1980	11.09	12.38	12.96	12.04	10.99	10.58
1981	12.81	13.35	13.33	13.88	14.32	13.75
1982	15.18	15.27	14.58	14.46	14.26	14.81
1983	11.79	12.01	11.73	11.51	11.46	11.74
1984	12.20	12.08	12.57	12.81	13.28	13.55
1985	12.08	12.13	12.56	12.23	11.72	10.94
1986	10.05	9.67	9.00	8.79	9.09	9.13
1987	8.36	8.38	8.36	8.85	9.33	9.32
1988	9.88	9.40	9.39	9.67	9.90	9.86
1989	9.62	9.64	9.80	9.79	9.57	9.10
1990	8.99	9.22	9.37	9.46	9.47	9.26
1991	9.04	8.83	8.93	8.86	8.86	9.01
1992	8.20	8.29	8.35	8.33	8.28	8.22
1993	7.91	7.71	7.58	7.46	7.43	7.33
1994	6.92	7.08	7.48	7.88	7.99	7.97
1995	8.46	8.26	8.12	8.03	7.65	7.30
1996	6.81	6.99	7.35	7.50	7.62	7.71
1997	7.42	7.31	7.55	7.73	7.58	7.41
1998	6.61	6.67	6.72	6.69	6.69	6.53
1999	6.24	6.40	6.62	6.64	6.93	7.23
2000	7.78	7.68	7.68	7.64	7.99	7.67
2001	7.15	7.10	6.98	7.20	7.29	7.18
2002	6.55	6.51	6.81	6.76	6.75	6.63
2003	6.17	5.95	5.89	5.74	5.22	4.97
2004	5.54	5.50	5.33	5.73	6.04	6.01
2005	5.36	5.20	5.40	5.33	5.15	4.96
2006	5.29	5.35	5.53	5.84	5.95	5.89
2007	5.40	5.39	5.30	5.47	5.47	5.79
2008	5.33	5.53	5.51	5.55	5.57	5.68
2009	5.05	5.27	5.50	5.39	5.54	5.61
2010	5.26	5.35	5.27	5.29	4.96	4.88
2011	5.04	5.22	5.13	5.16	4.96	4.99
2012	3.85	3.85	3.99	3.96	3.80	3.64
2013	3.80	3.90	3.93	3.73	3.89	4.27
2014	4.49	4.45	4.38	4.24	4.16	4.25
2015	3.46	3.61	3.64	3.52	3.98	4.19
2016	4.00	3.96	3.82	3.62	3.65	3.50
2017	3.92	3.95	4.01	3.87	3.85	3.68
2018	3.55	3.82	3.87	3.85	4.00	3.96
2019	3.93	3.79	3.77	3.69	3.67	3.42
2020	2.94	2.78	3.02	2.43	2.50	2.44
2021	2.45	2.70	3.04	2.90	2.96	2.79

* Source: Federal Reserve Bank of St. Louis, monthly data calculated as average of business days

MOODY'S SEASONED CORPORATE Aaa BOND YIELDS

JUL	AUG	SEP	OCT	NOV	DEC	
2.65	2.61	2.64	2.67	2.67	2.67	**1950**
2.94	2.88	2.84	2.89	2.96	3.01	**1951**
2.95	2.94	2.95	3.01	2.98	2.97	**1952**
3.28	3.24	3.29	3.16	3.11	3.13	**1953**
2.89	2.87	2.89	2.87	2.89	2.90	**1954**
3.06	3.11	3.13	3.10	3.10	3.15	**1955**
3.28	3.43	3.56	3.59	3.69	3.75	**1956**
3.99	4.10	4.12	4.10	4.08	3.81	**1957**
3.67	3.85	4.09	4.11	4.09	4.08	**1958**
4.47	4.43	4.52	4.57	4.56	4.58	**1959**
4.41	4.28	4.25	4.30	4.31	4.35	**1960**
4.41	4.45	4.45	4.42	4.39	4.42	**1961**
4.34	4.35	4.32	4.28	4.25	4.24	**1962**
4.26	4.29	4.31	4.32	4.33	4.35	**1963**
4.40	4.41	4.42	4.42	4.43	4.44	**1964**
4.48	4.49	4.52	4.56	4.60	4.68	**1965**
5.16	5.31	5.49	5.41	5.35	5.39	**1966**
5.58	5.62	5.65	5.82	6.07	6.19	**1967**
6.24	6.02	5.97	6.09	6.19	6.45	**1968**
7.08	6.97	7.14	7.33	7.35	7.72	**1969**
8.44	8.13	8.09	8.03	8.05	7.64	**1970**
7.64	7.59	7.44	7.39	7.26	7.25	**1971**
7.21	7.19	7.22	7.21	7.12	7.08	**1972**
7.45	7.68	7.63	7.60	7.67	7.68	**1973**
8.72	9.00	9.24	9.27	8.89	8.89	**1974**
8.84	8.95	8.95	8.86	8.78	8.79	**1975**
8.56	8.45	8.38	8.32	8.25	7.98	**1976**
7.94	7.98	7.92	8.04	8.08	8.19	**1977**
8.88	8.69	8.69	8.89	9.03	9.16	**1978**
9.20	9.23	9.44	10.13	10.76	10.74	**1979**
11.07	11.64	12.02	12.31	12.97	13.21	**1980**
14.38	14.89	15.49	15.40	14.22	14.23	**1981**
14.61	13.71	12.94	12.12	11.68	11.83	**1982**
12.15	12.51	12.37	12.25	12.41	12.57	**1983**
13.44	12.87	12.66	12.63	12.29	12.13	**1984**
10.97	11.05	11.07	11.02	10.55	10.16	**1985**
8.88	8.72	8.89	8.86	8.68	8.49	**1986**
9.42	9.67	10.18	10.52	10.01	10.11	**1987**
9.96	10.11	9.82	9.51	9.45	9.57	**1988**
8.93	8.96	9.01	8.92	8.89	8.86	**1989**
9.24	9.41	9.56	9.53	9.30	9.05	**1990**
9.00	8.75	8.61	8.55	8.48	8.31	**1991**
8.07	7.95	7.92	7.99	8.10	7.98	**1992**
7.17	6.85	6.66	6.67	6.93	6.93	**1993**
8.11	8.07	8.34	8.57	8.68	8.46	**1994**
7.41	7.57	7.32	7.12	7.02	6.82	**1995**
7.65	7.46	7.66	7.39	7.10	7.20	**1996**
7.14	7.22	7.15	7.00	6.87	6.76	**1997**
6.55	6.52	6.40	6.37	6.41	6.22	**1998**
7.19	7.40	7.39	7.55	7.36	7.55	**1999**
7.65	7.55	7.62	7.55	7.45	7.21	**2000**
7.13	7.02	7.17	7.03	6.97	6.77	**2001**
6.53	6.37	6.15	6.32	6.31	6.21	**2002**
5.49	5.88	5.72	5.70	5.65	5.62	**2003**
5.82	5.65	5.46	5.47	5.52	5.47	**2004**
5.06	5.09	5.13	5.35	5.42	5.37	**2005**
5.85	5.68	5.51	5.51	5.33	5.32	**2006**
5.73	5.79	5.74	5.66	5.44	5.49	**2007**
5.67	5.64	5.65	6.28	6.12	5.05	**2008**
5.41	5.26	5.13	5.15	5.19	5.26	**2009**
4.72	4.49	4.53	4.68	4.87	5.02	**2010**
4.93	4.37	4.09	3.98	3.87	3.93	**2011**
3.40	3.48	3.49	3.47	3.50	3.65	**2012**
4.34	4.54	4.64	4.53	4.63	4.62	**2013**
4.16	4.08	4.11	3.92	3.92	3.79	**2014**
4.15	4.04	4.07	3.95	4.06	3.97	**2015**
3.28	3.32	3.41	3.51	3.86	4.06	**2016**
3.70	3.63	3.63	3.60	3.57	3.51	**2017**
3.87	3.88	3.98	4.14	4.22	4.02	**2018**
3.29	2.98	3.03	3.01	3.06	3.01	**2019**
2.14	2.25	2.31	2.35	2.30	2.26	**2020**
2.57	2.55	2.53	2.68	2.62	2.65	**2021**

MOODY'S SEASONED
CORPORATE Baa*

	JAN	FEB	MAR	APR	MAY	JUN
1950	3.24	3.24	3.24	3.23	3.25	3.28
1951	3.17	3.16	3.23	3.35	3.40	3.49
1952	3.59	3.53	3.51	3.50	3.49	3.50
1953	3.51	3.53	3.57	3.65	3.78	3.86
1954	3.71	3.61	3.51	3.47	3.47	3.49
1955	3.45	3.47	3.48	3.49	3.50	3.51
1956	3.60	3.58	3.60	3.68	3.73	3.76
1957	4.49	4.47	4.43	4.44	4.52	4.63
1958	4.83	4.66	4.68	4.67	4.62	4.55
1959	4.87	4.89	4.85	4.86	4.96	5.04
1960	5.34	5.34	5.25	5.20	5.28	5.26
1961	5.10	5.07	5.02	5.01	5.01	5.03
1962	5.08	5.07	5.04	5.02	5.00	5.02
1963	4.91	4.89	4.88	4.87	4.85	4.84
1964	4.83	4.83	4.83	4.85	4.85	4.85
1965	4.80	4.78	4.78	4.80	4.81	4.85
1966	5.06	5.12	5.32	5.41	5.48	5.58
1967	5.97	5.82	5.85	5.83	5.96	6.15
1968	6.84	6.80	6.85	6.97	7.03	7.07
1969	7.32	7.30	7.51	7.54	7.52	7.70
1970	8.86	8.78	8.63	8.70	8.98	9.25
1971	8.74	8.39	8.46	8.45	8.62	8.75
1972	8.23	8.23	8.24	8.24	8.23	8.20
1973	7.90	7.97	8.03	8.09	8.06	8.13
1974	8.48	8.53	8.62	8.87	9.05	9.27
1975	10.81	10.65	10.48	10.58	10.69	10.62
1976	10.41	10.24	10.12	9.94	9.86	9.89
1977	9.08	9.12	9.12	9.07	9.01	8.91
1978	9.17	9.20	9.22	9.32	9.49	9.60
1979	10.13	10.08	10.26	10.33	10.47	10.38
1980	12.42	13.57	14.45	14.19	13.17	12.71
1981	15.03	15.37	15.34	15.56	15.95	15.80
1982	17.10	17.18	16.82	16.78	16.64	16.92
1983	13.94	13.95	13.61	13.29	13.09	13.37
1984	13.65	13.59	13.99	14.31	14.74	15.05
1985	13.26	13.23	13.69	13.51	13.15	12.40
1986	11.44	11.11	10.50	10.19	10.29	10.34
1987	9.72	9.65	9.61	10.04	10.51	10.52
1988	11.07	10.62	10.57	10.90	11.04	11.00
1989	10.65	10.61	10.67	10.61	10.46	10.03
1990	9.94	10.14	10.21	10.30	10.41	10.22
1991	10.45	10.07	10.09	9.94	9.86	9.96
1992	9.13	9.23	9.25	9.21	9.13	9.05
1993	8.67	8.39	8.15	8.14	8.21	8.07
1994	7.65	7.76	8.13	8.52	8.62	8.65
1995	9.08	8.85	8.70	8.60	8.20	7.90
1996	7.47	7.63	8.03	8.19	8.30	8.40
1997	8.09	7.94	8.18	8.34	8.20	8.02
1998	7.19	7.25	7.32	7.33	7.30	7.13
1999	7.29	7.39	7.53	7.48	7.72	8.02
2000	8.33	8.29	8.37	8.40	8.90	8.48
2001	7.93	7.87	7.84	8.07	8.07	7.97
2002	7.87	7.89	8.11	8.03	8.09	7.95
2003	7.35	7.06	6.95	6.85	6.38	6.19
2004	6.44	6.27	6.11	6.46	6.75	6.78
2005	6.02	5.82	6.06	6.05	6.01	5.86
2006	6.24	6.27	6.41	6.68	6.75	6.78
2007	6.34	6.28	6.27	6.39	6.39	6.70
2008	6.54	6.82	6.89	6.97	6.93	7.07
2009	8.14	8.08	8.42	8.39	8.06	7.50
2010	6.25	6.34	6.27	6.25	6.05	6.23
2011	6.09	6.15	6.03	6.02	5.78	5.75
2012	5.23	5.14	5.23	5.19	5.07	5.02
2013	4.73	4.85	4.85	4.59	4.73	5.19
2014	5.19	5.10	5.06	4.90	4.76	4.80
2015	4.45	4.51	4.54	4.48	4.89	5.13
2016	5.45	5.34	5.13	4.79	4.68	4.53
2017	4.66	4.64	4.68	4.57	4.55	4.37
2018	4.26	4.51	4.64	4.67	4.83	4.83
2019	5.12	4.95	4.84	4.70	4.63	4.46
2020	3.77	3.61	4.29	4.13	3.95	3.64
2021	3.24	3.42	3.74	3.60	3.62	3.44

* Source: Federal Reserve Bank of St. Louis, monthly data calculated as average of business days

MOODY'S SEASONED CORPORATE Baa* BOND YIELDS

JUL	AUG	SEP	OCT	NOV	DEC	
3.32	3.23	3.21	3.22	3.22	3.20	1950
3.53	3.50	3.46	3.50	3.56	3.61	1951
3.50	3.51	3.52	3.54	3.53	3.51	1952
3.86	3.85	3.88	3.82	3.75	3.74	1953
3.50	3.49	3.47	3.46	3.45	3.45	1954
3.52	3.56	3.59	3.59	3.58	3.62	1955
3.80	3.93	4.07	4.17	4.24	4.37	1956
4.73	4.82	4.93	4.99	5.09	5.03	1957
4.53	4.67	4.87	4.92	4.87	4.85	1958
5.08	5.09	5.18	5.28	5.26	5.28	1959
5.22	5.08	5.01	5.11	5.08	5.10	1960
5.09	5.11	5.12	5.13	5.11	5.10	1961
5.05	5.06	5.03	4.99	4.96	4.92	1962
4.84	4.83	4.84	4.83	4.84	4.85	1963
4.83	4.82	4.82	4.81	4.81	4.81	1964
4.88	4.88	4.91	4.93	4.95	5.02	1965
5.68	5.83	6.09	6.10	6.13	6.18	1966
6.26	6.33	6.40	6.52	6.72	6.93	1967
6.98	6.82	6.79	6.84	7.01	7.23	1968
7.84	7.86	8.05	8.22	8.25	8.65	1969
9.40	9.44	9.39	9.33	9.38	9.12	1970
8.76	8.76	8.59	8.48	8.38	8.38	1971
8.23	8.19	8.09	8.06	7.99	7.93	1972
8.24	8.53	8.63	8.41	8.42	8.48	1973
9.48	9.77	10.18	10.48	10.60	10.63	1974
10.55	10.59	10.61	10.62	10.56	10.56	1975
9.82	9.64	9.40	9.29	9.23	9.12	1976
8.87	8.82	8.80	8.89	8.95	8.99	1977
9.60	9.48	9.42	9.59	9.83	9.94	1978
10.29	10.35	10.54	11.40	11.99	12.06	1979
12.65	13.15	13.70	14.23	14.64	15.14	1980
16.17	16.34	16.92	17.11	16.39	16.55	1981
16.80	16.32	15.63	14.73	14.30	14.14	1982
13.39	13.64	13.55	13.46	13.61	13.75	1983
15.15	14.63	14.35	13.94	13.48	13.40	1984
12.43	12.50	12.48	12.36	11.99	11.58	1985
10.16	10.18	10.20	10.24	10.07	9.97	1986
10.61	10.80	11.31	11.62	11.23	11.29	1987
11.11	11.21	10.90	10.41	10.48	10.65	1988
9.87	9.88	9.91	9.81	9.81	9.82	1989
10.20	10.41	10.64	10.74	10.62	10.43	1990
9.89	9.65	9.51	9.49	9.45	9.26	1991
8.84	8.65	8.62	8.84	8.96	8.81	1992
7.93	7.60	7.34	7.31	7.66	7.69	1993
8.80	8.74	8.98	9.20	9.32	9.10	1994
8.04	8.19	7.93	7.75	7.68	7.49	1995
8.35	8.18	8.35	8.07	7.79	7.89	1996
7.75	7.82	7.70	7.57	7.42	7.32	1997
7.15	7.14	7.09	7.18	7.34	7.23	1998
7.95	8.15	8.20	8.38	8.15	8.19	1999
8.35	8.26	8.35	8.34	8.28	8.02	2000
7.97	7.85	8.03	7.91	7.81	8.05	2001
7.90	7.58	7.40	7.73	7.62	7.45	2002
6.62	7.01	6.79	6.73	6.66	6.60	2003
6.62	6.46	6.27	6.21	6.20	6.15	2004
5.95	5.96	6.03	6.30	6.39	6.32	2005
6.76	6.59	6.43	6.42	6.20	6.22	2006
6.65	6.65	6.59	6.48	6.40	6.65	2007
7.16	7.15	7.31	8.88	9.21	8.43	2008
7.09	6.58	6.31	6.29	6.32	6.37	2009
6.01	5.66	5.66	5.72	5.92	6.10	2010
5.76	5.36	5.27	5.37	5.14	5.25	2011
4.87	4.91	4.84	4.58	4.51	4.63	2012
5.32	5.42	5.47	5.31	5.38	5.38	2013
4.73	4.69	4.80	4.69	4.79	4.74	2014
5.20	5.19	5.34	5.34	5.46	5.46	2015
4.22	4.24	4.31	4.38	4.71	4.83	2016
4.39	4.31	4.30	4.32	4.27	4.22	2017
4.79	4.77	4.88	5.07	5.22	5.13	2018
4.28	3.87	3.91	3.92	3.94	3.88	2019
3.31	3.27	3.36	3.44	3.30	3.16	2020
3.24	3.24	3.23	3.25	3.28	3.30	2021

COMMODITIES

COMMODITIES — OIL - WEST TEXAS INTERMEDIATE CLOSING VALUES $ / bbl

	JAN	FEB	MAR	APR	MAY	JUN
1950	2.6	2.6	2.6	2.6	2.6	2.6
1951	2.6	2.6	2.6	2.6	2.6	2.6
1952	2.6	2.6	2.6	2.6	2.6	2.6
1953	2.6	2.6	2.6	2.6	2.6	2.8
1954	2.8	2.8	2.8	2.8	2.8	2.8
1955	2.8	2.8	2.8	2.8	2.8	2.8
1956	2.8	2.8	2.8	2.8	2.8	2.8
1957	2.8	3.1	3.1	3.1	3.1	3.1
1958	3.1	3.1	3.1	3.1	3.1	3.1
1959	3.0	3.0	3.0	3.0	3.0	3.0
1960	3.0	3.0	3.0	3.0	3.0	3.0
1961	3.0	3.0	3.0	3.0	3.0	3.0
1962	3.0	3.0	3.0	3.0	3.0	3.0
1963	3.0	3.0	3.0	3.0	3.0	3.0
1964	3.0	3.0	3.0	3.0	3.0	3.0
1965	2.9	2.9	2.9	2.9	2.9	2.9
1966	2.9	2.9	2.9	2.9	2.9	2.9
1967	3.0	3.0	3.0	3.0	3.0	3.0
1968	3.1	3.1	3.1	3.1	3.1	3.1
1969	3.1	3.1	3.3	3.4	3.4	3.4
1970	3.4	3.4	3.4	3.4	3.4	3.4
1971	3.6	3.6	3.6	3.6	3.6	3.6
1972	3.6	3.6	3.6	3.6	3.6	3.6
1973	3.6	3.6	3.6	3.6	3.6	3.6
1974	10.1	10.1	10.1	10.1	10.1	10.1
1975	11.2	11.2	11.2	11.2	11.2	11.2
1976	11.2	12.0	12.1	12.2	12.2	12.2
1977	13.9	13.9	13.9	13.9	13.9	13.9
1978	14.9	14.9	14.9	14.9	14.9	14.9
1979	14.9	15.9	15.9	15.9	18.1	19.1
1980	32.5	37.0	38.0	39.5	39.5	39.5
1981	38.0	38.0	38.0	38.0	38.0	36.0
1982	33.9	31.6	28.5	33.5	35.9	35.1
1983	31.2	29.0	28.8	30.6	30.0	31.0
1984	29.7	30.1	30.8	30.6	30.5	30.0
1985	25.6	27.3	28.2	28.8	27.6	27.1
1986	22.9	15.4	12.6	12.8	15.4	13.5
1987	18.7	17.7	18.3	18.6	19.4	20.0
1988	17.2	16.8	16.2	17.9	17.4	16.5
1989	18.0	17.8	19.4	21.0	20.0	20.0
1990	22.6	22.1	20.4	18.6	18.2	16.9
1991	25.0	20.5	19.9	20.8	21.2	20.2
1992	18.8	19.0	18.9	20.2	20.9	22.4
1993	19.1	20.1	20.3	20.3	19.9	19.1
1994	15.0	14.8	14.7	16.4	17.9	19.1
1995	18.0	18.5	18.6	19.9	19.7	18.4
1996	18.9	19.1	21.4	23.6	21.3	20.5
1997	25.2	22.2	21.0	19.7	20.8	19.2
1998	16.7	16.1	15.0	15.4	14.9	13.7
1999	12.5	12.0	14.7	17.3	17.8	17.9
2000	27.2	29.4	29.9	25.7	28.8	31.8
2001	29.6	29.6	27.2	27.4	28.6	27.6
2002	19.7	20.7	24.4	26.3	27.0	25.5
2003	32.9	35.9	33.6	28.3	28.1	30.7
2004	34.3	34.7	36.8	36.7	40.3	38.0
2005	46.8	48.0	54.3	53.0	49.8	56.3
2006	65.5	61.6	62.9	69.7	70.9	71.0
2007	54.6	59.3	60.6	64.0	63.5	67.5
2008	93.0	95.4	105.6	112.6	125.4	133.9
2009	41.7	39.2	48.0	49.8	59.2	69.7
2010	78.2	76.4	81.2	84.5	73.8	75.4
2011	89.4	89.6	102.9	110.0	101.3	96.3
2012	100.3	102.3	106.2	103.3	94.7	82.3
2013	94.8	95.3	92.9	92.0	94.5	95.8
2014	94.6	100.8	100.8	102.1	102.2	105.8
2015	47.2	50.6	47.8	54.5	59.3	59.8
2016	31.7	30.3	37.6	40.8	46.7	48.8
2017	52.5	53.5	49.3	51.1	48.5	45.2
2018	63.7	62.2	62.7	66.3	70.0	67.9
2019	51.4	55.0	58.2	63.9	60.8	54.7
2020	57.5	50.5	29.2	16.6	28.6	38.3
2021	52.0	59.0	62.3	61.7	65.2	71.4

* Source: Federal Reserve

- 195 -

OIL - WEST TEXAS INTERMEDIATE
CLOSING VALUES $ / bbl

COMMODITIES

JUL	AUG	SEP	OCT	NOV	DEC	
2.6	2.6	2.6	2.6	2.6	2.6	1950
2.6	2.6	2.6	2.6	2.6	2.6	1951
2.6	2.6	2.6	2.6	2.6	2.6	1952
2.8	2.8	2.8	2.8	2.8	2.8	1953
2.8	2.8	2.8	2.8	2.8	2.8	1954
2.8	2.8	2.8	2.8	2.8	2.8	1955
2.8	2.8	2.8	2.8	2.8	2.8	1956
3.1	3.1	3.1	3.1	3.1	3.0	1957
3.1	3.1	3.1	3.1	3.0	3.0	1958
3.0	3.0	3.0	3.0	3.0	3.0	1959
3.0	3.0	3.0	3.0	3.0	3.0	1960
3.0	3.0	3.0	3.0	3.0	3.0	1961
3.0	3.0	3.0	3.0	3.0	3.0	1962
3.0	3.0	3.0	3.0	3.0	3.0	1963
2.9	2.9	2.9	2.9	2.9	2.9	1964
2.9	2.9	2.9	2.9	2.9	2.9	1965
2.9	2.9	3.0	3.0	3.0	3.0	1966
3.0	3.1	3.1	3.1	3.1	3.1	1967
3.1	3.1	3.1	3.1	3.1	3.1	1968
3.4	3.4	3.4	3.4	3.4	3.4	1969
3.3	3.3	3.3	3.3	3.3	3.6	1970
3.6	3.6	3.6	3.6	3.6	3.6	1971
3.6	3.6	3.6	3.6	3.6	3.6	1972
3.6	4.3	4.3	4.3	4.3	4.3	1973
10.1	10.1	10.1	11.2	11.2	11.2	1974
11.2	11.2	11.2	11.2	11.2	11.2	1975
12.2	12.2	13.9	13.9	13.9	13.9	1976
13.9	14.9	14.9	14.9	14.9	14.9	1977
14.9	14.9	14.9	14.9	14.9	14.9	1978
21.8	26.5	28.5	29.0	31.0	32.5	1979
39.5	38.0	36.0	36.0	36.0	37.0	1980
36.0	36.0	36.0	35.0	36.0	35.0	1981
34.2	34.0	35.6	35.7	34.2	31.7	1982
31.7	31.9	31.1	30.4	29.8	29.2	1983
28.8	29.3	29.3	28.8	28.1	25.4	1984
27.3	27.8	28.3	29.5	30.8	27.2	1985
11.6	15.1	14.9	14.9	15.2	16.1	1986
21.4	20.3	19.5	19.8	18.9	17.2	1987
15.5	15.5	14.5	13.8	14.0	16.3	1988
19.6	18.5	19.6	20.1	19.8	21.1	1989
18.6	27.2	33.7	35.9	32.3	27.3	1990
21.4	21.7	21.9	23.2	22.5	19.5	1991
21.8	21.4	21.9	21.7	20.3	19.4	1992
17.9	18.0	17.5	18.1	16.7	14.5	1993
19.7	18.4	17.5	17.7	18.1	17.2	1994
17.3	18.0	18.2	17.4	18.0	19.0	1995
21.3	22.0	24.0	24.9	23.7	25.4	1996
19.6	19.9	19.8	21.3	20.2	18.3	1997
14.1	13.4	15.0	14.4	12.9	11.3	1998
20.1	21.3	23.9	22.6	25.0	26.1	1999
29.8	31.2	33.9	33.1	34.4	28.5	2000
26.5	27.5	25.9	22.2	19.7	19.3	2001
26.9	28.4	29.7	28.9	26.3	29.4	2002
30.8	31.6	28.3	30.3	31.1	32.2	2003
40.7	44.9	46.0	53.1	48.5	43.3	2004
58.7	65.0	65.6	62.4	58.3	59.4	2005
74.4	73.1	63.9	58.9	59.4	62.0	2006
74.2	72.4	79.9	86.2	94.6	91.7	2007
133.4	116.6	103.9	76.7	57.4	41.0	2008
64.1	71.1	69.5	75.6	78.1	74.3	2009
76.4	76.8	75.3	81.9	84.1	89.0	2010
97.2	86.3	85.6	86.4	97.2	98.6	2011
87.9	94.2	94.7	89.6	86.7	88.3	2012
104.7	106.6	106.3	100.5	93.9	97.6	2013
103.6	96.5	93.2	84.4	75.8	59.3	2014
50.9	42.9	45.5	46.2	42.4	37.2	2015
44.7	44.7	45.2	49.8	45.7	52.0	2016
46.6	48.0	49.8	51.6	56.6	57.9	2017
71.0	68.1	70.2	70.8	57.1	49.5	2018
57.4	54.8	57.0	54.0	57.0	59.9	2019
40.7	42.3	39.6	39.4	40.9	47.0	2020
72.5	67.7	71.7	81.5	79.2	71.7	2021

GOLD $US/OZ LONDON PM
MONTH CLOSE

	JAN	FEB	MAR	APR	MAY	JUN
1970	34.9	35.0	35.1	35.6	36.0	35.4
1971	37.9	38.7	38.9	39.0	40.5	40.1
1972	45.8	48.3	48.3	49.0	54.6	62.1
1973	65.1	74.2	84.4	90.5	102.0	120.1
1974	129.2	150.2	168.4	172.2	163.3	154.1
1975	175.8	181.8	178.2	167.0	167.0	166.3
1976	128.2	132.3	129.6	128.4	125.5	123.8
1977	132.3	142.8	148.9	147.3	143.0	143.0
1978	175.8	182.3	181.6	170.9	184.2	183.1
1979	233.7	251.3	240.1	245.3	274.6	277.5
1980	653.0	637.0	494.5	518.0	535.5	653.5
1981	506.5	489.0	513.8	482.8	479.3	426.0
1982	387.0	362.6	320.0	361.3	325.3	317.5
1983	499.5	408.5	414.8	429.3	437.5	416.0
1984	373.8	394.3	388.5	375.8	384.3	373.1
1985	306.7	287.8	329.3	321.4	314.0	317.8
1986	350.5	338.2	344.0	345.8	343.2	345.5
1987	400.5	405.9	405.9	453.3	451.0	447.3
1988	458.0	426.2	457.0	449.0	455.5	436.6
1989	394.0	387.0	383.2	377.6	361.8	373.0
1990	415.1	407.7	368.5	367.8	363.1	352.2
1991	366.0	362.7	355.7	357.8	360.4	368.4
1992	354.1	353.1	341.7	336.4	337.5	343.4
1993	330.5	327.6	337.8	354.3	374.8	378.5
1994	377.9	381.6	389.2	376.5	387.6	388.3
1995	374.9	376.4	392.0	389.8	384.3	387.1
1996	405.6	400.7	396.4	391.3	390.6	382.0
1997	345.5	358.6	348.2	340.2	345.6	334.6
1998	304.9	297.4	301.0	310.7	293.6	296.3
1999	285.4	287.1	279.5	286.6	268.6	261.0
2000	283.3	293.7	276.8	275.1	272.3	288.2
2001	264.5	266.7	257.7	263.2	267.5	270.6
2002	282.3	296.9	301.4	308.2	326.6	318.5
2003	367.5	347.5	334.9	336.8	361.4	346.0
2004	399.8	395.9	423.7	388.5	393.3	395.8
2005	422.2	435.5	427.5	435.7	414.5	437.1
2006	568.8	556.0	582.0	644.0	653.0	613.5
2007	650.5	664.2	661.8	677.0	659.1	650.5
2008	923.3	971.5	933.5	871.0	885.8	930.3
2009	919.5	952.0	916.5	883.3	975.5	934.5
2010	1078.5	1108.3	1115.5	1179.3	1207.5	1244.0
2011	1327.0	1411.0	1439.0	1535.5	1536.5	1505.5
2012	1744.0	1770.0	1662.5	1651.3	1558.0	1598.5
2013	1664.8	1588.5	1598.3	1469.0	1394.5	1192.0
2014	1251.0	1326.5	1291.75	1288.5	1250.5	1315.0
2015	1260.3	1214.0	1187.0	1180.3	1191.4	1171.0
2016	1111.8	1234.9	1237.0	1285.7	1212.1	1320.8
2017	1212.8	1255.0	1244.9	1266.4	1266.2	1242.3
2018	1345.1	1317.9	1323.9	1313.2	1305.4	1250.5
2019	1323.3	1319.2	1295.4	1282.3	1295.6	1409.0
2020	1584.2	1609.9	1609.0	1702.8	1728.7	1768.1
2021	1835.5	1742.9	1691.1	1767.7	1899.4	1763.2

* Source: Bank of England

GOLD $US/OZ LONDON PM MONTH CLOSE

COMMODITIES

JUL	AUG	SEP	OCT	NOV	DEC	
35.3	35.4	36.2	37.5	37.4	37.4	**1970**
41.0	42.7	42.0	42.5	42.9	43.5	**1971**
65.7	67.0	65.5	64.9	62.9	63.9	**1972**
120.2	106.8	103.0	100.1	94.8	106.7	**1973**
143.0	154.6	151.8	158.8	181.7	183.9	**1974**
166.7	159.8	141.3	142.9	138.2	140.3	**1975**
112.5	104.0	116.0	123.2	130.3	134.5	**1976**
144.1	146.0	154.1	161.5	160.1	165.0	**1977**
200.3	208.7	217.1	242.6	193.4	226.0	**1978**
296.5	315.1	397.3	382.0	415.7	512.0	**1979**
614.3	631.3	666.8	629.0	619.8	589.8	**1980**
406.0	425.5	428.8	427.0	414.5	397.5	**1981**
342.9	411.5	397.0	423.3	436.0	456.9	**1982**
422.0	414.3	405.0	382.0	405.0	382.4	**1983**
342.4	348.3	343.8	333.5	329.0	309.0	**1984**
327.5	333.3	326.5	325.1	325.3	326.8	**1985**
357.5	384.7	423.2	401.0	383.5	388.8	**1986**
462.5	453.4	459.5	468.8	492.5	484.1	**1987**
436.8	427.8	397.7	412.4	422.6	410.3	**1988**
368.3	359.8	366.5	375.3	408.2	398.6	**1989**
372.3	387.8	408.4	379.5	384.9	386.2	**1990**
362.9	347.4	354.9	357.5	366.3	353.2	**1991**
357.9	340.0	349.0	339.3	334.2	332.9	**1992**
401.8	371.6	355.5	369.6	370.9	391.8	**1993**
384.0	385.8	394.9	383.9	383.1	383.3	**1994**
383.4	382.4	384.0	382.7	387.8	387.0	**1995**
385.3	386.5	379.0	379.5	371.3	369.3	**1996**
326.4	325.4	332.1	311.4	296.8	290.2	**1997**
288.9	273.4	293.9	292.3	294.7	287.8	**1998**
255.6	254.8	299.0	299.1	291.4	290.3	**1999**
276.8	277.0	273.7	264.5	269.1	274.5	**2000**
265.9	273.0	293.1	278.8	275.5	276.5	**2001**
304.7	312.8	323.7	316.9	319.1	347.2	**2002**
354.8	375.6	388.0	386.3	398.4	416.3	**2003**
391.4	407.3	415.7	425.6	453.4	435.6	**2004**
429.0	433.3	473.3	470.8	495.7	513.0	**2005**
632.5	623.5	599.3	603.8	646.7	632.0	**2006**
665.5	672.0	743.0	789.5	783.5	833.8	**2007**
918.0	833.0	884.5	730.8	814.5	869.8	**2008**
939.0	955.5	995.8	1040.0	1175.8	1087.5	**2009**
1169.0	1246.0	1307.0	1346.8	1383.5	1405.5	**2010**
1628.5	1813.5	1620.0	1722.0	1746.0	1531.0	**2011**
1622.0	1648.5	1776.0	1719.0	1726.0	1657.5	**2012**
1314.5	1394.8	1326.5	1324.0	1253.0	1204.5	**2013**
1285.3	1285.8	1216.5	1164.8	1282.8	1206.0	**2014**
1098.4	1135.0	1114.0	1142.4	1061.9	1060.0	**2015**
1342.0	1309.3	1322.5	1272.0	1178.1	1145.9	**2016**
1267.6	1311.8	1283.1	1270.2	1280.2	1291.0	**2017**
1221.0	1202.5	1187.3	1215.0	1217.6	1279.0	**2018**
1427.6	1528.4	1485.3	1511.0	1460.2	1514.8	**2019**
1964.9	1957.4	1886.9	1881.9	1752.6	1887.6	**2020**
1825.8	1814.9	1742.8	1769.2	1804.4	1808.9	**2021**

FOREIGN EXCHANGE

	JAN		FEB		MAR		APR		MAY		JUN	
	US / CDN	CDN / US	US / CDN	CDN / US	US / CDN	CDN /US	US / CDN	CDN / US	US / CDN	CDN / US	US / CDN	CDN / US
1971	1.01	0.99	1.01	0.99	1.01	0.99	1.01	0.99	1.01	0.99	1.02	0.98
1972	1.01	0.99	1.00	1.00	1.00	1.00	1.00	1.00	0.99	1.01	0.98	1.02
1973	1.00	1.00	1.00	1.00	1.00	1.00	1.00	1.00	1.00	1.00	1.00	1.00
1974	0.99	1.01	0.98	1.02	0.97	1.03	0.97	1.03	0.96	1.04	0.97	1.03
1975	0.99	1.01	1.00	1.00	1.00	1.00	1.01	0.99	1.03	0.97	1.03	0.97
1976	1.01	0.99	0.99	1.01	0.99	1.01	0.98	1.02	0.98	1.02	0.97	1.03
1977	1.01	0.99	1.03	0.97	1.05	0.95	1.05	0.95	1.05	0.95	1.06	0.95
1978	1.10	0.91	1.11	0.90	1.13	0.89	1.14	0.88	1.12	0.89	1.12	0.89
1979	1.19	0.84	1.20	0.84	1.17	0.85	1.15	0.87	1.16	0.87	1.17	0.85
1980	1.16	0.86	1.16	0.87	1.17	0.85	1.19	0.84	1.17	0.85	1.15	0.87
1981	1.19	0.84	1.20	0.83	1.19	0.84	1.19	0.84	1.20	0.83	1.20	0.83
1982	1.19	0.84	1.21	0.82	1.22	0.82	1.23	0.82	1.23	0.81	1.28	0.78
1983	1.23	0.81	1.23	0.81	1.23	0.82	1.23	0.81	1.23	0.81	1.23	0.81
1984	1.25	0.80	1.25	0.80	1.27	0.79	1.28	0.78	1.29	0.77	1.30	0.77
1985	1.32	0.76	1.35	0.74	1.38	0.72	1.37	0.73	1.38	0.73	1.37	0.73
1986	1.41	0.71	1.40	0.71	1.40	0.71	1.39	0.72	1.38	0.73	1.39	0.72
1987	1.36	0.73	1.33	0.75	1.32	0.76	1.32	0.76	1.34	0.75	1.34	0.75
1988	1.29	0.78	1.27	0.79	1.25	0.80	1.24	0.81	1.24	0.81	1.22	0.82
1989	1.19	0.84	1.19	0.84	1.20	0.84	1.19	0.84	1.19	0.84	1.20	0.83
1990	1.17	0.85	1.20	0.84	1.18	0.85	1.16	0.86	1.17	0.85	1.17	0.85
1991	1.16	0.87	1.15	0.87	1.16	0.86	1.15	0.87	1.15	0.87	1.14	0.87
1992	1.16	0.86	1.18	0.85	1.19	0.84	1.19	0.84	1.20	0.83	1.20	0.84
1993	1.28	0.78	1.26	0.79	1.25	0.80	1.26	0.79	1.27	0.79	1.28	0.78
1994	1.32	0.76	1.34	0.74	1.36	0.73	1.38	0.72	1.38	0.72	1.38	0.72
1995	1.41	0.71	1.40	0.71	1.41	0.71	1.38	0.73	1.36	0.73	1.38	0.73
1996	1.37	0.73	1.38	0.73	1.37	0.73	1.36	0.74	1.37	0.73	1.37	0.73
1997	1.35	0.74	1.36	0.74	1.37	0.73	1.39	0.72	1.38	0.72	1.38	0.72
1998	1.44	0.69	1.43	0.70	1.42	0.71	1.43	0.70	1.45	0.69	1.47	0.68
1999	1.52	0.66	1.50	0.67	1.52	0.66	1.49	0.67	1.46	0.68	1.47	0.68
2000	1.45	0.69	1.45	0.69	1.46	0.68	1.47	0.68	1.50	0.67	1.48	0.68
2001	1.50	0.67	1.52	0.66	1.56	0.64	1.56	0.64	1.54	0.65	1.52	0.66
2002	1.60	0.63	1.60	0.63	1.59	0.63	1.58	0.63	1.55	0.65	1.53	0.65
2003	1.54	0.65	1.51	0.66	1.48	0.68	1.46	0.69	1.38	0.72	1.35	0.74
2004	1.30	0.77	1.33	0.75	1.33	0.75	1.34	0.75	1.38	0.73	1.36	0.74
2005	1.22	0.82	1.24	0.81	1.22	0.82	1.24	0.81	1.26	0.80	1.24	0.81
2006	1.16	0.86	1.15	0.87	1.16	0.86	1.14	0.87	1.11	0.90	1.11	0.90
2007	1.18	0.85	1.17	0.85	1.17	0.86	1.14	0.88	1.10	0.91	1.07	0.94
2008	1.01	0.99	1.00	1.00	1.00	1.00	1.01	0.99	1.00	1.00	1.02	0.98
2009	1.22	0.82	1.25	0.80	1.26	0.79	1.22	0.82	1.15	0.87	1.13	0.89
2010	1.04	0.96	1.06	0.95	1.02	0.98	1.01	0.99	1.04	0.96	1.04	0.96
2011	0.99	1.01	0.99	1.01	0.98	1.02	0.96	1.04	0.97	1.03	0.98	1.02
2012	1.01	0.99	1.00	1.00	0.99	1.01	0.99	1.01	1.01	0.99	1.03	0.97
2013	0.99	1.01	1.01	0.99	1.02	.098	1.02	0.98	1.02	0.98	1.03	0.97
2014	1.09	0.91	1.11	0.90	1.11	0.90	1.10	0.91	1.09	0.92	1.08	0.92
2015	1.21	0.82	1.25	0.80	1.26	0.79	1.23	0.81	1.22	0.82	1.24	0.81
2016	1.42	0.70	1.38	0.72	1.32	0.76	1,28	0.78	1.29	0.77	1.29	0.78
2017	1.30	0.77	1.32	0.75	1.33	0.75	1.37	0.73	1.35	0.74	1.30	0.77
2018	1.24	0.80	1.26	0.79	1.29	0.77	1.27	0.79	1.29	0.78	1.31	0.76
2019	1.33	0.75	1.32	0.76	1.34	0.75	1.34	0.75	1.35	0.74	1.33	0.75
2020	1.32	0.76	1.34	0.75	1.41	0.71	1.39	0.72	1.38	0.72	1.36	0.73
2021	1.27	0.79	1.27	0.79	1.26	0.80	1.25	0.80	1.21	0.82	1.22	0.82

Source: Federal Reserve: Avg of daily rates, noon buying rates in New York City for transfers payable in foreign currencies

US DOLLAR vs CDN DOLLAR
MONTHLY AVG. VALUES

JUL US/CDN	JUL CDN/US	AUG US/CDN	AUG CDN/US	SEP US/CDN	SEP CDN/US	OCT US/CDN	OCT CDN/US	NOV US/CDN	NOV CDN/US	DEC US/CDN	DEC CDN/US	Year
1.02	0.98	1.01	0.99	1.01	0.99	1.00	1.00	1.00	1.00	1.00	1.00	1971
0.98	1.02	0.98	1.02	0.98	1.02	0.98	1.02	0.99	1.01	1.00	1.00	1972
1.00	1.00	1.00	1.00	1.01	0.99	1.00	1.00	1.00	1.00	1.00	1.00	1973
0.98	1.02	0.98	1.02	0.99	1.01	0.98	1.02	0.99	1.01	0.99	1.01	1974
1.03	0.97	1.04	0.97	1.03	0.97	1.03	0.98	1.01	0.99	1.01	0.99	1975
0.97	1.03	0.99	1.01	0.98	1.03	0.97	1.03	0.99	1.01	1.02	0.98	1976
1.06	0.94	1.08	0.93	1.07	0.93	1.10	0.91	1.11	0.90	1.10	0.91	1977
1.12	0.89	1.14	0.88	1.17	0.86	1.18	0.85	1.17	0.85	1.18	0.85	1978
1.16	0.86	1.17	0.85	1.17	0.86	1.18	0.85	1.18	0.85	1.17	0.85	1979
1.15	0.87	1.16	0.86	1.16	0.86	1.17	0.86	1.19	0.84	1.20	0.84	1980
1.21	0.83	1.22	0.82	1.20	0.83	1.20	0.83	1.19	0.84	1.19	0.84	1981
1.27	0.79	1.25	0.80	1.23	0.81	1.23	0.81	1.23	0.82	1.24	0.81	1982
1.23	0.81	1.23	0.81	1.23	0.81	1.23	0.81	1.24	0.81	1.25	0.80	1983
1.32	0.76	1.30	0.77	1.31	0.76	1.32	0.76	1.32	0.76	1.32	0.76	1984
1.35	0.74	1.36	0.74	1.37	0.73	1.37	0.73	1.38	0.73	1.40	0.72	1985
1.38	0.72	1.39	0.72	1.39	0.72	1.39	0.72	1.39	0.72	1.38	0.72	1986
1.33	0.75	1.33	0.75	1.32	0.76	1.31	0.76	1.32	0.76	1.31	0.76	1987
1.21	0.83	1.22	0.82	1.23	0.82	1.21	0.83	1.22	0.82	1.20	0.84	1988
1.19	0.84	1.18	0.85	1.18	0.85	1.17	0.85	1.17	0.85	1.16	0.86	1989
1.16	0.86	1.14	0.87	1.16	0.86	1.16	0.86	1.16	0.86	1.16	0.86	1990
1.15	0.87	1.15	0.87	1.14	0.88	1.13	0.89	1.13	0.88	1.15	0.87	1991
1.19	0.84	1.19	0.84	1.22	0.82	1.25	0.80	1.27	0.79	1.27	0.79	1992
1.28	0.78	1.31	0.76	1.32	0.76	1.33	0.75	1.32	0.76	1.33	0.75	1993
1.38	0.72	1.38	0.73	1.35	0.74	1.35	0.74	1.36	0.73	1.39	0.72	1994
1.36	0.73	1.36	0.74	1.35	0.74	1.35	0.74	1.35	0.74	1.37	0.73	1995
1.37	0.73	1.37	0.73	1.37	0.73	1.35	0.74	1.34	0.75	1.36	0.73	1996
1.38	0.73	1.39	0.72	1.39	0.72	1.39	0.72	1.41	0.71	1.43	0.70	1997
1.49	0.67	1.53	0.65	1.52	0.66	1.55	0.65	1.54	0.65	1.54	0.65	1998
1.49	0.67	1.49	0.67	1.48	0.68	1.48	0.68	1.47	0.68	1.47	0.68	1999
1.48	0.68	1.48	0.67	1.49	0.67	1.51	0.66	1.54	0.65	1.52	0.66	2000
1.53	0.65	1.54	0.65	1.57	0.64	1.57	0.64	1.59	0.63	1.58	0.63	2001
1.55	0.65	1.57	0.64	1.58	0.63	1.58	0.63	1.57	0.64	1.56	0.64	2002
1.38	0.72	1.40	0.72	1.36	0.73	1.32	0.76	1.31	0.76	1.31	0.76	2003
1.32	0.76	1.31	0.76	1.29	0.78	1.25	0.80	1.20	0.84	1.22	0.82	2004
1.22	0.82	1.20	0.83	1.18	0.85	1.18	0.85	1.18	0.85	1.16	0.86	2005
1.13	0.89	1.12	0.89	1.12	0.90	1.13	0.89	1.14	0.88	1.15	0.87	2006
1.05	0.95	1.06	0.95	1.03	0.97	0.98	1.03	0.97	1.03	1.00	1.00	2007
1.01	0.99	1.05	0.95	1.06	0.95	1.18	0.84	1.22	0.82	1.23	0.81	2008
1.12	0.89	1.09	0.92	1.08	0.92	1.05	0.95	1.06	0.94	1.05	0.95	2009
1.04	0.96	1.04	0.96	1.03	0.97	1.02	0.98	1.01	0.99	1.01	0.99	2010
0.96	1.05	0.98	1.02	1.00	1.00	1.02	0.98	1.02	0.98	1.02	0.98	2011
1.01	0.99	0.99	1.01	.098	1.02	0.99	1.01	1.00	1.00	0.99	1.01	2012
1.04	0.96	1.04	0.96	1.03	0.97	1.04	0.96	1.05	0.95	1.06	0.94	2013
1.07	0.93	1.09	0.92	1.10	0.91	1.12	0.89	1.13	0.88	1.15	0.87	2014
1.29	0.78	1.31	0.76	1.33	0.75	1.31	0.76	1.33	0.75	1.37	0.73	2015
1.31	0.77	1.30	0.77	1.31	0.76	1.33	0.75	1.34	0.74	1.33	0.75	2016
1.25	0.80	1.25	0.80	1.25	0.80	1.29	0.78	1.29	0.78	1.25	0.80	2017
1.31	0.76	1.30	0.77	1.30	0.77	1.30	0.77	1.32	0.76	1.34	0.74	2018
1.31	0.76	1.33	0.75	1.32	0.76	1.32	0.76	1.32	0.76	1.32	0.76	2019
1.33	0.75	1.30	0.77	1.33	0.75	1.33	0.75	1.30	0.77	1.28	0.78	2020
1.25	0.80	1.26	0.79	1.27	0.79	1.24	0.80	1.26	0.80	1.28	0.78	2021

FOREIGN EXCHANGE — U.S. DOLLAR vs EURO MONTHLY AVG. VALUES

	JAN EUR/US	JAN US/EUR	FEB EUR/US	FEB US/EUR	MAR EUR/US	MAR US/EUR	APR EUR/US	APR US/EUR	MAY EUR/US	MAY US/EUR	JUN EUR/US	JUN US/EUR
1999	1.16	0.86	1.12	0.89	1.09	0.92	1.07	0.93	1.06	0.94	1.04	0.96
2000	1.01	0.99	0.98	1.02	0.96	1.04	0.94	1.06	0.91	1.10	0.95	1.05
2001	0.94	1.07	0.92	1.09	0.91	1.10	0.89	1.12	0.88	1.14	0.85	1.17
2002	0.88	1.13	0.87	1.15	0.88	1.14	0.89	1.13	0.92	1.09	0.96	1.05
2003	1.06	0.94	1.08	0.93	1.08	0.93	1.09	0.92	1.16	0.87	1.17	0.86
2004	1.26	0.79	1.26	0.79	1.23	0.82	1.20	0.83	1.20	0.83	1.21	0.82
2005	1.31	0.76	1.30	0.77	1.32	0.76	1.29	0.77	1.27	0.79	1.22	0.82
2006	1.21	0.82	1.19	0.84	1.20	0.83	1.23	0.81	1.28	0.78	1.27	0.79
2007	1.30	0.77	1.31	0.76	1.32	0.75	1.35	0.74	1.35	0.74	1.34	0.75
2008	1.47	0.68	1.48	0.68	1.55	0.64	1.58	0.63	1.56	0.64	1.56	0.64
2009	1.32	0.76	1.28	0.78	1.31	0.77	1.32	0.76	1.36	0.73	1.40	0.71
2010	1.43	0.70	1.37	0.73	1.36	0.74	1.34	0.75	1.26	0.80	1.22	0.82
2011	1.34	0.75	1.37	0.73	1.40	0.71	1.45	0.69	1.43	0.70	1.44	0.69
2012	1.29	0.77	1.32	0.76	1.32	0.76	1.32	0.76	1.28	0.78	1.25	0.80
2013	1.33	0.75	1.33	0.75	1.30	0.77	1.30	0.77	1.30	0.77	1.32	0.76
2014	1.36	0.73	1.37	0.73	1.38	0.72	1.38	0.72	1.37	0.73	1.36	0.74
2015	1.16	0.86	1.14	0.88	1.08	0.92	1.08	0.92	1.12	0.90	1.12	0.89
2016	1.09	0.92	1.11	0.90	1.11	0.90	1.13	0.88	1.13	0.88	1.12	0.89
2017	1.06	0.94	1.07	0.94	1.07	0.94	1.07	0.93	1.11	0.90	1.12	0.89
2018	1.22	0.82	1.23	0.81	1.23	0.81	1.23	0.81	1.18	0.85	1.17	0.86
2019	1.14	0.88	1.13	0.88	1.13	0.89	1.12	0.89	1.12	0.89	1.13	0.89
2020	1.11	0.90	1.09	0.92	1.10	0.91	1.09	0.92	1.09	0.92	1.13	0.88
2021	1.22	0.82	1.21	0.83	1.19	0.84	1.20	0.84	1.21	0.82	1.20	0.83

Source: Federal Reserve: Avg of daily rates, noon buying rates in New York City for cable transfers payable in foreign currencies